RED
BARON

RED
BARON

THE LIFE AND DEATH OF AN ACE

PETER KILDUFF

David and Charles

This book is dedicated to my longtime "co-pilot" Karl F. Kilduff, who knows the best route in many areas, and shares his expertise with me with boundless generosity.

A DAVID & CHARLES BOOK
Copyright © David & Charles Limited 2007

David & Charles is an F+W Publications Inc. company
4700 East Galbraith Road
Cincinnati, OH 45236

First published in the UK in 2007

Text copyright © Peter Kilduff 2007

Peter Kilduff has asserted his right to be identified as author of this work
in accordance with the Copyright, Designs and Patents Act, 1988.

A catalogue record for this book is available from the British Library.

ISBN-13: 978-0-7153-2809-5 hardback
ISBN-10: 0-7153-2809-3 hardback

Printed in Finland by WS Bookwell
for David & Charles
Brunel House, Newton Abbot, Devon

Commissioning Editor: Emily Pitcher
Desk Editor: Demelza Hookway
Senior Designer: Sarah Clark
Production Controller: Kelly Smith

For Chevron Publishing Ltd
Editor: Robert Forsyth
Design & Illustrations: Tim Brown

Visit our website at www.davidandcharles.co.uk

David & Charles books are available from all good bookshops; alternatively you
can contact our Orderline on 0870 9908222 or write to us at FREEPOST EX2 110,
D&C Direct, Newton Abbot, TQ12 4ZZ (no stamp required UK only); US customers
call 800-289-0963 and Canadian customers call 800-840-5220.

CONTENTS

INTRODUCTION

Manfred von Richthofen was more than the most successful fighter pilot of World War I. While he shot down 80 enemy aeroplanes, a score not equalled by any other pilot in that conflict, he also received more high decorations than any other German combatant in World War I and set a standard for leadership in combat. At the height of his career, he held the rank of *Rittmeister* [Cavalry Captain], which inferred boldness. Richthofen's choice of having his aircraft painted red to make him identifiable in the air, along with his aristocratic stature as a *Freiherr* [a form of baron], led to his being called 'the Red Baron' by Germans and non-Germans alike. That *nom de guerre* enhanced his reputation in life and helped to perpetuate his memory in the nearly nine decades since he was killed in combat at noon on Sunday, 21 April 1918.

Manfred von Richthofen became a living legend and had an effect on German culture that extends to the present time. Imperial German Government propagandists equated him to heroes in Richard Wagner's Teutonic myth-based operas and to philosophical ideals in Friedrich Nietzsche's writings, both of which enjoyed wide popularity in Germany at the time. The legend continued during World War II when a fighter wing [*Jagdgeschwader*] carried his name into aerial combat to inspire another generation of airmen. It was resurrected during the Cold War and continues to the present with democratic Germany's *Luftwaffe* operating a '*Richthofen Geschwader*' to help maintain peace in the skies over members of the North Atlantic Treaty Organization (NATO).

Manfred *Freiherr* von Richthofen has been the subject of many books, including a translation of his memoirs and four other volumes about him written by this author alone. Many of his contemporaries mentioned him in their accounts of the aerial conflict in the skies during what has been called The Great War. So why is there yet another book about him? Because Richthofen remains a fascinating figure and questions about him and his exploits continue to be raised. The interest has also been fuelled by the reunification of Germany beginning in 1989, which has led to the discovery of new material from former East German state archives and other sources. Continued inquiry and source examination has also led to new insights. For example, this author discovered a first-hand German-language document that finally allows analysis of a long mentioned but otherwise undocumented contention that Manfred von Richthofen was killed – executed – by British Commonwealth troops after his last crash-landing. Additionally, a review of Richthofen's little-seen medical records sheds light on the after-effects of his being shot down and badly injured on 6 July 1917, including informed commentary by modern medical specialists, to whom I express my deep gratitude: *Prof Dr Med* Henning Allmers of the medical faculty of the Universität Osnabrück in Germany, Dr Andrew Bamji of Great Britain, Dr Dieter H.M. Gröschel, a retired professor at the University of Virginia School of Medicine, and Dr M. Geoffrey Miller of Australia, who also very kindly allowed me to quote from his article 'The death of Manfred von Richthofen: Who fired the fatal shot?' which appeared in *Sabretache*, the Journal and Proceedings of the Military History Society of Australia. Additional insights come from a newly discovered World War I German Air Force [*Luftstreitkräfte*] report on the effects of flying on the human body that is likely a pioneering effort in the (then) new field of aviation medicine and how it was applied to early 20th century combat airmen.

The author is grateful to a number of aviators who survived World War I and, via correspondence and/or personal visits beginning some 45 years ago, provided insights into the times and events in which *Rittmeister* Manfred *Freiherr* von Richthofen became such a notable part. They have long since departed this life, but live on in memory: Wing Commander Ronald Adam, OBE, former *Leutnant der Reserve* Oscar Bechtle, Major Carl A. Dixon, former *Leutnant der Reserve* Johannes Knauer, Major Clayton Knight, OBE, former *Leutnant der Reserve* Oskar Kuppinger, and *Oberstleutnant der Reserve a.D.* Hanns-Gerd Rabe.

The author expresses sincere gratitude to succeeding generations of German friends linked in one way or another to airmen of World War I, especially to: Fritzcarl Prestien, son of a Richthofen flying comrade; Donat *Freiherr* von Richthofen; Hartmann *Freiherr* von Richthofen, nephew of the illustrious flyer; *Botschafter aD.* Prof (hc) DLaws (hc) Dr Hermann *Freiherr* von Richthofen, GCVO; Manfred *Freiherr* von Richthofen, nephew and namesake of the ace; and Wolf-Manfred *Freiherr* von Richthofen, son of Lothar and nephew of *Rittmeister* Manfred *Freiherr* von Richthofen. For helping an American learn more about the intricacies of German military and civilian customs and traditions, the author offers special thanks to the late *Dipl.-Ing* Klaus B. Fischer, Alfred von Krusenstiern, and Klaus Littwin.

The author is grateful to the late Cole Palen, founder of The Old Rhinebeck Aerodrome, for providing the experience of being in the air, in the backseat of an open cockpit two-seat biplane during mock combat between replica and original World War I aircraft. Special tribute is due to another Rhinebeck flyer, the late Dave Fox, who, like Richthofen, flew and died in a Fokker Dr.I Triplane. Other resources, only slightly less adrenalin-producing and just as valued, were provided by *Major Dr* Harald Potempa, Director of the Luftwaffenmuseum der Bundeswehr in Berlin, and Falk Hallensleben, Director of the Richthofen-Geschwader Museum in Wittmund, and by helpful people at the Bayerisches Hauptstaatsarchiv, the Bayerische Staatsbibliothek, and Bundesarchiv facilities in Berlin, Dresden, Freiburg and Potsdam, as well as the Elihu Burritt Library at my Alma Mater, Central Connecticut State University. Special thanks for comments, observations, photographs and much other help goes to: Charles H. Donald, the late Ed Ferko, Norman L.R. Franks, the late Peter M. Grosz, Adrian Hellwig, Colin Huston, Dr Eberhardt Kettlitz, *Dr* Volker Koos, Carl-August *Graf* von Kospoth, Paul S. Leaman, James F. Miller, the late Neal W. O'Connor, Lothair Vanoverbeke, Gregory VanWyngarden, the late George H. Williams, and the late H. Hugh Wynne.

Continued thanks go to Roderick Dymott, who encouraged me to develop a 'zero-base' research approach in my first Richthofen biography, and to my friends Trudy and Jules Baumann, and David E. Smith, whose comments on the manuscript have been invaluable. To my sons Clayton and Karl, I express special gratitude for their help with intricacies of 21st century technology and for generously providing other skills that go far beyond mine. And, from my own generation, grateful acknowledgement to my wife Judy for being a persevering proofreader and sounding board as this book was developed.

Finally, nearly five decades of research and a variety of sources, listed in the bibliography, preceded the writing of this book. The rationale for producing a volume about *Rittmeister* Manfred *Freiherr* von Richthofen and early air warriors connected to him is found in *They Fought for the Sky* by the late American journalist Quentin Reynolds (1957), one of the books that attracted the author to study World War I aviation history. Reynolds' introduction, titled 'Confessions of a Thief,' characterizes a writer's pursuit of such stories and expresses views with which I concur and wish to share with the reader:

'Now that the book is finished I am disturbed by the thought that I didn't really write it – I merely typewrote it. I picked the brains of hundreds of men, dead and living, and this is the result ... The material in this book was for the most part written by those who figure in it, and I, the predatory professional writer, have stolen their thoughts, their emotions and in some cases their very words. I make no apology – I think they bear repeating.'

Peter Kilduff
New Britain, Connecticut, USA
June 2007

FOREWORD

In 1892, my uncle Manfred *Freiherr* von Richthofen came into the world in Breslau (Silesia). He served the last German Kaiser as an aviator and flew in the last year of the war until his death. The fame he attained among friend and foe alike during the war has meanwhile become a legend. The memory of Manfred von Richthofen remained even after World War II, which otherwise obliterated everything else, so strong and alive that the democracy and the republic that emerged from the rubble of the illegal German state did not hesitate to give his good name as the official designation to a squadron of the German *Luftwaffe*.

In World War II, everything that was German was so tarnished by the Nazi leaders that even now we struggle for explanations for the incomprehensible, horrible deeds that were committed at the time.

But, for all that, the 'Red Baron' is for the succeeding generation abroad a concept that stands for flying skill, for bravery and also for gallantry. After Manfred von Richthofen fell, he was laid to rest with military honours by Germany's enemies of World War I. The Headquarters of the British Royal Air Force sent to his formal funeral a wreath with a ribbon bearing the inscription: 'To Captain von Richthofen, the brave and worthy opponent.'

There is an explanation for this discriminate attitude towards a military opponent: especially in war, with all of its unimaginable carnage, there is a need for an ultimate order of moral values. And there was the need for good examples that support these orders of moral values, figures that embody these moral values for friend and foe alike, role models to prevent millions of soldiers from becoming blind and berserk.

Likewise, the gallant combat flyer von Richthofen from World War I came to honours, both unexpectedly and singularly in Anglo-Saxon countries after World War II. Perhaps here he also resonated the idea that carpet bombings such as in Dresden and the atomic bomb attacks on Hiroshima and Nagasaki, which at the end were carried out against civilians, were not only senseless, but also upset the soldierly order of moral values.

What was reported to us about my uncle – his sense of duty, his comradeship, his gallantry and his courage in battle, his devotion to his mission, the necessity of which he was convinced, his patriotism and his moral sense of protecting his own homeland and countrymen – are also today components of responsible thinking civil conduct.

Only from the distance of many decades and the experiences that we had to accumulate did we come to the realization that seldom is a young life so richly fulfilled as that of Manfred von Richthofen, the great German aviator.

Manfred von Richthofen
Berlin, Germany
June 2007

1
FIRST BLOOD

From the beginning of my career as a pilot I had only one ambition and that was to fly a single-seat fighter-plane.

Manfred von Richthofen would do anything to achieve his goal and ignored other pilots who scoffed at his idea of having a forward-firing machine gun rigged to the top wing of his Albatros two-seat biplane. Without it, the aeroplane was defended only by the observer, sitting in the back seat, armed with a swivel-mounted machine gun. 'People laughed at the gun arrangement because it looked very primitive,' he wrote later, 'but soon I had the opportunity to put it to practical use'. He wanted to be more than an aerial 'chauffeur' for his observer and, with his own machine gun, Richthofen could be aggressive in aerial combat, more like a fighter pilot. The prospect excited him as he headed down the grass runway and took off for a morning offensive patrol on 26 April 1916, to keep French aeroplanes from attacking German rear areas. His new Albatros C-type two-seater, which was sleek looking and very sturdy, with a wood-covered fuselage, climbed steadily as he steered it westward toward Verdun, where one of the war's most horrific artillery and ground battles had been raging for months. Approaching the battle zone, Richthofen and his observer test-fired their guns to assure they were ready to fight.

As they crossed the front lines, a French Nieuport fighter came into view. Earlier encounters with Nieuports, which were armed with machine guns attached to the top wings specifically to fire over the propeller arc, inspired Richthofen to have his plane rigged the same way, right down to the firing cable linking the gun to the pilot. Taut with anticipation of the air battle to come, he stayed calm enough to observe that, like himself, the Nieuport pilot was:

... apparently also a beginner, because he acted foolishly fearful. I flew towards him, whereupon he flew away. Evidently his gun had jammed. It seemed that I would not be able to engage him.

Then, I thought: "What would happen if I fired at him?" I flew
after him and, for the first time and from an ever-closing distance,
I pressed the machine gun firing button. A short series of well-
aimed shots and the Nieuport reared up and rolled over. At first
my observer and I thought it was one of the many tricks the
Frenchmen go in for. But this "trick" did not stop; he went lower
and lower. Then my observer tapped my helmet and yelled:
"Congratulations! He is going down!" In fact, he fell in a forest
behind Fort Douaumont and disappeared among the trees. It was
clear to me that I had shot him down. But on the other side of the
lines! I flew home and reported nothing more than "an aerial
combat, one Nieuport shot down." A day later I read of my deed in
an Army Report. I was very proud of it, but this Nieuport is not
counted among the number of enemy planes that I brought down.

The downed Nieuport was not confirmed as an aerial victory because it fell
within enemy lines and there were no independent witnesses, only the two
German airmen. But Richthofen's pride compelled him to dash off a note to
his mother: 'Look at the Army Report of 26 April! My machine gun is
responsible for one of the two aeroplanes brought down.' His achievement
was reported – obliquely – in the popular press: 'Two enemy aeroplanes were
shot down in aerial combat over Fleury, one south of Douaumont, and one
west of it.' The family knew that their Manfred had achieved the first success
in his self-appointed mission to become an aerial warrior.

An avid hunter, Richthofen would have prized a souvenir of his first air
combat triumph, which was not possible due to the location of the Nieuport's
crash site. Over nine decades later, modern research can only suggest that he
may have accounted for the Nieuport 11 fighter that appeared on that day's
French casualty list; its pilot, *Maréchal des Logis* [Sergeant-Major] Jean Casale
of *Escadrille N.23*, was reported as wounded. All of Richthofen's subsequent
victims were British airmen, who were often on the offensive and driven by
circumstances to venture over German territory, which made it easier to
confirm those victories.

In the spring of 1916, however, Richthofen still flew with *Kampfstaffel 8*
[Combat Squadron 8] of *Kampfgeschwader der Obersten Heeresleitung Nr 2*
[Combat Wing of the Supreme High Command 2], based outside Metz. The

city was only 50 kilometres (31 miles) within the Lorraine province that France had been forced to cede to Germany after the War of 1870 and, since then, the French Government had heavily fortified Verdun and the surrounding hills to offset the German stronghold. Richthofen was glad that the fierce pace of the Battle of Verdun required more activity for *Kasta 8*'s two-seat aircraft, which usually provided visual and photographic reconnaissance, and bombing missions. New orders called for 'barrier flights', using two-seaters to stop enemy aircraft from flying over German ground positions. Erwin Böhme, a pilot in neighbouring *Kasta 10*, who later became a good friend and squadron-mate of Richthofen's, described the situation in a letter to his fiancée:

> Now we have been entrusted with a new mission, which is more to
> my liking than those awful bomb-flinging, "barrier flights"
> against Verdun. I must explain the word to you. Often our infantry
> and artillery have had to grit their teeth that French flyers have
> been unhindered in bothering them from above and directing
> enemy artillery fire against them. Now that is prevented by our
> aircraft flying back and forth over the Front and hindering
> enemy aircraft.

Richthofen's hopes of becoming a fighter pilot were raised after he completed pilot training and was assigned to *Kasta 8*. That unit's commanding officer was an experienced pre-war flyer, *Hauptmann* [Captain] Victor Carganico, but its sister squadron, *Kasta 10*, was led by *Hauptmann* Wilhelm Boelcke, brother of Germany's second-highest-scoring fighter pilot of the time, *Oberleutnant* [First Lieutenant] Oswald Boelcke. Indeed, the famous air fighter had arrived at *Kampfgeschwader 2*'s airfield outside Metz to visit his brother only a few days before Richthofen's encounter with the Nieuport. If fate were kind enough to arrange for the two men to meet, Richthofen could talk to him about air combat on a first-hand basis. With luck, he might persuade Boelcke to request him for his unit, the *Kampfeinsitzer Kommando* [Single-Seat Fighter Detachment] at nearby Sivry, as a replacement for the ace's wingman, who had been killed in a training accident on Good Friday, 21 April. Boelcke and his friendly rival, Germany's highest-scoring fighter pilot, *Oberleutnant* Max Immelmann, were the first airmen to be decorated with the *Orden Pour le Mérite*, Prussia's highest combat bravery award for officers, which commanded respect throughout the German Empire. Boelcke and Immelmann were considered to be the best pilots in the German *Fliegertruppe* [Flying Service] and Manfred von Richthofen, then a *Leutnant* [Second Lieutenant], aspired to join this air warrior *élite*.

But Boelcke flew back to Sivry and Richthofen understood he had to prove himself as a member of *Kasta 8* before he could move on to what he regarded as a higher calling. Boelcke's name and deeds continuously reminded him of the opportunities for air combat success that awaited pilots lucky enough to be assigned to single-seat fighter units. Richthofen read the Army daily reports which noted on 28 April that Boelcke shot down his 14th enemy aeroplane and, on 1 May, his 15th victim fell.

The *Kampfgeschwaders* were the 'rapid reaction force' of their day, provided with their own trains to move men, aircraft and equipment to various sectors as needed. Thus, a few days later, Richthofen and his comrades headed north-west to Mont. The new airfield there was closer to Verdun, the ancient fortress city straddling the Meuse River as it flowed southward. Once settled in, Richthofen was dispatched back to Metz to attend to minor administrative chores. It was an easy enough behind-the-lines flight, only about 35 kilometres (22 miles), with the observer replaced by a 100-kilogram (220-lb) ballast sack secured in the rear compartment to balance the aircraft. The return flight the following day, however, turned out to be a nerve-wracking yet instructional experience with the forces of nature let loose by bad weather.

Richthofen later wrote:

> As I pulled my machine out of the hangar the first signs of an approaching thunderstorm became apparent. The wind blew up the sand and a pitch-black wall arose from the north. Old, experienced pilots urged me not to fly. But I had already promised to return, and I would have appeared timid if I had not come back due to a stupid thunderstorm. Therefore, I increased power ... [and] right at the outset it began to rain. I had to take off my goggles in order to see anything. The trouble was that I had to go over the Moselle Mountains, straight through the valleys where the thunderstorm was raging. I thought to myself: "You will be lucky to get through," and got closer and closer to the black

clouds that reached down to the earth. I flew as low as possible. I had to "jump" over houses and trees in some cases. I no longer knew where I was. The storm seized my machine like a piece of paper and tossed it around. My heart sank lower. I could not land among the hills. I had to press on.

All around me it was black. Beneath me, the trees bent under the storm. Suddenly a wooded height appeared before me. I had to go over it and my good Albatros got me through. I could only fly straight ahead ... like riding a steeplechase over trees, villages, church spires and chimneys that, at most, I cleared by five metres (about 16 feet), in order to see anything through the black thunderclouds. Lightning flashed all around me ... I believed that death would come at any moment, and surely the storm would throw me into a village or a forest. Had the engine quit, I would have been done for.

Then all at once I saw a light place in front of me. The thunderstorm had already passed there; if I could reach this point, I would be saved. Gathering all my energy, as only a reckless man can, I steered toward the light.

Suddenly, as if wrenched out, I was free of the thunderclouds. I flew through streaming rain, but otherwise I was out of danger. Despite the ... rain, I landed at my home field, where everyone waited anxiously for me. A report had come from Metz as soon as I departed that I had disappeared on the way out.

Richthofen was little chastened by the experience, as he later noted with his usual daring spirit:

In retrospect, everything was beautiful ... there were some beautiful moments that I would not have wanted to miss ...

Despite lack of recognition and dangerous thunderstorms, Richthofen surely felt linked to one of the war's most important operations. One connection was to the leader of the German 5th Army that stood opposite Verdun, 33-year-old Crown Prince Wilhelm of Prussia, the heir to the dynasty of Frederick the Great, who had elevated the Richthofen family to the aristocracy. Another was Richthofen's oath of allegiance to the House of Hohenzollern, the Kaiser's family, rather than the state, as he was a product of the Royal Prussian Cadet Corps. Further, this fierce battle to inflict French casualties that would 'bleed them white' was proposed by German General Staff Chief Erich von Falkenhayn, whose son 'Fritze' was a flying comrade of Richthofen's during an earlier squadron assignment. Finally, even the maps were inspirational, identifying Crown Prince Wilhelm's battlefront as the 'Kriemhilde Line' in honour of the Teutonic heroine who avenged the death of the mythical hero Siegfried. Richthofen firmly believed that Germany was under attack by enemies on its eastern and western borders, and he felt bound by a deep sense of honour and the weight of history to fight them to the death.

He hungered to be part of this epic battle, but understood that he could not fulfil his personal goals by continuing to fly *Kasta 8*'s bulky reconnaissance and bombing aircraft. The unit also had one Fokker E.III single-seat monoplane fighter and a pilot designated to fly it when the larger planes required a fighter escort. Richthofen planned to become *Kasta 8*'s second fighter pilot, as he later wrote:

> After annoying my commanding officer for a long time, I finally received permission to go up in a Fokker ... [and at first] it felt strange to be completely alone in a small aeroplane. I shared the Fokker with my friend *Leutnant der Reserve* [Second Lieutenant, Reserves] Hans Reimann ... I flew it in the morning and he in the afternoon. Each of us was afraid the other would smash the crate to pieces. On the second day we flew against the enemy.
> I encountered no Frenchman in the morning [and] in the afternoon it was [Reimann's] turn. He did not return [and] there was no news of him. Nothing.
>   Late in the evening the infantry reported an air fight between a Nieuport and a German Fokker, in the course of which the German had apparently landed on *La Mort Homme* [Dead Man's Hill, west of Verdun]. It could only be Reimann, as all the other flyers had returned. We were feeling sorry for our brave comrade, when all of a sudden, in the middle of the night, came a telephone report that a German flying officer had suddenly appeared at the

forward trenches of Dead Man's Hill. It turned out to be Reimann. His engine had been shot to pieces ... and he had to make an emergency landing. He could not reach our lines and landed between the enemy and us. Quickly, he set fire to the machine and then hid in a bomb crater several hundred metres away. During the night he managed to sneak over to our trenches. Thus ended our first Fokker joint venture.

Several weeks later, another Fokker monoplane arrived at *Kasta 8* and, as Richthofen was a career officer and two years older than Reservist Reimann, he claimed the new aircraft. All went well, Richthofen noted, until:

It was perhaps my third flight in the small, fast machine. The engine quit on take-off. I had to land and went right into a hayfield. In a flash, the once proud, beautiful machine was an unrecognizable mass. It is a miracle nothing happened to me.

Not to be denied his destiny, Richthofen pestered Carganico for a replacement. His superior later recalled:

At the time he came to my *Staffel* as a two-seater pilot, he was already urging that I send him for two or three days to ... the head of the Air Park in Montmédy ... for single-seat fighter instruction. After his return, I placed my own single-seater at his disposal as, due to engine failure and through no fault of his own, he had had to "set down" his own aircraft.

Richthofen marked his 24th birthday with several air fights – all without success – and a visit to an old friend from his first squadron assignment almost a year earlier. The following day, 3 May 1916, he wrote to his mother:

Most sincere thanks for your kind wishes on my birthday, which I spent here very pleasantly. In the morning, I had three very nerve-wracking aerial combats, and in the evening I sat with

[*Oberleutnant* Georg] Zeumer ... until one o'clock in the morning, enjoying a May wine under a blossoming apple tree. I feel very happy in my new occupation as a combat pilot; I believe that no posting in the war could be as challenging as this one. I fly a Fokker ... the type of aeroplane with which Boelcke and Immelmann have had their enormous successes ...

With time to gain experience and luck to stay alive, Richthofen would go on to outshine Boelcke, Immelmann and all other *Pour le Mérite* aviators.

2
THE GLORY OF ITS NAME

Visitors to St. Nikolai's Church in eastern Berlin rarely recognize the epitaph in one wall honouring Paulus Praetorius (1521-1565). He was the progenitor of the Richthofens, a family of many accomplished members in German society, but which since World War I has become best known for its link to Manfred *Freiherr* von Richthofen, arguably the most famous German aviator in history. A look at his family tree shows that Manfred's relentless drive to succeed was foreshadowed in roots that go back to the German province of Brandenburg in the 16th century.

The Richthofen family originated with Paulus Praetorius, who, in his 44-year lifespan, became a man of wealth and influence in Brandenburg. He was Councillor to the Elector of Brandenburg, Privy Councillor to the Archbishops of Magdeburg and Halberstadt, and hereditary feudal lord and supreme legal authority in several dominions. He was the son and grandson of mayors of Bernau, a Brandenburg town that once was larger than Berlin, and he became an educated man and renowned judge. Old engravings of him bear this tribute in Latin: '*Vir prudens et orator gravissimus*' [an intelligent man and a distinguished speaker].

There is a slight twist to the story in that the bloodline began with Sebastian Schmidt (1515-1553). As a 27-year-old theologian who had studied under Martin Luther in Wittenberg, Schmidt left his home town of Koblenz in the Rhineland in 1542 and travelled eastward to become Lutheran archdeacon in Bernau. A year later, he was appointed rector at St. Nicolai's in Potsdam. Following the custom of the time, Schmidt Latinized his surname to Faber und Fabricius. He also married the daughter of a Berlin city councillor, Barbara Below, a cousin of Paulus Schultze, who was better known by his Latinized family name, Praetorius.

Paulus Praetorius, successful in all of life's other endeavours, had no male heirs, and so it was agreed that he adopt Sebastian and Barbara Schmidt's son Samuel. After Paulus died in 1565, 22-year-old Samuel inherited considerable wealth, many responsibilities and a coat of arms granted in 1561 by Holy Roman Emperor Ferdinand I. The prominent figure in the heraldry is a black-robed judge seated on a tribunal chair [*Richterstuhl*] and, after Samuel Praetorius completed his education, he entered the practice of law. Subsequently, he moved east to Frankfurt an der Oder, where he became a city councillor, city judge and Mayor.

His son Tobias Praetorius (1576-1644) expanded the family's holdings and acquired the family's first property in Silesia by marrying a local nobleman's daughter. Silesia was then a state of the Holy Roman Empire of the German Nation, as Charlemagne's legacy was known in its final iteration, and closely linked to Brandenburg. Thus, it was a natural development for Tobias's son, Johann Praetorius (1611-1664), to move his entire family to Silesia, which was rich in natural resources and offered a more favourable social climate for Lutherans. Indeed, he advanced to a point that, in 1661, he was elevated to hereditary Bohemian Knighthood under the name Johann Praetorius von Richthofen by Holy Roman Emperor Leopold I. Richt-Hofen is a Germanization of Praetorius, meaning 'court of judgment.'

The family grew and settled in the Silesian districts of Striegau, Jauer, Schweidnitz and Liegnitz. While the area was significantly Catholic, early Richthofens maintained their Protestant links to Brandenburg and naturally sided with King Friedrich II of Prussia, best known as Frederick the Great, in the First Silesian War (1740-1742). That conflict wrested Silesia from the Habsburg dynasty that eventually absorbed the Holy Roman Emperor's court in Vienna. The Richthofen family's service and support were rewarded on 6 November 1741, with the Prussian monarch's decree elevating them to the baronial ranks; men were granted the hereditary title *Freiherr*, and their spouses and unmarried sisters the title *Freifrau*.

Richthofens were raised to be active in society, with the accent on leadership, and for generations they have held key civic and education posts throughout Germany. The world traveller and geographer Professor Ferdinand *Freiherr* von Richthofen (1833-1905), published an extensive body of work based on his explorations in every hemisphere; Oswald *Freiherr* von Richthofen (1847-1906), held many posts in the Royal Prussian Government, including as Foreign Minister under Chancellor Bernhard Prince [Prinz] von Bülow; members of the National Assembly during the Weimar Republic included *Freiherren* Karl, Ernst, Hartmann and Praetorius von Richthofen; and, in more recent times, the now retired career diplomat *Botschafter aD* Dr Hermann *Freiherr* von Richthofen, GCVO, Professor (hc) of Central Connecticut State University and Doctor of Laws (hc) of the University of Birmingham, has served as the Federal Republic of Germany's Ambassador to the Court of St. James and to the North

Atlantic Alliance. Two of the *Rittmeister*'s [Cavalry Captain's] nephews also figure prominently in contemporary German society: Manfred *Freiherr* von Richthofen, Honorary President of the German Olympic Sports Association, and Hartmann *Freiherr* von Richthofen, Managing Director of the Associations of Casinos in Baden-Baden and Konstanz.

Family military heritage stems from Manfred von Richthofen's paternal great-grandmother, Thecla von Berenhorst, a granddaughter of Prussian Field Marshal *Fürst* [Prince] Leopold von Anhalt-Dessau. The Prince, who closely served King William III of England (1650–1702) and, later, John Churchill, the first Duke of Marlborough (1650–1722), was described as:

> ...a daring, dashing commander, who ... loved to swoop down on the unsuspecting foe ... and [who] helped to lay the foundations of Prussia's military reputation ...

Manfred's mother's family also had notable martial connections. His maternal grandmother hailed from the distinguished Falckenhausen family, whose progenitor, *Markgraf* [Margrave] Karl Wilhelm Friedrich von Ansbach, was descended from a Frankish line of the House of Hohenzollern and who married a sister of Frederick the Great. The Richthofen family's long and illustrious heritage was rendered into verse by the 19th century German envoy Emil *Freiherr* von Richthofen:

> Reaching back not into grey antiquity, the family tree
> Is nevertheless of an indeed old and worthy lineage;
> Crystal-clear, unclouded remains the glory of its name,
> Held high for all time in truth, honour and justice.
> True to ancestral ways, devout, brave, honest and modest,
> Has by God's gracious favour been protected from harm.
> Oh, waver not from the path of Christian duty,
> Further your name proudly in the manner of true knights!
> Even as the lineage flowers heartily, the very picture of honour,
> Never shall a shadow fall upon this noble escutcheon!

Manfred also noted:

Among the present generation of Richthofens there are, of course, many more soldiers. In war, every Richthofen capable of bearing arms is on active service. Right at the beginning of [World War I] I lost six cousins of various ranks. All were cavalrymen, but my father is actually the first in our branch of the family who became a professional soldier. At an early age he entered the [Royal Prussian] Cadet Corps and from there joined Uhlan Regiment Nr 12. He is the most conscientious soldier imaginable. But he became hard of hearing after saving one of his men from drowning in a horse pond and ... continuing his duties without regard to being cold and wet.

At that time, a soldier could spend his career in his home area and *Major* Albrecht Phillip Karl Julius *Freiherr* von Richthofen and his wife Kunigunde (*née* von Schickfuss und Neudorff) settled into life in Breslau, where his first three children were born: Elisabeth Therese Luise Marie (called Ilse) on 8 August 1890, Manfred Albrecht on 2 May 1892 and Lothar Siegfried on 27 September 1894. Manfred's godfather and namesake was an uncle who, in peacetime, had been adjutant to *Kaiser* [Emperor] Wilhelm II and Commander of the Corps of the Guards. During World War I, *General der Kavallerie* [Cavalry General] Manfred *Freiherr* von Richthofen commanded the 6th Division in the 3rd Army Corps on the Western Front.

Ultimately, *Major* von Richthofen's damaged hearing required him to retire early and, while he had no estate or personal fortune, he was able to maintain a pleasant villa in the town of Schweidnitz. His third son, Karl Bolko, called Bolko, was born there on 16 April 1903. Manfred was tutored until he was nine years old and after that he attended school for a year in Schweidnitz.

Kunigunde *Freifrau* von Richthofen, had fond memories of her oldest son's childhood, including an early attraction to moving targets that portended things to come:

We passed our vacations in the country with Grandmother. One day Manfred could not suppress his fast-developing passion for hunting. He had his first air rifle and with it killed three or four of Grandmother's tame ducks that he found swimming in a little pond near the house. He proudly related his exploit to his grandmother, and I started to reprimand him. His good old grandmother stopped me from scolding him because, as she said, he had been right in confessing his misdeed.

Manfred's misadventure took another turn when he created his first hunting trophy from amongst the day's 'bag'. He used a dab of red sealing wax to fasten a feather from each duck to a small piece of brown pasteboard. It was the first – but not the last – time he sought proof of his hunting prowess.

Major von Richthofen encouraged his sons to pursue the manly arts of horsemanship and athletics. Manfred's favourite sports were swimming and shooting, and the woods in the Weistritz Valley, stretching from Silesia to the Czech border, offered him many thrilling chases and hunting triumphs.

This lifestyle was funded by *Major* von Richthofen's modest Army pension and The Old Gentleman, as he was called affectionately, could assure his sons' higher educations only by having them follow his path and qualify for admission to the Royal Prussian Cadet System. Thus, in August 1903, three months after his 11thbirthday, Manfred left the beautiful Weistritz Valley and its many memories of sport and exploration. It was time for him to begin preparing for his future career by entering the prestigious Cadet Institute at Wahlstatt, which had produced such outstanding Prussian generals as Paul von Beneckendorff und von Hindenburg (best known as Hindenburg), who would be recalled from retirement at age 66 and eventually become Germany's great Field Marshall and Chief of the General Staff in World War I. Wahlstatt offered Germany's future warriors a Spartan existence, many long hours of study and much rigid discipline to instil in them now the value of learning to obey in order to gain the maturity needed to command later. Manfred wrote:

I was not particularly eager to become a cadet, but it was my father's wish, so I was barely consulted. The strict discipline and order were especially difficult for such a young pup. I did not particularly care for the instruction. I was never a great scholar. I did what was necessary to pass. Consequently, my teachers did not have high regard for me. On the other hand, I liked sports very much, especially gymnastics, soccer and the like. I believe there was not a movement on the horizontal bar that I could not do and soon the School Commandant awarded me several prizes.

> I had a great liking for risky tricks. So one fine day, for example,
> with my friend Frankenberg, I climbed the famous steeple of
> Wahlstatt by going up the lightning rod wire and tied my
> handkerchief to the top of the steeple. I remember vividly how
> difficult it was to negotiate the gutters. When I visited my little
> brother at Wahlstatt about ten years later, I saw my handkerchief
> still tied high in the air. My friend Frankenberg was the first victim
> of the war who I knew personally.

Manfred's slight build concealed an athletic ability that enabled him to perform many physical tasks. By excelling in such activities, he learned the value of teamwork. Indeed, his physical abilities and a certain aloof bearing made him less vulnerable to older boys who bullied younger, smaller boys. And when bigger boys picked on Manfred, they only toughened his resolve. Despite bullying and relentless drilling on the parade ground, Manfred nurtured an inner strength that enabled him to endure six years at Wahlstatt, as well as other privations and disappointments to come. According to his medical records, however, he seems to have experienced normal physical growth – standing 1.395 metres (4 feet 5 inches) and weighing 32.8 kilograms (72.3 lbs) in April 1903, and growing to 1.72 metres (5 feet 6 inches) and 67 kilograms (147.7 lbs) by November 1910.

A year earlier, in 1909, he was graduated to the Senior Cadet Academy at Gross-Lichterfelde, not far from Berlin. There, he wrote:

> I liked it considerably better. I was not cut off from the world and
> began to live a bit more like a human being. My happiest memories
> of Lichterfelde are those of the great sporting events when my
> opponent was *Prinz* Friedrich Karl of Prussia. The Prince won many
> first prizes and other awards beyond mine, as I had not trained as
> carefully as he had.

The two young men also had another link. *Prinz* Friedrich Karl, a distant cousin of *Kaiser* Wilhelm II, also became a pilot during the war. Almost a year younger than Manfred, the Prince died a year before his schoolmate. But such grim events were far off when they graduated from Gross-Lichterfelde during the Easter season of 1911. Both men were posted to choice light cavalry units, the Prince to Life Hussar Regiment Nr 1 garrisoned in Langfuhr, outside Danzig, and Richthofen to the lance-bearing Uhlan Regiment Nr 1 in Militsch in Silesia. While the Prince left the Senior Cadet Academy with the rank of *Fähnrich*, [Army Ensign], Manfred, who had failed the Ensign's examination, headed to duty as a *Sergeant*. He qualified for officer's rank only after his second examination, which made him junior to his peers and placed him behind them in future promotions.Very likely, this stinging – and quite public – disappointment led to his drive to take greater risks which would result in career success and recognition of his later achievements.

He was detached from his unit to attend the Military Academy in Berlin, after which he was commissioned a Regular Army *Leutnant* [Second Lieutenant] in 1912. While he was behind his career-oriented peers on the rank list, Richthofen was at least a social notch above Reserve and Home Guard officers. He returned to his unit, based north east of Breslau, not far from his home.

> **Finally I received the epaulettes,** he recalled joyfully. **It was about the proudest feeling I ever had to be addressed as** "*Herr Leutnant.*"

Upon receiving his commission, marking the true beginning of his military career, Manfred's father presented him with a beautiful mare named 'Santuzza'. It was a practical gift, as the horse would enable the young officer to maintain athletic and equestrian skills needed in wartime. Manfred and his Gross-Lichterfelde classmate, regimental comrade and best friend Erich-Rüdiger von Wedel, who owned a charger named 'Fandango', trained their horses together for a jumping competition and cross-country race in Breslau. 'Santuzza' was a good jumper, but the day before the event, she hit a high fence and bruised her shoulder; Manfred tumbled off her and cracked his collarbone. Not one to admit defeat, he got back in the saddle and continued to ride. "Fandango' did gloriously,' he noted.

> **In training, I demanded speed and performance from my good stout mare "Santuzza" and was very surprised when Wedel's thoroughbred beat her.**

As a devoted sportsman, Manfred was caught up in the nascent modern Olympics movement, which had been revived with increasing fervour from the middle to late 19th century. When an Olympiad event was held in Breslau in 1913, with its promise of glory and recognition to compensate for his lower ranking among his Senior Cadet Academy peers, Manfred had the good fortune to ride a beautiful chestnut bay gelding named 'Felix,' whose abilities seemed to match his ambitions. He wrote:

> The cross-country race began and in the second third of the course my horse was doing so well that I had high hopes of success. Then came the final obstacle. From a distance I saw that it must be something special, as a crowd of people had gathered there. I thought to myself: "Cheer up, there is worse to come!" and came winding up over the embankment, on top of which was a brace. The people there waved to me and shouted not to ride so fast, but I saw and heard nothing more. My horse jumped and took the brace right off and, to my great astonishment, on the other side there was a steep slope toward the Weistritz River. Before I could act, the animal fell with a gigantic leap into the river, and horse and rider disappeared in the torrent ... "Felix" came out of the river on one side and I on the other. At the weigh-in at the end of the race, people were astonished that I weighed ten pounds more instead of two pounds less, as usual. Thank God no one noticed that I was soaking wet.

Not fazed by his poor showing, Manfred also competed in that year's Kaiser's Prize Race, a cross-country event that would test the extents of his courage.

Manfred's brief time of glory soon ended and in autumn 1913 he returned to his Uhlan regiment, on patrol near the town of Ostrovo, ten kilometres [six miles] west of the Prosno River border with Russian Poland. Initially, the murder of Austrian Archduke Franz Ferdinand and his wife Sophie in Sarajevo, the Bosnian capital, on 27 June 1914 had no visible impact on troops in the field. But over the coming weeks the assassination of the heir to the Austro-Hungarian throne became a focal point for underlying conflicts between the Triple Alliance of Germany, Austria-Hungary and Italy, and the Triple Entente of Great Britain, France and Russia. Two of Europe's oldest royal houses stood shoulder to shoulder, reinforced by Kaiser Wilhelm's pledge of 'Nibelungen loyalty' to the Habsburgs of Austria. With such support, the powers in Vienna imposed harsh demands on Serbia that led to events resulting in battle lines being strengthened across Europe. Richthofen wrote:

> In all the newspapers at this time there was nothing but inflated stories about the [impending] war. But for some months we had been accustomed to "war talk." We had packed our service kits so often that it had long since become boring and no longer believed there would be war. We who were on the border, "the eyes of the Army," as the commander of my cavalry patrol called us, believed least of all that there would be war.

The men in the field were not privy to message traffic and other exchanges between Berlin and Vienna and were surprised when, on 28 July 1914, Austria-Hungary declared war on Serbia. The Imperial Russian Army was mobilized and, drawing on the emotional power of Teutonic mythology, Germany supported its 'Nibelungen' ally by declaring war on Russia on 1 August. The German Government declared war against France two days later, the same day that its erstwhile ally, Italy, proclaimed its neutrality. Germany's violation of Belgian neutrality was one stated reason for Britain to declare war on Germany and Austria-Hungary on 4 August.

On the eve of war with Russia, Richthofen and some friends held a party in their regimental mess. They dined on oysters, drank champagne and gambled while Europe tottered on the brink of a catastrophe that would assume global proportions and set the stage for a second worldwide conflagration. Then a knock at their door announced the arrival of the royal magistrate of the Öls district, which encompassed Ostrovo, August *Graf* [Count] von Kospoth. At 50 years old, the stately aristocrat was a wise and credible father figure to the young officers, most of whom were less than half his age. His visits were always welcome, but always with some occasion attached to them, and this time was no different. Richthofen recalled:

> The Count had a frightful look on his face. We greeted our old friend with a rousing "Hallo!" And then he explained that he had come personally to the border to see for himself whether rumours of an impending war were true. He assumed, quite correctly, that the best information could be obtained at the border. He was more

than a bit astonished by our party's picture of peace. We learned from him that all the bridges in Silesia were patrolled by the military and that fortification of other positions was being considered. We quickly convinced him war was out of the question and continued our festivities.

The next day, we rode off to battle. The word "war" was certainly familiar to us border cavalrymen. Each of us knew to the smallest detail what to do and what to leave undone. But nobody had any idea what would happen next. Every soldier on active duty was eager to show his personal worth and knowledge. We young cavalry *Leutnants* had the most interesting task, to be sure: reconnoitring the enemy's rear areas, destroying important installations; all tasks that require real men.

Just before the first shots were fired, however, *Freifrau* von Richthofen and her other three children were trying to enjoy an uneasy late July vacation at Zoppot, a suburb of Danzig. With all the disturbing news, there was concern that the tranquil Baltic Sea coast setting could quickly become a Russian naval target. Clouds of war were hard to see against bright sunny sky and clear blue water, but many guests were leaving the popular resort early. Lothar, who had completed his public school education in Breslau and was now enrolled in military training at the War College in Danzig, urged his mother to telegraph Manfred for advice. The response was swift and to the point: 'Advise you leave immediately.' Early on Friday morning, 31 July 1914, *Freifrau* von Richthofen took Ilse and Bolko on an early train back to Schweidnitz. Lothar returned to his regiment at Lüben.

Freifrau von Richthofen's book, *Mein Kriegstagebuch* [My War Diary], is a treasury of information about the home town view of World War I. A telling entry describes what the first days of war meant to her family:

While the garrison [at Breslau] with its unexpected abundance of people ... became a feverishly agitated scene and thoughts of what would happen swirled, Manfred as a young Uhlan *Leutnant* rode against the enemy in the East. And carrying him was "Antithesis," the English thoroughbred that I had presented to the gifted, passionate horseman. On the day the horse should have carried him to victory at the racecourse in Posen, he carried him over the border – on patrol against Russia. On 3 August we learned that Uhlan Regiment Nr 1 and Infantry Regiment Nr 155 had occupied the village of Kalisch. The first armed conflict, the first victory, and Manfred had been in it. There was concern all around and yet a proud feeling.

Every night for a week, Manfred led patrols across the Prosna River into enemy territory. The 22-year-old officer had spent half his life preparing for these missions and now he saw the proof of the rigorous Prussian military system that moulded boys and young men into modern Germanic warriors. On several occasions he and his men were nearly caught by troops of the advance enemy force. Steely discipline and resourcefulness helped them outwit even the wily Cossacks. Manfred sent daily dispatches back with the latest information until, finally, he was the only one left to bring back a report. Upon his return to the unit, he wrote:

> Everyone stared at me as if I were a ghost, not only due to my unshaved face, but there had been a rumour that Wedel and I had fallen at Kalisch. The time and place and all the circumstances of my death had been reported in such detail that the report had spread throughout Silesia. My mother had already received condolence visits. All that was lacking was my obituary in the newspaper.

Manfred's letter of 5 August assured his mother that he was alive and successful, despite some minor physical privations:

> ... There is little to eat; only with threats of violence can one get anything [from the local population]. None of my men has yet been wounded. When you receive this letter I will perhaps already be at the French border. The cannons are thundering near Kalisch, [and] I must see what is going on.

Surely, the Uhlan Regiment's superiors had informed its officers that the main Eastern Front battle was far to the north, in East Prussia. There, the German 8th Army prepared to engage a major Russian fighting force that threatened to lock the province in a massive pincer movement. Hence, German forces in the West, driving swiftly through France, needed more fast-moving cavalry forces, which the Kalisch sector could spare, and Uhlan Regiment Nr 1 was soon on a train heading west to German fortifications in the former French province of Lorraine, now marked as 'Lothringen' on Manfred's map. As he described it, the regimental officers travelled in relatively fine fashion:

> I converted part of a baggage car into a living- and bedroom for greater comfort. I had air, light, and plenty of space. I obtained straw at a station stop and covered it with a tent cloth. I slept as well in my improvised sleeping car as I had in my bed in Ostrovo. The journey lasted for a day and a night, through all of Silesia and Saxony, always moving. We seemed to be going in the direction of Metz and at every railway station, we were greeted by a sea of people, overwhelming us with cheers and flowers. The Uhlans were especially admired. The train that passed through the station before us had probably reported that we had met the enemy – and we had been at war only for a week. In addition, my regiment had been mentioned in the first army communiqué ... Therefore, we were celebrated heroes and felt as such. Wedel had found a Cossack sword and showed it to wide-eyed girls. It made a big impression. Finally, we disembarked near Diedenhofen [north of Metz].

While Manfred's unit was moving through Luxembourg toward Belgium, Lothar's unit, the rifle-armed horse-mounted Dragoon Regiment Nr 4, had been mobilized and sent west to join the assault on Belgium. In his first letter from France, on 19 August 1914, Manfred wrote to his mother:

> We Uhlans are unfortunately attached to the infantry; I say unfortunately, for surely Lothar has already taken part in great battles on horseback, as we would hardly be assigned to do. I am often sent out on patrol and try very hard to come back with the Iron Cross. I believe that it will be another eight to 14 days before we are in a great battle ...

That letter revealed the first evidence of Manfred's sibling rivalry with Lothar in their military endeavours, as well as Manfred's interest in the recognition value of military awards. The latter point brings to mind an old soldier's saying: 'A man won't sell you his life, but he'll give it to you for a piece of coloured ribbon.' And the ribbon that Manfred had in mind was made of silver and black thread, was some 30 centimetres [1/8 inches] wide and attached to a medal in cross *patée* form, cast in iron, with a silver edge to make it stand out against dark uniform colours. Similar in form to the battle emblem worn by the Teutonic Knights seven centuries earlier, in World War I the Iron Cross became a distinctive symbol of Prussia's – and now Imperial Germany's – recognition of valour. The medal was established in 1813 by Prussian King Friedrich Wilhelm III and tapped into German history to honour bravery in combat during the Napoleonic Wars and, later, the War of 1870. Eventually it lost some value in World War I, with over 5,000,000 presentations of the Second Class award made, but the Iron Cross was still a significant honour in 1914 and it was distinctive in being the first award of a European monarchy to be presented to officers and enlisted men equally. The Iron Cross was so prized that Manfred von Richthofen and millions of other German soldiers were inspired to fight fearlessly for the award.

As Manfred's regiment advanced northward through Luxembourg and into Belgium, he saw something else that captivated his thoughts: aeroplanes. He noted:

> At the time, I had not the slightest idea what our flyers did.
> I considered every flyer to be an enormous faker. I could not tell
> whether it was a German or an enemy airman. I had no idea that
> German machines were marked with [black] crosses and the
> enemy's with [multi-coloured] cockades. Consequently, we fired at
> every aeroplane we saw. The old flyers still tell us how painful it
> was to be fired at by friend and foe alike.

Uhlan Regiment Nr 1 plodded ever north and Manfred's dreams of epic horseback battles were frustrated by the reality of newly evolving forms of warfare. Encounters with uniformed forces gave way to sniping attacks by armed 'irregular' forces called *franc-tireurs*, whose street clothes made them indistinguishable from civilians. There were even confrontations with local villagers, whose behaviour was contrary to what Manfred knew about warfare. He became hardened by the experience, as he described the dilemma he faced at Arlon, just inside the Belgian border with Luxembourg:

> One day, I had ridden no less than 110 kilometres (68 miles) with my entire patrol. Not a horse failed us; a splendid achievement by my animals. In Arlon, I climbed the church tower steeple using peacetime tactical principles. Of course, I saw nothing, as the nasty enemy was still far away.
>
> At that time we caused relatively little harm. So, I had my patrol stay outside the city and rode alone on bicycle right through the city to the church tower. When I came down again from the tower, I was in the midst of a bunch of grumbling, hostile-looking young men. My bicycle had, of course, been pilfered and I had to go on foot for half an hour. But it amused me. I would like to have got in a scuffle. I felt absolutely secure with a pistol in my hand. Later I learned that inhabitants had rioted against our cavalry, and then our hospitals. A number of these gentlemen had been stood against a wall [and shot]. In the afternoon I reached my destination and learned that three days earlier my cousin Wolfram had fallen nearby.

Manfred's first real combat with French forces occurred on 21 August, when he and over a dozen men reconnoitred an area some 20 kilometres (12.5 miles) west of Arlon. At the edge of a huge rocky forest, they spotted the steel breastplates of a band of French Cuirassiers. The sighting promised an interesting fight between Uhlan lances and cavalry swords. The Germans charged after their foe at full speed. But within a few moments the Cuirassiers seemed to have disappeared. As the Uhlans emerged from the other end of the

forest, they saw only a rock wall and a stream, with a broad meadow beyond the water. The Uhlans had taken the bait for a clever French trap, as Manfred wrote home:

Just as I put the field glasses to my eye, a volley of fire cracked from the edge of the forest about 50 metres (160 feet) away. There were about 200 to 250 French riflemen over there. We couldn't move to the left or forward because the enemy was there, and to the right was the wall of rock; therefore we had to go back. Yes, but it was not so simple. The way was quite narrow and it led right by the enemy-fortified forest's edge. Taking cover was also useless; I had to go back. I was the last one out. Despite my orders, all the other men had bunched together and offered the Frenchmen easy targets. I brought back only four men. This baptism of fire was not as much fun as I thought. That evening some of the others came back, although they had to come by foot, as their horses were dead.

The following evening, however, Manfred von Richthofen and his men tasted victory. Lucky survivors of the French riflemen's ambush returned as Richthofen and other Uhlans joined the mobilization for a divisional strength assault on Virton. As other units of *General* Otto von Below's 9th Infantry Division moved into place, Richthofen's horsemen were alongside the Grenadiers commanded by *Prinz* Oskar of Prussia, the 26-year-old fifth son of Kaiser Wilhelm II. Armed with a variety of hand grenades, the members of Grenadier Regiment Nr 7 were an impressive force. Richthofen was awestruck as he observed *Prinz* Oskar standing 'on a pile of rocks and urging his regiment onward, looking each grenadier in the eye. A splendid moment before the battle.'

Following a hard two-day fight against a vastly superior French force, the German Division won a decisive victory. During the fighting, Richthofen was greatly inspired by the son of Germany's Supreme War Lord, as he noted in letter home:

In this battle *Prinz* Oskar fought at the head of his regiment and remained unscathed. I spoke with him right after the battle, as he was presented with the Iron Cross [Second Class].

Richthofen learned good lessons from these encounters. First, to exercise more caution before rushing off to battle. Second, the example of leadership evident in the way *Prinz* Oskar's determined gaze steeled his grenadiers for the difficult task ahead. Third, battlefield success has tangible rewards, as when the Prince was awarded the high honour of the Iron Cross.

The proof of the lessons came on 23 September 1914, when the young Uhlan officer's further successes resulted in his receiving the Iron Cross Second Class - only a month after it had been pinned to the breast of an heir to the Hohenzollern soldier kings. Manfred von Richthofen had truly arrived and this was only the beginning of his combat career.

3
THE SKY ARENA

The day after Manfred von Richthofen was awarded the Iron Cross, his father received good news from the military establishment. *Major* Albrecht *Freiherr* von Richthofen, at age 55 and partially deaf, was recalled to active duty and assigned to an administrative post at the Silesian Reserve Hospital in Kattowitz, near Krakow. With two sons at the Front, his daughter serving as a Red Cross nurse, and even the family servant, Gustav Mohaupt, serving with a local rifle battalion, the *Major* was itching to be back in uniform.

Freifrau von Richthofen welcomed his good news, as noted in her diary:

> My husband has realized at least a part of his ardent wish ... He has been – one must say – very cranky and unhappy lately and has had us all thoroughly annoyed. He wanted so much to be at the Front, but that was out of the question due to his hearing impairment ... Now, as a result of the Kattowitz command, at least he has something to do for the time being and does not see himself as being in the way.

The *Major* was not the only unhappy Richthofen at that time. Only two months into the war and with one coveted medal on his chest, Manfred began complaining that the front line situation was becoming boring. He wanted to be active in the cavalry tradition, galloping over obstacles, gathering information for local area commanders to use. Unfortunately for him, Uhlan Regiment Nr 1's recent transfer from Belgium to Verdun offered Manfred only a boring view of the dissolution of mobile warfare, for which he had been trained, and devolution to static warfare. There was little opportunity for fast-charging uhlans, dragoons and hussars to function among the network of trenches and fortifications then under construction. Richthofen's numbing boredom was broken only by bursts of artillery fire from batteries far behind enemy lines. From the relatively secure German fortress at Metz, he wrote home:

> A cavalry division has been assembled opposite Paris for about eight days. I believe that Lothar has the good fortune to be with that division. He has certainly experienced more than I have here near

Verdun. The Crown Prince's army will surround Verdun from here
northwards until it surrenders ... The fortifications are too strong
and would require excessive amounts of munitions and lives to take
by storm. It is too bad that we of Uhlan Regiment Nr 1 are tied up
here and the war will most likely end here. The battle for Verdun is
very hard and claims an immense number of lives daily.

Manfred's mood soon turned to impatience and envy that his younger brother
was seeing more combat action than he. Further, he feared the war would end
before he could use the martial skills he had spent half of his life learning. As
he described his position:

At first, I was in the trenches in a location where nothing was going
on. Then I became an assistant adjutant and believed I would
experience more. But I was sadly mistaken. The fighting men looked
down on me as a "paper shuffler." I was not really that low, but ...
I was allowed to advance only up to 1,500 metres (4,900 feet) behind
the front lines. There I sat for weeks on end in a bombproof, heated
dugout. I carried things back and forth, from here to there. That was
a great physical strain; for I went uphill, downhill, criss-cross,
through an unending number of trenches and mud holes until
finally I came to where the men were firing. After a short visit with
the fighting men, my job felt like a dumb thing for me to be doing
with my healthy bones.

   At that time they began digging underground. It was not yet clear
to us what it meant to build a dugout or to extend a trench. We
knew the terms from fortification lessons at the Military Academy,
but it was a subject for combat engineers. Up at the Combres
Heights, everyone ... had a spade and a pick, and gave unending
effort to dig in the ground as deeply as possible. It was quite funny
that in many places the French were only five paces away from us.
We could hear them talk and see them smoke cigarettes, and now
and then they threw a piece of paper at us. We conversed with them,
but still sought to annoy them in every way possible, especially with
hand grenades.

Despite the hazards, soldiers on both sides continued their mole-like work, looking into earth that had never been opened by human beings. Around them, great patches of the once beautiful wooded hills of the Côte Lorraine had become deserts of timber uprooted and carelessly harvested by the savage exchange of bullets and artillery shells. The logs did not go to waste; they became the side and roof beams of the growing network of earthen bunkers on both sides of the lines. For Manfred von Richthofen, the avid hunter and woodsman raised in the strong German traditional love of the outdoors, it must have been deeply depressing to see so much destroyed forest land during his early morning rounds around the mud fields that developed without tree roots to keep the earth intact. During afternoons, he had to telephone those reports to higher echelons, but at least he was in a dugout, away from the random devastation above ground. In his off-duty time, Richthofen hunted wild boars in La Chaussée Forest and his successes added welcome variety to otherwise bland meals from the field kitchen.

Letters from home informed Manfred that his brother had also had a close call, when he was nearly hit by a sniper. That incident was brushed aside when, in mid-October, Lothar was awarded the Iron Cross Second Class and, shortly thereafter, his unit was transferred to the Eastern Front, where there was still plenty of activity in a truly mobile war. Manfred continued to grumble:

> **We are now in and out of the trenches, like the infantry. Some shells come back and forth in singular exchange; that is all I have experienced in the last four weeks. It is too bad we are not employed in the major battle ... I would like very much to have got the Iron Cross First Class, but there is no opportunity here. I would have to go to Verdun dressed as a Frenchman and blow up a gun turret.**

Sitting in his dugout, Manfred could only read war dispatches and news summaries to follow the course of what he perceived to be 'the real war,' where German forces were beating back the Russians at every opportunity. The best news came from the precarious situation on the Eastern Front, where *General* Paul von Hindenburg's forces had achieved several stunning victories. A veteran of the Austro-Prussian War of 1866 and the Franco-Prussian War of 1870, Hindenburg had been recalled from retirement on 22 August 1914. Five days later he was promoted to *Generaloberst* [Colonel-General] and given command of the German 8th Army, which defeated the Russian 2nd Army at the Battle of Tannenberg. By mid-September, Hindenburg's army had routed the Russian 1st Army at the Battle of the Masurian Lakes, thereby fending off the threat to East Prussia. And, following his elevation to Supreme Commander of German Forces in the East, Hindenburg led the November victory at Łodz that halted the Russian advance toward Silesia. His success was rewarded with his promotion to the army's highest commissioned rank, *Generalfeldmarschall* [Field Marshal], on the 27th of the month.

As winter approached, Manfred became more frustrated in his dugout in France, especially after learning about Lothar's successes in Poland and in Hungary and as Hindenburg's achievements inspired more German victories across the Eastern Front. Manfred knew only that the war continued to drag on, as he noted in a letter to his mother:

> Now I have been sitting opposite Verdun for three months. Here,
> nothing changes. Last night, we were playing cards when a shell ...
> banged on the roof of the house next door. I never jumped up from
> a table so fast as I did then. Normally, we spend every other day in
> the trenches. I have figured out that we will relieve the other shift
> the evening of 24 December, and so from 24 to 25 December I will
> make my stealth patrol of the enemy trenches. This is the first
> Christmas Eve that I have not spent in the family home. Hopefully,
> it will be the only one I spend in enemy territory.

In early January 1915, Manfred was posted as an orderly officer with the 18th Infantry Brigade. With no need for soldiers on horseback, he was a dispatch carrier with a fancy title. The advent of spring rains made matters worse, creating rivers of mud between the trench positions. Battles raged in Flanders and along the Marne River, but Manfred's situation at Verdun grew bleaker with an endless stream of minor events that got on his nerves. On his 23rd birthday – 2 May 1915 – he sat in a dugout, counting the days until he could go on leave and be with his family.

Totally frustrated by Western Front ground warfare, which once promised opportunities to prove himself a fearless warrior in the long military tradition of individual combat, Manfred looked into the future almost every time he glanced skyward. He saw more and more German aeroplanes crossing the battle lines to reconnoitre hostile rear areas and make direct contact with the enemy by dropping bombs on them or strafing them with machine gun fire. Aeroplanes offered the mobility he once enjoyed on horseback. With nothing to lose by inquiring about a change in his status, he wrote to his commanding general:

> Dear Excellency, I did not go to war to gather cheese and eggs, but for another purpose.

That cheeky introduction may have helped him vent his frustration, but it did him no good in higher echelons. His request to transfer to the Flying Service was promptly denied.

Then, perhaps after some perceptive bureaucrat realized that cavalry officers had reconnaissance training and skills that would make them good aerial observers, Manfred's request came back again and this time it was approved. He was granted a brief home leave and then ordered to report to an aviation training centre.

He announced the good news with a dramatic entry at home bright and early on the morning of Friday, 21 May 1915. Arriving at the family house in Schweidnitz, Manfred found the garden gate still locked, but easily surmounted by a man of his physical agility. In no time, he stood at the foot of his mother's bed, sporting a broad smile. Despite the abrupt awakening, *Freifrau* von Richthofen soon had breakfast organized and carried out to the garden, in the shade of the old nut trees, so she could hear the latest news from her oldest son. Based on newspaper accounts, she cited the many German victories reported and opined that the war must at last be coming to an end. She noted the conversation in her diary, beginning with Manfred's glum assessment:

> "I do not believe that we will win this war ... You have no idea how strong our enemy is". But we continue to win [I replied].
> Have you never heard anything about our retreat at the Marne?"
> No, we knew nothing at all about it.
> And Manfred concluded: "It would be, at best, a stalemate".
> Then we spoke about this and that, exchanged views and arguments; as always, his mature, sensible opinions surprised me. Then, unexpectedly, Manfred said: "I am going to join the flyers".

There was something nice and happy in his voice as he said it; I understood nothing about it, could imagine very little, and yet I knew that once he spoke about it, it was an established fact to him, irrevocably. Therefore, I said nothing against it. We would get used to it and, despite Manfred's youth, respect it. I listened with much more interest as he said what he knew about his new weapon. As we walked from the garden into the house, I sensed with certainty that a new and great mission had taken root in him.

Four days later, Manfred went off to war again.

The German Flying Service's 16 flying schools were dispersed throughout the country, to provide basic training for hundreds of pilots, observers and ground crewmen at any one time. Manfred von Richthofen was assigned to the training unit *Flieger-Ersatz-Abteilung 7* at Cologne, during the last week in May, to determine whether he would be suitable for aviation duties. In joining the Flying Service his 'greatest wish was fulfilled' and he approached the new challenge in his usual orderly and disciplined manner. He was soon surprised, as he wrote:

The night before, I went to bed earlier than usual to be fresh the next morning, as at seven o'clock I was to fly for the first time as an observer. Naturally, I was very excited, as I could not at all imagine what it would be like. Everyone I asked about it told me something different. We were driven to the airfield and then I sat in an aeroplane for the first time. The blast of wind from the propeller bothered me enormously. It was impossible to make myself understood by the pilot. Everything flew away from me. If I took out a piece of paper, it disappeared. My crash helmet slipped off, my scarf loosened too much, and my jacket was not buttoned securely; it was miserable. Before I knew what was happening, the pilot got the engine up to full speed and the machine began rolling, faster and faster. I held on frantically. All at once, the shaking stopped and the machine was in the air. The ground slipped away beneath me.

The pilot flew left and right and here and there until Manfred was totally disoriented. He had no idea where he was and he did not care. This ride across the sky was as exhilarating as being on a new horse. He continued to cling to the side of his seat, but peered over the side to observe the Rhine River stretching as far as he could see like a blue ribbon with sparkles of early morning sunlight dancing along it. On one bank he spotted the city of Cologne, with the twin spires of its landmark cathedral reaching to the sky, but still looking as small as a toy. This was a view unlike any he had ever seen on the back of even the highest horse. In the aeroplane, Manfred von Richthofen found his muse:

> It was a glorious feeling to sail over everything. Who could have touched me? No one! I did not care where I was and I was quite sad when my pilot thought it was time to land ... In an aeroplane one has a feeling of absolute security; one sits as peacefully as in an easy chair ... one does not become giddy in an aeroplane. But it is a damned nervous sensation to whistle through the air, especially when the aeroplane suddenly dips ... the engine stops running, and then there is a tremendous silence. I held on frantically and thought, of course, "now you are going to crash." But everything went along so naturally and simply – even the landing when we again touched the ground – that the feeling of fear was completely absent. I was very enthusiastic about it and could have stayed in the aeroplane all day. I counted the hours until the next take-off.

Of the 30 officers who began the short introductory course, Richthofen was one of the few who passed all the tests and, on 10 June, he was sent eastward to *Flieger-Ersatz-Abteilung 6* at Grossenhain in Saxony for training as an aerial observer. He could have applied for pilot instruction, but elected the two-week observer programme because, as he pointed out:

> I wanted to go to the Front quickly, for I was afraid that I would be too late for the war. Three months were required to become a pilot. By then peace could have come; therefore, the longer course was out of the question.

No longer devoting minimal efforts to his education, as he had in his cadet days, Manfred von Richthofen completed his observer's training quickly and, on 21 June, he was assigned to *Feldflieger-Abteilung 69* [Field Flying Section 69], which was being assembled on the Eastern Front. It was fully ready for duty on 3 July 1915, during newly promoted *Generalfeldmarschall* August von Mackensen's successful use of a combined German, Hungarian and Bulgarian army group to smash Russian forces along the southern part of the Eastern Front. Richthofen recalled:

> I joined [Mackensen's] army during the siege at Rawa Ruska [in Western Ukraine, due south of Brest-Litovsk]. I spent a day at the aviation field headquarters and then I was sent to *Feldflieger-Abteilung 69*. As a beginner I felt very foolish, but my pilot, *Oberleutnant* Georg Zeumer, was very well known. Actually, this was my nicest time. It had many really great similarities to the cavalry. Every day, morning and afternoon, I could fly reconnaissance missions and bring home reports.

Manfred was very happy, flying reconnaissance missions throughout July and August as Mackensen's forces pushed north toward the heavily defended fortress at Brest-Litovsk. And Manfred saw plenty of action with his pilot, *Oberleutnant* Zeumer, who flew him on daily morning and afternoon patrols in a big sturdy Albatros B.II two-seat biplane, known to be a fast and reliable reconnaissance aircraft. Manfred sat in the front cockpit and made his observations by peering between the wings. He was armed with a rifle, which limited his defensive capability, but a weapon in the hands of a skilled, motivated and experienced hunter such as Manfred von Richthofen made the aircraft a true fighting machine.

Zeumer shared Richthofen's desire for action and was a skilled pilot who usually took his observer down for a close look at important ground installations that the higher-ups needed to know about. Zeumer's reputation for such daring flying earned him the nickname 'the black cat' because he seemed headed for disaster. He knew that he had tuberculosis, and was determined to die gloriously. While Richthofen focused on living to defend his country for as long as he possibly could, he recognized that Zeumer had traits that made him the perfect pilot at the time.

Manfred's letter of 20 July 1915 sums up his now joyful mood:

> Now we are again right into completely mobile warfare. I fly over the
> enemy almost daily and bring back reports. I reported the retreat of
> the Russians three days ago. It is so much more enjoyable for me, in
> any case more than playing Assistant Adjutant ... I am especially
> happy to be right here, in the most important theatre of operations,
> and to be able to participate in it.

In the ebb and flow of deployments, Zeumer was abruptly transferred back to
Flanders. He had come to the Eastern Front to provide experienced personnel
to *Feldflieger-Abteilung 69* and now he was sent back to his unit. Richthofen was
concerned about finding another pilot with Zeumer's skills and sense of
daring. The new man, 29-year-old *Rittmeister* [Cavalry Captain] Erich *Graf* von
Holck, a veteran of Dragoon Regiment Nr 9, filled the bill perfectly. In addition
to being a fellow cavalryman, Holck had been a successful racing car driver
before the war, so there was no question about his tolerance for high risk to
achieve his objectives, as Richthofen wrote:

> *Graf* von Holck was ... a pilot of rare ability and most especially and
> importantly, he was in a class far above the enemy. We made many
> splendid reconnaissance flights – who knows how far? – into Russia.
> I never had any feeling of insecurity with him; on the contrary, at the
> critical moment he gave me support. When I looked into his
> determined face, I had even more courage than before.

Their last flight together almost ended in disaster. Richthofen and Holck were
assigned to determine the size of a retreating Russian troop force that was
applying a scorched earth policy to everything in its wake. Their Albatros
approached Wicznice, a Polish town completely covered by a column of thick
black smoke some 2,000 metres (6,500 feet) high. Their aeroplane was at about
1,500 metres (4,900 feet) altitude, so Richthofen, who, as the observer, was in
charge of the aircraft, motioned to Holck to fly around the pillar of smoke.

But, as Richthofen pointed out:

The greater the danger, the more attractive it was to Holck. Therefore, he went right into it! It was fun to be with such a plucky fellow. But our carelessness soon cost us dearly; for barely had the tail of the aircraft disappeared into the cloud when I noticed the aeroplane swaying. I could see nothing more, the smoke stung my eyes, the air was significantly warmer and beneath me I saw only an enormous sea of fire. Suddenly the aeroplane stalled and plunged spiralling downward. I could only grab on to a strut to brace myself; otherwise I would have been tossed out. The first thing I did was look into Holck's face. I regained my courage, for his bearing was of iron confidence. My only thought was: it is so stupid to die ... in such a needless way.

The plane was caught in a maelstrom-like swirl of thermal currents that no pilot of the time could master with such a lightly constructed machine; its 100-horsepower engine was no match for fire-fuelled air blasts. Richthofen and Holck were seconds away from falling into the inferno when, by sheer luck, their Albatros dropped out of the cloud and Holck was able to regain control. Using the full power of the Benz engine, he pulled up to 500 metres (1,600 feet) altitude and steered the aeroplane directly for German lines. But at such a low altitude, the plane was an easy target for columns of retreating Russian soldiers, armed with machine guns which they quickly directed against the hapless Albatros. The bullets hitting the plane 'sounded like chestnuts popping in a fire,' Richthofen recalled. Then the aeroplane's engine quit and Holck had to set it down near an abandoned Russian artillery position. Just when it seemed that matters could not get worse, Richthofen and Holck saw a swarm of soldiers running toward them. Holck carried no sidearm and Richthofen had only a pistol and six bullets to defend them. But their fear quickly dissolved when they recognized the troops as German.

They were even more surprised to learn the men were from Grenadier Regiment Nr 2, which was commanded by *Prinz* Eitel Friedrich of Prussia, the 32-year-old second son of Kaiser Wilhelm II. Moments later, the main force appeared, along with its commander. Exercising Prussian frugality and a concern for government-owned property, the Prince ordered horses and a cart for his aviation guests so they could return to their unit with what was left of their aeroplane. Richthofen quipped:

Once again we two cavalry flyers were mounted on "oat burning" engines.

They arrived back at their airfield just after sundown. The Albatros B.II was written off as a total loss, but its type was about to be replaced by the similar-looking but improved C.I, in which the observer, in the rear cockpit, was better able to perform his duties and defend the aircraft. Before they received a new aeroplane, however, the two airmen were transferred to different units. Holck was assigned to the newly forming two-seater artillery support squadron *Flieger-Abteilung (A) 203*, at Montmédy in the Champagne Sector. The unit had a contingent of Fokker monoplane fighters then appearing in front line service and Richthofen could easily imagine which aircraft the daring Holck would find a way to fly while at Montmédy. Richthofen could not have imagined or appreciated that Holck's comrades at *Flieger-Abteilung (A) 203* included the newly promoted but still relatively unknown *Oberleutnant* Oswald Boelcke, who would go on to build a formidable reputation flying Fokker fighters.

The early Fokkers' importance was summarized by the late Peter M. Grosz, the world authority on German aircraft of World War I:

> Machine gun synchronization, introduced with the appearance of the Fokker monoplane fighters (of which the E.III was the most popular model) in June 1915, changed if not revolutionized the war in the air. German pilots flying nimble, single-seat Fokker fighters armed with a fixed machine gun firing through the rotating [propeller] arc gained lasting fame when they caught the Allies by surprise and took an alarming toll of British and French [aircraft].

Meanwhile, Richthofen packed his luggage and headed to a unit bearing the odd and certainly outmoded cover name *Brieftauben-Abteilung Ostende* [Carrier Pigeon Section Ostend] on the English Channel coast of the 4th Army Sector in Flanders. En route to Ostend, he managed a brief stopover at Schweidnitz, where, his mother recalled:

> We fetched him from the train station at about midnight; he was accompanied by his orderly, the ever faithful Menzke, who had

been with him since peacetime. Manfred looked splendid, he beamed and related his experiences at the Front, each one more interesting than the other. We listened breathlessly.

Richthofen and Menzke arrived in Ostend on 21 August and were met at the train by Georg Zeumer, the frail, but ever-enthusiastic 'black cat' of the Eastern Front. On the way to their quarters in a luxurious resort hotel right on the beach, Zeumer described at length the types of British and French aviation units that operated against them and the British warships that were so bold as to sail fairly close to their splendid beach and lob a few shells at them.

Richthofen was most interested in the *Abteilung*'s new aircraft. The unit had recently been relieved of its old B-type aircraft, which were passed down to training schools, and had received new C-type machines, as well as two-engined AEG G.II biplane bombers. In the G-type – the designation for '*Grosskampfflugzeug*' [Large Combat Aeroplane] – Richthofen would be the observer/bombardier, sitting in what flyers called the 'pulpit,' a forward-protruding cockpit. Unobstructed and forward of the pilot, Richthofen would have the same offensive capability as new German E-type monoplane fighters, which were then the only aircraft armed with forward-firing synchronized machine guns. At last, Richthofen would go from a defensive to a new, truly offensive role in aerial combat and he embraced it eagerly.

During his orientation flight in the AEG, the initials of the plane's manufacturer, *Allgemeine Elektrizitäts-Gesellschaft* [General Electric Company], Richthofen saw elements of the extensive system of trenches and barbed wire barriers being erected by the opposing armies from the Swiss border near the Vosges Mountains in southern France to the North Sea near Holland. This aerial view of the Western Front revealed how effectively the trench network walled off the battle lines that cavalry units had once leaped over with impunity to reconnoitre enemy positions. Now, hydrogen-filled balloons tethered to the ground by a steel cable were sent up as aerial vantage points from which to spy on the enemy, but they were limited by the strength of the balloon observers' binoculars. The aeroplane, however, could easily cross the lines to gather information and bombard rear areas. As a natural development of that process, single-seat fighters interdicted reconnaissance aircraft attempting to carry out their mission.

Richthofen wrote:

> Now I really had a very nice time; it had little to do with the war,
> but it was essential to my apprenticeship as a combat flyer. We
> flew a great deal, seldom had aerial combats and never had any
> successes. The other life, however, was alluring. We had
> expropriated a hotel on the beach at Ostend and there we
> sunbathed every afternoon. Unfortunately, other soldiers were the
> only holiday visitors there. We sat on the terraces of Ostend,
> wrapped in our brightly coloured bathrobes and drank coffee in
> the afternoon.
>
> One day, as we sat as usual on the beach ... suddenly came the
> sound of a trumpet signalling the approach of a British naval
> squadron. Naturally, we did not allow our comfort to be disturbed
> and continued drinking our coffee. Someone called out: "There
> they are!" And we could actually see on the horizon, although not
> very distinctly, first some puffing smokestacks and later some
> ships. Quickly, we fetched binoculars and observed them. We saw
> quite an imposing number of ships. It was not clear to us what
> they intended to do, but we soon found out.

Richthofen and his comrades went up to the roof of their hotel for a better
view of the approaching enemy warships, and soon recognized their error.
One gunboat fired a shot that landed and exploded exactly where the
Germans had been lying on the beach. The men quickly ran for the air raid
shelter, which in the tradition of wartime gallows humour was called the
'*Heldenkeller*' [heroes' cellar]. They remained there for some time, waiting for
the British naval force to cease firing.

Having endured that baptism of fire, Richthofen and Zeumer eagerly
volunteered for an early evening flight out to sea to test an experimental
steering device to enable the two-engined AEG bombers to fly in a straight
line even on one engine. Ordinarily the loss of one engine's power would
cause a two-engine aeroplane to drift off course in the direction of the non-
functioning engine; hence, the new device, if workable, would have greatly
aided night flight operations by AEG and other multi-engined German
bombers. Richthofen recounted the flight:

[After a time] I suddenly noticed that the water was gradually disappearing from our radiator. It seemed a bit scary to me and I brought it to my pilot's attention. He made a long face and prepared to go home. However, we were roughly 20 kilometres (12.5 miles) from the coast and first we had to fly that distance. One engine began to quit and I quietly prepared myself for a cold and humid bath. But we made it! The giant "apple barge" made it with one engine and the new steering device, and we reached the coast and landed very nicely at our airfield.

Following that over-water flight, Richthofen and Zeumer concentrated on operations over land, often flying five or six hours a day to drop bombs on a variety of enemy targets. After expending their bombs, they were free to search for enemy aircraft to attack. During a morning flight on 1 September 1915, they had an opportunity. Looking off in the distance, Manfred spotted what he took to be a British Farman, a type of biplane that German airmen called 'Gitterschwanz' [lattice-tail] because the engine was mounted at the back of a stubby fuselage between the wings, with twin tail booms – like latticework – that swept back to the rear control surfaces.

Zeumer headed straight for the kite-like aeroplane while, as Richthofen recorded, he prepared to fight:

My heart was pounding as Zeumer approached him. I was excited about what was about to happen. I had never seen an aerial combat and had only a very vague conception of it. All of a sudden, the Englishman and I were rushing toward each other. I got off at most four shots, while the Englishman suddenly got behind us and shot the whole works at us. I must say that I did not feel in danger because I could not imagine how such a battle would turn out. Time and time again we circled each other until finally, to our great astonishment, the Englishman, quite satisfied, turned away and flew off. I was greatly disappointed, as was my pilot.

Back at Ostend, both men were in a foul mood about the missed opportunity for a successful fight in the air. Zeumer accused Richthofen of having shot badly, while Richthofen countered that Zeumer's piloting skills failed to put him in a good position to fire. Finally, they went back to the aeroplane to see what it might 'tell' them about the fight. They saw that 'the apple barge,' as they called the AEG, had taken a respectable number of hits without being disabled and concluded that the flimsy-looking Farman may have been just as rugged. It became clear to both novice air warriors that there was more to shooting down an enemy aeroplane than simply firing a gun at it and hitting it.

Up to that point, Richthofen had endured the war without a scratch. There were some close calls – a bullet through his fur-lined boots, another through his scarf and still another into the arm of his leather flight jacket – but no combat-related wounds that drew blood. That illusion of Siegfried-like invincibility changed during a routine bombing mission, which he later described:

> We reached the target and dropped the first bombs. It is, of course, very interesting to watch the results of such a mission ... But my *Grosskampfflugzeug*, which was well suited for carrying bombs, had a stupid peculiarity that made it hard to see the explosion; for, immediately after the bomb was dropped, the aeroplane moved over the target and covered it completely with its wings. This always angered me, as there was so little enjoyment because of it. When the bomb bursts below and one sees the lovely greyish-whitish cloud of the explosion near the target, it is very pleasing. So I signalled to my good friend Zeumer to fly so that the wings were off to the side. In so doing I forgot my infamous "apple barge" had two propellers that turned to the right and left of my observer seat. I was showing him whereabouts the bomb had struck and – smack! – my little finger was nicked by a propeller blade. I was surprised at first that it had been injured, but Zeumer had noticed nothing.
>
> I was sick of dropping bombs and quickly let my last one go so we could make for home. My love for the large combat aircraft, which had been weak at best, suffered seriously from this bomb drop. I could not fly again for a week. Now my finger has only a beauty blemish, but at least I can say with pride: "I, too, have a war wound."

At Ostend, Richthofen was in the company of several German military aviation pioneers and he learned from them. He became close friends with *Leutnant* 'Fritze' von Falkenhayn, who started in aviation in 1913 as an observer and became a pilot the following year. The lesson in career mobility in the new Air Service was not lost on Richthofen, who ultimately followed the same path. 'Fritze' was the son of *General der Infanterie* Erich von Falkenhayn, the Chief of the German General Staff, and Richthofen would later benefit from his friend's access to people in high places.

For the moment, though, activity in Flanders was mild compared to the new French offensive in the Champagne region that began on 25 September 1915. German lines began to crack and *General* von Falkenhayn himself raced from Berlin to the scene to restore order. To help hold the line, crews from *Brieftauben-Abteilung Ostende* were quickly sent by train to the 3rd Army Sector. Four *BAO* C-type aircraft and two Fokker monoplane fighter aircraft were assigned to *Feldflieger-Abteilung 22*'s airfield at Vouziers to cover large German troop formations in that area and then two more *BAO* two-seaters were provided to escort other 3rd Army aircraft.

Richthofen and Zeumer were among *BAO* crews sent to Vouziers, where there was an opportunity to return to smaller, more manoeuvrable single-engine C-type aircraft. Zeumer was impressed by field reports about the air combat successes of Oswald Boelcke and Max Immelmann, Germany's emerging master combat pilots. But, despite his physical frailty, Zeumer focused on joining their ranks by flying a Fokker monoplane at Vouziers. Indeed, he soon became so proficient with the Fokker that Richthofen had to find a new flying partner.

Again, Richthofen's good luck held and he was assigned to fly with 27-year-old *Oberleutnant* Paul Henning von Osterroht, who, like Richthofen, was a product of cadet training at Wahlstatt and Gross-Lichterfelde. Further, Osterroht, a pre-war military flyer, had long viewed the aeroplane as a weapon and sought opportunities to prove the point. Now they flew in an Aviatik C.I two-seat biplane, and, while Osterroht scouted for targets, Richthofen stood by his machine gun, ready to fight. But the French offensive failed and, with the German 3rd Army holding fast, some of the hastily called German reinforcements were redeployed to assure adequate coverage in other sectors. Initially, several *BAO* aircrews, including Richthofen and Osterroht, were sent back to Ostend and then, on 1 October, quickly ordered to Rethel, some 30 kilometres

(18.6 miles) north-east of Vouziers, to help counter increasing French aerial activity around Verdun.

As usual, the BAO train carried aircrews, ground personnel and aircraft to the new operational area. At one point in the journey, Richthofen was in the dining car when he recognized an officer of his rank and about his own age at a nearby table. There was nothing special about the other *Leutnant's* uniform, the same dull field grey colour worn by most ground units. But his strong, rugged-looking face was becoming well known due to ever more frequent appearances in newspapers and magazines. Then it came to Richthofen – the other man was Oswald Boelcke, who by now had shot down four enemy aircraft. Richthofen's interest in him soared, as he recorded:

> He had been mentioned by name in the dispatches. He impressed me because his experiences were quite exciting. Even though I had taken great pains up to that point, I had not destroyed a single enemy plane; that is, I had not been credited with any. I wanted to find out how this *Leutnant* Boelcke had really accomplished it.
>
> So I asked him: "Tell me honestly, how do you really do it?"
>
> He laughed, although I was quite serious. Then he replied: "Yes, good heavens, it is quite simple. I fly as close as I can, shoot, and then he falls down." I just shook my head and thought to myself that I had done the same thing, but my opponent had not fallen down. The difference, to be sure, was that Boelcke flew a Fokker monoplane and I an AEG *Grosskampfflugzeug*.
>
> I took the trouble to become better acquainted with this nice, unassuming person who had impressed me so much. We often played cards together and went for walks during which I would question him. After that I made up my mind and told myself: "You must learn to fly a Fokker yourself, then perhaps it will be better."

Once settled in at the new airfield at Rethel, Richthofen persuaded Zeumer to teach him how to fly aeroplanes. Zeumer obtained a two-seater, most likely an old B-type, in which the student sat in the front seat while the instructor demonstrated the controls from the pilot's seat behind him. Of course, this instruction took place on slow days or after both men had flown their regularly assigned missions. Richthofen proved to be a tireless pupil and, after some 25 hours of instruction, Zeumer told him he was ready for his first solo flight. Light enemy activity on the afternoon of 10 October 1915 offered the perfect opportunity.

Richthofen recalled:

> There are few moments in life that produce as nervous a sensation as the first solo flight. When Zeumer announced "So, now go and fly by yourself," I must say I would rather have answered: "I am afraid." But this word should never come from the mouth of a defender of the Fatherland. Therefore, good or bad, I had to swallow my cowardice and sit myself in the machine.
>
> Once again, he explained every theory of movement to me. I scarcely heard what he said, for I was firmly convinced that I would forget half of what he told me.
>
> The engine started with a roar. I gave it power and the machine began to pick up speed and suddenly I could not help but notice that I was actually flying. Finally, it was no longer an anxious feeling; rather, it was one of daring. Now it was all up to me. No matter what happened, I was no longer frightened. With contempt for death I made a wide curve to the left, shut off the engine precisely over the designated tree and waited to see what would happen. Then came the most difficult part, the landing. I remembered the essential manipulations; I performed them mechanically. However, the machine reacted differently than when Zeumer sat in it. I lost my balance, made some wrong movements, and landed nose-first with what was once the "instruction machine." Very sadly, I looked at the damage that I had done, which was not very great, but I had to endure laughter from all sides.
>
> Two days later I went back to my flying lessons with mad passion and suddenly everything went wonderfully well.
>
> Two weeks later [26 October] I took my first examination to become a pilot. I flew the prescribed figure eights and made the ordered number of landings, whereupon I proudly got out of the machine and heard, to my great astonishment, that I had failed.

There was nothing else to do but to try once more to pass the initial examination.

That afternoon, however, Richthofen's luck changed when an irresistible French target presented itself within its own lines over Somme Py, east of Reims.

As Richthofen wrote:

> I flew as an observer with Osterroht, who also had an aeroplane smaller than our "apple barge," the *Grosskampfflugzeug*. About five kilometres [three miles] behind the front we encountered a Farman two-seater. He let us calmly approach him and for the first time I saw an aerial opponent at quite close range. Osterroht flew very skilfully and so close to him that I could easily bring him under fire. The opponent had not noticed us at all; for he did not begin to fire back until I had my first gun jam.
>
> After I had fired my entire drum of a hundred rounds, I could not believe my eyes, as all of a sudden the opponent went down in a peculiar spiral. I followed him with my eyes and tapped Osterroht on the head [to take note of it]. He fell and fell and in fact went into a big shell crater; we saw it, standing on its nose, with the tail pointing to the sky. According to the map, it lay five kilometres behind the Front, on the other side of the lines. At that time aeroplanes shot down behind enemy lines did not count; otherwise, I would have one more on my victory list today. But I was very proud of my success; for in other respects the main point is that [an enemy] is brought down, not that one receives credit for doing it.

Determining credit for aerial victories was very complicated. Eyewitness accounts by only the crewmen involved were not accepted. Confirmation by either another friendly aircrew or some credible person on the ground was essential to receiving credit for success in an air battle. This practice was followed by all the World War I belligerents – and there were always exceptions to the rule, as will be pointed out later in this book – because of the variables involved. Fictionalised accounts presented one problem, misjudgements another and final results could be misleading. In the case of the French Farman claimed by Richthofen over Somme Py, the latter seems to be the case. French records show no losses along the entire Western Front on 26 October 1915.

On many subsequent occasions, Richthofen obtained or had someone else gather physical proof of his aerial prowess. The highly-prized duck feathers at the family home in Schweidnitz would be joined by many other trophies of war – patches of fabric bearing the serial numbers of downed enemy aircraft, captured machine guns, flare pistols and other souvenirs – and the house would become a museum dedicated to his unprecedented success in aerial combat.

After German 3rd Army forces recovered territory lost during the abortive French offensive in the Champagne region, there was much less air activity there and Richthofen was posted to the aviation training unit *Flieger-Ersatz-Abteilung 2* at Döberitz, east of Berlin. Despite his aggressive displays in the air, Richthofen was considered to be a multi-engined large aircraft crewman and his assignment to Döberitz was to prepare him for flight in the next development in that area, the new R-types (the designator for *Riesenflugzeuge* or Giant Aeroplanes) that were soon to enter service.

In a letter dated 2 November 1915, he wrote to his mother:

> ... I am preparing to leave the beautiful Champagne country in the near future. I have received orders to [learn to fly] fly a *Riesenflugzeug*, but, unfortunately, it is not yet ready. Therefore, my pilot, *Herr* von Osterroht, and I must go to Berlin to become familiar with the giant barge. It can hold almost as many bombs as a Zeppelin. Five or six men fly in it: mechanic, machine-gunner, two pilots and an observer. I am very curious about the crate.

4
WINDS OF CHANGE

Manfred von Richthofen became a man of his time, moving easily from warfare on horseback to fighting in new military equipment powered by internal combustion engines. His interest in such new developments as German *Riesenflugzeuge* ['Giant' or R-type aircraft] can be explained by these lines from the definitive book on the subject:

> In World War I, technology played a ... dramatic role in advancing the science of aeronautical engineering ... No small part of this progress belonged in the field of giant aircraft development, particularly in Germany. German engineers in a few short years had spanned the gulf between crude wooden biplanes and all-metal, multi-engined, monoplane giant bombers.

Much of that progress was concentrated outside Döberitz, which became the fountainhead of German military aviation in 1900, when the nation's first airship battalion and military flying field were established there. Lighter-than-air craft soon gave way to engine-powered aircraft and, located on a broad, empty heath, Döberitz was an ideal location for aviation developments throughout the next two decades and beyond; the area was away from city distractions, and the soft heath could absorb many faulty landings. The site also became home to Germany's first Giant aircraft training facility, and Richthofen's determination to learn more about the new aircraft – and his evaluation of their role in his future – is evident in his commentary about being assigned to the flying school:

> ... From the beginning I took a great interest in the *Riesenflugzeug*. Strangely enough, flying in the gigantic thing made it clear to me that only the smallest aeroplane would serve my purpose as a combat pilot. Such a big "apple barge" is not responsive enough for combat, and that is the main point in my business. The difference between a Large Combat Aeroplane and a Giant plane is that a Giant plane is considerably bigger and is more suitable for bombing and less for fighting.

Richthofen's knack for meeting prominent people continued at Döberitz, where he became friends with *Oberleutnant* Bodo *Freih*err von Lyncker, whose father was the Kaiser's adjutant general and chief of the military cabinet. Lyncker came from an illustrious family at a much higher social level, was two years younger and a rank higher than Richthofen. The key to their friendship was that Lyncker, also a former cavalryman, shared Richthofen's passion for combat flying and adventure. Richthofen described some of their exploits:

> Our shared objective was to fly Fokkers in a *Jagdstaffel* [fighter unit] on the Western Front ... We spent many enjoyable hours at Döberitz. One of them, for example, involved "off-field landings and take-offs." I used the opportunity to combine the necessary with the agreeable. My favourite off-field landing place was the Buchow Estate, where I had been invited to hunt wild boar. On nice evenings I would have preferred to fly, except for my passion for hunting. Therefore, I arranged my off-field landing place so that I could comfortably reach my hunting grounds.
>
> I flew a two-seater and took a second pilot with me as an observer, and sent him back in the evening. During the night I set out after the boar and the next morning this pilot fetched me. If I had not been fetched, I would have been in trouble, as I would have had to march by foot for about ten kilometres (six miles) back to Döberitz. So I needed a man who would fetch me from my high perch in any weather. Not everyone will fly in foul weather; yet, I found one such hearty, daring fellow.
>
> One morning after I had spent the night outside, a tremendous snowstorm began. I could not see more than 50 metres (160 feet) ahead of me. It was just eight o'clock, the designated time the pilot was to pick me up. I silently hoped this time he would not come back for me. But suddenly I heard a droning sound – although I could see nothing – and five minutes later my beautiful bird crashed and lay in front of me, in a heap, all twisted out of shape.

The unnamed pilot was not injured in the crash and had to join Richthofen in the long walk back to Döberitz to explain the loss of the aeroplane, which was no doubt an obsolete former front line machine, but still government property that had to be accounted for. Who was this brave pilot who risked his life and career to make an unauthorized flight in a snow squall which resulted in the apparent total loss of a training aircraft just so Richthofen could make his nocturnal hunting excursions?

The answer might have come when Richthofen was on leave in May 1917 and began dictating his memoir *Der rote Kampfflieger* [The Red Combat Flyer], but he did not reveal the man's name due to wartime censorship or his own selective memory. It could be conjectured that the pilot was Bodo von Lyncker, who could easily have arranged for such an indiscretion to be overlooked. By the time the book appeared, Bodo had already been killed in combat and, indeed, he was the second of *Generaloberst* Moritz *Freiherr* von Lyncker's sons to die in the war. There was nothing to be gained by reminding the mass market for Richthofen's book that two young aristocrats with lofty connections could 'bend the rules' presumably without punishment. And if there were some form of disciplinary action, no record of it has yet surfaced. Once again, good luck saved the day for Richthofen.

It is known, though, that Manfred von Richthofen enjoyed a very pleasant Christmas in 1915. He received a passing grade on his third and final pilot's examination on 25 December and he was able to fly off to a quick home leave with his family. Part of the test was a long-distance flight with his mechanic, first from Döberitz about 150 kilometres (90 miles) north-west to Schwerin. Once there, a visit to the Fokker factory only whetted Richthofen's appetite for the small, trim-looking monoplanes that Germany's enemies called 'the Fokker Scourge.' After enjoying some holiday cheer, Richthofen flew a much longer stretch of over 400 kilometres (250 miles) south-west to Breslau, where he was able to park the aeroplane in a secure place and go by train to Schweidnitz. It was the last time that he celebrated Christmas with his entire family.

Freifrau von Richthofen was thrilled to have her husband and all of her children at home for the holiday. She was the only family member not in uniform, as they all gathered around the Christmas tree, bright with lighted candles, to sing Christmas carols. Her youngest son, Bolko, proudly wore his cadet uniform to fit in with the men in the family, in their Army uniforms, and her daughter Ilse was in crisp white Red Cross nurse's garb. But as the unofficial 'commander' of the family, Kunigunde von Richthofen understood her young 'troops' very well, as revealed by her insightful diary entries, beginning with Manfred's combined passion of flying and hunting:

He had the phenomenal eye and steady hand of my husband. Often – when Manfred was just a boy – they both went into the thickets. Manfred was always with him; the word "hunt" fascinated him; I could wake him in the middle of the night with it. Only once, when my husband got him out of bed in the dewy morning darkness, Manfred muttered a bit: "Well, just wait until my kids are this big, and then I will throw them out of the hatch so early." But then he jumped out of bed with both feet and the two hunters were off. His marksmanship was the mutual heritage of both my husband's and my family. I was not surprised when Manfred wrote that he wanted to be a *Jagdflieger* [fighter pilot].

He always had his eye right on the target. Frantic recklessness was absolutely not Manfred's style. His way of doing things was to "look before you leap." In his clear mind, he would analyse the problem, form a plan and stay with it and not be distracted. He does not lack courage and energy to carry out his plans. He could make a split-second decision and know immediately what to do. He never wavered in his view ... He saw things with amazing clarity.

... "Manfred is always right" was also Lothar's incontestable view ... He felt comfortable beneath and near his brother and there he would stand – with a full, undivided heart. Lothar loved Manfred more than himself ... and if it came to that, Lothar would have given his life for his brother.

By this time, Manfred was past his envy of Lothar's early combat exploits. During the rounds of correspondence between the two brothers and their mother, news circulated about Manfred's success in the Flying Service and Manfred resumed being the older sibling who looked out for the younger. Indeed, in February 1915, after Lothar became so ill during the Russian winter that he had to be sent to the *Charité* in Berlin, one of the oldest and finest convalescent hospitals in Germany, Manfred encouraged him to join the Flying Service. Just as Manfred had followed the example of his friend 'Fritze' von Falkenhayn and progressed from the observer's seat in the back of the aeroplane to the pilot's seat in the front, over the summer Lothar followed his advice and became an observer.

Manfred wrote:

> Just a year later he was a pilot.

But the brief Christmas leave time passed all too quickly and Manfred was soon off to Breslau to reclaim his aeroplane and fly it back to Döberitz. And Lothar returned to his aviation training. On 1 February, however, Manfred returned to Schweidnitz, this time with Lothar as his passenger. It was good that Manfred had called ahead to ask local officials for permission to land in the parade ground across the street from the family home. Landing an aeroplane within the city limits caused quite a stir, as most Schweidnitz residents had never seen one and, after the engine was shut off, there were many questions for the brothers who climbed out of it. All of this fuss was new to Manfred and Lothar, but they would become accustomed to it.

While the Richthofen brothers were in their respective training courses, German combat aviation units were undergoing a major reorganization to assure the Air Service a more important role in combat operations. On 1 December 1915, two *Kampfgeschwader der Obersten Heeresleitung* [Combat Wings of the Supreme High Command], abbreviated as *Kagohl,* were established. As a consequence, on the 20th of that month, the *Brieftauben-Abteilung* at Ostend was renamed *Kagohl 1* and the *Brieftauben-Abteilung* at Metz (*BAM*) became *Kagohl 2*. At the same time, the new *Kagohls 3, 4* and *5* were established. Each *Kagohl* was composed of six *Kampfstaffeln* [Battle Squadrons] or *Kastas* of six aircraft each and was led by a *Geschwader-Kommandeur* [Wing Commander], who reported to *Major* Hermann von der Lieth-Thomsen, the Chief of Field Aviation. Leaping over a large section of the normal chain of command, *Major* Thomsen, a protégé of *Generalleutnant* [Lieutenant-General] Erich Ludendorff, was responsible to the Supreme High Command – in essence, to the General Staff and, nominally, the Kaiser, whose influence steadily waned as the war continued.

Upon Manfred von Richthofen's arrival in Metz on 16 March 1916, he did not return to *Kagohl 1*; rather, he was assigned to *Kampfstaffel 8* of *Kagohl 2*, based at Mont-Murville, east of Landres. Ultimately, Lothar reported to *Kasta 23* of *Kagohl 4*, operating in the Somme and Verdun Sectors, the latter being close to Manfred's unit. As an observer, Lothar flew in the back seat of a new

C-type two-seat reconnaissance aircraft, but Manfred, now sitting in the pilot's seat of his two-seater, quickly noticed that his squadron also had a Fokker single-seat monoplane fighter and his primary objective became to fly in that more aggressive combat machine.

Manfred von Richthofen's interest in becoming a fighter pilot was heightened by news of the rising number of aerial victories achieved by the pilot he had met on the train from Ostend to Rethel, Oswald Boelcke, and his fellow fighter pilot Max Immelmann. Their achievements, unique at the time, led to their receiving high awards and growing recognition, which fuelled Richthofen's ambitions. Boelcke and Immelmann enjoyed a very special Christmas in 1915 when von der Lieth-Thomsen sent each of them a one-litre silver goblet inscribed 'To the Victor in Aerial Combat' and dramatically illustrated with a scene of one eagle defeating another in the air. Named the *Ehrenbecher* [Goblet of Honour], this distinction was subsequently awarded to all German pilots, observers and aerial gunners after they were credited with shooting down their first enemy aeroplanes. The impressive silver goblet became another incentive to encourage German airmen to deal aggressively with enemy aircraft.

Even more noteworthy, on 12 January 1916, after Boelcke and Immelmann each had eight confirmed aerial victories to their credit, they were presented with the Kingdom of Prussia's oldest and highest award for bravery in combat, the *Orden Pour le Mérite*. Established by Frederick the Great in 1667 and worn at the neck for maximum visibility, the Order's handsome Maltese cross badge of deep blue enamel with gold trim became broadly recognized and accepted as the German Empire's highest decoration for bravery for commissioned officers.

Consequently, when Manfred von Richthofen reached *Kasta 8* in March, he was pleased to learn that the commanding officer of neighbouring *Kasta 10* was Oswald Boelcke's older brother, Wilhelm. Looking for an opportunity to again meet with – or come to the attention of – the celebrated combat pilot surely motivated Richthofen to order a forward-firing machine gun fitted to his Albatros two-seater and attack a French two-seat reconnaissance plane on 26 April, as described in Chapter 1.

Lothar von Richthofen tried to attack a French aeroplane two days later, but with less fortunate results, as he recounted in a letter home:

Manfred visited me for an hour recently. It was very nice to see him again, here in the field. A few days later [26 April] he shot down a Frenchie. Unfortunately, I have not yet succeeded at that, although I already have a few aerial combats behind me. Once, on 28 April, I saved one of our aircraft from the clutches of two Frenchmen. The observer, *Leutnant* von Schwerin of my *Staffel*, was mortally wounded and could no longer defend himself. Unfortunately, he later died. The pilot was only lightly wounded.

Two days later, Manfred von Richthofen also tried to intervene in an aerial combat when, off in the distance near Verdun, he saw a Fokker monoplane attacking a flight of French two-engined bombers. He wrote:

I was a new pilot on a "barrier" flight over Fort Douaumont when it came under a fierce artillery barrage. I watched a German Fokker attacking three Caudrons. But, to my misfortune, there was a strong west wind blowing against me. In the course of the fight, the Fokker was driven over the city of Verdun. I brought this to the attention of my observer, who thought that the German must be a very daring fellow. We wondered whether it could be Boelcke and wanted to go there to find out. But then I saw to my horror that the attacker became the defender. The Frenchmen, whose strength had meanwhile been increased to at least ten aeroplanes, forced the German lower and lower.

I could not come to his aid. I was too far from the combatants and, besides, my heavy machine could not overcome the wind. The Fokker defended himself desperately. By now the enemy had driven him down to at least 600 metres (1,900 feet). Then suddenly, his pursuers renewed their attack. He disappeared in a dive into a cumulus cloud. I breathed easily, for in my view that was his salvation.

When I returned home I reported what I had seen and learned that it was my old comrade in arms from the Eastern Front, Holck, who had become a fighter pilot shortly before the Verdun offensive. He had plunged straight down with a shot through the head. I was affected very deeply by his death, for he was not merely a model of energy, he was also a person of character, of whom there are only a few.

Three days later, Richthofen flew a short distance westward to Sivry-sur-Meuse airfield for *Graf* von Holck's funeral, just one of many such sad events that he would attend within the next two years.

Manfred von Richthofen's and Hans Reimann's misadventures with Fokker monoplane fighters in the spring and early summer, noted earlier, were insignificant compared to the major loss suffered by the German Air Service on 18 June 1916. Germany's second-highest-scoring fighter ace, *Oberleutnant* Max Immelmann, was flying a Fokker E.III monoplane when he crashed to his death while fighting with a British two-seater. The event became even more ominous when a Flying Service investigation commission determined Immelmann's demise may have been caused by failure of his machine gun synchronisation mechanism, which caused him to shoot off his own propeller and tumble down out of control. The loss of a top fighter pilot in a Fokker was bad for Dutch-born aircraft builder Anthony H.G. Fokker. To make matters worse, at the time, Germany's other leading combat flyer, Oswald Boelcke, was testing a Fokker biplane fighter, a proposed improved successor to the monoplanes, and a new source of business for Fokker.

Richthofen's reaction to the news and suspected cause of Immelmann's death was typical of the shaken confidence in Fokker monoplanes, especially after the loss of *Hauptmann* Ernst *Freiherr* von Gersdorff, a pre-war flyer and well-regarded Fokker pilot, shortly after Immelmann's fall. Richthofen wrote home on 22 June:

> What do you have to say about Immelmann's death? In the long run everyone believes it – even Boelcke. The commander of Lothar's *Kampfgeschwader 4* has also not returned from a photographic reconnaissance mission. A day before, the commander of my old *Kampfgeschwader 1*, formerly the *BAO*, was shot down. He was *Freiherr* von Gersdorff, probably the most qualified commander a *Kampfgeschwader* ever had. I always liked him very much.

In an attempt to stop any further erosion of German combat pilot morale in the event of another prominent loss, direct orders from Kaiser Wilhelm II removed Oswald Boelcke from flight status. He was dispatched to Eastern sectors to visit German and local allied units.

Meanwhile, overall war strategy far beyond a junior officer's comprehension catalysed events that would result in rapid changes for Manfred von Richthofen. Italy renounced its earlier neutrality and declared war on Austria-Hungary on 23 May 1915, and France appealed to Russia for help against their Central Powers adversaries. Consequently, Russian General Aleksei Alekseievich Brusilov's South-West Army Group opened an offensive on 4 June to draw German units away from France and Austro-Hungarian forces away from the Italian Front. Russian forces achieved the desired effect, but the German units sent east inflicted a series of defeats on the Russians.

Kagohl 2 soon joined the German counter-offensive and none too soon for Richthofen, who had had no luck in achieving a credited aerial victory, either with a Fokker monoplane or his machine gun-equipped Albatros C.III two-seater. He was frustrated and impatient, as evident in his letter of 6 July:

> A few days ago I nose-dived my Fokker into the ground. Witnesses
> were more than a little astonished when, after quite some time,
> I crawled out of the heap of rubble totally unhurt. My good friend
> Zeumer has already gone one better than me. First he was shot
> down by the French but received only light grazing shots, and then
> three days later he broke his thigh ...
>
> I am entertaining the thought of going to Boelcke and asking
> about becoming his student. I always need a change. That would
> be something new again and would not hurt me.

At the time Richthofen wrote home, however, Boelcke was on his way to Turkey. Very shortly thereafter, *Kagohl 2*'s men and equipment were heading to the Eastern Front on their special train. Four days later the train pulled up to an airfield outside the Ukrainian city of Kovel, which was threatened by Brusilov's forces. The convenience and mobility of the train made barracks and some shop facilities unnecessary. But the summer heat beating down on the cars soon drove many of the *Kagohl* crews out of the train.

Richthofen and two comrades, *Leutnants* Alfred Gerstenberg and Franz Christian von Scheele from *Kasta 11*, set up a tent in a nearby forest, so they would be thoroughly rested when it was time for long bombing flights over Russian positions.

Richthofen described one such mission:

> Our entire Combat Wing set out to bomb a very important railway station at a place called Manjewicze, east of Kovel, about 30 kilometres (20 miles) behind the Front. The Russians were planning an attack, so the station was crammed with trains, side by side; a long stretch of rails was covered with trains. We could see them nicely from the air; there were troop trains at every junction.
>
> There are many things to be enthusiastic about in flying and for a time I was much interested in bombing. It gave me a sinister pleasure to plaster our "friends" down below. Often, I went out twice a day on such flights. This day Manjewicze was the target. Each *Geschwader* prepared to set out against the Russians.
>
> The machines rolled with difficulty to the flight line. They were filled to capacity with bombs. Many times I hauled 150-kg (300-lb) bombs with an ordinary C-type aeroplane. Moreover, I even had with me a heavy observer, who had apparently not suffered at all from the meat shortage, and, "just in case," I had two machine guns, although I never got to try them out in Russia. It is a shame that not a single Russian is in my collection of air combat souvenirs. His cockade would have looked very colourful on the wall.

On the way back from Manjewicze, Richthofen and his observer flew over a Russian airfield just as an aeroplane was taking off.

> Did he have it in mind to attack us? Richthofen mused. I believe not. More likely, he sought security in the air, for most certainly that is the most comfortable place to be to avoid personal mortal danger during bombing attacks on an airfield.

The summer wore on and the *Kagohls* attacked the Russian forces relentlessly, helping to push them off to the north and east. There, German and Austro-Hungarian army units achieved victory after victory under *Generalfeldmarschall* von Hindenburg, who had become commander of all German forces in the east. The Brusilov offensive, which had made great gains at one point, was now finished. In the words of one military expert, the battle:

> ...became a race between excellent German-Austrian lateral communications and the inferior Russian railroads.
> The Germans won.

Russian withdrawals in the face of German successes on the Eastern Front offered no respite to Hindenburg's forces. The British offensive in the Somme Sector and increased French efforts at Verdun and along the Meuse River called for a redirection of the German war effort. Appropriate changes also occurred in the Flying Service, where newly promoted *Oberstleutnant* [Lieutenant Colonel] Hermann von der Lieth-Thomsen, was implementing a reorganization which included new units called *Jagdstaffeln* [fighter squadrons] or *Jastas* to coordinate with and tactically support each Army. Thomsen re-designated *Kampfeinsitzer Kommando Nord*, an existing Fokker unit based at Park Vélu in the 1st Army sector, as *Jasta 1* under its current commanding officer, *Hauptmann* Martin Zander. At the same time, he directed *Hauptmann* Oswald Boelcke, Germany's highest-scoring fighter ace at the time, to establish and command *Jasta 2* at Bertincourt, then in the 2nd Army Sector.

Boelcke was visiting his brother Wilhelm in Kovel when Thomsen's telegraphed orders arrived on 12 August. Richthofen recalled the events that led to a seminal moment in his career:

> The August sun was almost overpowering on the sandy airfield at Kovel. We were chatting among ourselves when one of my comrades said: "Today the great Boelcke is coming to visit us, or, rather, his brother." That evening the famous man appeared and, much to our surprise, told us many interesting things about his journey to Turkey, from where he was returning on the way to Grand Headquarters. He spoke of going back to the Somme to continue his work and of setting up a *Jagdstaffel*.

I did not dare to ask him to take me with him. I did not want
to leave our *Kampfgeschwader* on the basis of its being too boring.
On the contrary, we made extensive and interesting flights, and
peppered many a Russki train station with our bombs. But the
thought of fighting again on the Western Front appealed to me.
There is nothing finer for a young cavalry officer than flying off
on a hunt.

Just before leaving three days later, Boelcke invited two pilots to join him in
France. The first was *Leutnant der Reserve* Erwin Böhme, who at age 37 was 12
years older than Boelcke and considered to be an 'old man' in *Kasta 10*, but
who was known to be a courageous and dependable pilot. The second was
Richthofen, whose aggressive nature was well known. Richthofen recalled:

Suddenly there was a knock at my door early in the morning and
there stood the great man with the *Pour le Mérite*. I did not know
what he wanted of me. I knew him, as previously mentioned, but I
did not think that he would come to ask me to become his pupil.
I could have hugged him when he asked whether I wanted to go
with him to the Somme sector.

Three days later I sat in the railway train and travelled through
the whole of Germany directly to my new field of activity. At last
my greatest wish was fulfilled. Thus began the finest time of my
life. At that time I did not dare to hope that I should be as
successful as I have been. When I left my quarters in the East, a
good friend of mine called out after me: "See that you do not come
back without the *Orden Pour le Mérite*."

Manfred von Richthofen did not report directly to his new unit,
formally known as *königliche preussische Jagdstaffel 2* [Royal Prussian Fighter
Squadron 2]; the Prussian distinction is noteworthy, as the Kingdoms of
Bavaria, Saxony and Württemberg also had squadrons, staffed mostly by
their own subjects, but integrated within the total German war effort.
Richthofen arrived in Schweidnitz on 25 August and spent a few quiet days
at home. Within a month he and his *Jasta 2* comrades were flying with
Boelcke, hunting for aerial quarry in the skies over France.

5
FLYING WITH BOELCKE

Oswald Boelcke was widely honoured as the 'Creator of Fighter Aviation' in the German Flying Service. He led squadrons in battle, test-flew new types of fighter aircraft and drew on his experiences to develop and teach basic air combat tactics – called 'Boelcke's Dicta' – which remain valid for 21st century fighter pilots. His personal charisma and leadership style were equally as effective and he became the mentor – indeed, the idol – to Manfred von Richthofen and other early fighter pilots.

Born in the Prussian town of Giebichenstein on 19 May 1891, Boelcke was always a fighter. He overcame whooping cough as a child and maintained top physical strength as a vigorous sports enthusiast. He followed his older brother Wilhelm into Army officer training and, as with the Richthofen brothers, into the Flying Service. In June 1914, Oswald Boelcke was completing pilot training when the war began. He was posted to an advance German airfield at Trier and, while waiting for orders to a front line unit, he flew to Montmédy, France, to visit his brother at *Feldflieger-Abteilung 13*. Wilhelm arranged for Oswald to remain with his unit for a time and, together, the brothers reconnoitred the Argonne and Champagne regions. They flew together so often that other crews complained they 'monopolized' one Albatros B.II as if it were their personal property. That tenacity was rewarded when, within weeks of each other in late 1914, the brothers received the Iron Cross Second Class and First Class awards. Oswald was then posted to Döberitz, where the soon to be famous *Feldflieger-Abteilung 62* was being established. He was joined a short time later by *Fähnrich* Max Immelmann, a pilot with whom he developed a friendly rivalry over air combat victories which propelled both men to national prominence, with both of them receiving the coveted *Orden Pour le Mérite*, acknowledged as Germany's highest bravery award.

The era of German fighter aces had begun and, by the time Manfred von Richthofen was en route to *Jagdstaffel 2*'s airfield at the town of Bertincourt, south-west of Cambrai, in late August 1916, an additional seven names had been added to the list of fighter pilots who had earned the *Pour le Mérite*. Like Boelcke and Immelmann, those pilots also became the subjects of newspaper stories and portrait postcards collected by a public in need of heroes, and encouraged by a government in need of propaganda symbols.

When Richthofen reached his new airfield, other major changes had taken place within the German military establishment. On 29 August, *General der Infanterie* Erich von Falkenhayn, Chief of the General Staff and leading proponent of the disastrous Verdun campaign, asked to be relieved of command after losing an internal Army political struggle over strategy with *Generalfeldmarschall* Paul von Hindenburg, the celebrated overall commander of the Eastern Front. Hindenburg's ascendancy benefited the Flying Service, as Chief of Field Aviation Hermann von der Lieth-Thomsen was a protégé of Hindenburg's chief of staff, Erich Ludendorff, who had just been appointed Quartermaster General of the Army.

While *Jagdstaffel 2* was formally established on 10 August 1916, it was over two weeks before the unit's various elements were brought together in the 2nd Army Sector. According to the unit's official war diary entry of 28 August:

> *Jagdstaffel 2* has been assembled under the leadership of *Hauptmann* Boelcke. Officers and enlisted men are coming from various other units. On hand: three officers (in addition to Boelcke and *Leutnants der Reserve* von Arnim and Günther), 64 non-commissioned officers and non-rated men. Billets: officers live in [houses in] Bertincourt, enlisted men in barracks. Aeroplanes: none have yet arrived. Current activity: setting up the airfield.

During the next few weeks, pilots from other units filled the *Staffel* roster. On 1 September, *Leutnant* Manfred von Richthofen and his one-time Fokker monoplane 'co-owner' *Leutnant der Reserve* Hans Reimann reported in from *Kasta 8*. The first aircraft to arrive was a new Albatros D.I biplane fighter that *Vizefeldwebel* [Sergeant Major] Leopold Reimann (no relation to Hans Reimann) brought with him when he was posted from *Jasta 1* to bolster *Jasta 2*'s number of experienced pilots. The 2nd Army Air Park provided two new dual-machine gun-equipped Fokker D.III biplane fighters, one of which Boelcke himself flew from the Air Park to Bertincourt. The following day, he was at the controls of the same Fokker when he shot down his 20th enemy aircraft.

The Battle of the Somme, which began on 1 July, drew German forces away from Verdun and was soon being fought at a furious pace which would result in more losses on both sides than the Verdun stalemate. While Anglo-French ground and air forces gained strength daily, Boelcke waited for more and better aircraft to arrive. Initially, he could only gather his men and tell them what he had learned about aerial combat. During these talks, he hammered away at key tactical points needed for success in air combat, which became known as Boelcke's Dicta:

– Before attacking, look for an advantage.
– Look for the most favourable moment to attack, such as when the sun is behind you.
– Once the attack has been launched, carry it out quickly and resolutely.
– Open fire only at close range and only when you have your opponent in your sights.
– Keep your eye on your opponent at all times.
– Do not allow yourself to be deceived by any manner of ruse.
– When your opponent comes down on you from above, do not turn away from him; rather, fly right at him.
– Over enemy territory, never forget your own escape route.

Boelcke also knew that his new unit was going into battle at a point in time when British and French aviation efforts were making great progress in countering the early German technological superiority that had aided his own success. *Oberstleutnant* Wilhelm Siegert, a pre-war flyer and early proponent of an independent German air arm who became Inspector General of the Flying Service, wrote after the war:

The beginning of the Battle of the Somme also coincided, unfortunately, with the nadir in the technical development of our aeroplanes. Our absolute air superiority in early 1916 with Fokker monoplanes passed in March and April to enemy Nieuport, Vickers and Sopwith aeroplanes.

To meet that growing threat, Boelcke used his experiences to teach and motivate his air warriors, who listened eagerly on the ground and followed him intently in the air. They practised individual flying, as well as the ineffective two-aircraft 'barrier flights' to keep enemy aircraft from penetrating German lines. Boelcke also had them practise close formation flying so they could penetrate enemy formations when they flew over German positions.

Meanwhile, Boelcke continued to make solo flights over the lines, adding to his victory score and using the encounters as the day's lesson in aerial combat. On the early evening of 2 September, he shot down a British single-seat fighter north-east of Thiepval, noting that after his target hit the ground, 'the pilot jumped out of the burning machine and clapped his hands all over his arms and legs, as he was also on fire.' The pilot, Captain Robert Wilson of No. 32 Squadron, Royal Flying Corps, provided a lesson in survivor's luck to *Jasta 2* pilots when Boelcke invited him to their officers' mess the following afternoon. Wilson regaled the Germans with his account of crash-landing a burning aeroplane. His heavy flying suit saved him from serious injury, which was a valuable lesson; at the time, parachutes were not yet assigned to aviation crewmen, who had two choices if their aircraft caught fire in the air: ride it down and risk being burned alive, as Wilson had done, or jump to certain death.

Wilson's downing was credited as Boelcke's 20th aerial victory. Within the next two weeks, Boelcke used his new Fokker D.III to shoot down six more British aircraft. Upon returning from a flight, if Boelcke's chin had been blackened by gunpowder residue, the men knew he had shot down an enemy aeroplane, as he used ammunition sparingly and effectively. Unfortunately, the Fokker D-Type biplanes did not prove to be worthy successors to the E-Type monoplanes which had given German airmen their earlier aerial superiority. The German Air Service's fortunes changed, however, with the advent of the new Albatros D.I and D.II single-seat biplanes. Produced by the Albatros *Flugzeugwerke* [Aeroplane Works] and descended from pre-war racing biplanes, the D-Types:

> ...were the first German fighters fitted with a 160-hp engine thus providing sufficient power to carry two Spandau [7.92 mm] machine guns and 790 rounds of ammunition for each gun and yet maintain performance parity with Allied fighters.

On Saturday, 16 September six of the new fighters arrived at *Jasta 2*. From its rounded propeller nose spinner to the end of its streamlined, plywood-covered fuselage, the Albatros was so sleek in appearance it was immediately called the '*Haifisch*' [shark]. Boelcke's pilots had one day to become proficient in their new aircraft, and the following day, he took them with him on a hunting mission in the skies over Bertincourt, as ever-bolder British airmen brought the air war to German territory.

Jasta 2's opponents that day turned out to be a flight of Royal Aircraft Factory FE2b two-seat biplanes which appeared to be awkward with their so-called 'pusher' engines mounted behind their fuselages, but, as one expert has noted, 'they had to do a good deal of fighting ... [and] in this they acquitted themselves well ... The FE2b owed its success chiefly to the wide and unobstructed field of fire in all forward directions provided by the pusher layout.' Also known as 'Fees,' these aircraft were formidable opponents. Indeed, some Germans believed that the legendary German fighter ace Max Immelmann had been shot down by an FE2b during his last and fatal aerial combat exactly 12 weeks earlier.

The following summer, by which time Richthofen had gained the level of fame to write an eagerly awaited wartime memoir, he described the encounter that led to his receiving official credit for his first aerial victory:

> The next morning, 17 September, was a wonderful day ... We had just arrived at the Front when, over our lines, we recognized by the explosions of balloon defence guns that an enemy formation was heading for Cambrai. Boelcke was of course the first to see it, as he always saw more than other people. Each of us struggled to stay close behind Boelcke. It was clear to all of us that we had to pass our first test under the eyes of our revered leader.
>
> We approached the enemy formation slowly, as it could no longer escape us ... If they wanted to go back, they had to get by us. We counted their aeroplanes – there were seven in all. There were only five of us. All the Englishmen flew big two-seat bombers. In a few seconds it would all begin.
>
> Boelcke was the first to get close to an enemy, but he did not open fire. I was the second and close to me were my comrades. The Englishman nearest to me was in a big darkly painted barge.

I did not ponder long and took aim at him. He fired and so did I, but we both missed. Then the fight began. I tried to get behind him because I could only fire in the direction I was flying. This was not necessary for him, as his observer's flexible machine gun could fire in all directions.

But this fellow was no beginner, for he knew very well that the moment I succeeded in getting behind him, it would be his last hour. At that time I was not yet convinced that he must fall; rather, I was much more anxious to see whether he would fall, and that is a significant difference.

Richthofen's combat report, described the conclusion of the fight:

Suddenly the enemy went gliding down and I followed until I had killed the observer, who had not stopped firing until the last minute. Now my opponent went downwards in tight turns. At about 1,200 metres (3,900 feet), a second German machine came along and attacked my victim right down to the ground and then landed next to the British aeroplane.

The pilot, even though mortally wounded, managed to land his aeroplane at the German airfield at Flesquières. There it was learned that Richthofen's victims were Second-Lieutenant Lionel B.F. Morris, age 19, and Captain Thomas Rees, age 21, of No. 11 Squadron, RFC. Whenever possible under combat conditions at the time, enemy combatants were given medical treatment and, as warranted, some form of religious burial. In this case, Morris was taken to a field hospital at Cambrai and was subsequently buried near it; Rees was interred in Villers Plouich, not far from where he fell.

Not to be deprived of his victory, Richthofen also made a hasty landing near the crashed FE2b. He wrote:

I was so excited that I could not resist coming down and landed with such eagerness on this strange ground that I almost went over on my nose ... A group of soldiers was already streaming toward the fallen enemy. Arriving there, I found that my assumption was correct. The engine was shot to pieces and both crewmen were severely wounded ... Later, I erected a stone on his grave to the memory of my honourably fallen opponent.

By the time Richthofen flew back to Bertincourt, Boelcke and his students were reviewing the morning's work over a late breakfast. The new victor explained his tardiness proudly:

One Englishman shot down!

Jasta 2 had much to celebrate that day: Manfred von Richthofen's and Erwin Böhme's first confirmed victories, a second kill for Hans Reimann, and Oswald Boelcke's 27th aerial victory. In the evening, Boelcke had the added pleasure of presenting Böhme with the Iron Cross First Class, which had arrived for him that day.

With paperwork yet to be processed, it was too soon for Richthofen and Böhme to each receive the silver *Ehrenbecher* from the Chief of Field Aviation in recognition of their first aerial victories, but Richthofen noted the achievement in his own way. He wrote to a jeweller in Berlin and ordered a 'victory memento' of his own design: a plain silver cup about an inch wide at the top and two inches tall, with the lip sloping slightly toward the base. He directed that it be inscribed '1. Vickers 2. 17.9.16' to commemorate his first victory, achieved over what he identified as a 'Vickers' -type two-seat 'pusher' aircraft (for which the FE2b was commonly mistaken) on 17 September 1916. It was the first of 60 such cups he would order to commemorate his victories.

A ground mist on the morning of 23 September did not prevent Boelcke and five comrades, including Richthofen, from flying over the main road from Bapaume to Cambrai. Over Bapaume they spotted six ungainly Martinsyde G.100 'Elephant' single-seat biplanes, which proved to be aptly named as they plodded along and came under the guns of the sleek, fast and manoeuvrable Albatros fighters of *Jasta* 2. Knowing just what to do, Manfred von Richthofen pounced on his prey and quickly sent it down.

Richthofen's second victim was Sergeant Herbert Bellerby, age 28, of No. 27 Squadron, RFC. Apparently, infantrymen buried the body of the 28-year-old Essex native where he fell, as British records indicate he has no known grave.

Richthofen's success, however, was marred by *Jasta 2*'s loss of *Leutnant* Hans Reimann. After shooting down a Martinsyde, subsequently credited as his fourth victory, Reimann was rammed by another Martinsyde; the British pilot managed to escape in the badly damaged aeroplane and make his way to a British airfield. Reimann's Albatros fell to the ground and the pilot, age 25, was killed in the crash.

That evening, while *Jasta 2* was being moved a short distance north to the airfield at Lagnicourt, Richthofen ordered a second silver cup from the Berlin jeweller and had it inscribed: 2. Martinsyde 1. 23.9.16.

A week later, Richthofen achieved his third victory, another FE2b. On 30 September, British ground forces were in the process of retaking Pozières Ridge and the Ancre Valley. The Royal Flying Corps reinforced the offensive by sending Nieuport and Morane fighters and 'Fees' to bomb *Jasta 2*'s airfield at Lagnicourt. Richthofen caught one of the 'Fees' over Frémicourt and sent it down in flames, killing the crew. He described that victory and thoughts about his career aspirations in a letter home:

> The heart beats a little faster when the opponent, whose face one has just seen, goes roaring down from 4,000 metres (13,000 feet). When I arrived down below, of course nothing remained of the men or the machine.
>
> I removed a small national insignia as a souvenir. From my second victory, I took the machine gun as a souvenir. It has a bullet of mine in the bolt and is useless. My Frenchman from Verdun does not count, unfortunately.
>
> Earlier, one received the *Pour le Mérite* after the eighth victory, but no longer, even though it is becoming ever more difficult to shoot down enemy aircraft. In the last four weeks since the establishment of *Jagdstaffel Boelcke* we have lost five of our ten aircraft.

On 1 October, Boelcke shot down his 30th opponent and then a run of bad weather restricted flight operations and the opportunity for other combat triumphs. On Saturday, 7 October however, despite 'stormy, cloudy and misty' conditions,' Boelcke flew and scored again. Richthofen logged his fourth victory, which was the first to be described in an Army report:

The biplane single-seater (Lt Fenwick) shot down by *Ltn Frhr* von Richthofen near Equancourt belonged to the 21st Squadron and, indeed, according to the papers [found in it] to a BE Flight. The airplane is apparently one of new construction.

Events of Sunday, 8 October 1916 marked significant changes in the overall structure of Germany's air arm and the effects would be felt right down to squadron level.

The Flying Service was upgraded as a command by having a general officer placed in charge and renamed the *Luftstreitkräfte* [Air Force] and *Generalleutnant* Ernst von Hoeppner proved to be a good choice to become the Commanding General of the Air Force. He was not a flyer, but an old cavalryman accustomed to leading widely deployed forces over a broad area (roughly analogous to aviation units) and he had been advanced to lead the 75th Infantry Division, thereby gaining the larger command experience needed for what would become the pinnacle of his career. The Flying Service's loose command structure 'for aviation, tethered observation balloons, Army airships and the Army Weather Service, as well as the anti-aircraft and home defence units,' was succeeded by a more cohesive structure.

Under *General* von Hoeppner's command, some air units were expanded, reassigned or consolidated into other, larger units. The *Jagdstaffeln*, currently 15 in number, were to be augmented by another 22 units in preparation for the anticipated Anglo-French spring 1917 offensive. Hoeppner continued to allow lone aircraft patrols, seeking targets of opportunity, but the emphasis was placed on developing strategies and tactics for massed air strength.

Boelcke proved the value of coordinated attacks during a slight break in the bad weather on 10 October, when he and his men repeatedly attacked British aircraft trying to bomb German airfields and other targets.

The day began with Boelcke's pronouncement 'Weather fit for pigs!' as he surveyed the dark clouds batted about by wind gusts over *Jagdstaffel 2*'s airfield. But in recent weeks the elements had been just as harsh on his enemies and had aided Boelcke and his most successful protégé, Richthofen, since they had shot down nine British aeroplanes between them during that short time.

Reports of an enemy formation heading toward their airfield had Boelcke and his eager subordinates suiting up for another opportunity to stop the invaders and, they hoped, add to their personal scores of aerial victories. Their sleek Albatros D.II fighters could out-dive and out-run any British aeroplanes and, following Boelcke's example, the new pilots were becoming more skilled in using the D.II's features to their advantage. Pilots who learned quickly could expect medals and other rewards beyond the self-satisfaction of serving their country's cause; those who did not learn Boelcke's lessons were transferred out of the unit, if they survived long enough for the paperwork to go through. Among the early pilots 'rotated out' was Richthofen's old friend *Oberleutnant* Bodo von Lyncker, who after a short time with *Jasta 2*, was posted to the Balkans, where he was subsequently killed. Since beginning flight operations a month earlier, four *Jasta 2* pilots had already fallen in combat.

Those thoughts, however, were far from minds of the six airmen as they took off into the morning mist. They remained focused on their leader, making a steady climb toward the advancing dark specks in the air. Moments later, the specks became visible as a formation of big, lumbering British FE2b two-seat reconnaissance aircraft and smaller Airco DH2 fighters, which, like the 'Fees', were rear-engined aircraft with a totally unobstructed forward view. The big 'Fees' were not easy targets; what they lacked in speed and manoeuvrability they made up for in firepower. The observers' flexible machine guns and the pilots' fixed forward-firing guns could be a lethal combination. The presence of nimble DH2 scouts added another obstacle to hitting the reconnaissance machines, which had to be prevented from photographing and observing events behind German lines. Or at least not allowed to return home with such valuable intelligence material.

Boelcke's crew claimed six British aircraft that day, including Boelcke's 32nd victory and what should have been credited as Richthofen's fifth 'kill'. Despite having flown several missions that day, Richthofen was fully alert when he closed in on an FE2b, carefully staying out of range of the observer, who used his gun to squeeze every advantage out of his pilot's steep banks and turns. Richthofen fired about 300 rounds at the British two-seater and then, as he later wrote:

[It] began to smoke and then started to glide steeper and steeper. I followed, continuing to fire ... [until his] propeller was turning very slowly, and clouds of black smoke were coming from the engine. The observer no longer fired at my machine.

Just then, Richthofen himself came under attack and, sensing that his adversary was finished, he pulled up to engage the new enemy threat, which quickly retreated. In any event, the stricken FE2b continued to lose altitude and its predicament was further complicated by the appearance of a German two-seater, whose crew also fired at it.

Richthofen flew home, confident that he had bagged his fifth victory, thereby qualifying as an 'ace,' to use a word initiated by the French, picked up by the British and slowly coming into use by German airmen. Best of all, the FE2b went down near his airfield. Once again, Richthofen might have been able to salvage some remnant of the British aeroplane as a trophy of his success. He came up empty-handed in more ways than one. The following day, Richthofen learned that credit for shooting down the FE2b was awarded to the two-seater crew, which seemed to him to be administering the *coup de grâce* to his hard-won victory. Witnesses on the ground saw only the two-seater firing at the British aircraft, without knowing who initially disabled it. Richthofen could have contested the claim to the Staff Officer in Charge of Aviation for the German 1st Army Sector, but he accepted the reality of the situation and, with nothing to show for his efforts, he did not mention the incident further. Nor did he ever again allow anyone else to 'sweep up' after his work.

The coveted fifth confirmed victory came six days later, when fine weather with occasional clouds offered British squadrons an opportunity to attack German positions. In response, Boelcke led a four-plane flight that included Richthofen against a larger enemy formation trying to bomb Ruyaulcourt, just south of the Bapaume-Cambrai road. As usual, Boelcke led the way, focusing on a slower and all-too-steady BE2 two-seater. His four protégés sought out their own targets – with no pestering German two-seaters to get in the way this time – and Richthofen opened fire on a BE12, the equally hard-to-manoeuvre single-seat version of the plane that Boelcke was pursuing. His opponent did not have a chance, as Richthofen noted in his combat report:

Together with four planes, above Bertincourt I singled out an enemy ... at 2,800 metres (just over 9,000 ft) altitude. After firing 350 shots, I brought down the enemy aeroplane ... [which] crashed to the ground ... [near Ytres].

He proudly wrote to his mother to proclaim his fifth confirmed victory, but the credit that mattered to him appeared in Boelcke's letter home, which was published during Richthofen's lifetime. Despite wartime censorship, it is not difficult to determine who was singled out for praise when Boelcke wrote:

The day was in other respects also good for the *Staffel*. *Leutnant* R[ichthofen] shot down his fifth ... so that in all we finished off five.

The wreckage of the BE12 was salvaged for souvenirs and Richthofen received a patch of fabric bearing the aircraft serial number 6580. He had absolute proof of this victory claim. The body of the luckless British pilot, 23-year-old Second-Lieutenant John Thompson of No. 19 Squadron, RFC, was buried at a cemetery nearby.

Heady with the success of the time, Richthofen recalled:

I have never found a more beautiful hunting ground than in the skies over the Somme Battle. In the morning, as soon as I had got up, the first Englishmen arrived, and the last did not disappear until long after the sun had set. "An El Dorado for fighter pilots," Boelcke once said. That was when Boelcke increased his victories from 20 to 40 in only two months. We beginners did not have the experience that our master did and we were quite satisfied when we ourselves did not catch a thrashing. But it was beautiful! Not a mission without an aerial combat. Often there were great air battles of 40 to 60 Englishmen against, unfortunately, fewer Germans. They did it with quantity and we did it with quality ...

The day after Richthofen's fifth confirmed victory, 17 October 1916, *Jasta 2* coordinated operations with *Jasta 1* and, during the subsequent air fight, Boelcke shot down his 35th opponent. The Master, as Boelcke was often called, scored his 36th, 37th and 38th victories over the next week. On 25 October, the day Boelcke easily dispatched his 39th opponent, Richthofen had a more difficult time achieving his sixth victory, which was also claimed by another fighter pilot and a two-seater crew. But Richthofen had fought too hard to let the credit go to anyone else, as indicated in his combat report:

> About 0900 hours, I attacked an enemy aeroplane over the trenches near Lesboeufs. [There was] unbroken cloud cover at about 2,000 metres (6,500 feet). The aeroplane came from the German side and after [I fired] some 200 rounds, it went down in big right-hand turns and was forced back by the strong wind south of Bapaume. Finally, it crashed ...
>
> When I first saw the enemy aeroplane, there was no other German machine in the area and, during the fight, no machine approached the scene of the action. As the enemy aeroplane began to go down, I saw a German Rumpler [two-seat] machine and several Halberstadt [single-seat] aeroplanes. One of the latter came down to the ground ... He claims to have opened fire first at 300 metres (980 feet) and then, at 1,000 metres' (3,300 feet) distance, some 500 rounds at the enemy aeroplane.
>
> Afterwards, his gun jammed and he flew away. Quite apart from these curious circumstances, even a child knows that one cannot hit an aeroplane from such a ridiculous distance. Then a second aeroplane, a Rumpler, came down, also claiming his share of the booty. But all other pilots were quite certain that it had not taken part in the fight.

Richthofen prevailed and he was credited with his sixth victory. The aircraft, a BE12, came down north of Bapaume and was the same type as his two previous victories. The pilot, Second-Lieutenant Arthur J. Fisher, age 21, died of his wounds.

The significance of counting shot-down enemy aircraft – even to the extent of calling them 'victories' – was put into words by Richthofen's and Boelcke's close mutual friend Erwin Böhme in a letter to his fiancée:

For us, every [air] fight is a personal fight of man against man, with the same weapons and the same chances. That is the splendid part of fighter aviation, that in this time of mass murder by machines, technology and chemistry, which modern warfare has become, individuals still conduct an honourable manly fight, eye to eye with the opponent. Consider when I am in a swirling flight, circling my opponent, I recognize him precisely and many times come so close that I can look him in the eye.

Every fight is for us a knightly joust, or to say it more modernly, a sportsman-like duel. I have nothing at all against the individual man with whom I "fence" – I want only to put him and his aeroplane out of the fight so they cannot harm us any more. Whenever my opponent must make an emergency landing within our territory, if he has fought honourably and bravely, I will gladly extend my hand to him, I respect him – but nonetheless he will be recorded as a "number." Therefore, as you see, there is no disrespect to the opponent.

That one records his victories is perhaps now understandable: because every fight is personal, one writes down his success personally and when the successes increase, one must count them ... [Furthermore] every victory I achieve is counted not only for me, but also for my *Staffel* ...

Hauptmann Oswald Boelcke shot down his 40th – and last – enemy aircraft on Thursday, 26 October. With that achievement, he became the highest-scoring fighter pilot in the world at the time, rivalled only by Britain's 20-year-old Captain Albert Ball, whose score stood at 31 and who, very wisely, had been posted back to Britain for a tour of duty as an instructor. Otto von Below, Commanding General of the 1st Army, urged – but did not order – Boelcke to go on leave. The *Hauptmann* stubbornly responded, 'I am needed here' and the General accepted his choice.

Bad weather on 27 October led to cancellation of virtually all flight operations on both sides of the lines. But a slight improvement in the following day's weather offered an opportunity neither side could afford to miss.

Erwin Böhme described the day's events:

On Saturday afternoon we sat around in a state of readiness inside our little cottage at the airfield. I had just begun a game of chess with Boelcke – when shortly after [1600 hours] we were called up to the Front during an infantry attack. Boelcke himself led us, as usual. Very soon we were over Flers and attacking several British aeroplanes, fast single-seat fighters that ably defended themselves.

In the fierce aerial combat that followed, during which we had only a brief time to fire, we sought to drive them down by alternately cutting them off, as we had done so often with success...

Boelcke and I had an Englishman right between us, when another opponent pursued by friend Richthofen cut in front of us. During the simultaneous lightning-quick evasive manoeuvre, Boelcke and I, obstructed by our wings, did not see each other for an instant and that is when it happened.

How can I describe for you my feelings at that instant when Boelcke suddenly appeared a few metres to my right, dived down, while I pulled up, and yet we grazed each other and had to return to the ground! It was only a gentle touch, but at such a furious speed it was also a collision.

The other participant in this immediate action, Richthofen, made no mention of chasing a target at the moment that Boelcke and Böhme bumped each other. According to Richthofen:

... I looked around and observed Boelcke about 200 metres (650 feet) away from me, settling in behind his opponent.

It was again the usual thing. Boelcke shoots down his opponent and I look on. Close to Boelcke flew a good friend of his. It was an interesting battle. Both men were firing and at any moment the Englishman had to fall. Suddenly I observed an unnatural movement by both German aeroplanes. The thought flashed through my brain: collision! I had never seen a collision in the air and I imagined that it would look quite different. It was ... a mere touching. But at the great speed of an aeroplane, even a slight touching is a violent concussion.

Boelcke immediately pulled away from his victim and headed for the ground in great spiralling curves. I still did not feel he would crash, but as he descended below me, I noticed that part of his wings had broken off. I could not observe what happened next, but in the clouds he lost a whole wing. His aeroplane became uncontrollable and he plunged down accompanied by his faithful friend. When we got home, the report was already there: "Our Boelcke is dead!" We could hardly believe it ...

... It was a strange phenomenon that I have observed only in Boelcke. He never had a personal enemy. He was equally friendly to everyone, no more to one, no less to another. The one person who was perhaps closest to Boelcke was the one who had the accident with him.

News of Boelcke's death spread quickly on both sides of the battle lines and, in an unusual move, a British aeroplane flew over *Jasta 2*'s airfield and dropped a parachuted wreath with the inscription: 'To the memory of Captain Boelcke, our brave and chivalrous foe. From the British Royal Flying Corps.' Often, German and Allied flyers dropped canisters with notes about airmen who had been captured or killed, but nothing on the order of this tribute to the most successful fighter pilot of the time.

Indeed, Boelcke's funeral set a new standard for German tributes to fallen heroes. His parents were brought from their adopted home town of Dessau to Notre Dame Cathédral in Cambrai. There, they were reunited with their surviving three sons in uniform for the church service, which Richthofen likened to 'that of a reigning prince.' Boelcke was raised in the Lutheran faith and his biographer, Professor Dr Johannes Werner, noted a special aspect of the arrangements:

On the afternoon of 31 October, the funeral rites for Oswald Boelcke took place in Cambrai. The coffin was borne to the altar of the vaulted cathedral. It was the first time that one of the biggest cathedrals in northern France – not without resistance from the archbishop – was used for the funeral service of a German hero. Dignified silence prevailed in the lofty chamber, while outside, at the nearby front lines, there was heavy fighting.

Appearing at the head of the general officers was Crown Prince Rupprecht of Bavaria and, representing the Kaiser, *Generalleutnant* von Below, leader of the 1st Army. Following remarks by *General* [Hermann] von Stein ... the chaplain for the 4th Guards Infantry Division, [Rev] Stelter, began with a reading from 1 Machabees 9:10: "... but if our time be come, let us die gallantly for our brothers, and let us not stain our honour."

At the conclusion of the service, Manfred von Richthofen led the procession, carrying the black velvet awards pillow [*Ordenskissen*] displaying the *Pour le Mérite* and other high honours accorded to Boelcke, whose coffin was borne out of the cathedral to a waiting gun carriage drawn by six brightly scrubbed black horses. Stone-faced and looking straight ahead during the one-kilometre-long journey to the train station, Richthofen gave no hint of his inner turmoil about Boelcke, which would become nearly obsessive during the next 17 months until his own death in combat. Richthofen would often compare his performance to Boelcke and even hint at feelings of inadequacy and envy when he exceeded – indeed, doubled – his mentor's air combat achievements.

There were final front line honours at the train station, where Boelcke's coffin was placed aboard a special train to carry it and his family to an official state funeral in Dessau. Under a steady stream of German aircraft gliding with engines turned off in criss-cross patterns in the skies above, a gun salute by troops of front line soldiers broke the silence with the snapping of their volleys. Boelcke's deputy squadron leader, *Oberleutnant* Stephan Kirmaier, offered the unit's farewell remarks.

Richthofen, who had been designated as *Jasta 2*'s representative to the official funeral cortège in Dessau, missed the train and returned to his flying duties. He never explained how, as one of the first members of the funeral procession to reach the railway station, he managed to miss the train. But he attained his seventh aerial victory a few days later, when he would otherwise have been in Germany, which leaves room for speculation that he wanted to honour his mentor with action rather than ceremony.

Flying with Boelcke

6
PREPARING FOR COMMAND

As expected, *Oberleutnant* Stephan Kirmaier was advanced from deputy leader to commanding officer of *Jagdstaffel 2*. He was the *Staffel*'s senior officer and highest-scoring fighter pilot, with seven aerial victories to his credit, the last five achieved under Boelcke's tutelage. Kirmaier, according to Manfred von Richthofen, modestly maintained that his piloting skills were limited and 'he could fly only straight ahead,' and he soon proved that aerobatics were not required to be a successful combat pilot and that he was a worthy successor to Boelcke.

On the afternoon of 1 November, Kirmaier led a *Jasta 2* flight and shot down a 'BE single-seater' over Le Sars, south-west of Bapaume. Richthofen and other *Staffel* comrades congratulated their leader on his eighth confirmed victory, knowing that now the 27-year-old Kirmaier could be considered for the *Pour le Mérite*.

Two days later, Kirmaier led *Jasta 2* in a combined operation with *Jasta 5* against FE2b reconnaissance aircraft heading for Bapaume. Kirmaier and his crew caught the 'Fees' over Grévillers, where Richthofen shot down one of the intruders, as he recorded in his combat report:

> Accompanied by two aeroplanes of the *Staffel*, I attacked a low-flying aeroplane at 1,800 metres (5,900 feet). After I fired 400 rounds, the adversary crashed to the ground. The aeroplane was smashed to pieces, occupants killed.

Richthofen received credit for his seventh aerial victory. His eighth victory came just over a week later, on 9 November, when he took part in a combined formation of *Jastas 1* and *2* aircraft defending a choice target, the German ammunition dump at Vraucourt, north-east of Bapaume. Richthofen and his 18-year-old comrade *Leutnant der Reserve* Hans Imelmann (no relation to the famed Saxon fighter pilot Max Immelmann) dived on a pair of Royal Flying Corps bombers. Richthofen described the fight:

> Just short of the target, I caught up with the last of the opponents. Right away my first shots put the gunner in the enemy aeroplane

out of action and probably tickled the pilot a bit also; in any case he decided to land with his bombs. I burned him a little around the edges and because of that the speed with which he sought to reach the ground became somewhat greater ... he tumbled down and fell near our airfield at Lagnicourt.

The morning's fight was virtually over and, with *Leutnant* Hans Wortmann pursuing the last of the British fighters in the group, Richthofen and Imelmann departed and landed quickly. Scarcely out of their aeroplanes, they jumped into a small staff car and headed for the crash site to confirm their handiwork. This victory could put Richthofen in consideration for the *Pour le Mérite* and he was very keen to secure his claim to it. He and Imelmann drove as close to the crash site as they could and then raced across a great muddy field to gather souvenirs from the downed bombers before anyone else could beat them to it.

Many soldiers in the area had seen the fight and, with ground combat at a lull, a large number of them flocked to the site of the crashed aeroplanes and their German victors. In a burst of youthful enthusiasm, Richthofen asked broadly if anyone in the crowd had seen the fight and what they thought of it. A staff officer with the 38th Infantry Division, *Rittmeister* von Schack, stepped out, approached Richthofen and simply said his superior wanted to speak with the flyer.

Richthofen was not suitably dressed to be in the company of senior officers, but, as he wrote, he made the best of it:

It was not very pleasant for me, for I had ... mussed up my clothes. And the gentlemen I was now to be with were all fastidiously dressed. I was presented to a personage who made a strange appearance to me. He wore a general's trousers, and had a high award hanging at his neck, but for all that a relatively youthful face, and with indefinable epaulettes ... I sensed something exceptional about him and in the course of the conversation straightened out my shirt and trousers and took on a more military bearing. I did not know who he was. I took my leave of him and went home.

That evening the telephone rang and I learned that he was His Royal Highness, Duke Carl Eduard of Saxe-Coburg-Gotha. I was ordered to report to him [the next day]. It was known that the

British had intended to drop bombs on his headquarters. To that
end I had helped keep the assailants away. For that I received the
Oval Silver Duke Carl Eduard Bravery Medal.

Duke Carl Eduard, at age 32 the head of an old European noble house related
to the House of Windsor and other royalty, was the first of many crowned
heads and titled dignitaries to present honours to Manfred von Richthofen. In
addition to receiving the Duke's high award, Richthofen also gained another
highly placed friend. The young Duke was very interested in flying as, prior to
the war, he financed aviation activities and sponsored the Duke Carl Eduard
Flying School in Gotha, one of the two capital cities in his duchy. With the
outbreak of war, the flying school became a primary military aviation training
facility, *Flieger-Ersatz-Abteilung 3*. The Duke was too important to be allowed to
fly on his own, but he enjoyed being with flyers and later hosted many of them
at his ducal residence and hunting lodge.

Of course, Richthofen was pleased by the decoration from the young Duke,
but he had set his sights on a higher award: the *Pour le Mérite*, which he had not
received following his eighth victory. As he wrote:

In Boelcke's time, eight victories was quite a respectable number.
Those who hear of the colossal numbers of victories [later in the
war] must think that shooting down aeroplanes is becoming easier.
I can assure them that it is becoming more difficult from month to
month; indeed, from week to week. Of course, there are more
opportunities now, but, unfortunately, the enemy's armament is
getting better and his numbers are getting larger. When Max
Immelmann shot down his first opponent, he had the good fortune
to find an enemy who had no machine gun. Now, such novice
aviators are found only over Johannisthal [aviation training centre
near Berlin].

It also became clear that criteria for receiving Prussia's highest bravery award
were changing. Two fighter pilots, *Leutnant der Reserve* Albert Dossenbach and
Oberleutnant Hans Berr, were credited with achieving their ninth aerial victories
in early November 1916, but only Dossenbach subsequently received the *Pour
le Mérite*. Two weeks earlier, he had been awarded the Royal Order of the House

of Hohenzollern in the grade of the Knight's Cross with Swords, but Berr had not yet received it. Almost without exception, the Hohenzollern House Order became the required intermediate award between the Iron Cross First Class and the *Pour le Mérite*, and the aerial victory requirement for the latter honour would be raised even higher in the future.

Consequently, when the same 1st Army Report that announced Dossenbach's *Pour le Mérite* award also mentioned that Richthofen was to receive the Hohenzollern award, the Baron's family understood the importance of the high honour from the *Kaiser*'s own royal house. *Freifrau* von Richthofen recorded that and another piece of good news in her diary:

> Manfred telegraphed that he had received the Hohenzollern House Order ... We were very pleased and were very proud of our youngster. Lothar [also] informed us that he is going to the flying school in Cambrai and wants to fly single-seat fighters.

By not accompanying Boelcke's funeral group to Dessau, Richthofen lost an opportunity for a few days' home leave. He made up for that missed visit by showing up unannounced at home on 14 November 1916, as his mother noted in her diary:

> A great, unexpected joy! At the crack of dawn, Manfred arrived. He looked trim and fit. And all that he had experienced! He told us about it all day long. Boelcke's death affected him deeply. He praised once again the inner clarity and complete self-mastery of the man, the friendly evenness of his personality that also suppressed thoughts of favouritism. (Above all else, I believe I sensed that, by nature, Boelcke and Manfred had many similarities.)
>
> Abruptly, Manfred gives descriptions of his own fights. Every time, it is a duel of you or me. Manfred sees it differently; it is for him the last vestige of an old chivalry in this battle of man against man. He does not think much of aerobatic tricks in the air. "That is only something for the eye," he opines. Usually, he flies at 5,000 metres (16,000 feet) altitude, closes in and first opens fire at 30 metres (less than100 feet) distance. One need not be a marksman, he believes. (Although he himself is certainly an excellent shot.)

Referring to Boelcke – they went hunting together a few times –
[Boelcke] never hit anything. And he always hits them in the air! The
heart makes the fighter pilot – on that point they agreed very well.

The next morning, Manfred and his mother attended the wedding of one of her
nieces. Despite this happy occasion, Manfred felt the call of duty. Before the
young couple left for their honeymoon, Manfred was on his way back to the
Front. He must have borrowed an aeroplane for the trip home and back, as he
was back at *Jasta 2*'s airfield in time to congratulate *Oberleutnant* Stephan
Kirmaier on his tenth victory, a Sopwith two-seater on 16 November.

The Battle of the Somme ended on a rain-filled cloudy Saturday,
18 November 1916. The victory, such as it was, went to British and French
forces, which recorded casualties of 420,000 and 195,000, respectively, while
German casualties were put at 650,000. Most of all, Anglo-French efforts
successfully relieved the German Army's pressure on Verdun and kept the
German Air Force on the defensive.

Unaware of the battle's frightful toll on the ground, Kirmaier took advantage
of the first day of good weather two days later and led *Jasta 2* in two fights in
which three British aeroplanes were shot down. Two of them were credited to
Manfred von Richthofen. According to German 1st Army records, Kirmaier
shot down a BE2 at 0900 hours over Miraumont and, 40 minutes later,
Richthofen downed a BE2 south of Grandcourt. That afternoon, at 1615,
Richthofen scored another victory, an FE2b over Guedecourt, south of
Bapaume. He ordered two more commemorative silver cups from his Berlin
jeweller and, expecting to build a large collection of them, from that point
forward he ordered every tenth cup in a larger size so he could tally his victories
at a glance. In haste, however, this time he reversed the order of the victories.
Thus, the normal-sized cup for the day's first triumph was inscribed: 9. Vickers
2. 20.11.16 and Richthofen's first tenth cup erroneously chronicled that victory
as: 10. B.E. 1. 20.11.16.

With 11 aerial victories to his credit, Stephan Kirmaier was only one ahead of
Richthofen and that thought may have been in his mind on 22 November
when he led four *Jasta 2* Albatroses west of Bapaume to engage a flight of RFC
fighters and bombers crossing German lines. In the mêlée that followed,
Leutnant der Reserve Erich König scored *Jasta 2*'s only victory that day, a
DH2 fighter, while Erwin Böhme reported last seeing Kirmaier diligently

pursuing 'a smoking "Vickers two-seater" [FE2b]' into British territory. Böhme, König, Richthofen and another pilot flew back to Lagnicourt, but Kirmaier failed to return. It was later learned that he was shot down and killed in combat behind British lines. A basic lesson was not lost on Richthofen and his comrades. Kirmaier's focus on pursuing the stricken FE2b ignored Boelcke's eighth dictum: 'Over enemy territory, never forget your own escape route.'

Oberleutnant Karl Bodenschatz, *Jasta 2*'s chief administrative officer, nominally headed the unit for a week, until a new commanding officer arrived. In the absence of a combat pilot to organize missions, Richthofen, the highest-scoring, highest-decorated officer in the unit, became the *de facto* air leader.

The use of 'curve' as a verb is commonly found in German air combat reports, such as those quoted below and elsewhere. The verb derives from a German noun coined during World War I – *Kurvenkampf* or 'battle of curves' – to describe the twisting and turning involved in combat between aircraft. The colourful English equivalent word 'dogfight' is also used as a noun and a verb.

Richthofen equalled Kirmaier's victory score the following afternoon during one of 19 air fights reported in the vicinity of Bapaume that day. His combat report noted that, at 1500 hours, south of Bapaume, together with *Leutnants* Hans Wortmann and Dieter Collin, he attacked a 'Vickers single-seater' at about 3,000 metres (9,800 feet) altitude. Richthofen wrote:

> After a long curving fight of three to five minutes, I forced my adversary down to 500 metres (1,600 feet). Now he tried to escape, flying toward the Front. I pursued and brought him down after firing 900 rounds.

Following the usual crash site inspection and 'souveniring', Richthofen learned that his adversary had been the distinguished flyer Major Lanoe George Hawker, a nine-victory ace, master air tactician and the first pilot to receive Britain's highest award for bravery in combat, the Victoria Cross, specifically for his air fighting achievements. Hawker's plane fell some 250 metres (820 feet) east of Luisenhof Ferme, a war-ruined farm alongside a road south of Bapaume. German troops examined Hawker's body, reported he had taken one shot in the back of the head, and buried him where he fell, with his final monument being the DH2 wreckage. Richthofen received patches of fabric bearing the aircraft's serial number and the machine gun for his trophy collection. Indeed, both were prominently displayed between the World Wars at the Richthofen Museum in Schweidnitz.

Richthofen proudly wrote about the fight to his mother on 25 November:

> My 11th Englishman is Major Hawker, 26 years old and commander of a British squadron. Prisoners have said that he is "the British Boelcke." I had the most difficult fight with him that I have ever had up to now. Finally I shot him down. Unfortunately, we lost our *Staffel* leader [Kirmaier] three days ago and eight days before that we lost an aeroplane.

A Bavarian pre-war military pilot, *Oberleutnant* Franz Josef Walz, was a ppointed as the new commanding officer of *Jasta 2*. He had leadership and air combat experience, having commanded a *Kampfstaffel*, and while a two-seater pilot, he was credited with six aerial victories within three months. He had also trained new pilots and overseen the formation of *Jagdstaffel 19* in the 1st Army area. Despite his organizational abilities, Walz was not as aggressive an air fighter as Boelcke and Kirmaier had been. He shot down only one additional enemy aeroplane while with *Jasta 2* and when he finally received the *Pour le Mérite*, on 9 August 1918, the award recognized primarily his long service and outstanding leadership of a two-seater unit in Palestine and less for his aerial combat skills and for having shot down enemy aircraft.

Jasta 2 moved from Lagnicourt to Pronville, five kilometres away, on 5 December, but a week's worth of fog and rain kept the unit from any further aerial triumphs. Clear weather on the morning of Monday, 11 December 1916 provided Richthofen the opportunity for his 12th victory, an Airco DH2 that he forced down. In his combat report he wrote:

> At about 1145 hours, at 2,800 metres altitude and south of Arras, I attacked with *Leutnant* Wortmann a flight of eight single-seat Vickers machines. I singled out one machine and, after a short curving fight, I ruined the adversary's engine and forced him to land behind our lines near Mercatel. Occupant not seriously wounded.

The engine behind the fuselage – or 'pusher' – design of the Airco DH2 no doubt saved the pilot's life, as the engine stopped many of Richthofen's bullets from hitting the wood and canvas-constructed fuselage.

Generalleutnant Ernst von Hoeppner, the Commanding General of the Air Force, was touring air units in the 1st Army Sector at the time and, that evening, he was invited to dine with *Jagdstaffel 2*. His visit became an occasion to celebrate Richthofen's 12th – and the *Staffel's* 69th – victories, and for the General to bolster morale, as *Leutnant der Reserve* Erwin Böhme noted in a letter:

> He spoke very flatteringly for the highest authority about orders for our *Staffel* having highest priority, which was welcome news to us, regarding all sorts of wishes that would otherwise remain hung up in official channels, for example to help obtain ever faster aeroplanes, more automobiles, and so forth. The old gentleman was especially pleased with the original way we fitted out our Officers' Mess: on the ceiling were hung two chandeliers made from captured British propellers and the like.

As a further tribute to the importance of *Jasta 2*, its heroic first leader was to be remembered even in death. Less than a week after *General* von Hoeppner's visit to the *Staffel*, an official message disseminated throughout the German Air Force announced:

> On orders of His Majesty [the Kaiser], *Jagdstaffel 2* will henceforth bear the name *Jagdstaffel Boelcke*.

However, any battle fervour that the honour might have inspired was dampened by bad weather. Except during brief breaks, flight operations on both sides of the lines were greatly reduced. Taking advantage of the bad weather at the Front, the Chief of Field Aviation, *Oberstleutnant* Hermann von der Lieth-Thomsen, summoned Richthofen to meet with him, in Kattowitz, an industrial centre in Upper Silesia. It was a long flight from France to the eastern edge of Germany, but such a summons from the Number Two man in the Air Force signalled to Richthofen that, like Boelcke before him, he had become an important asset to the military establishment. His 12 aerial victories reflected a growing body of experience that, combined with his professional officer's training, made Richthofen more than just one of a few surviving successful fighter pilots. Like Boelcke, he would be called on to test new aircraft and recommend areas of improvement in overall air combat operations. The first mention of Richthofen's enhanced standing in the Air Force organization surfaced in a brief note in his mother's diary, as the trip east offered an opportunity for a brief stop near his hometown:

> In the middle of [December], I saw Manfred in Breslau for a few hours on a stopover. He was en route to ... see the Chief of Field Aviation about new machines [and] he was very hurried, one noticed that he was pressed to travel on ...

Manfred von Richthofen was back at the Front by 20 December, when the bad weather broke and Royal Flying Corps patrols and attacks resumed. *Jagdstaffel Boelcke* responded vigorously and sought out targets behind British lines. On that day's morning patrol, Richthofen led four Albatros D.IIs against six Airco DH2s and shot one down over Monchy-au-Bois, within German lines. His comrades forced down four others, including three over their own aerodrome and one in the trenches.

Unknown to Richthofen, his 13th victory had a curious twist to it. He shot down and killed a pilot who was linked to Boelcke's death just over three weeks earlier. Richthofen's combat report notes only:

> About 1130 hours... after some curving fighting, I managed to press [my] adversary down to 1,500 metres (4,900 feet), where I attacked him at the closest range (a plane's length away). I saw immediately that I had hit the enemy: first, he went down in curves and then he dashed to the ground. I pursued him until I was 100 metres (320 feet) above the ground. This aeroplane had been attacked only by me.

The dead pilot was subsequently identified as 21-year-old Captain Arthur Gerald Knight, a member of No. 29 Squadron, RFC. An eight-victory ace and recipient of the Distinguished Service Order and Military Cross, Knight had been Boelcke's intended 41st victory on 27 October, when Erwin Böhme had to swerve to avoid hitting a DH 2 pursued by Richthofen. That is when Böhme's aeroplane grazed Boelcke's Albatros, causing it to lose its top wing and fatally crash. Knight slipped away that time, but not on 20 December 1916, when Richthofen followed him right to the very end of the Canadian's ill-fated flight. Knight was buried at what became the British Cemetery at Douchy-les-Ayette.

Richthofen was credited with a second aerial victory that day, an FE2b of No. 18 Squadron, RFC. He led an attack against a flight of 'Fees' north-east of Bapaume and made it quite clear in his combat report that only *Jasta 2* was involved in this fight:

> About 1335, I attacked, together with four aeroplanes of our *Staffel*, at 3,000 metres (9,800 feet) altitude, an enemy formation above Moreuil. The British squadron had thus far not been attacked by Germans and was flying somewhat apart. Therefore, I had the opportunity to attack the last machine [in the formation].
>
> I was foremost of our own people and other German aeroplanes were not to be seen. After the first attack, the enemy's engine began to smoke; the observer had been wounded. The aeroplane went down in great curves. I followed and fired at closest range. As was ascertained later, I had also killed the pilot. Finally the aeroplane crashed into the ground ... between Quéant and Lagnicourt.

Later, Richthofen was presented with two fabric patches, including one bearing the serial number A.5446 as proof of his 14th aerial victory. According to the *RFC Combat Casualty List*, that FE2b had been crewed by 28-year-old Second-Lieutenant Lionel G. D'Arcy and Sub-Lieutenant Reginald C. Whiteside, age 21, whose deaths that day were confirmed by the German Red Cross, although neither man has a known grave site. The fabric patches were later displayed at the Richthofen Museum in Schweidnitz, photographs of which have led historians to conclude that the two Britons were victims of *Jasta 2*'s new star.

Lothar von Richthofen followed his brother's advice and gave up flying as an observer with *Kampfstaffel 23*; in the summer of 1916, he was allowed to transfer from the two-seater unit to a pilot training centre. He capped his Christmas holiday by making his first solo flight in the presence of Manfred and their father, who commanded a small garrison outside Lille and joined his sons for a brief holiday together. Manfred's letter of 28 December relayed the latest good news:

> Papa and Lothar were both with me for Christmas Eve. It was a memorable celebration. A Christmas in the field was even more fun than you at home might think. Our celebration consisted only of a Christmas tree and a very good meal. The day after [Christmas], Lothar made his first solo flight. Now the next big event will be his first aerial victory. Yesterday, I shot down my 15th Englishman ...

Uncertainty remains as to whether Manfred von Richthofen succeeded in shooting down a rear-engined 'pusher' (so-called 'Vickers') biplane, as claimed in his note, on the afternoon of Wednesday, 27 December 1916. According to his combat report:

> At 1615 [hours], five aeroplanes of our *Staffel* attacked an enemy flight south of Arras. The enemy approached our lines, but was thrown back. After some fighting, I managed to attack a very courageously flown Vickers two-seater. After [I fired] 300 rounds, the enemy aeroplane began dropping, uncontrolled. I pursued the aeroplane up to 1,000 metres (3,200 feet) above the ground.
> The enemy aeroplane crashed to the ground on the enemy side, one kilometre (0.6 mile) behind trenches near Ficheux.

The *RFC Combat Casualty List* for that day contains no FE2b losses, especially not an aircraft that allegedly 'crashed to the ground' within British lines. A likely scenario identified the British aircraft as a similarly configured Airco DH2 rear-engined 'pusher' single-seat fighter flown by [then] Sergeant James T.B. McCudden, whose superior flying skills tricked his German opponent into thinking he was hit, and simply slipped away. McCudden went on to attain the rank of Major, become a 57-victory ace and receive the Victoria Cross and other high decorations. Small wonder that Richthofen noted his intended target was 'very courageously flown.' But one has to wonder about the German pilot's ability to 'see' an aeroplane crash into the ground from 1,000 metres' distance. In any event, Richthofen was credited with his 15th victory.

The new year 1917 did not get off to a bright start for *Jasta Boelcke*. First, the much-anticipated successor to the Albatros D.II fighters had not yet reached front line units to be tested in combat. Second, better aircraft were beginning to appear in British squadrons, including one pointed out by Royal Air Force historian H.A. Jones:

> It was noticeable, in much of the fighting at this period, that, probably owing to lack of experience, many of the German pilots did not get the best out of their superior aeroplanes, and their dominance was to that extent discounted. Furthermore, there was one British aeroplane that could stand up to the best of the German fighters ... the Sopwith "Pup" with which No. 54 Squadron [RFC] and No. 8 (Naval) Squadron were equipped.

Officially named the Sopwith Scout, the new aeroplane appeared to be a scaled-down single-seat version of the successful Sopwith Two-Seater (given the odd appellation of '1½ Strutter') and was considered to be the larger aircraft's 'pup,' a name that stuck to it.

On the afternoon of Tuesday, 4 January 1917, a flight of *Jasta 2* Albatros D.IIs encountered the new British aircraft. Richthofen recorded in his combat report:

> About 1615 [hours], we were just starting out when we saw above us at 4,000 metres (13,000 feet) altitude four aeroplanes unmolested by our artillery. As our anti-aircraft guns were not firing, we took them for our own.
>
> Only when they approached did we notice that they were British. One of [them] attacked us and we saw immediately that [it] was superior to ours. Only because we were three against one did we detect the enemy's weak points.
>
> I managed to get behind him and shoot him down. The aeroplane broke up while falling.

The pilot, Flight-Lieutenant Allan S. Todd, at age 30 relatively old for an air combatant, was found dead in the wreckage at Metz-en-Coûture, some 13 kilometres (8 miles) south-south-east of *Jasta Boelcke*'s airfield at Pronville.

Once again, the aeroplane's serial number – N.5193 – was acquired for Richthofen's souvenir collection, although Todd's body has no known grave.

Lothar von Richthofen, still on his Christmas leave, was out on the airfield at Pronville and watched through a telescope as Manfred shot down the Sopwith 'Pup.' Obviously, he did not see all the details with perfect clarity, but he saw enough to observe the nuances of Manfred pressing the attack and getting into the 'kill' position behind the British aeroplane. In that moment, history repeated itself as Lothar learned from Manfred in the same way Manfred had learned by watching Boelcke in action.

On 7 January, the men of *Jasta Boelcke* were very pleased when their first batch of Albatros D.III aircraft arrived from the replacement depot. Very similar in appearance to their predecessors, the D.IIIs had streamlined reinforced wood fuselages and were equipped with the same 160-hp Mercedes engines used in the D.IIs. Instantly noticeable on the D.IIIs, however, were the narrower-width lower wings, as opposed to the equal width wings of the D.I and D.II types. Captured French Nieuport sesquiplanes (biplanes with narrow width bottom wings) had impressed the Inspectorate of Military Aviation engineers, whose reports encouraged Albatros designers to adapt their wing designs and make other changes to add speed and a faster climb rate to the D.III, while retaining the D.II's manoeuvrability.

Of course, Manfred von Richthofen received one of the first Albatros D.IIIs, as befits a man whose career was about to ascend dramatically. But before he could lead his *Jasta 2* comrades into battle again, on 14 January he was transferred northward to the 6th Army Sector to serve as new commanding officer of *Jagdstaffel 11*, a unit based outside Douai, north-east of Arras. That sector was of special interest because German commanders believed it was 'where the British spring offensive was to be staged' and where the most aggressive *Staffel* leaders would be needed to repel British air units.

To Richthofen, the assignment was the supreme challenge, as he recalled:

> My 16th foe had fallen. Consequently, I was at the top of all [living German] fighter pilots. This was the goal I wanted to achieve. It was what I had said a year earlier to my friend Bodo von Lyncker when we trained together and he asked: "What is your goal? What do you want to achieve as a pilot?" Half in jest I answered: "Well, to be the leading fighter pilot must surely be quite nice." Neither I nor anyone

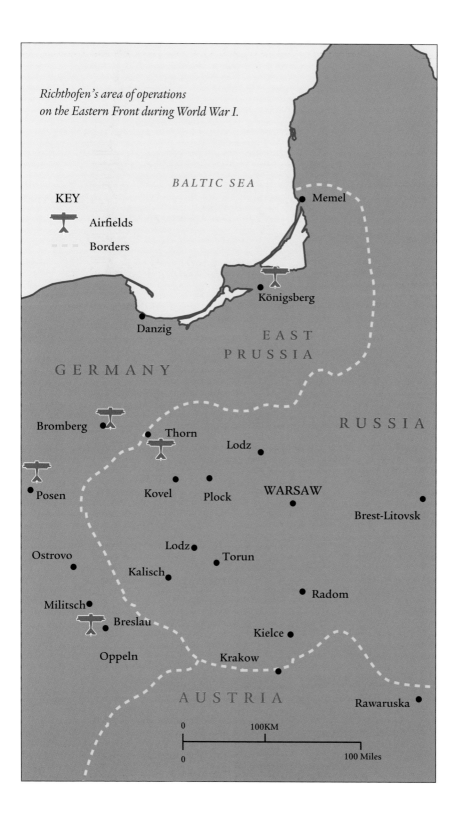

Richthofen's area of operations
on the Eastern Front during World War I.

BALTIC SEA

KEY

✈ Airfields

--- Borders

Memel

Königsberg

Danzig

EAST
PRUSSIA

GERMANY

RUSSIA

Bromberg

Thorn

Lodz

Posen

Kovel

Plock

WARSAW

Brest-Litovsk

Ostrovo

Lodz

Torun

Kalisch

Militsch

Radom

Breslau

Kielce

Oppeln

Krakow

AUSTRIA

Rawaruska

0

100KM

0

100 Miles

Manfred Freiherr *von Richthofen at home in Schweidnitz, wearing his Army cadet uniform, with younger brothers Bolko and Lothar.*

Manfred in 1912, after earning the epaulettes of a Fähnrich *[Ensign] of Uhlan Regiment Nr 1.*

An AEG G.II bomber with the open 'pulpit' of the type in which Manfred von Richthofen injured his right little finger due to close contact with a propeller arc; later models of this aeroplane had screens to protect observers from making such errors.

Richthofen's bandaged digit is seen in this photograph with comrades (from left) Rittmeister *Hans* Freiherr *von Könitz*, Leutnant *Hans* Reichsfreiherr [*Baron of the Holy Roman Empire*] Haller von Hallerstein and Leutnant *von Katte* at Brieftauben-Abteilung *Ostende's* airfield at Ghistelles, Belgium.

Kampfgeschwader 2 *on the Eastern Front undergoing inspection by the 9th Army Commander, Prince Leopold of Bavaria, seen here speaking with* Leutnant Manfred von Richthofen.

Oberleutnant *Max Immelmann flew this* Fokker Eindecker *[monoplane], numbered E 3/15, in combat. After World War I it was displayed at the Saxon Army Museum in Dresden and was destroyed during an Allied bombing raid in World War II.*

Hauptmann Boelcke und Oberleutnant Immelmann
im Kreise ihrer Kameraden.

The first two German pilots to receive the Orden Pour le Mérite *– Oswald Boelcke (fourth from left) and Max Immelmann (third from right) – wore the medal at the base of the neck of their uniform jackets while posing with other* Feldflieger-Abteilung 62 *members for a popular postcard photograph.*

The look of satisfaction indicates Manfred von Richthofen found his true calling at the controls of a Fokker monoplane fighter, seen behind him.

Imprudently smoking cigarettes in front of a Jagdstaffel 11 *Albatros D.I at La Brayelle airfield are (beginning with second from left):* Leutnant *Konstantin Krefft, the* Staffel's *Technical Officer;* Oberleutnant *Hans Helmuth von Boddien, a pilot from* Feldflieger-Abteilung 18 *who later joined* Jasta 11; Leutnant *Kurt Wolff, who ultimately shot down 33 enemy aircraft;* Leutnant der Reserve *Kurt Küppers, a pre-war pilot who flew on the Eastern Front; and* Leutnant *Carl Allmenröder, a Richthofen protégé who became a leading fighter pilot.*

The Ehrenbecher *[Honour Goblet], established to reward combat aviators for shooting down enemy aeroplanes, was first presented to Oswald Boelcke and Max Immelmann on Christmas Eve 1915. Bearing the inscription 'Dem Sieger im Luftkampf' [To the Victor in Aerial Combat], the one-litre silver goblets were produced at the direction of Kaiser Wilhelm II by Godet, an exclusive gold and silversmith in Berlin. The goblets were presented to officers and enlisted men alike on the occasion of their first air combat success.*

Built by the Royal Aircraft Factory, the awkward-looking FE2b two-seater was a worthy opponent that caused the demise of many German pilots. Manfred von Richthofen's first confirmed aerial victory, on 17 September 1916, was a 'Fee' and he had great respect for the type. He shot down 12 FE2s.

The Royal Aircraft Factory's BE2 was an effective two-seat reconnaissance aeroplane, but no match for a skilled German combat pilot. Some 13 of Richthofen's 80 'kills' were BE2s, plus three single-seat BE12 fighter variants.

The Bristol F2A, a fast and agile two-seat fighter, offered a wide field of vision for the pilot's forward-firing gun and less restriction of the observer's gun due to the low rudder design. Operating problems on the type's first offensive patrol, on 5 April 1917, was disastrous for the Royal Flying Corps and a bonanza for Manfred von Richthofen's Jagdstaffel 11, *which brought down four brand-new F2As that day.*

Manfred von Richthofen's all-red Albatros D.III was instantly recognizable and led to his being called the Red Baron. German airmen called the sleek-looking fighter the 'Haifisch' *[shark].*

A hawk's eye view of a favourite target of German fighter pilots, the Royal Aircraft Factory's RE8 two-seat reconnaissance aeroplane. Manfred von Richthofen shot down six RE8s.

Leutnant der Reserve *Erwin Böhme, a close friend of Richthofen's, was involved in the mid-air accident that led to the death of* Hauptmann Oswald Boelcke.

Manfred von Richthofen's shyness in the company of women is apparent in this contemporary newspaper photograph of the flyer at a popular horse racing event in the Grunewald area of Berlin.

German propagandists were not shy about creating a popular postcard by using the same image of Richthofen against a combat-related background. Here, the famed pilot is portrayed as being modest about his accomplishments.

When his red Albatros D.III was temporarily out of service, Richthofen flew a Halberstadt D.II fighter similar to this one, but painted red.

Richthofen stands by his all-red Halberstadt D.II as he talks to a long-time friend, Leutnant *Alfred Gerstenberg, who served with him until the famous ace's death in 1918. Gerstenberg became a general during World War II.*

Lieutenant William A. Bishop, who became the highest-scoring Allied fighter pilot of World War I, shown demonstrating the top wing-mounted Lewis machine-gun on his Nieuport. Early in his career, Richthofen had a gun similarly mounted on his Albatros two-seat reconnaissance aeroplane. Bishop and Richthofen were involved in at least one aerial combat, on 30 March 1917, which was inconclusive.

This Albatros D.V 2059/17 is reportedly the only aeroplane flown by Richthofen to survive World War I. The all-red Albatros helped perpetuate the legend of the Red Baron between the wars when it was displayed in the Zeughaus [Armoury] in Berlin. The aeroplane was destroyed during a World War II Allied bombing raid.

Manfred von Richthofen's Albatros D.III suffered wing flutter and breakage, as seen in this photograph of 24 January 1917. The sesquiplane design led to nearly continual operational problems, even with the later Albatros D.V fighter.

Leutnant *Werner Voss was nearly five years younger than Richthofen, but just as courageous and determined to shoot down enemy aeroplanes.*

An early postcard hailed Manfred von Richthofen as 'our most successful combat flier' and portrayed him in his parade tunic, wearing the Pour le Mérite, *Iron Cross First Class, Knight's Cross with Swords of the Royal House Order of Hohenzollern, Duke Carl Eduard Medal with Date Clasp and Swords of Saxe-Coburg-Gotha, and the Austro-Hungarian Military Merit Cross Third Class with the War Decoration.*

A later postcard view of Richthofen showed him wearing his field cap and with his overcoat open just enough to display the Pour le Mérite *at the base of his neck.*

Jagdstaffel 11 *members were also popular postcard subjects, as they achieved high victory numbers during 'Bloody April.' Seen here are (from left):* Vizefeldwebel Sebastian Festner *(who scored 10 victories that month),* Leutnant Karl-Emil Schäfer *(15 victories),* Obeleutnant Manfred von Richthofen *(21 victories),* Leutnant Lothar von Richthofen (15 victories) and Leutnant Kurt Wolff *(20 victories). Festner died in aerial combat on 23 April 1917.*

Richthofen's 'Red Baron' image extended to his non-combat flying. As did other air units, Jagdstaffel 11 had a 'hack' aircraft for behind-the-lines flights and the Albatros C.IX two-seater was painted all red. Richthofen flew in this aeroplane to Germany to meet Kaiser Wilhelm II *in May 1917.*

Postcard fans were treated to a view of Richthofen's meeting at Supreme High Command Headquarters in Bad Kreuznach, Germany with Oberstleutnant *Hermann von der Lieth-Thomsen, Air Chief of Staff (left)*, and Generalleutnant *Ernst von Hoeppner, Commanding General of the Air Force.*

After meeting many high-ranking personages at Supreme High Command Headquarters, Richthofen enjoyed a lighter moment in nearby Bad Homburg vor der Höhe. He seems charmed by the elder von Forkenbeck-Gablenz sister (left), while his friend Fritz von Falkenhayn teased the younger sister. Both women were part of the German Empress's entourage.

Following his visit to Bad Kreuznach, Richthofen mistakenly believed that by taking an early Saturday train, he could slip into Schweidnitz unnoticed. His life had changed and, as seen here on 19 May at 7 a.m., crowds gathered wherever he appeared.

As his fame grew, Manfred von Richthofen attracted the attention of noted German artists, such as Arnold Busch, who created this life portrait just prior to the flyer's near-fatal crash on 6 July 1917. The inscription reads: 'Im Felde – Juli 1917' [In the field – July 1917]. Adding Richthofen's signature at the bottom of the illustration bolstered the drawing's appeal as a postcard.

While flying during Jagdgeschwader I's first extensive aerial operations, on 6 July 1917, Richthofen was wounded in aerial combat and had to make a forced landing. His aircraft, Albatros D.V 4693/17, was repaired and, after being hospitalized, Richthofen flew this aircraft on subsequent missions. It was distinctive in that only the nose, wheel covers and tail were painted red.

else believed it would ever come to that. Boelcke, when once asked "Who looks as though he has a chance to become a good fighter pilot?" is supposed to have pointed his finger at me and said - of course, not to me personally, but as it was told to me by another – "That is the man!"

Boelcke and Immelmann received the *Pour le Mérite* after their eighth victories. I had doubled that number. What would happen to me? I was very excited. It was whispered I would be given command of a *Jagdstaffel*. Then one day came the telegram: "*Leutnant* von Richthofen has been appointed to be the leader of *Jagdstaffel* 11." I must say I was more annoyed than pleased. I had become so thoroughly acquainted with my comrades in *Jagdstaffel Boelcke* that now to have to begin settling in anew was bothersome. Besides, I would rather have the *Pour le Mérite*.

Two days later – we were sitting cosily together at *Jagdstaffel Boelcke* and celebrating my leaving – and a telegram came from Headquarters announcing that the *Pour le Mérite* had been awarded to me. Naturally, there was great joy all around...

There seems to be a time discrepancy in Richthofen's relating of these events. The official documentation with his *Pour le Mérite* bears the date 12 January 1917, exactly a year after the same high honour had been authorized for Oswald Boelcke and Max Immelmann. In addition to announcing the latest recipient of Prussia's highest bravery award, the notice distributed to 6th Army aviation also noted an important criterion for it by clearly stating that Richthofen's *Pour le Mérite* was 'bestowed for the successful confirmed downing of 16 enemy airplanes.'

Once again, the price of glory had risen.

7
THE RED BARON ARISES

Germany's highest-scoring living fighter pilot and the latest Knight of the *Orden Pour le Mérite*, Manfred von Richthofen, commanded his new *Staffel* with absolute, unquestioned authority. Royal Air Force Historian H.A. Jones assessed the air combat leadership and tactics that Richthofen instilled in his men, many of whom graduated to *Staffel* commands of their own to begin the training cycle anew:

> ... Richthofen was a ruthless opponent, but ... he was never reckless. He was courteous and entirely without ill will towards those of his victims who were made prisoners, but in the air he showed no mercy, nor does it appear that he found any aspect of his duty distasteful. He was fond of hunting and his tactics, more especially in the early part of his career, showed the influence of his sporting experiences. He would stalk his adversary with calculated patience, making the most of every advantage of height, wind, cloud, or sun, to place himself in a favourable position ..."
>
> [Richthofen's tactics were] perfectly suited to the conditions under which the German armies fought on the Western Front. Those armies were, for the greater part of the war, on the defensive and the German air service was numerically weaker than the combined air services of the Allies. Richthofen's task was to inflict the greatest damage with the minimum of loss to his own service, and he knew that on any day suitable for flying, great numbers of aeroplanes of the Royal Flying Corps would be over the German lines. He seldom had to seek combat. It was offered to him and he could make his choice, and if it were ... to avoid or to break off a fight, Richthofen would never hesitate [to do so].
>
> ... [Richthofen] showed great acumen in his choice of [pilots] and was stern but patient in his schooling of them, inspiring them with his own high courage, confidence and sense of proportion, so that they became one of the most efficient fighting forces of the war.

Despite Richthofen's comments about not wanting to leave his comrades in *Jagdstaffel Boelcke*, he needed to step out from his mentor's shadow and prove his own worth. Being assigned to command *Jagdstaffel 11* was the perfect challenge for him. Since its establishment on 28 September 1916, *Jasta 11* had been the least successful of the three fighter units attached to the 6th Army. Under its first commander, 27-year-old *Oberleutnant* Rudolf Lang, the *Staffel* was briefly mentioned once in the 6th Army Weekly Aviation Report for its involvement in a protracted aerial battle with 27 enemy aircraft on 23 November 1916, but had no air combat successes to show for its efforts. In fact, after arriving at his new post, Richthofen learned that a neighbouring reconnaissance two-seater unit, *Flieger-Abteilung 18*, had a higher victory score than his new *Jagdstaffel*. Moreover, in the latest 6th Army Weekly Aviation Report, he read that, a week earlier, a *Flieger-Abteilung 18* crew had forced a British two-seater to land within its own lines, as confirmed by a German anti-aircraft unit. He made note of the pilot, *Leutnant* Friedrich Wilhelm Lübbert, who turned out to be the younger brother of Eduard Lübbert, a promising flyer Richthofen inherited from his predecessor, Rudolf Lang. Perhaps the Lübbert brothers had hunting blood in their veins – like the Richthofens. *Jasta 11* already had a full complement of ten flying officers and two enlisted pilots, but, following Boelcke's example, Richthofen continued to look for aggressive flyers to become successful fighter pilots. The reasoning was simple for anyone in command: normal combat attrition would take its toll and some original members might not perform to his satisfaction. Plus, Richthofen's new association with *Oberstleutnant* von der Lieth-Thomsen, the Chief of Field Aviation, would assure he received the resources needed to make *Jasta 11* successful.

To get off on the right foot, Richthofen made a dramatic appearance at *Jagdstaffel 11* on Saturday, 20 January 1917. He arrived at La Brayelle, just northwest of Douai, in the new Albatros D.III that he had received at *Jagdstaffel Boelcke*. His aeroplane's sleeker top wing and narrow bottom wing made it instantly recognizable from the rugged, square-winged D.I and D.II types parked at the airfield. According to preliminary reports, the D.III was 'easy to fly, possess[ed] no nasty traits and ... was a fighter that the average pilot, fresh from single-seater school, could feel comfortable in.' Thus, Richthofen was clearly the leader of the future of fighter aviation, equipped with the leading German aeroplane for that mission. Shortly, the entire *Staffel* would be flying the new fighters.

As he was getting settled in, Richthofen found another way to make an impression on his new subordinates. The Albatros *Flugzeugwerke* [Aeroplane Works], in a clumsy attempt to camouflage the D.IIIs, delivered most of them with natural wood finish fuselages and a pattern of olive green and brown (or lilac mauve) on the upper wing surfaces. Recognizing the futility of trying to camouflage an aeroplane in the air, Richthofen took the opposite approach, and, as he wrote, he had his aeroplane '...painted glaring red. The result was that absolutely everyone could not help but notice my red bird. In fact, my opponents also could not help but notice it.'

A leading German aircraft markings expert has noted:

> Richthofen's choice of red no doubt stemmed from its high visibility and it was also the regimental colour of his old [West Prussian cavalry] unit ...

To be sure, Richthofen's early orientation flights in his all-red Albatros D.III had a startling effect on friend and foe alike, as he subsequently learned from one of the few surviving opponents with whom he was able to speak. During his first combat missions – incorrectly identified as his first days at *Jasta 11* in the following letter to his mother – he demonstrated his ability in air combat, as well as mastery of the new Albatros fighter in a tight situation:

> I was lucky. On my first day here I shot down Number 17 and on the second day Number 18. As I shot down my 18th, one of my [lower] wings broke during the air battle at 3,000 metres (9,800 feet) altitude. It was only through a miracle that I reached the ground without going *kaput*. On the same day, three new aeroplanes of *Jagdstaffel Boelcke* fell ... It is possible that the same [wing problem] that happened to me also happened to them.

Richthofen's 18thvictory, scored at midday on 24 January 1917, was not as easy as the ace made it seem in the letter. He was on a mentoring patrol with *Sergeant* Hans Howe, who had experience with a two-seater unit and then *Jasta 10* and was still unsuccessful in aerial combat. When Richthofen saw a flight of FE2bs west of Vimy Ridge, less than 20 kilometres (12 miles) from Douai, he motioned for Howe to follow him in a classic 'kill' position, with the sun directly behind them to make it nearly impossible for their victims to see them coming. They dived on the lead aircraft and, as Richthofen later wrote:

> My opponent never had a chance to turn and had to hasten to get down to earth, as he had already begun to show suspicious signs of burning [trailing fuel vapour]. When an aeroplane is in such a condition, we say: "He stinks." As it turned out ... his time was up, as, shortly before the machine came to earth, it burst into bright flames.
>
> I felt compassion for my opponent and decided not to send him crashing down, but, rather, to force him to land, as I had a feeling that he was already wounded, for he had not fired a shot.
>
> At about 500 metres (1,600 feet) altitude, during a normal glide, a malfunction in my machine forced me to land before making another turn. Now something quite comical happened. My enemy in his burning machine landed smoothly, while I, the victor, turned over on the barbed wire of a reserve emplacement trench.
>
> A sporting reception followed with both Englishmen, who were more than a little surprised at my crash, as ... they had not fired at me and they could not imagine why I had made a forced landing. They were the first Englishmen I had brought down alive. Therefore, I enjoyed talking with them. Among other things, I asked whether they had ever seen my machine in the air. "Oh yes," one of them said, "I know it quite well. We call it '*Le petit rouge*' [the little red one]."

The wounded but lucky-to-be-alive FE2b crewmen – Lieutenant John E. MacLennan, age 20, and Captain Oscar Grieg, age 28, members of No. 25 Squadron – were taken to a medical aid station. After treatment for their wounds, they remained prisoners for the remainder of the war.

In his combat report, Richthofen noted that he had landed quickly after a lower wing cracked when he was at about 300 metres (980 feet) altitude. The wing weakness could not have been caused by the observer's defensive machine gun fire; in a brief conversation made possible by Richthofen's rudimentary cadet school English, he learned that MacLennan's gun had jammed.

Richthofen's experience, in addition to the loss of the two *Jasta Boelcke* Albatros D.IIIs due to wing failure the previous day, caused him to raise concerns about the new aeroplane.

Drawing on his budding association with the Chief of Field Aviation, Manfred urged officials at the Inspectorate of Military Aviation in Berlin to find a solution for the Albatros wing-cracking problem. Initially, quality of workmanship and materials were the obvious points of study. The new science of aerodynamics had not yet advanced to include such sub-specialties as aero-elasticity, which would have enabled Inspectorate and Albatros engineers to understand that an inherent design flaw caused a 'fluttering' effect on the D.III's reduced-width, single-spar bottom wing, and that this problem would continue with the Albatros D.III and even its successors, the D.V and D.Va. Conversely, French Nieuport designs, which inspired Albatros engineers to incorporate reduced-width lower wings in successors to the D.II, continued to provide the advantages of 'significant improvement in downward view for ... the pilot... [and] combined the manoeuvrability of a monoplane with the stability of a biplane.' Later in the war, however, the Nieuport 28 design returned to equal-chord (width) for both wings, but the lesson was lost on Albatros engineers.

After receiving complaints from Richthofen and other *Staffel* leaders, the Commanding General's Office grounded the Albatros D.IIIs on 27 January. The aeroplanes were sent to Army Air Depots to be fitted with modifications then being made at the factory. Landing gear was strengthened, auxiliary braces were added to the bottom portion of the V-shaped interplane struts connecting the bottom and upper wings, and to alleviate cooling problems, radiator changes were made.

Until the Albatroses were returned to their units, Richthofen flew a Halberstadt D.II, an early single-seat biplane successor to the Fokker monoplanes. Once again he proved his skill as a fighter pilot, even with an older, less capable aircraft, by scoring his 19th aerial victory on the afternoon of 1 February 1917. But, there was no trophy to be obtained from this success, as the British two-seater crashed within German forward lines and the wounded crewmen reportedly were just clear of the wreckage when a Canadian artillery battery destroyed it to keep the Germans from salvaging anything useful from it. The crewmen died of their wounds the following day in a field hospital. During that fight, Richthofen was mentoring *Leutnant* Carl Allmenröder, an original *Jasta 11* member who went on to shoot down 30 enemy aeroplanes, to command his own *Jagdstaffel* and receive the coveted *Pour le Mérite*.

Following his 19th aerial victory, Richthofen felt comfortable enough with his protégés' progress to take a short home leave. He arrived in Schweidnitz very early on Sunday, 4 February 1917, the day the United States of America severed diplomatic relations with Imperial Germany, making America's entry into the war a certainty.

But global politics were far from mind when *Freifrau* Kunigunde von Richthofen was awakened by the sound of the doorbell. She turned on a light and looked at the clock, which showed it was 7 a.m. Then, she recalled:

> ... the door is quickly opened and Manfred stands before my bed, fresh and happy, [with] no trace of fatigue after the long night's journey. The blue [Maltese Cross] glitters at his collar – the *Pour le Mérite*. I take his hand and speak as I would when praising a boy: "Bravo, you have done well, Manfred ... But how did you get in? Was the garden gate open?" No, that was not it, but it did not matter. The Knight of the *Orden Pour le Mérite* climbed over the fence.
>
> As quickly as possible, [Manfred, Ilse and I] are at breakfast, for morning coffee. No wartime substitute coffee, please! A handful of coffee beans were scraped together. They were saved for a special festive occasion. That hour was now here.
>
> An inexhaustible question and answer time commences ... I look at him with pride. His face seems to me to have become more closed. A face of will. But the lovable, well-defined mouth still has its charm.
>
> [The question] "Where have you been, Manfred?" [resulted in a] ... complicated, less pleasant subject. In recent times, it has happened more often that German flyers have had wings break away in the air. He wanted to call attention to competent authorities in Berlin about these construction faults. (Or was it perhaps faulty materials?)

In any case, Manfred was certain that the Albatros D.III bottom wing flutter problem was being corrected and it would cause no further disruption in his air combat operations. The conversation changed, as *Freifrau* von Richthofen's diary shows:

Manfred told us ... the enemy calls his aeroplane *"Le petit rouge"* because he had it painted bright red. I found that frivolous, but he believed: "One cannot make his aeroplane invisible in the air, and so at least our [people] recognize me."

Manfred, Ilse and *Freifrau* von Richthofen huddled by the hearth to ward off the bitter cold outside that even chilled the house and talked for hours. Later in the evening, Manfred proudly showed his mother and sister a Berlin newspaper article about his 19th aerial victory; it provoked a response from his mother:

"Why do you risk your life like this every day? Why do you do it, Manfred?"
He looks at me intently, with great seriousness written on his face.
"For the man in the trenches," he says simply. "I want to ease his hard lot in life by keeping enemy flyers away from him."

His mother and sister understood why Manfred empathized with the countless thousands of ordinary front line soldiers; he had experienced the trench network, where death could be a step away or at the end of the shrill whistling of an incoming artillery shell. For the most part, those soldiers were not individually praised in battle reports and did not receive high honours.

By bedtime, the women understood Manfred's view that war was more than glorious actions and the perverse satisfaction of cheating death once again. As his mother concluded in her diary entry:

I understood from this night what made up the nature of combat flyers and what enabled these young people, who were barely out of their adolescence, to accomplish such feats within death's shadow.

As was an established practice, Richthofen spent only a few days at home and then returned to his new duties at Douai. He was eager to resume working with his pilots and to begin to judge their merits. En route to Douai in the Halberstadt D.II in which he had scored his most recent victory, Richthofen stopped at Pronville, home of his former unit, *Jagdstaffel Boelcke*. One of his best friends there, Erwin Böhme, responded to news of the *Jasta 11* assignment:

I am happy about it, for without a doubt Richthofen has been called to play a great role in aviation – but in our *Staffel* he has left a great hole.

During the flight from Pronville to Douai, Richthofen assured a dramatic return to duty by shooting down his 20th enemy aeroplane, a BE2 two-seat biplane. According to his combat report, at about noon:

> After flying back from ... *Jasta Boelcke*, I spotted an enemy artillery-ranging aeroplane at an altitude of 2,000 metres (6,500 feet) west of Loos. I ... approached him unnoticed to within some 50 metres (160 feet). After firing several hundred rounds [at it], the aeroplane dashed down, falling into our trenches. The pilot was killed in the air, the observer was seriously injured when landing.

Although the weather was turning bad, Richthofen and five of his men later returned to the skies west of Loos and, later that afternoon, attacked another flight of BE2 artillery-spotters. Richthofen went after one of them and claimed to have sent it down within British lines. Realizing he was drifting over enemy territory, Richthofen reported that he continued firing at the two-seat biplane until both wings on the left side of the aeroplane fell off. In his combat report, he wrote:

> ... I could observe that the enemy aeroplane touched the ground south-west of Mazingarbe. I could see a heavy cloud of smoke in the snow arising from the place where the aeroplane was lying. As it was foggy and already rather dark, I have no witnesses, either from the air or from the ground..

It is interesting – and certainly unusual – that with 'no witnesses, either from the air or from the ground,' nor any physical evidence to support his claim, Richthofen received official credit for his 21st aerial victory.

American journalist Floyd Gibbons, whose landmark book *The Red Knight of Germany* (1927) is based on very good access to British and German archival sources, as well as surviving veterans, relatively soon after the war, wrote that Richthofen's 21st victory was:

... the only one of Richthofen's early claims that was acknowledged and credited to him when there were no witnesses to the event. After his 60th victory in the air, witnesses were no longer required to the reports he made of his combats, because, after that time, he seldom appeared with [fewer] than 20 planes with him.

The best that can be said of the incident is that the German ace 'might' have shot down BE2c 2543 of No. 2 Squadron, RFC, as many of the circumstances match its crash-landing within British lines near Mazingarbe that day. The pilot, 26-year-old Captain George C. Bailey, was wounded in the fight, while the observer, Second Lieutenant George W.B. Hampton, age 31, emerged from the wreckage unscathed.

Richthofen's growing reputation, enhanced by repeated mention in Army reports and newspaper articles, did more than give him distinctive credibility. It made him – like Boelcke – a magnet for aspiring fighter pilots. The same day he scored his first double victories, he received a telegram from a man whose name he recognized, *Leutnant der Reserve* Karl-Emil Schäfer. He had heard that Schäfer had been badly wounded early in the ground war, resulting in his left leg being slightly shorter than his right, but that impairment had not stopped him from joining the Flying Service. Indeed, less than a month earlier an Army report noted the 25-year-old Rhinelander scored his first aerial victory while flying a two-seater reconnaissance plane.

Schäfer's telegram simply asked: 'Can you use me?' Richthofen responded with a similarly terse response: 'You have already been requested.' He had the aggressive spirit and indomitable will that Richthofen wanted and, a week later, Schäfer arrived at *Jasta 11*, ready to go to work.

Conversely, Richthofen determined that *Sergeant* Hans Howe was not an asset to the *Staffel*. For the past three months, Howe had not shot down an enemy aeroplane, nor distinguished himself in any way; hence, he was posted out on 17 February. Although other long-term non-scorers were allowed to remain, Richthofen usually gave men a relatively short time to add to *Jasta 11*'s victory score or demonstrate in some way that they shared his dedication to the *Jagdstaffel's* mission.

And to clarify how he thought a *Jagdstaffel* should operate, Richthofen sent a series of reports to the Chief of Field Operations on 16 February. In one, he expanded on Boelcke's dislike of stunt flying and the need for strict discipline:

The best method of flying against the enemy is as follows: The officer commanding the [unit], no matter how large, should fly lowest, and should keep all machines under observation by turning and curving.

No machine should be allowed either to advance or to keep back. More or less, the whole squadron should advance curving.

Flying straight on above the front is dangerous, as even ... the same type of aeroplane develop different speeds. Surprises can be avoided only when flying in close order. The commanding officer is responsible [to assure] that neither he nor any of his pilots is surprised by the enemy. If he cannot see to that, he is no good as a leader.

As *Jasta 11* became more successful under Manfred von Richthofen, the pilots became concerned that their leader's notoriety as *'Le petit rouge'* could make him a distinctive target. Lothar von Richthofen, who subsequently joined the *Staffel*, noted:

Every flyer on the other side knew him, for at the time he alone flew a red-painted aeroplane. For that reason ... [his pilots wanted] to have all *Staffel* aeroplanes painted red and implored my brother to allow it so he would not be so especially conspicuous. The request was granted; for ... everyone knew ... it attracted attention. Consequently, one had to really perform ... My brother's crate was glaring red. Each of the rest ... had some additional markings in other colours ... as recognition symbols. Schäfer, for example, had his elevator, rudder and most of the back part of the fuselage [painted] black; Allmenröder used white [on the nose and spinner], Wolff used green ... In the air and from the ground, as well as from the enemy's view, we all looked to be red, as only small other parts were painted in another colour.

An early British Richthofen biographer added:

... the distinctive second colour enabled members of the *Staffel* to recognise each other in the air. As each of them developed his own fighting individuality, it was helpful for a pilot to identify his neighbours in a dogfight because he knew what they would do under certain given circumstances and could adapt his own tactics accordingly. This [identification system] made for good teamwork, and so the main background with distinctive personal subsidiary colours was subsequently adopted by other *Jagdstaffeln*.

Unfortunately, weather conditions did not offer much opportunity for *Jasta 11*'s colourful war birds to take to the air. Rain and snow are normal for February and March in northern France and Belgium, which helps to explain why, after Richthofen's victory on 14 February, he did not score again until 4 March. Air activity on both sides of the battle lines increased only on good-weather days. German ground commanders anticipated an Anglo-French spring offensive and the inevitable opposing ground and air probes of German lines as the weather allowed. *Jasta 11* and other *Staffeln* were busy, trying to keep British air units from reconnoitring their side's preparations for the coming offensive.

Modest successes – *Vizefeldwebel* Sebastian Festner's second victory on 15 February and Allmenröder's first the next day – were positive signs to their leader. Often, however, the winter flights did more to educate the fledgling combat pilots than to keep German lines free of their aerial adversaries. As Lothar von Richthofen commented about his brother's early combat patrols with Carl Allmenröder and Kurt Wolff, both of whom became leaders of their own *Staffeln* and later received the *Pour le Mérite*:

In the first days, my brother flew out with them, attacked numerous British [aircraft], and his machine received an enormous number of hits, without successes to make up for it, and both of them did not help. Of course my brother came back somewhat annoyed, but did not reproach them; on the contrary, he did not say a word about it. As Wolff and Allmenröder ... told me, that influenced them more than the harshest dressing-down.

Manfred von Richthofen understood that new pilots at the Front need practice, skill and luck in their early flights to enable them to mature and survive in the crucible of air combat. He once told a General Staff officer:

I have never had anything to do with ... combat-proven, experienced flyers. Just beginners. I do not always receive [the quality of men] I request, as may be generally imagined. My gentlemen always come fresh out of flying school ...

The most important elements of flying, in my view, are skill in taking off and landing, and the personal courage with which a man goes after the enemy. To me, it is a thousand times better to have a daring fellow who might have difficulty making a left turn, but who goes hell-bent for leather after the enemy, than the most elegant ... air show flyer who I cannot bring over the Front. We need daredevils, not aerial acrobats!

I once flew with a gentleman who tore through dashing turns and made an absolutely marvellous impression. But in aerial combat, it seemed to me that he did not go after the enemy so smartly. And once when I was working with him, paying special attention to him – he was gone. I was in a damned tight spot and shot down an enemy, but got away by a hair. When I returned home, he reported to me that the moment the fight began he became so ill that he had to break off immediately. You could tell that when you looked at him. Aerial combat requires a special kind of nerve. [I said to him:] "Then I ask that you disappear immediately. I cannot use people who leave their comrades in the lurch. And when you feel sick, then you damned well better tell us at once." There are, of course, always people who try to delay things and think: no one will take any notice of it.

The German 6th Army's weather office forecasted a 'break in the previously foggy and stormy weather' for Sunday, 4 March 1917, as did its British counterpart, and airmen from both sides were out in force. In the early afternoon, Richthofen scored *Jasta 11*'s first victory of the day, a two-seater that he shot down north of Loos, in the no-man's-land just ahead of German lines. The aircraft was a BE2 of No. 2 Squadron, RFC, piloted by 20-year-old Lieutenant James B.E. Crosbee, with Flight Sergeant John E. Prance, age 32, in the observer's seat. Prance's combat report stated they were on a photo-reconnaissance mission north of Lens when they were attacked 'from right out of the glare of the sun' by what Prance identified as a very fast 'Halberstadter' single-seater. Richthofen's first burst of machine gun fire hit Prance, who continued to fire at their pursuer. Through the sheerest of luck Crosbee managed to fly out of German territory.

Richthofen stated:

> My adversary dived, but in such a steep way that I could not follow. According to our infantry observations, the aeroplane crashed to the ground in front of our trenches.

About three hours later, Richthofen and five of his men attacked a flight of Sopwith 1½ Strutter two-seaters over Acheville, east of Vimy. This crew was not as lucky as Crosbee and Prance, as Richthofen coolly recorded in his combat report:

> The Sopwith I had singled out flew for quite a while in my [stream of] fire. After [my] 400th shot, the aeroplane lost a wing while making a turn. The machine hurtled downwards. It is not worthwhile to have the aeroplane taken back, as parts are all over Acheville and the surrounding area.

The Sopwith's single Lewis and Vickers two machine guns were taken to *Jasta 11* as souvenirs of Richthofen's 23rd aerial victory.

Due to snowfall on 5 March, most flight operations on both sides of the lines were suspended. The following day, Tuesday, the weather was 'fine,' but resulted in mixed blessings. During a late morning patrol over Lens, Schäfer shot down two Sopwith two-seaters. In the course of the fight, however, *Leutnant* Eduard Lübbert was wounded in the shoulder and made a forced-landing. His aeroplane had been shot up in nearly every fight he had been in. Once he came back with 64 holes in his machine. But he had yet to shoot down an enemy aeroplane and so his comrades made a little joke of it and called him *'Kugelfang'* [bullet catcher]. Lübbert, that day's only recorded air casualty in the German 6th Army Sector, was not seriously wounded. He landed his undamaged aircraft so skilfully that, a few hours later, Richthofen was driven to the landing site to fly it back to La Brayalle.

Later that day, Richthofen shot down his 24th enemy aeroplane. He reported that he:

...and Allmenröder ... attacked two [BE2] ...artillery flyers at low altitude over the other side. The wings on the plane I attacked came off. [The aeroplane] ... smashed into the ground.

The return of bad weather on 7 and 8 March made flying nearly impossible. But later the following morning conditions improved and Richthofen led a flight in which he received a personal reminder of how easily death comes to those in the air. From a distance, he spotted a flight of 'lattice-tail' rear-engined biplanes that looked to be an advantageous target, as he wrote in his memoirs:

> I was in my formation and saw an opponent who likewise was in formation over our artillery positions in the vicinity of Lens. I had a bit yet to fly until I would reach the area. It is a very stimulating moment when the opponent approaches, when one sees the enemy and still has a few minutes' time until the battle begins. I believe that my face becomes pale, but, unfortunately, I do not have a mirror with me. I find this moment beautiful. For it is extremely stimulating and I love it all. One observes the opponent from a distance, recognizes the formation as the enemy, counts the number of enemy machines and weighs the unfavourable and favourable factors. For example, the wind plays an enormous role, whether the wind pushes away or toward my front lines ...
> We were five and the opposition three times as strong. The Englishmen flew together like a great swarm of gnats. It is not easy to disperse such a swarm ... It is out of the question for one machine to do it and is extremely difficult when the difference in numbers is so unfavourable, as it was in this case. But one feels so superior to the enemy that one does not doubt success for a moment ...

Almost intuitively, the British pilot focused on Richthofen, who related:

> Now I am almost upon him, about a hundred metres (300 feet) away, the safety catch is off my gun, I ... fire some shots, the guns are in working order ... In my mind I see the opponent already

falling. The previous excitement is gone. I think quite calmly and objectively now, weighing the probabilities of hitting him and being hit. On the whole, the fight itself is usually the least exciting aspect and whoever gets excited makes mistakes. He will never shoot down anyone. But self-control is indeed a matter of habit.

Now I am about 50 metres (150 feet) away and, with some good shots, success cannot fail to come. So I thought. All of a sudden ... I have barely got off ten shots when ... there is a smack on my machine. It is clear ... my machine has been [hit, although] I personally have not. At the same moment it stinks something terrible of gasoline, also the engine has slowed down. The Englishman notices it, for now he shoots even more. I must break off immediately.

I go straight down. Instinctively, I switch off the engine. Just in time. If the fuel tank is punctured and the stuff squirts around my legs, the danger of fire is indeed great. Up front there is an internal combustion engine over 150 "horses" strong, glowing hot. One drop of fuel on it and the whole machine goes up in flames. I am leaving behind me a trail of white mist. I know it very well from having seen it in opponents ... just before an explosion.

Then, Richthofen's luck improved. Abruptly, his opponent flew off, considering the German pilot to be finished. But, gliding down without power, Richthofen was still in danger. As he wrote:

Suddenly, there is a rocket [heading toward me]. Is it an enemy signal flare? No. It is too big for that. It is getting bigger and bigger. One of the aircraft is burning. But what kind? The machine looks exactly like [one of] ours. Thank God, it is an opponent. Who could have shot it down? Right after that, a second aeroplane falls from the flight, [and] like mine, it goes straight down, spinning, continuously spinning – and then – it recovers. It flies right toward me. It is also an Albatros ...

The other Albatros pilot, Schäfer, came down to check on his leader and, once assured, headed back to their airfield. Meanwhile, Richthofen landed smoothly on a small meadow along the road to Hénin-Liétard. An Army officer driving by saw Richthofen come down and offered to drive him to the city, a few minutes away. There, he called *Jasta 11* and was quickly picked up. In little over an hour, Richthofen was flying another Albatros and heading south toward Arras to cut off any of the 'lattice-tails' that might be left from the morning fight.

At about noon, Richthofen and three comrades pounced on a single-seat rear-engined fighter. The leader sent it down in flames near Roclincourt, a few kilometres north of Arras. He noted that 'the aeroplane is lying on our side [of the lines], but cannot be salvaged as it is nearly completely burned and too close to the Front.'

Richthofen marked his 25th victory in grand style:

> In the evening I [called and] assured my kind host at Hénin-Liétard that I had increased my "bag" to a quarter-hundred.

The following day, *Jasta 11* welcomed a new member, *Leutnant* Lothar von Richthofen. After completing pilot training, he worked himself into a state of exhaustion while perfecting his flying skills and was sent home for recuperative leave in February. He was all too aware of whose trail he followed and he felt he had to prove himself worthy of the name.

As Richthofen's first British biographer observed:

> In the ordinary course of events, [Lothar] should have been put in a number of Front patrols as a two-seater pilot before applying for a transfer to the *Jagdstaffel* school, but luck was with him. Manfred was fast making a name, while German aces were still too few and far between. Probably the prospect of two brothers as champions of the air promised good material for home propaganda, which was so badly needed.
>
> At any rate, Lothar was sent to *Jagdstaffel 11* as soon as he ...[finished] his final tests. There, Manfred gave him some sound theoretical instruction of the type he had received from Boelcke and made him practise behind the lines. A fortnight later he was taken out for his first patrol, with strict injunctions to keep close behind Manfred and avoid fights.

Ever since his service in the cavalry, Lothar always carried a riding crop for good luck. There was no room for this talisman in the tight space of an aeroplane cockpit, so he had to fly without it. He later recalled:

> ... soon I got my hand on another talisman. After I arrived ... at my brother's *Staffel*, Manfred gave me [the Albatros] with which he had attained ten aerial victories. Likewise, he gave me a pair of old leather gloves, with which at just the right moment he had so often pressed the machine gun triggers. As luck would have it, I shot down my first ten Englishmen armed with these gloves and [in that] machine ...

But before Lothar von Richthofen could join his brother in combat, Manfred and his men went on to continue redeeming the reputation of the once lacklustre *Jasta 11*. Shortly before noon on 11 March, the *Staffel's* technical officer, *Leutnant* Konstantin Krefft, scored his first aerial victory, shooting down a single-seater while his leader watched the results of his training. Then, Manfred von Richthofen went after the BE2 reconnaissance aeroplane that the fighter had been escorting and, some 15 minutes later, shot it down and scored his 26th victory.

Another run of bad weather curtailed flight operations across *Jasta 11*'s sector. Using those conditions as cover, between 16 and 20 March, German ground forces withdrew to the *Siegfriedstellung* [Siegfried Line], which the British called the Hindenburg Line, running from Arras south to St. Quentin. The new battle line offered the advantage of prepared defensive systems, from which the Germans could advance again when it was advantageous. Meanwhile, British ground and air forces were stretched further in the area, which also benefited the Germans. As one historian has noted:

> The German withdrawal to the Hindenburg Line ... invalidated the Allied plan for their 1917 offensive.

One benefit occurred near midday on Saturday, 17 March, when *Jasta 11* made two successful attacks against British two-seaters north of Arras. In his combat report, Richthofen noted the large extent of the forces involved:

... I attacked with nine of my machines an enemy formation of
15 aeroplanes. During the fight I managed to force a "Vickers"
two-seater to one side and then, after [firing] 800 rounds, brought
it down. In my machine gun fire, the aeroplane lost its ... [lattice-
like] tail.

The 6th Army Weekly Air Report confirmed Richthofen's 27th aerial victory
and, for their achievements in the same fight, Kurt Wolff and Carl
Allmenröder were each credited with their third 'kills'.

Richthofen went up again later that afternoon and, west of Vimy, he saw a
lone BE2 ranging artillery fire using wireless telegraphy. At first it looked like
an easy target, but then he saw that the two-seater had escort aircraft flying
above it. His favoured position, an attack from above, would not work. He took
a riskier course, as his combat report relates:

... I went down to 700 metres (2,300 feet) and attacked my
adversary, who was flying at 800 metres (2,600 feet), from below.
After a short fight, my opponent's aeroplane lost both wings and
fell. The machine crashed into no-man's-land and was fired upon
by our artillery.

Despite continued bad weather on 21 March, Richthofen and his men went up
in the afternoon to counter Royal Flying Corps probing flights that were trying
to determine new German positions and troop strengths. Allmenröder shot
down a Sopwith two-seater at 1530 hours, which was logged as his fourth 'kill'
and, almost two hours later, Richthofen sent down a BE2 for his 29th, which
fell within British lines and, therefore, he felt required to file the following
more detailed account:

Messages came through that enemy aeroplanes had been seen at
1,000 metres (3,200 feet) altitude in spite of bad weather and a
strong east wind. I went up by myself, intending to bring down a
[low-level reconnaissance] or artillery [ranging] flyer.
    After one hour, I spotted at 800 metres (2,600 feet) a large number
of enemy artillery flyers beyond our lines. They sometimes
approached our front, but never crossed it. After several

unsuccessful attempts, I managed, half hidden by clouds, to take one of these BEs by surprise and to attack it at 600 metres (1,900 feet) beyond our lines.

The adversary made the mistake of flying in a straight line when he tried to evade me, and thus he was just a wink too long in my machine gun fire (500 rounds). Suddenly, he made two uncontrolled turns and dashed, smoking, to the ground. The aeroplane was completely ruined ...

Manfred von Richthofen's singular bravery had already been rewarded on 12 January when Kaiser Wilhelm II personally signed the document awarding him the *Pour le Mérite*. On 23 March, Richthofen's leadership skills were recognized when, on special orders from the Royal Cabinet of Ministers, he was granted an early promotion to *Oberleutnant*. The irony of that advancement was not lost on Richthofen, who had been the last man in his cadet class to be commissioned and was now ahead of all of his peers. He proudly wrote to his mother:

I have therefore gained a good half-year's seniority.

Manfred von Richthofen, having long since shaken off the lethargy of his cadet days, was a fierce competitor by nature and he knew that every aerial victory scored by *Jasta 11* put his unit that much closer to the greatness achieved by the unit founded by his late and always lamented mentor. As he wrote in his memoirs:

At the time I was trying very hard to compete with *Jagdstaffel Boelcke*. In the evening, we compared our mutual "bags." There were some devilish fellows there, and they were never to be outdone. At best, one could but equal them. They already had the advantage of having downed a hundred enemy aeroplanes. I must concede this advantage for the present. The chances for victory all depend on which opponent one faces – the sneaky Frenchman or those plucky fellows, the Englishmen. I prefer the Englishmen. The Frenchman flinches, the Englishman seldom does ...

The Englishman ... shows some of his Germanic blood.

These sportsmen take readily to flying, but they lose themselves in sport. They have enough amusement by looping, diving, flying upside down and demonstrating similar stunts for our men in the trenches ...

On 24 March, *Jasta 11* reflected its leader's enthusiasm by recording two more 'kills.' At 1055, Schäfer shot down his eighth victory, a Sopwith two-seater north of Arras. An hour later, Richthofen forced down a SPAD S.7, a fast, rugged French-built biplane fighter that the Royal Flying Corps had begun to use to supplement its inventory of fighters capable of battling the new Albatroses. According to Richthofen's combat report:

As the fight had taken place above the trenches, my adversary tried to escape, but I managed to force him to land behind our lines near Givenchy. The aeroplane turned completely over, in a small shell hole and remained upside down. It was taken by our troops [and its pilot was captured].

The following day, Richthofen was the only *Jasta 11* member to successfully shoot down an opponent, in this case a French-built Nieuport 17 flown by a British pilot, who was taken prisoner. Having achieved his 31st victory, the *Staffel* leader devoted his time to administrative matters for the few remaining days of the month, including adapting his operations as part of a refined organizational effort to support ground troop movements. On 28 March 1917, *Hauptmann* Maximillian Sorg, the 6th Army's *Kommandeur der Flieger* [Officer in Charge of Aviation] announced he would be aided by three new sub-commanders, each of whom would coordinate flying activities for an Army Corps. As applied to *Jagdstaffel 11*, Richthofen and the *Jasta 3* leader would work with the air group leader *Gruppenführer der Flieger 12*, who would also be responsible for four two-seat reconnaissance units and three two-seat low-level close air support units working for the 1st Bavarian Reserve Corps in an area directly north of Amiens. While the move added a layer of command between Richthofen and the *Kommandeur der Flieger*, it also set the stage for a further organizational refinement that would add to the *Rittmeister*'s command responsibilities.

Lothar von Richthofen achieved his first confirmed victory on 28 March, when he forced down an FE2b south of Lens. The aircraft was salvaged for evaluation. Two days later, Wolff and Allmenröder each shot down a British Nieuport fighter and on the 31st, Wolff scored his fifth victory to bring *Jasta 11*'s total victory score up to that time to 36 confirmed 'kills.' It was far short of *Jagdstaffel Boelcke*'s impressive tally of nearly three times that number, but a very promising beginning.

The month ended on a sad note when *Jasta 11* lost its first pilot on 30 March. *Leutnant* Eduard Lübbert, the hard working but unsuccessful 'bullet catcher' of the unit, was shot down and killed in a fight over Gavrelle. Richthofen singled out Lübbert for praise in his memoirs, where he wrote:

> ... this outstanding officer ... had the stuff to become a Boelcke, [and] died a hero's death for the fatherland ...

Manfred von Richthofen had yet another combat-related loss to cope with and, in his usual stoic manner, he honoured lost friends by focusing on the promise of achievements yet to come. He had received a letter from his close friend from their pilot training time a year earlier, *Oberleutnant* Bodo *Freiherr* von Lyncker. He had departed *Jasta 2* and gone on to score two victories with *Jasta 25* on the Macedonian Front. Now, Lyncker sought transfers back to the Western Front for himself and a promising comrade, *Leutnant* Otto Brauneck. Shortly thereafter, Richthofen learned that Lyncker had been killed in a mid-air collision with an enemy aircraft. But his fallen friend's legacy was the recommendation of Brauneck, who had shot down three enemy aircraft and four balloons and had already received the Hohenzollern House Order. Richthofen was sure that the man would be a perfect fit for *Jasta 11* and he set in motion the transfer process, which he spelled out in a letter to Brauneck:

> I recall that Lyncker had already written to me about you and a recommendation from this fine man is good enough for me. Therefore, I am ready to request you immediately. Today a telegram is going to [the Officer in Charge of Aviation] in your [area], followed by a telegram to the [Office of the Commanding General of the Air Force]. It is up to you to pressure your superior, so that he

will release you from there; for, without consent on his part, nothing can be done at the [high level].

There is plenty going on here. We shoot down at least one a day during good flying weather.

Also you will find here a very nice circle of comrades. I await your answer as soon as possible.

8
BLOODY APRIL 1917

April 1917 became the most successful month in Manfred von Richthofen's career. His personal victory score climbed from 32 to 52 British aeroplanes shot down, thereby surpassing the 40-victory score of his mentor Oswald Boelcke, and making Richthofen the world's top-scoring fighter ace of the time. April 1917 also became Britain's second worst month for aviation casualties in World War I, with the loss of one-third of its airmen then at the Front, 316 pilots and observers in 50 Squadrons. It is no small wonder that month is known in British aviation history as 'Bloody April.'

After completing a successful strategic withdrawal behind strong defensive positions, German commanders reorganized their forces in the face of the anticipated Anglo-French offensive. Moreover, German air units still fielded superior aircraft that they could advance or withdraw as needed, generally in aerial combat over their own lines. The Allied air arms had no advantage; only the task of trying to conserve their forces for the offensive while also sending out aircraft – in an unusually stormy month marked with many snowfalls – to try to attack and to disrupt German communications.

Sunday, 1 April was a total washout due to the weather, but, the following day, despite prospects of wind and rain, Richthofen scheduled two flights of four aircraft each to be ready to fly at 0500 hours. However, it was almost three hours later before the battle call was sounded and Richthofen could return to combat in a strengthened and refitted Albatros D.III.

He wrote in his memoirs:

> I was still in my bed when the orderly rushed in exclaiming: "*Herr Oberleutnant*, the British are here already!" Still a bit sleepy, I looked out of the window and, there, circling over the airfield were our "dear friends." I got out of bed and quickly put on my things. My red bird was ready to begin the morning's work. My mechanics knew that I would not let this favourable moment pass without taking advantage of it. Everything was ready. I quickly donned my fur-lined flight suit and was off.
>
> Even so, I was the last to take off. My comrades were already closer to the enemy. I feared that my prey would escape and that I would

have to watch from a distance while the aerial battles took place
before my eyes. Suddenly, one of the cheeky [British] characters
dived on me from above, trying to force me down. Calmly, I let him
come on and then [we] began a merry dance. Soon my opponent
flew on his back, then he did this, then that ... I was superior to him
and he soon realized he could not escape me. During a pause in the
fighting, I made sure that we opposed each other alone. Therefore,
he who shot better, remained the calmest and had the best
perspective at the moment of danger would win.

With his usual skill, Richthofen got into the 'kill' position above and behind his
tenacious adversary. Just when it looked as though the British pilot would land
and surrender, he made a run for it and went flat out, straight ahead. Richthofen
pursued him at treetop height and opened fire. Undaunted by a hit to his own
engine, he chased the two-seater until it crashed into a block of houses in
Farbus, a village north-east of Arras.

Richthofen concluded:

Very pleased with the results of my red "bicycle" in the morning's
work, I returned [to La Brayelle]. My comrades were still in the air
and were very surprised when, as we later sat down to breakfast,
I told them of my No. 32. A very young *Leutnant* had shot down his
first [that morning] and we were all happy.

Jasta 11 logged four more victories that morning before receiving a visit by
another fast-rising air combat celebrity, *Leutnant der Reserve* Werner Voss. Then
19 years old, Voss joined *Jagdstaffel Boelcke* just before Richthofen left that unit
to take command of *Jasta 11* and the two men became friends. Voss soon
showed himself to be a formidable air fighter, having shot down more than 20
enemy aeroplanes within less than four months, irrespective of the generally
unfavourable weather conditions. Not to be outdone, Richthofen modestly
informed his guest that the morning's work had produced another victory. As
he later wrote: 'Voss had dispatched his 23rd the day before. He was, therefore,
right behind me and was at the time my strongest competitor.'

Voss was not familiar with *Jasta 11*'s operational area, so Richthofen invited
him to accompany the *Staffel*'s next patrol, in the direction of Arras, where Voss

could find landmarks and get his bearings to return to Lagnicourt. Richthofen led the way and finished the morning's work at about 1120, when he, his brother Lothar and Voss attacked eight Sopwith two-seaters, most likely flying back from photographing Vimy Ridge. Manfred forced down one Sopwith some 300 metres (980 feet) east of Givenchy. According to his combat report:

> But, as yet my adversary would not surrender, and even when his machine was on the ground, [the observer] kept firing at me, thereby hitting my machine very severely when I was only five metres (16 feet) above the ground. Consequently, I attacked [the aeroplane] on the ground once more and killed one of the occupants.

The Sopwith's observer was certainly tenacious, fighting to the bitter end – but his continued resistance justified Richthofen's return fire to a grounded adversary whom he would otherwise ignore.

The following afternoon, Manfred von Richthofen led his brother Lothar and Karl-Emil Schäfer in an attack on three FE2bs near Méricourt, south-east of Lens. Manfred shot down his 34th victim near Liéven.

On 4 April, five days before the abortive Anglo-French offensive began, the Royal Flying Corps initiated an aerial assault along the British front lines in the hope of drawing German aircraft away from the intended battle area so that RFC reconnaissance and bombing aircraft could operate unhindered. The effort was a disaster. From 4 to 8 April, 75 British aircraft were shot down in combat, resulting in 19 dead, 13 wounded and 73 missing airmen; to make matters worse, there was 'an abnormally high number of flying accidents,' resulting in the loss of another 56 aircraft. German 6th Army Sector reports recorded two first-day British combat losses and showed no German casualties.

Despite foul weather on 5 April, during the late morning, Richthofen and four of his men attacked six Bristol F.2A two-seat fighters of No. 48 Squadron on their very first offensive patrol. The newly arrived fighters were led by the much-celebrated Captain William Leefe Robinson, the first airman to earn the Victoria Cross within United Kingdom territory. Despite the top talent assigned to the flight, the Bristol Fighters' first foray over the lines came undone when their machine guns failed during the fight, thereby giving *Jasta 11* the advantage.

Richthofen took the opportunity to praise his newly returned and strengthened Albatros in his combat report for the first of two victories he scored that day:

> The D.III, both in speed and ability to climb is undoubtedly superior [to the F.2A]. Of the enemy squad, which consisted of six aeroplanes, four were forced to land on our side by my *Staffel*.

Richthofen shot down his first F.2A at 1115 hours over Lewarde and the second 15 minutes later over Cuincy. *Leutnant* Georg Simon scored his first victory that day, downing a Bristol F.2A over Auchy. Meanwhile, near Méricourt, *Vizefeldwebel* Sebastian Festner logged his fourth victory, F.2A A.3337 piloted by Captain Leefe Robinson, VC, with Second-Lieutenant Edward D. Warburton as his observer; both men were uninjured and taken prisoner.

Despite it being Maundy Thursday, an otherwise solemn occasion, the day's string of victories and the capture of Captain Leefe Robinson were cause for a celebration for every member of *Jagdstaffel 11*, from the lowest enlisted man to the commanding officer. It was an unusual event in the hidebound German military establishment, but one that occurred more frequently in Germany's youngest military arm, the Air Force, where close relationships between pilots and ground crews required such camaraderie.

While the *Staffel's* victory party was under way, a flight of 18 British night bombers headed for the Douai area to exact their own toll for the day's losses. When German front line observers alerted *Jasta 11* that enemy bombers were heading their way, Richthofen interrupted the festivities and quickly arranged a 'surprise party' of his own. He had all *Staffel* members armed with rifles to defend their airfield, and then had the airfield searchlights turned on.

Richthofen described the air raid on La Brayelle:

> [One] Englishman seemed to fly very high. First, he flew once around the entire airfield. We thought he was looking for another target. Then all of a sudden he switched off his engine and dived down ... We each fetched a carbine and began to fire at [him]. Then we could not see him. But just the noise of the shooting calmed our nerves.

Then he came into the searchlight beam. From everywhere on the airfield there was a great hullabaloo. It was quite an old crate. We recognized the type precisely. He was at most a kilometre (0.6 mile) away from us. He flew right toward our airfield ... lower and lower. Then he switched the engine back on and came flying right at us. Kurt Wolff opined: "Thank God, he is looking for the other side of the airfield." But it was not long before the first and then other bombs rained down. It was a wonderful fireworks display ... put on for us. Only a frightened rabbit would have been impressed by it. I find that, in general, bombing at night has significance only on morale. If one fills his pants, then it is very embarrassing for him, but not for the others.

On Good Friday, *Jasta 11* logged two victories – one by Wolff, the other by Schäfer – and, that evening, Richthofen, expecting another air raid, ordered his defensive perimeter reinforced. *Staffel* enlisted men drove poles into the ground at key locations and, ironically, mounted captured British machine guns on them, ranged to hit incoming aircraft.

Richthofen wrote in his memoirs:

The first one came over, just as on the previous evening, at very high altitude, then came down to about 50 metres (160 feet) and, to our greatest joy, this time he aimed right for the side of our barracks. He was right in the searchlight beam ... at most 300 metres (980 feet) away from us. One of our men began firing at him and then ... everyone opened fire. A massive assault could not have been better warded off ... A raging burst of fire greeted him. He could not hear the machine gun fire over the sound of his own engine, but he saw all the muzzle flashes and I think he was very daring in not veering off, but, rather, staying on course for his mission. He flew right over us and then went off.

At the moment that he flew over us, of course we all quickly jumped into the bomb shelter, for to be hit by a stupid bomb would be a foolish hero's death for a fighter pilot. Scarcely had he gone over us when we were again at our guns, firing away at him. Of course, Schäfer maintained: "I hit him." The fellow shot very well, but in this case I did not quite believe him and, besides, every one of us had as good a chance to hit [the enemy].

But at least we accomplished something, as the enemy dropped his bombs haphazardly thanks to our firing at him. Nevertheless, one bomb landed a few metres away from *"le petit rouge"* but did not damage it.

Other Good Friday news would not be fully appreciated by *Jasta 11* and other front line units for some months: US President Woodrow Wilson announced America's formal declaration of war against Germany and Austria-Hungary.

The following afternoon, Richthofen and four comrades crossed the lines, looking for enemy aircraft south of Arras. They spotted and attacked a flight of six British Nieuport 17 single-seat fighters. The Albatros pilots outperformed their opponents; each German aeroplane, armed with two synchronized machine guns, practically sliced through the less manoeuvrable Nieuports, each fitted with a single machine gun. Richthofen's victim, his 37th, fell in flames near Mercatel. Wolff, Schäfer and Festner each brought down one.

Improved weather on Easter Sunday led to considerable flight activity. As the RFC came out for final preparations for the beginning of the Battle of Arras, *Jastas 4* and *11* combined forces in the vicinity of Arras. Together, they shot down seven British aircraft; included in that number were Richthofen's 38th and 39th victories. *Vizefeldwebel* Sebastian Festner, who began the day's scoring by shooting down his seventh victim, almost became a victim himself when, during the fight, his Albatros D.III's bottom left wing broke. He made a safe landing, but Richthofen was livid at the recurrence of a problem that should have been resolved. Disgusted, he wrote in his report to the Inspectorate of Military Aviation: 'The machine is being sent home as useless for combat.'

Part of Kaiser Wilhelm II's Easter festivities included the signing of a Supreme Military Cabinet order for awards and advancements which only he could authorize. First were awards of the *Orden Pour le Mérite*, which, in addition to being Prussia's highest military honour for merit and bravery in wartime, was also awarded to senior officers in recognition of exemplary performance in positions of high responsibility. The 8 April 1917 recipients in the latter category were the Air Force's two top officers: *Generalleutnant* Ernst von Hoeppner, the Commanding General, and his Chief of Staff, *Oberstleutnant* Hermann von der Lieth-Thomsen.

A *Pour le Mérite* combat-related award was bestowed on 20-year-old *Leutnant der Reserve* Werner Voss of *Jagdstaffel Boelcke*. He was the first fighter pilot to receive that high honour since Manfred von Richthofen almost three months earlier. Voss, who was awarded the Hohenzollern House Order on 17 March, had attained 24 aerial victories (vs. Richthofen's 16) at the time he received the coveted blue enamel and gold Maltese cross. Yet again, the stakes had been raised for those seeking glory.

And Manfred von Richthofen, who had been promoted to *Oberleutnant* by a similar imperial decree 16 days earlier, was advanced again in the latest decree, this time to *Rittmeister*. Even though he currently served in the Air Force, in keeping with tradition, he received his captaincy in the cavalry. In one stroke of the Kaiser's pen, Richthofen, the man who had come bottom in his cadet class, was elevated to the new rank years before most of his peers would be.

At 0530 hours on Easter Monday, 9 April, the British First and Third Armies attacked German forces along a line some 13 kilometres (eight miles) south of Arras to 11 kilometres (seven miles) north of the city. Intended as a diversion to precede a French offensive on the Aisne Sector, the British assault was strongly supported by RFC air units. For most of the day, however, the flyers' efforts were hampered by snow and strong winds. Accordingly, German air opposition was very light, with the only 6th Army air success that day being a BE two-seater that *Leutnant* Karl-Emil Schäfer shot down behind German lines west of Lens. More strong wind and snow the following day allowed RFC units to cross the lines to support the ground advance with practically no German air resistance.

Jastas 4 and *11* made up for the previous day's lull on 11 April, when they logged nine victories between them and suffered no losses. Manfred von Richthofen attacked a low-flying BE2 infantry support aircraft over Willerval, north-east of Arras, and sent it crashing into a shell hole. That fight, which was witnessed by *Leutnant* Kurt Wolff, was recorded as Richthofen's 40th aerial victory, thereby making the newly promoted *Rittmeister* equal in every respect to his mentor, *Hauptmann* Oswald Boelcke.

The following evening, Richthofen welcomed a special civilian guest to *Jasta 11*. The holder of the exalted academic title *Herr Professor Doktor*, Georg Wegener had turned to more lucrative and exciting work as a war correspondent for *Die Kölnische Zeitung* [The Cologne News]. He had been cleared by the War Ministry in Berlin to tour various battlefronts and provide his war-weary readers with positive, uplifting articles about the men who were fighting for their fatherland. Recognizing Wegener's value to the war effort, Richthofen accommodated his guest fully. In what would be an inspired public relations move, Richthofen had a telescope set up for Wegener to watch the *Staffel's* preparations for an early morning take-off the following day. Unbeknown to anyone, the journalist would have a spectacular view of a great aerial triumph.

The article that appeared in Wegener's newspaper was just what the War Ministry wanted Germans to read and, today, remains a sharp-eyed account of the colourful aircraft and the aerial warriors who went to war in them:

> From a distance they looked like iridescent giant insects, like a swarm of gaily-coloured butterflies with their wings spread out, sunning themselves on the ground. The principle of looking as much as possible like the colour of the sky was entirely abandoned. "Invisibility cannot be achieved," it was explained to me, "but one does indeed run the risk of a mix-up between enemy and friendly aeroplanes. These different markings on the fuselages are clearly visible in the air, and one recognizes them during combat and can assist a comrade."
>
> For this reason every pilot has his personal machine, in which he always flies and to which he is so closely attached as if with a living creature, giving it a special marking that enables his comrades to keep him in sight during combat and to know at all times who controls the machine. One machine has white or red or some other coloured stripes, another carries them diagonally or longitudinally, etc. From Richthofen's eyes shine the pride of the warrior knight, whose shield and helmet ornament are known and feared by the opponent. "I make sure that my flight sees me wherever I am."
>
> In fact, we perceive very strongly how much the old knightly gallantry has come alive again in the conduct of modern aerial combat; here the personal markings of the armaments by emblems visible from a distance heighten the impression. These young combatants have a bearing quite like that of the medieval lords, of whom the [14th-century chivalric heraldry] chronicler Jean Froissart so colourfully recounted, with their shimmering banners, coats of arms and battle flags, which they displayed with pride ...

One after the other until the take-off time was determined, they climbed into their flight clothing, which looked like a combination of a diver's suit and a Dutch fisherman's outfit, and, with their hands in their deep pockets, laughing and joking, [the pilots] sauntered amongst their ground crews preparing their machines for take-off or over to the big telescope to carefully observe the sky. Even Richthofen had already put on his gear and carefully scrutinized the heavens with his naked eye.

All of a sudden – I myself saw not the slightest movement up in the clear blue – quickly he turned to a bell hanging nearby and sounded the alarm. In an instant, all of the mechanics ran to their machines; each pilot hurried to his own aircraft, climbed into the seat, as the propellers thundered, and one after the other the small, fast aeroplanes ran along a stretch of the ground, lifted up and quickly climbed up into the blue. The last one was [*Rittmeister* von] Richthofen's machine.

The flyers remaining behind, the ground crewmen, the orderlies and sentries – all followed with the greatest excitement the events in the sky. Now I recognized, first through the telescope and then without it, a squadron of British aircraft; at least six, perhaps more. I had to watch them very close, otherwise I would lose them in the glimmering brightness.

The flyers on the ground saw other things. They recognized and named the various types and they shouted indignantly: "What nerve! They come over here at barely 2,000 metres (6,500 feet)! What do they think they are doing?"

The objects of interest were six RE8 two-seaters. From the ground, the spectators watched as, less than ten kilometres (six miles) away from them, *Jasta 4* and *11* fighters attacked the interlopers. Within a brief time, all six were shot down. In the encounter, *Rittmeister* Manfred von Richthofen scored his 41st aerial victory. Other RE8s were brought down by *Leutnant* Kurt Wolff and *Vizefeldwebel* Sebastian Festner, and two were shot down by *Leutnant* Lothar von Richthofen.

Manfred von Richthofen later wrote:

The good friend down on the ground was more than a little
astonished. He had imagined the event would be ... much more
dramatic. He thought it all looked quite harmless until suddenly
some of the aeroplanes, one of them burning like a rocket, came
crashing down. I have gradually become accustomed to the sight,
but I must say that the first Englishman I saw go roaring down made
a frightful impression on me and I dreamed about it for a long time.

Wegener described the return of the victorious air warriors in his article:

Scarcely half an hour had passed and they were all there again.
The combatants climbed out of their seats and – laughing, proud,
happy, recounting events animatedly – stood amidst their well-
wishing comrades and enlisted men who shared the enthusiasm of
their officers.

No one was injured. It all looked like it could have been a
successful sporting event. But Richthofen's machine showed how
little it was really like that. An enemy machine gun burst hit the left
lower wing and, for about a metre and a half (five feet), the fabric
looked like it had been slashed open by the swipe of a big knife.
And on the outer wooden covering close to the pilot's seat ran a
second scar showing that another shot came close to taking his life.

While Richthofen ate a late breakfast, the ground crew was still working on his
damaged Albatros. It was not ready, so he climbed into another aeroplane and
led the day's second flight over British lines. Just past midday, he spotted an
FE2b east of Arras and '...fired on it immediately.' His combat report described
his 42nd victory:

After rather a long fight, during which I manoeuvred in such a way
that my adversary could not fire a single shot at me, the enemy plane
plunged to the ground between Monchy and Feuchy.

That evening, Richthofen achieved his 43rd victory, which marked 13 April as
the first day in which he shot down three enemy aeroplanes. He and three other

Jasta 11 pilots attacked six FE2bs over the German troop train debarkation station at Hénin-Liétard. His combat report noted:

> After a short fight, my adversary began to glide down and finally plunged into a house near Noyelles-Godault. Both crewmen were killed and the machine was destroyed.

Richthofen devoted a chapter of his memoirs to the events of 13 April 1917. Under the title 'My Most Successful Day Thus Far,' he noted proudly how his red Albatros was being discussed amongst his adversaries:

> One of the Englishmen we had shot down [that day] was captured and we had a conversation with him. Of course, he inquired about the red aircraft. It is known even to the troops down in the trenches and it is called *"le diable rouge"* [the red devil]. In his squadron the rumour had been spread that a girl [flew] the red machine ... similar to Joan of Arc. He was very surprised when I assured him that the alleged girl stood before him right then. He was not trying to be funny; rather, he was convinced that only a young girl could sit in the extravagantly painted crate.

Manfred von Richthofen was amused by his notoriety among enemy flyers, but he did not dwell on it. He continued to lead his men into combat, chalking up victory after victory and suffering no personnel or aircraft losses. On 14 April, *Jasta 11* was credited with eight enemy aircraft shot down, including Richthofen's 44th victory. Richthofen's chances for combat success were much improved when, on 15 April, a cloudy, rainy Sunday, *Jasta 11* moved out of their quarters at La Brayelle and headed to a new airfield at Roucourt, a little over 20 kilometres (12 miles) south-west of Douai, and just behind the front lines. Richthofen wanted to be as close as possible to the fighting.

His quarters at the previous airfield were replicated as much as possible at the new location. These accommodations included what German war correspondent Georg Wegener described as a room

> ...decorated with the trophies of his career, the colourful national insignias and other parts of the aircraft he shot down. From the

ceiling hung an enemy Gnôme rotary engine sent back [and] modified into a multi-armed chandelier, [and] over the door ... the machine gun of his most dangerous opponent, the British Major Hawker ... one of the most successful British combat pilots.

While the men settled in at Roucourt, the next day the pilots added four more aerial victories to *Jasta 11*'s score, including Richthofen's 45th, thereby raising to 92 the number of enemy aircraft brought down since the *Staffel* began flight operations under Richthofen in January.

The following day, Saxony became the first of the other major German states to honour Germany's new ace of aces. On that day, King Friedrich August III of Saxony authorized the Knight's Cross of the Military Order of St. Henry be awarded to Manfred von Richthofen 'in recognition of his 30 air victories.' That milestone had been reached weeks earlier, but Richthofen's award was significant as he was one of only four non-Saxons with no Saxon military service to receive the kingdom's highest military honour. The award elevated him to the status enjoyed by the first flyer to receive this high honour, Saxon native Max Immelmann. Even the illustrious Boelcke, who grew up in the Saxon Duchy of Anhalt, had not been so highly decorated.

On the other side of the battle lines, 16 April was no day for celebration. The British ground offensive at Arras stalled due to worsening weather and the French offensive against German forces at Chemin des Dames sputtered to a halt. To make matters worse, heavy French losses and general failure in the doomed campaign led to widespread mutinies among French forces which crippled their spring offensive. But for *Jasta 11*, April 1917 was a glorious month, filled with further successes – five victories on 21 April, and three on the 22nd, including Manfred von Richthofen's 46th and Kurt Wolff's 20th air combat triumph, the latter being recorded as *Jasta 11*'s 100th aerial victory, which led to yet another milestone for the *Staffel*.

In recognition of the unit's quick and stunning success, the weekly service-wide information report published by the Commanding General of the Air Force's office included this notice signed by General von Hoeppner:

In the time from 23 January until 22 April 1917, *Jagdstaffel 11* has shot down 100 enemy aeroplanes. I am pleased to be able to announce this singularly unrivalled [rate of] success to the aviation forces. Here a small band of brave pilots has been trained and led into battle by an outstanding leader, *Rittmeister Freiherr von Richthofen*, who alone has contributed 39 of these 100 aircraft, for the benefit of the hard fighting troops on the ground, and accomplished feats which redound to the highest honour of the German Air Force.

May such a spirit, the spirit of Boelcke, remain always and in all respects with the German Air Force.

Manfred and Lothar von Richthofen each scored again on 23 April. They attacked a pair of BEs north-east of Arras. Although both aircraft came down within British lines, Manfred would be credited with his 47th and Lothar his tenth. There was always a lag from the time an aerial victory was claimed until it was officially confirmed or denied. Hence, Manfred quoted a lower victory number – no doubt reflecting confirmations – in a letter he wrote to his mother that evening:

> I intend to come home at the beginning of May... At that time I have been invited to breakfast with the Kaiser. I have now reached No. 44 and will stop at 50 ...

Despite his seeming nonchalance, Richthofen would have been honoured and excited to be invited to visit Kaiser Wilhelm at the Supreme Headquarters, then located in the palatinate spa city of Bad Kreuznach. Perhaps in anticipation of the visit, on 26 April, *Jasta 11* received word that the Kaiser had ordered the unit to be called *Jagdstaffel Richthofen*. *Jasta 11* was only the second air unit to bear such a distinction, but it lasted only three weeks, according to 6th Army Weekly Aviation Reports, and after that all references to the unit appeared simply as *Jagdstaffel 11*.

Richthofen concentrated on his main mission: demonstrating how to shoot down enemy aeroplanes, while running up his own score. He logged his 48th victory on 28 April and, the following day, wrapped up the month's work with an unprecedented quadruple victory: Numbers 49, 50, 51 and 52.

His 52nd victory is of particular interest, as it marked an early German encounter with one of the new Sopwith Triplanes deployed with two Royal Naval Air Service squadrons operating with the Royal Flying Corps.

Powered by a 130-hp Clerget rotary engine, the Sopwith Triplane was reported to have outperformed an Albatros fighter in a 20-minute fight on 23 April. According to a British source, while '... the German pilot showed great skill in manoeuvring his machine ... the Triplane could out-manoeuvre and out-climb the hostile machine.'

But Richthofen would have known about the new British aircraft, since the 6th Army Weekly Aviation Report published an announcement about it before his encounter on 29 April: 'The number of enemy triplanes sighted has increased. They are said to surpass the Albatros D.III in manoeuvrability and above all in climbing ability.'

As the technology advantage tipped back in Britain's favour, it is clear that superior piloting skills saved the day for Manfred von Richthofen. Best of all, much of the day's success had been witnessed by his father, *Major* Albrecht *Freiherr* von Richthofen, who commanded a garrison near Lille, about 30 kilometres (18 miles) from the airfield. The 'Old Gentleman', as Richthofen's comrades called him, picked a good day for his first visit to Roucourt.

Manfred wrote that his father arrived at the airfield a half hour later in time to see the morning patrol return. At the sight of his father, Lothar von Richthofen sprang from his aeroplane and reported with pride: 'Hello, Papa, I have just shot down an Englishman.'

A moment later, Manfred said the same words and noted:

> The Old Gentleman was happy; one could see that he was amused
> [by this report]. He is not one of those fathers who worries about his
> sons; on the contrary, he would just as soon have got into the
> machine and shot one down – at least I believe that. We had
> breakfast with him and then flew again.

In an important shift in German air fighting tactics, on 30 April, Douai-based *Jastas 3, 4, 11* and *33* were directed to operate together, perhaps as a test for the first *Jagdgeschwader* [fighter wing] that had been discussed within the German Air Force, but had not yet been commissioned. Following the appearance of that German group operation, British units dubbed the mass of various-coloured aircraft the 'Richthofen Circus.' The 20 Albatros fighters deployed in two formations, with the first taking off early in the morning. Lothar von Richthofen shot down two British two-seaters.

The afternoon patrol was not so fortunate. Back over Drocourt, looking for more British bombers, Manfred von Richthofen and three *Jasta 11* comrades did not see the approaching little bright glints behind them, racing at them like fish in a sun-swept pond. In an instant, a silver-coloured Nieuport 17 of No. 60 Squadron, followed by three more of the deadly aerial minnows, dived from 3,300 metres (11,000 feet) and charged through the flight of red Albatroses.

Manfred von Richthofen did not score in the ensuing clash, but he very likely had a brief fight with Captain William A. Bishop, MC, then a 14-victory Canadian ace. Bishop went on to become the British Commonwealth's highest-scoring fighter pilot of World War I, with 72 aerial victories to his credit.

Bishop, the deputy flight leader, described the encounter:

> This ... quartette, I believe was made up of Baron von Richthofen and three of his best men. However, although we knew who they were, we had been searching for a fight, and ... so after the four we went. The Major [Alan J.L. Scott] reached them first and opened fire on the rear machine from behind. Immediately, the leader of the scouts did a lightning turn and came back at the Major, firing at him and passing within two or three feet of his machine. In my turn I got in two or three good bursts at the Baron's "red devil" ... 00Around we went for cyclonic minutes, here a flash of the Hun machines, then a flash of silver as my squadron commander would whiz by ... [and] every now and then ... a red machine [was] in front of me ... I was glad the Germans were scarlet and we were silver. There was no need to hesitate about firing when the right colour flitted by your nose.
>
> Once my gun jammed, and while manoeuvring to the utmost of my ability, I had to "fuss" with the weapon until I got it right again. I had just got going again when von Richthofen flashed by me and I let him have a short burst. As I did so, I saw up above me four more machines coming down to join in the fight. Being far inside the German lines, I at once decided they were additional Huns, so I "zoomed" up out of the fight to be free for a moment and have a look around ... [and see] the approaching machines were [RNAS] triplanes ... coming for all they were worth to help us against the Albatroses. The latter, however, had had enough of the fight by now,

and ... they dived and flew away toward the earth.

The German group's tally for the day's work was one victory each for *Jastas 3, 4* and *33*, and two for *Jasta 11*. While the group operation had not succeeded as hoped, within a few months Manfred von Richthofen would prove the value of combining several *Jagdstaffeln* under the command of one overall leader. In any event, Lothar's double victory was a joyful event, worthy of a few bottles of wine. The party was interrupted later that evening by an important telephone call for the *Staffel* leader. What could this be? Surely, not an urgent order to attempt night-time flight operations! With the dulling effect of alcohol coursing through his men's veins? Ever the correct professional soldier, Manfred answered in his command voice, but his sternly set lips quickly turned to a broad grin, as the call turned out to be from an officer at Supreme Headquarters, with information Manfred had been waiting for.

> Among other things I received the pleasant news that His Majesty
> [the Kaiser] expressed the wish to speak with me personally and,
> indeed, the date was already set for the 2nd of May,' he announced.

A few more bottles of wine deserved to be consumed that evening to toast so much good news. Indeed, there was also good news for Lothar. In Manfred's absence, common sense would have dictated that 27-victory ace Kurt Wolff would become the temporary commander of *Jasta 11*. But wiser heads in the command structure recognized Lothar's greater 'name' value; even though he had 17 victories to his credit, the younger Richthofen was put in command.

Lothar wrote to his mother:

> Manfred is going on leave ... Hopefully, he will stay for a long time,
> for he must absolutely get away from this strenuous business for
> once. For me, of course, [his leaving] ... is unfortunate, for I could
> learn much from him. And yet I am happy that he can take it easy.

Brotherly care aside, Manfred's departure offered Lothar an opportunity to demonstrate his own abilities as an air fighter, as a leader, and as a worthy successor.

9
DEUTSCHLAND ÜBER ALLES

As April 1917 came to an end, Manfred von Richthofen prepared to go on leave at the height of success. Under his leadership, *Jagdstaffel 11* had distinguished itself throughout April. The 6th Army's Weekly Aviation Report noted prominently that, of 40 enemy aircraft shot down in the last week of that month, '23 [were credited] to *Jagdstaffel Richthofen.*'

Additionally, a tactical experiment on the last day of the month proved to be a harbinger of things to come, as described by RAF Historian H.A. Jones:

> The 30th of April was notable for a change in German air fighting tactics. The fighter flights [*Jagdstaffeln*] attached to the Arras Corps at Douai (3rd, 4th, 11th, and 33rd) were combined to form one group which could, as occasion demanded, operate as a massed fighting formation. This group, which made its first sweep on the morning of the 30th, was promptly named ..."Richthofen's Circus," although, in fact, the first fighting squadron under Richthofen was not formed until June. The original idea seems to have arisen from a desire to link up a number of fighting formations for occasional combined sweeps, whereas Richthofen's circus was a homogeneous [air wing that] operated under the German leader's personal command.

The group exercise had been mildly successful – six of the day's 12 confirmed victories were awarded to *Jasta 3* (1), *Jasta 4* (1), *Jasta 11* (3), and *Jasta 33* (1) – and reinforced senior commanders' commitment to remain flexible and employ various tactics to counter growing Anglo-French numerical superiority.

On Tuesday, 1 May 1917, Manfred von Richthofen transferred command of *Jasta 11* to his brother Lothar with no more formality than a handshake and a smile. Indeed, other pilots in the unit were senior to Lothar, had more flight time and had shot down more enemy aeroplanes. But war planners and propagandists needed to exploit the growing value of the Richthofen name. And, Manfred was confident the *Staffel* was in good hands; he knew that Lothar would work hard to maintain the family honour.

In Roman times, a warrior leader who had attained Manfred von Richthofen's level of success in battle would have been crowned with a laurel wreath, fitted out in the finest raiment and transported in a golden chariot to be received by his Caesar. The dirt, smoke and grime of World War I, however, allowed Richthofen to begin his victory tour humbly clad in a well-worn fur-lined leather pilot's helmet and a basic service uniform (made slightly distinctive by his side-buttoned Uhlan's tunic) covered by an oil-spattered flight suit. The passenger's seat in an older utility aircraft, normally used to haul supplies from depots behind the lines – the aviation equivalent of a tramp steamer – would carry him to Supreme Headquarters to be received by his Kaiser. Richthofen, who had been forbidden to fly and take unnecessary chances during the visit to his Supreme War Lord, was chauffeured by his Technical Officer, *Leutnant der Reserve* Konstantin Krefft, who was heading home on leave and now had a faster way to get there.

Such an imperial summons was a rarity for a junior officer and Richthofen recorded some of the events:

Fifty [enemy aircraft] had been shot down. I liked [the number] 52 better. Therefore, on the same day [29 April] I shot down two more. Actually, that was against orders. In fact, I had been allowed only 41; anyone can guess why the number 41 was set and precisely for that reason I wanted to completely avoid it. I am no record-keeper; in general, records are far from our thoughts in the Flying Service. One only fulfils his duty. [By now] Boelcke would have shot down a hundred if the accident had not happened ... But it was still fun to have got half a hundred. Now I had finally reached it ... before I went on leave.

Hopefully, I will be able to celebrate the second 50.

[After] ... I received the delightful news that His Majesty expressed the wish to speak with me personally and specifically set the day of 2 May...[further details] reached me at nine o'clock in the evening of 30 April. It would not have been possible to go by train to comply with the wish of the All-High Warlord, so I decided to do what was more desirable, to make the trip by air. The next morning I started out, not in my single-seat *"Le petit rouge,"* but, rather, in a big fat two-seater.

Given such short notice for the trip, Richthofen recalled:

> I could take nothing more than a toothbrush with me in the
> aeroplane; therefore, I had to appear at Supreme Headquarters
> dressed as I was. And, in the field, a soldier does not have many
> beautiful items of clothing; in any event, not such a poor Front Hog
> as myself.

Once the aeroplane was aloft and heading east, Richthofen relaxed. The sounds
and sights of the war zone slipped away and the scenery below became more
verdant and tranquil as the aeroplane progressed homeward. By noontime, he
noticed the aeroplane descending toward Cologne, where he and Krefft were
greeted by an enthusiastic reception. News of Richthofen's 52nd victory made
headlines in the previous day's newspapers through effective government
propaganda and, alerted to the hero's arrival in their city, local residents gave
the young airman a fitting welcome. His uniform was dull, but Richthofen was
illuminated when he removed his flying helmet and flight suit; sunlight danced
along his crown of blonde hair and the glimmering enamel Maltese cross of his
Pour le Mérite at his neck. In the reserved way that Richthofen comported
himself in public, he observed:

> This was the first furlough I had taken "armed" with the *Pour le
> Mérite* and the first time I had come back home since I made a
> name for myself. For this reason it still felt rather strange that
> people looked at me ... But I soon became accustomed to it and
> felt good about it.

After lunch and a refreshing nap, Richthofen and Krefft were in the air again,
taking a leisurely aerial tour of the Rhine Valley and up the Nahe River tributary
leading to Bad Kreuznach, the quiet little spa city that was now the site of
Supreme Headquarters. Krefft set the plane down on a broad lawn just outside
the city limits of Bad Kreuznach. He wrote:

> There I was warmly greeted by all of the flyers on the staff of the
> Commanding General of the Air Force. I knew them all by sight; for
> the most part they had come from the [early air units] *Brieftauben-*

Abteilungen at Ostend and Metz. I also got to know the others better. I was greeted with bouquets of flowers and with a thundering cheer.

Amongst all of these smiling faces, surely there were new friends to be made; people who might do a small favour in return for a personally signed postcard from *'eine grosse Kanone'* [a big shot]. Now however, he wanted to help his old friend and informal flight instructor from the *Brieftauben-Abteilung* Ostende, *Oberleutnant* Georg Zeumer. Like the 'black cat' for which he had been nicknamed, Zeumer's luck had turned bad and he needed help. After he was shot down and lightly injured near Fort Vaux in June 1916, while being transported to a medical aid station, his car was involved in an accident, and Zeumer broke a thigh bone. It had not healed properly, leaving him with one leg nine centimetres shorter than the other and forced to use a cane. Already diagnosed as being tubercular and diabetic, Zeumer did not want to die at a desk job. The 27-year-old pilot wanted to be back in the air, where his recklessness offered the glory of a hero's end. Zeumer's motivation did not fit Richthofen's methodology and so a posting to *Jasta 11* was out of the question – even for an old friend. Richthofen hoped to – and did – arrange for Zeumer to fulfil his ominous destiny with another very active unit, *Jagdstaffel Boelcke*.

Few visitors came to the spa city during the war, and military officers had Bad Kreuznach's accommodation to themselves and at bargain rates set and paid for by the Government. Richthofen and Krefft were assigned rooms in a fine hotel within a short walk of the *Kurhaus*, the elegant spa and casino complex that, as the finest house in the city, became the Imperial residence. Richthofen had a brief meeting with his nominal host, *General* von Hoeppner, and then settled into comforts that were hardly imaginable in wartime. There seemed to be no shortage of fine food and drink.

The following day, Manfred von Richthofen was invited to have breakfast with Kaiser Wilhelm. The flyer recalled:

> It was my birthday and someone must have divulged that to His Majesty and so he congratulated me. First on my success, [and] then on my 25th year of life. He also surprised me with a small birthday present.

The gift was not small in size or significance. The young hero Richthofen received a full-size bronze and marble bust of the Kaiser in martial splendour. It was a memento fit for someone of very high status and Richthofen accepted it graciously. For many years this sculptural masterpiece was on public display when the family home became the Richthofen Museum, but, as with all of the Richthofen family treasures, it has not been seen since the departure of the Red Army from Schweidnitz after World War II.

Then the Kaiser wagged his finger at Richthofen playfully and chided: 'I have heard that you are still flying. You be careful that nothing happens to you!'

Turning to his aide-de-camp, *Kapitän zur See* [Naval Captain] Nikolaus *Graf* zu Dohna-Schlodien, the monarch asked: 'How could that be? Have I not forbidden him to fly?'

The aide responded: 'Majesty, in the interests of the whole situation, we cannot do that. We need Richthofen as an example and as a *Geschwader-Kommandeur* [Wing Commander], we need him as a combat pilot ...'

Richthofen was more surprised by the person who gave the answer than the response itself. The Kaiser's aide-de-camp, a 38-year-old Silesian nobleman and one-time commander of the surface raider *SMS Möwe* [Sea Gull] wore the *Pour le Mérite* and the highest bravery awards of Germany's other three kingdoms. Richthofen wondered how such a man of action could stand the dull pace of court life. Of all the other high-ranking and distinguished aides in the imperial retinue, Richthofen recalled, '... this small-statured, inconspicuous-looking man made by far the best impression on me. One could see that he was a front line soldier and no courtier.'

Before any other premature announcements slipped out, the conversation shifted again. According to Richthofen: 'The Kaiser conversed with me for about a half hour after the meal. The conversation was very one-sided. The theme ... was anti-aircraft guns.' In any event, for Richthofen, the defining moment of that conversation, often repeated, was that he would remain a warrior and never abandon his front line comrades for a safe and comfortable staff position. With that epiphany burned into his mind, the meeting was suddenly over. As if on cue, everyone left the table.

Later that morning, Richthofen came in to contact with more of Germany's most important people, beginning with a courtesy call at the elegant Hotel Oranienhof, now serving as the General Staff Headquarters. He waited for an hour outside *General* Erich Ludendorff's office, watching an almost choreographed sequence of uniformed functionaries entering and departing, carrying what he knew to be the fuel of bureaucracy: bundles of paperwork.

From reading newspapers, he recognized the faces of German luminaries who, at that moment, had no reason to be interested in a young *Rittmeister* in his drab service uniform with the *Pour le Mérite* at his collar. Foreign Minister Arthur Zimmermann accompanied Chancellor Theobald von Bethmann-Hollweg and was followed by Karl Helferrich, Secretary of the Imperial Treasury. Albert Ballin, *Generaldirektor* of the Hamburg-America Shipping Line, was involved in an animated but hushed discussion with a high-ranking member of the General Staff.

Several generals and ministers later, it was Richthofen's turn to be escorted in. A white-haired officer, looking like a great hero with row upon row of medals on his chest, but still just another functionary, waved Richthofen past the other dignitaries and ushered him into Ludendorff's office.

Ludendorff, a stern-looking man who appeared to have neither time nor inclination for pleasantries, muttered the obligatory 'Hello, how are you?' and directed his guest to a chair. Then, he came right to the point and sought the *Rittmeister's* professional views on air operations over the Arras Sector. A brief recitation of the facts would have been sufficient, but, even in his reserved, direct way, Richthofen was a social creature and he sought to engage the Quarter-Master General in a more conversational way. Ludendorff's reaction was apparently edited out of the 1917 edition of Richthofen's memoirs, but was saved for use a few years later. Richthofen wrote:

> I began to tell him and drifted into a little chat that had little military importance. Then he simply cut off my conversation and came [back] to things I had already mentioned. One noted he went all-out. After he elicited from me what he wanted to know about operations on the main battlefront at Arras, I was abruptly dismissed. I must say that I was quite satisfied [with that arrangement], for this serious, professional [and] dispassionate-thinking person seemed strange to me.

Richthofen had faced some tough opponents in his brief life, but none as formidable as *General* Ludendorff. Being able to leave that intimidating atmosphere and stepping out into the sunshine and fresh air of Kaiser-

Wilhelmstrasse was as much a relief as a safe return from combat. He could not resist a short walk to Elisabethenstrasse, where, at the end, was the Kaiser's residence, framed by a commanding view of the Nahe River.

That evening, Richthofen was the guest of honour at a dinner party hosted by *General* von Hoeppner. Ludendorff was among the invitees, but, by good fortune, Richthofen was seated to the right of *Generalfeldmarschall* von Hindenburg. Richthofen recalled:

> At dinner, [Hindenburg] made a speech about me. The whole place fell silent. In the course of the conversation, he asked me in his good-natured, calm way that inspired absolute confidence: "Now, tell me, Richthofen, have you also been a cadet?"
>
> I told him that I had been in the 2nd Company at Wahlstatt and, indeed, began my military career in Barracks Room 6.
>
> Then the old gentleman said: "Well, look at this, I also began to play soldier in Barracks Room 6, and presented the barracks my photograph as a memento."

That day ended pleasantly enough and the next morning Richthofen's old friend *Oberleutnant* Fritze von Falkenhayn flew him for a brief visit to nearby Bad Homburg vor der Höhe, another old spa city and one-time playground for Europe's rich and royal families. Bad Homburg still boasts a Kaiserbahnhof, the special wing of the main train station where the most important guests were met by limousines and carriages. The arrival of Falkenhayn and Richthofen in an old two-seater on a great open field away from everything else was a sign of the new developments in the old town.

As related by Lothar von Richthofen, Manfred's reception went smoothly:

> The Kaiserin [Empress Auguste Victoria] had such interest in aviation that she herself appeared at the airfield. During the flight my brother wore the old leather jacket in which he had achieved all of his aerial victories. Right after landing he reported to the Empress. In order to justify to some extent that he had dressed in his old leather jacket for this ceremonious occasion, he told her that he had won 52 aerial combats with it. The Empress stroked the jacket and said: "The good jacket, you have gone through 52 aerial victories with it."

Empress Auguste Victoria presented Richthofen with a belated birthday present, 'a gold and white enamelled cigarette case inscribed with her name,' which added more pleasant memories of his visit. As he recalled:

> One had a [nice] feeling, as it was with Hindenburg; one was in the
> presence of a charming old lady, with whom one could compare
> an old aunt or his own grandmother, and easily forget that she
> is the Empress.

A few hours later, Richthofen flew back to Bad Kreuznach and spent his last evening there at a formal dinner hosted by *Generalfeldmarschall* von Hindenburg. The guests included some of Richthofen's peers from other military units. He observed:

> Together at one table, were no fewer than eight Knights of the *Orden*
> *Pour le Mérite*. I would never again see so many in one house unless the
> war lasted so long that the Pour le Mérite became as common as the
> Iron Cross Second Class.

Caught up in the reverie of Bad Kreuznach nightlife, Richthofen would not have been aware of a major British land success of the Battle of Arras that day, with the capture of Vimy Ridge by the Canadian Corps. The land triumph was coupled with the less immediately tangible victory of British airmen persevering until more new aircraft and better equipment arrived at the Front. As events have shown, both would be problematic for Richthofen.

Further, the failure of the French Aisne offensive and the shake-up in the French High Command freed Field-Marshal Sir Douglas Haig, Commander-in-Chief of the British armies in France, to pursue his earlier plans for a major offensive in Flanders. In May he began to shift ground and air units northward, thereby forcing his adversaries to likewise prepare for the Battle of Messines, which would require Richthofen's *Jasta 11*'s move to a new and more intense combat environment in Northern France and Belgium.

While others worked on grand strategies, the following day, Manfred von Richthofen was concerned mainly with shooting at small, elusive wood grouse in the Black Forest. He was kept posted of significant *Staffel* developments and soon received very good news about his brother. Lothar's 19th victory, in the early evening of 7 May, resulted from an aerial combat with Britain's top-scoring fighter pilot, Captain Ball, DSO, MC. Ball, 20 years old at the time of his death, was credited with shooting down 44 German aircraft and had been proposed for Britain's highest award for valour, the Victoria Cross.

Lothar's Albatros had been hit in the fight, after which he had been forced to land, leaving little doubt that he was also Ball's 45th – but unacknowledged – aerial victory. Lothar was neither wounded nor injured and resumed flying the following day, but Ball was found dead in his crashed SE5 fighter. German authorities were quick to credit the younger Richthofen with downing the celebrated British ace. The German Air Force's weekly news bulletin mentioned Lothar's victory in the summary of events for 7 May and included the name of his prestigious victim.

Albert Ball's Vickers machine gun, flare pistol and other crash site trophies were sent home to Schweidnitz for eventual display in the Richthofen Museum. To further establish Lothar von Richthofen's victory claim, for obvious propaganda reasons, photographs of Albert Ball's grave and a note of disingenuous tribute were dropped over British lines: 'RFC Captain Ball was brought down in a fight in the air on the 7th of May, 1917, by a pilot who was of the same order as himself. He was buried at Annoeullin.'

Lothar's recent achievements prompted Manfred to write to his mother on 9 May, making his usual apologies for delaying his visit to her:

> Surely you are angry that I have been sitting here in Germany for almost eight days without writing to you. I am in Freiburg hunting for wood grouse and will stay here until the 14th. Then I must go to Berlin to look at new aeroplanes, which will take about three days, [and] then I will come to Schweidnitz. You must excuse me that it is so long.
>
> From Schweidnitz I will go to [the estate of] *Fürst* von Pless and shoot a bison. Toward the end of the month I will tour other Fronts in the Balkans, and so forth. That will take about three to four weeks. Meanwhile, Lothar leads my *Staffel* and will indeed be the next [flyer] to receive the *Pour le Mérite*. What do you say now about both of your wayward sons?

The next news about Lothar was not the joyous announcement anticipated. Manfred von Richthofen received an urgent telegram from the Front, saying only: 'Lothar wounded, not life-threatening.' According to later information, at midday on Sunday, 13 May, Lothar and Carl Allmenröder shot down a pair of British two-seaters at low altitude within British territory. The two Germans became separated during the fight and, as Lothar approached German lines, he was hit, probably from the ground. The last thing he remembered was approaching a flat meadow before him. When he awoke, he was in a field hospital. Treatment and convalescence for more than five months would interrupt his impressive aerial combat achievement of 24 victories in just over six weeks.

Even Manfred had not been so successful, admitting:

> Had my brother not been wounded on [13] May, I believe that after my return from leave, he likewise would have gone on leave with 52 [enemy aircraft] having been dispatched.

Lothar had a superstitious bent – reflected in his interest in talismans and good luck charms – and, after being shot down on 13 May, his fear of the supernatural grew. Perhaps with good cause, as he would be shot down twice more – on both occasions on the 13th of the month.

Leutnant Carl Allmenröder succeeded Lothar as acting commanding officer of *Jasta 11*. And the following day, Lothar's fortunes improved, when he became the 20th aviation recipient of the *Orden Pour le Mérite*. By this time, the criterion for a fighter pilot was 20 confirmed aerial victories, which Lothar had attained on 6 May.

Satisfied that his brother was not in mortal danger, Manfred continued his leave, proceeding from Freiburg to Nürnberg, most likely with Fritze von Falkenhayn as his pilot, as Konstantin Krefft had gone on leave. On the next leg of their flight, they were caught in bad weather, made a forced-landing outside Leipzig and continued on to Berlin by train. Richthofen must have looked like just another weary combat pilot, walking through Berlin's cavernous Anhalter Bahnhof, but the staff at the Inspectorate of Military Aviation soon had him scrubbed, trimmed and otherwise transformed into the polished, well-dressed hero whom they wanted Germany to idolize. Then, the handsome young pilot was off to the noted studio of C.J. von Dühren for a new formal portrait photograph to enable the Sanke printing company to produce thousands of copies of a new photo-postcard; their earlier Richthofen card grew in popularity as Richthofen's victory list swelled.

After a meeting at the major publisher Verlag Ullstein, where arrangements were finalized for him to begin work on his memoir *Der rote Kampfflieger* [The Red Combat Flyer], Richthofen was finally free for his main purpose in Berlin: a tour of the aeronautical test centre at the Adlershof airfield, just outside the capital. He was keen to fly the new LFG Roland D.III, another sleek, plywood-fuselaged fighter aircraft being considered for production. He continued to be disturbed by the incidence of lower wing failure in the Albatros D.IIIs and, if the problem could not be corrected, he urged – in an ever more authoritative voice – that designs be sought from other manufacturers.

Once his business in Berlin was concluded, on Friday, 18 May, Richthofen headed for the train station. There was no need to wait until the next morning, as there was a night train to Schweidnitz. He dozed on the train, probably imagining that he could slip into his home town as easily as he entered the enormous train station in Berlin. He was in for a rude surprise. When the train pulled into Schweidnitz, promptly at 0700 hours, his sister Ilse was there to meet him and accompany him on the short walk to their home. But word of the great air hero's arrival spread quickly and, even at that early hour on a Saturday he attracted a crowd of admirers. His mother recalled:

> Scarcely had the news of his arrival spread when a flood of floral bouquets and small presents rained down upon us. The whole city seemed to be mobilized. I knew how very much Manfred opposed being honoured [like this]. But now it could not be helped and he found himself reluctantly in [this] role. There was no lack of tributes, neither from the *Wandervogel* [Bird of Passage youth movement] with the whirring imitation of a whooping crane, nor the day nursery school children with paper helmets and tassels.
>
> ...Delegations came and went. The *Jung-Deutschland* [youth movement], the Youth Defence Corps, the local elementary school, speeches, serenades ... [and] military bands resounded – and again I watch Manfred as he busies himself with the children; how they are devoted to him, how it gives him such joy to look into so many young faces glowing with enthusiasm.

At the end of the long day, Richthofen was nearly exhausted. He understood that part of his public role was inspiring his fellow Germans and he patiently obliged many requests from old and young to sign their Sanke postcards. But he also drew a line between inspiration and exploitation.

Freifrau von Richthofen remembered:

> One time ... a woman showed up with a hundred postcards and asked him to autograph them, he said gruffly: "I will not sign a single one." Startled by this almost brusque tone of the refusal, I gave him a wounded look. He explained ever more resentfully that in another city someone once asked him to sign 50 photo postcards [and] he did it. Later he watched from his window as the 50 postcards were sold on the street.

When the volume of visitors did not decrease, *Freifrau* von Richthofen informed the newspapers that Manfred was away, 'travelling.' In fact, she and Ilse took him by car to a beautiful old game preserve a short distance away. But, even there, the villagers crowded the main street for a glimpse of their famous neighbour. Finally, her son's long time friend and fellow hunter, *Herr* Schwanitz, appeared and whisked Manfred into the safety of the forest for the rest of the day.

Manfred von Richthofen never claimed to be a master of prose, so when it came time for him to begin work on his book, his publishers sent a stenographer to Schweidnitz. She stayed at the Hotel Crown, in the city centre, where Manfred visited her in the mornings to dictate stories about his life that could be edited into book form. After the stenographer typed her notes, every afternoon she brought them to the house, where Manfred, his mother and sister reviewed them.

The working sessions were perfectly proper and business-like, but after enough people heard about meetings between the young, pretty stenographer and the handsome flyer, there was much idle curiosity about their relationship. Never one to miss an opportunity for mischief, Manfred arranged for a way to cap the growing public speculation, as his mother wrote:

> Once, just when Manfred brought her to the garden gate, a pair of inquisitive ladies passed by. Hesitating, with barely restrained curiosity they came to a standstill and greeted Manfred cordially,

while their eyes did not move from the modest, smiling young woman at his side. A gleam came to Manfred's eyes; he was again quite the boy. He gestured toward her with his hand and in all seriousness introduced [the stenographer] as: "My fiancée."

I stood in the garden and watched as the attractive Berliner bit her lips, and I also had to laugh. For their part, with the guarded mistrust that is usually bound up with inquisitiveness, the ladies turned aside somewhat coolly and strode away.

"Yes," asserted Manfred laughing, "at least that settles the situation."

After leaving the stenographer with much material to transcribe, Manfred quietly departed Schweidnitz to hunt with a member of the old-line landed nobility of Silesia, Hans Heinrich XI, *Fürst* [Prince] of Pless. The Prince's domain was isolated among some of the last thick woodlands of Europe's Forest Primeval and had served as a well protected site for the Supreme Headquarters from 1915 until the Kaiser's entourage moved westward to Bad Kreuznach in 1917.

Richthofen was especially devoted to marksmanship, and gloried in the thrill of the hunt and the triumph of the kill, both in the forest and in the air. His comments on shooting a rare bison reflect the omnivorous and amoral hunting appetite that characterize a fighter pilot's dedication:

I stood on the high spot where, the head gamekeeper told me, His Majesty had stood numerous times and had bagged many bisons ... [Then] ... suddenly I saw, in the high timber, a giant black monster trundling along right toward me ... and, I must say, I had hunting fever. It was a mighty bull. At 250 paces away, he sniffed the air for a moment. I was too far away to shoot ... He probably noticed the drivers, for suddenly he made a sharp turn and came directly toward me at remarkable speed for such an animal ...

... I had the same feeling ... when the bull came at me, the same hunting fever that grips me when I sit in an aeroplane, see an Englishman and must fly along for five minutes to come at him. The only difference is that the Englishman defends himself ...

Five minutes later the monster was finished. The hunt was ended and *"Hirsch tot"* ['dead stag' = a successful hunt] was trumpeted. All three shots were right above his heart – a very good sign.

The furlough was soon to end and the victorious hunter returned to Schweidnitz, where, early on the morning of 31 May, a two-seater and a single-seat aircraft landed on the parade ground near the Richthofen home. The Halberstadt single-seater was for Richthofen to maintain his flying proficiency on the way to Vienna, for a 'tour' that had been arranged.

After breakfast, Manfred bade farewell to his family and was off in the Halberstadt. But the flight was fraught with problems, beginning halfway between Schweidnitz and Breslau, when Richthofen let go of the control column for a moment. Normally, with all controls in a neutral position, the aeroplane would almost 'fly' itself. In an instant, however, the Halberstadt rolled inverted and Richthofen was flying upside-down, held in the aeroplane only by the seat harness. The Halberstadt turned out to be nose-heavy and the moment the pilot let go of the controls, it went 'wheels-up' on him. Richthofen quickly regained control of the aeroplane and brought it back to the right position. After landing, he admitted to being 'very shaken by the experience.'

During a refuelling stop, the Halberstadt's engine quit and could not be restarted. A short time later, a severe storm with hail and gale-force winds blew in. Richthofen knew better than to tempt fate, so he sent a telegram to his orderly, Menzke, telling him they would meet at Vienna's main train station. Ostensibly, Richthofen was to begin a tour of Central Powers' aviation facilities, first in Austria and then in Turkey. But he knew that, like Boelcke before him, he was being sent out of harm's way, to keep him alive for his symbolic value. Germany already had enough dead heroes.

On the afternoon of 5 June 1917, it gained another one when *Leutnant* Karl-Emil Schäfer, a Richthofen protégé who had gone on to command *Jasta 28*, was shot down and killed. His body was sent back to his home town of Krefeld in Westphalia. Richthofen cancelled the rest of his appointments in Vienna and went to Berlin by *Schnellzug* [express train] to attend Schäfer's funeral.

Richthofen felt compelled to go to Berlin to use his position and prestige to goad his contacts in the Inspectorate for Military Aviation into providing a successor to the Albatros fighters. Too many pilots had complained that even the improved D.V series continued to suffer wing failures and were becoming less and less of a match for newer British and French fighters.

At the same time, moreover, the perseverance of British air units was beginning to pay off, as RAF Historian H.A. Jones noted:

> The pilots of the fighting squadrons equipped with the new type aeroplanes, the S.E.5, the Bristol Fighter ... and the Sopwith Pup, had gained confidence and experience in handling their craft, and the squadron mechanics had come to understand the new engines and equipment. There was, from May [1917] onwards, a marked diminution of engine and gun trouble, which, throughout April, had been a source of irritation to many pilots and had too often led to a breaking-off of combat ... From the beginning of May, therefore, the casualties to the corps' aeroplanes dropped appreciably, and the air fighting was pushed away from the lines towards the German back areas.

And there was a radically new aeroplane in the British inventory, the Sopwith Triplane. Three-winged aircraft were not totally new, but no British triplane demonstrated the Sopwith's '...phenomenal rate of climb and manoeuvrability [which, in turn] apparently suggested to the Germans that there must be some extraordinary quality inherent in the triplane configuration.' Anxious to regain the aerial superiority their pilots had enjoyed in April, the German Inspectorate of Military Aviation seized on the triplane design as a means to achieve that objective – just as they had tried to marry the French Nieuport sesquiplane feature with the otherwise solid Albatros D.II biplane design.

Inspectorate aeronautical engineers were motivated by reports of the new Sopwith's performance against such a skilled pilot as Manfred von Richthofen, whose 52nd and most recent victory had been a triplane. When a Sopwith Triplane landed with engine trouble within German lines on 6 April, it offered a perfect example for study and inspired the Inspectorate to order '*Dreidecker*' [triplane] prototypes from the Pfalz, Siemens-Schuckert and Fokker factories. Ultimately, the Fokker Dr.I was selected as Germany's full-production triplane fighter and went on to great fame as an 'acrobatic champion, quite unlike any contemporary fighter.'

Richthofen's flying restriction had been lifted to expedite his return to the Front. He piloted his *Staffel*'s two-seater from Berlin to Krefeld to be there in time to lead the honour guard at Schäfer's funeral. As his pilot, Krefft, was still on leave, Richthofen was accompanied by one of his former instructors from Wahlstatt, *Hauptmann* Erich von Salzmann, who at age 40 had not flown previously. The loss of one good friend was balanced by the company of a mentor.

While mourning Schäfer, Richthofen became even more convinced of the ineffectiveness of the Albatros series when he learned that his 23-year-old cousin, *Leutnant* Oskar von Schickfuss und Neudorff, an Albatros pilot with *Jasta 3*, had been shot down in flames behind British lines only hours after Schäfer perished. Oskar had followed Manfred's example and gone from a horse-mounted unit into the Air Force. *Freifrau* von Richthofen informed Manfred that Oskar's last letter described a recent aerial combat and 'mentioned that often he had to break off the fight due to a jam in his guns; also in some cases the British aircraft seemed to be better than ours ...'

Despite Richthofen's urgent need to return to the Front, he was ordered to fly from Krefeld to Bad Kreuznach. But a good soldier follows orders, even when social niceties came during the opening of the Battle of Messines, an all-out assault against German forces in Flanders. In his and Lothar's absence, *Jasta 11*'s overall successes, while the best of any fighter unit on the 6th Army Sector, were down. It was obvious to Manfred von Richthofen that *Jasta 11* was too far from the new battle lines. And, on 9 June, the day before he arrived at Bad Kreuznach, *Jasta 11* was moved northward from Roucourt to Harlebeke, north-east of Courtrai, in the 4th Army Sector which included most of Belgium. Between the move and the arrival of new Albatros D.V aircraft, however, *Jasta 11* would achieve no further victories until Richthofen returned.

Richthofen covered highlights of his visit and a bit of family business in a letter to his mother:

> On my way back [to the Front], I stopped at Kreuznach, where I was again invited to lunch with His Majesty, and I met the King of Bulgaria, who decorated me with his Bravery Order 4th Class 1st Degree. It is worn like the Iron Cross and looks very nice. I was introduced to the Chancellor ... and some other ministers.
>
> As regards Oskar [von Schickfuss und Neudorff], I have been able to determine with certainty that he is dead, as he either fell or jumped out of his aeroplane at about 500 metres (1,500 feet). He lies close to the Front, but on the other side. I have inquired by messages

dropped over the British lines whether his body was recovered. In this respect the Royal Flying Corps is extremely noble ...

Yesterday (17 June 1917), Zeumer fell in aerial combat. It was perhaps the best that could have happened to him. He knew he had not much longer to live ... How he would have hated to drag himself on toward the inevitable end ... As it is, he died a heroic death before the enemy. During the next few days, his body will be brought home.

I visited Lothar [at a hospital in Hamburg] ... He looked tanned and very well, stretched out full length on a divan. He was fully dressed and wore the *Pour le Mérite* around his neck. He is already able to stand and will fully recover ...

On Sunday, 10 June, Manfred von Richthofen made his first landing at Harlebeke airfield. Five days earlier, while patrolling northward of their [then] 6th Army Sector boundaries, three *Jasta 11* pilots – *Leutnant* Carl Allmenröder and *Leutnants der Reserve* Otto Brauneck and Alfred Niederhoff – shot down a trio of Sopwith two-seaters and thereby scored *Jasta 11*'s first aerial victories in the 4th Army Sector. Richthofen could be pleased that, even when he was 'otherwise distracted' by Air Force public relations endeavours, his men got off to a roaring good start in their new operational area.

Allmenröder's victory that day was logged as his 26th and so it was hardly surprising that, on 14 June, he became the fourth member of *Jasta 11* to receive the *Pour le Mérite*. Staffel leader von Richthofen took the occasion to encourage all of his pilots – new arrivals and old-timers alike – to aspire to Allmenröder's level of achievement.

Among the new pilots who came to Richthofen's attention was *Leutnant* Wilhelm-Gisbert Groos. The two men had much in common; both were veterans of the Prussian cadet system and Uhlan regiments, and wanted to shoot down aeroplanes.

Groos later recalled:

Richthofen was a born leader. Sharp as a razor in service matters; at all times fair, especially in the air over the Front. He saw everything. He gave new men in the *Jasta* every chance to score a victory. He gave away many victories, if by doing so the young pilot was able to score his first kill. He protected every member of the flight [as much as] possible, but there was no pardon if a pilot sneaked away from a fight. That pilot would be transferred immediately.

Richthofen knew he had chosen Groos wisely, when the young Uhlan *Leutnant's* first two victories were new Sopwith Triplanes. He proved one of Richthofen's highest ideals: any enemy could be bested by a brave and determined fighter pilot.

10
GATHERING OF EAGLES

By the time Manfred von Richthofen returned to the Flanders Sector, the British breakthrough in the Ypres area in southern Belgium enabled General Herbert G.O. Plumer's Second Army to outflank German defences and clear Messines Ridge, which had provided an ideal post for German observation of British activities south of Ypres. The loss of Messines Ridge placed a heavier burden on German aerial reconnaissance units, which, in turn, required more *Jagdstaffel* [fighter unit] protection over the air combat zone. Increased British air operations were the logical response to that move to assure continuation of their ground successes.

Likewise, German commanders adapted to the changing situation on the ground and in the air. In the 4th Army Sector, for example, the aviation chain of command was altered so that fighter units no longer reported to a *Gruppenführer der Flieger* [Group Aviation Commander]. Now, massed fighter support by the four *Jastas* would be directed by the *Kommandeur der Flieger* [Officer in Charge of Aviation] for the Sector, *Hauptmann* Otto Bufe. At first, the abbreviated command structure appeared to favour the *Jagdstaffel* commanding officers, who regained direct access to the 4th Army's senior aviation officer, but, in this case, the change led to a clash between *Rittmeister* Manfred von Richthofen and *Hauptmann* Bufe. Both were of equal rank and their antipathy became a contest of wills that mainly affected their subordinates.

At 33, Otto Bufe had a promising future as a career officer. One of the top graduates of the Prussian cadet corps system, he joined the Flying Service before World War I began. By November 1914, he had been promoted to *Hauptmann*, qualified as an aviation observer and was given ever increasing command responsibility. Now, with four fighter units to direct, including the celebrated *Jagdstaffel 11*, Bufe had an opportunity to advance his career by demonstrating his leadership and tactical abilities. An important part of that challenge would be to successfully manage or at least accommodate the glittering 'star' of German fighter aviation, *Rittmeister* Manfred von Richthofen. Bufe had already missed one chance to motivate flying officers under his command and to flatter egocentric fighter pilots when he failed to use his widely read weekly activity report to mention Carl Allmenröder receiving the *Pour le Mérite*. Seemingly small, this oversight was the first of a series of organizational errors or personal blunders by Bufe.

Jagdstaffel 11 made another mark of progress in its new operational area in the mid-morning of Monday, 18 June 1917. Manfred von Richthofen led a flight toward the lines, no doubt hoping to encounter the vaunted new Sopwith Triplanes, but coming upon three old Nieuport 17 Scouts, one of which Allmenröder shot down over Verlorenhoek for his 27th victory.

North of Ypres a few hours later, Manfred von Richthofen shot down an RE8, his 53rd aerial victory, which, he reported, was 'driven by the wind, [and] fell into Struywes's [sic] farm, where it began to burn.'

On the evening of 23 June, Richthofen attacked a British SPAD single-seater from above and behind. He fired a stream of bullets into the SPAD and reported:

> **My adversary ... did nothing to evade my fire. At first the aeroplane began to smoke and then it fell, turning and turning, to the ground ... north of Ypres ...**

Richthofen was credited with his 54th victory.

The following morning, Richthofen and six comrades dived on two Airco DH4 two-seat reconnaissance aircraft and ten Sopwith Triplane fighter escorts near Moorslede. Richthofen was credited with shooting down a DH4 near Beceleare for his 55th aerial victory, while Carl Allmenröder and Wilhelm-Gisbert Groos each shot down triplanes.

Hauptmann Bufe's brief overall leadership of *Jagdstaffeln 6, 7, 11* and *26*, ended on 24 June 1917. That day, the area Army Group Commander, Crown Prince Rupprecht of Bavaria, ordered the four *Staffeln* to operate as a new group unit designated *Jagdgeschwader I* [Fighter Wing 1] and to be commanded by *Rittmeister* Manfred *Freiherr* von Richthofen. The first of several such self-contained units to be created to achieve aerial superiority over critical battle areas, *JG I* was made immediately subordinate to the 4th Army High Commander – in effect, to Bufe's superior. Two days later, Air Force Commanding General Ernst von Hoeppner added his imprimatur to the order and noted the:

...ever-increasing number of aircraft which the opposition deployed to reach a target made it seem desirable for us to combine several *Jagdstaffeln* into a *Jagdgeschwader* ... [and] in the personage of *Rittmeister* von Richthofen . . . [it] received a commander whose steel-hard will in relentlessly pursuing the enemy was infused in every member of the Geschwader.

Richthofen's chances for success were bolstered when two of the original *JG I Staffeln* were replaced: *Jasta 7* commanded by a little known pilot with one aerial victory to his credit, and *Jasta 26* led by five-victory ace *Oberleutnant* Bruno Loerzer, whose prominence was yet to come. Those units were replaced by *Jasta 4*, which had had three *Pour le Mérite* recipients among its leaders, and *Jasta 10*, with two *Pour le Mérite* holders during its short operational life.

Late on the afternoon of 25 June, new *Jagdgeschwader-Kommandeur* [Air Wing Commander] von Richthofen accompanied a patrol led by *Leutnant* Carl Allmenröder, who succeeded the *Rittmeister* as leader of *Jasta 11*. Richthofen demonstrated his aerial combat skills once again by shooting down an RE8 two-seat reconnaissance aircraft, which was credited as his 56th victory.

This otherwise laudable achievement marked another procedural error by Bufe. Normally, the Army Corps Officer in Charge of Aviation [*Kommandeur der Flieger*, abbreviated '*Kofl*'], in this case Bufe, would include all aerial victories in the Sector in his weekly report to his superior. As these reports were disseminated throughout the Army Corps, the '*Kofl*' could showcase 'his' fighting flyers, from the lowest *Gefreiter* [Private] to the most illustrious *Rittmeister*. But, with the 29 June 1917 issue of the '*Meldung über die Tätigkeit der Flieger der 4. Armee*' [Notification about Activity of Flyers in the 4th Army Sector], the format was changed and individual aerial victories were listed as a collective score of aerial combats that 'took place' involving a specific enemy aircraft type on the day, time and location noted, but with no mention of the German airmen involved. Conversely, German air combat casualties were listed in considerable detail. In short: the report offered little good news and much bad news. And, in this instance, Richthofen's 56th victory was not noted at all, although there was brief mention of a Sopwith Triplane brought down that day, but its victor (*Leutnant* Carl Allmenröder) was not identified.

The 28 June issue of the Air Force Commanding General's weekly *Nachrichtenblatt der Luftstreitkräfte*, disseminated throughout the German air arm, mentioned only that Richthofen achieved his 56th victory and Allmenröder his 30th. Three weeks later, the *Nachrichtenblatt* summary of aerial victories noted all German air combat successes for the period. Allmenröder's brief leadership of *Jasta 11* ended less than two weeks after he was awarded the *Pour le Mérite*. On the morning of Wednesday, 27 June 1917. Carl Allmenröder was shot down and killed. According to a German eyewitness account, he was very likely hit by British anti-aircraft fire. His body was returned to his home town for a national hero's funeral. *Leutnant der Reserve* Otto Brauneck was assigned to represent the *Staffel* and to carry his comrade's black velvet *Ordenskissen*, crowned by the *Pour le Mérite* that the 21-year-old Rhinelander wore when he died.

Manfred von Richthofen was visiting his brother Lothar, who was recuperating in a hospital in Hamburg, when news of Allmenröder's death arrived. Unable to attend the funeral, Manfred wrote to Allmenröder's father:

A British aeroplane, that was at least 800 metres (2,600 feet) away, fired just a few shots from this enormous distance (the usual fighting distances are 100 or 50 metres (330 or 165 feet) or only an aircraft's-length away). Carl's machine immediately made a left turn in the direction of our lines. That was a sign that [Carl] was still in control of the machine. His comrades observed that he had turned off his fuel [to minimize the danger of fire] and was heading down in a glide ... [from which] he went into a dive that could no longer be averted ...

I myself could not wish for a more beautiful death than falling in aerial combat; it is a comfort to know that Carl felt nothing at the end ...

Jasta 11's next leader was certainly worthy of the honour: *Leutnant* Kurt Wolff. Like Allmenröder, Wolff was a 30-victory ace and a top Richthofen protégé. With this adjustment to the *Geschwader* roster, Richthofen's unit commanders were:

- *Jasta 4*: *Oberleutnant* Kurt-Bertram von Döring, age 28 and a former cavalry officer, who transferred to aviation in June 1913 and a year later, completed pilot training. Promoted to *Oberleutnant* in 1915,

Döring flew two-seaters before being assigned to command *Jasta 4* on 8 April 1917.

- *Jasta 6*: *Oberleutnant* Eduard Dostler, age 25, had flown with two-seater units and the Bavarian *Jasta 34*. He was credited with 12 victories.

- *Jasta 10*: *Oberleutnant* Ernst *Freiherr* von Althaus, age 27, entered the aviation service in April 1915 and flew Fokker monoplane fighters. After quickly scoring eight victories, he became the eighth aviation *Pour le Mérite* recipient, but had not shot down an aeroplane since 1916. He faced an uncertain future under the results-oriented Richthofen.

- *Jasta 11*: *Leutnant* Kurt Wolff, age 22, had been a two-seater pilot and, while with *Jasta 11*, became the 18th aviation recipient of the *Pour le Mérite*. With 31 aerial victories to his credit, Wolff was *JG I*'s brightest star.

Manfred von Richthofen was granted a broad charter to staff *JG I* with people he felt best suited to make the *Geschwader* successful. Thus, he had only to request that *Jasta 11*'s Technical Officer, *Leutnant der Reserve* Konstantin Krefft, be assigned the same post in the *Jagdgeschwader* and the transfer was approved. Likewise, Richthofen was able to lure away *Jasta Boelcke*'s adjutant, a 26-year-old former Bavarian infantry officer, *Oberleutnant* Karl Bodenschatz.

Geschwader quarters and facilities were established at Marcke, a town south-west of Kortrijk [Courtrai]. The broad green lawns, comfortable castle and nearby buildings comprising the estate of *Baron* Jean de Bethune were summarily expropriated and converted to *JG I*'s use.

When the men and matériel arrived, it was first-come first-served. *Jastas 11* and *4* were assigned to Marcke, while *Jasta 6* went to Bisseghem, just across the Lys River from Marckebeke. *Jasta 10* was set up at nearby Heule airfield.

With *JG I* settled into its new facilities, on the morning of Monday, 2 July 1917, Richthofen went up with a *Jasta 11* flight and joined their attack on a pair of RE8 reconnaissance biplanes some 20 kilometres (12 miles) south-west of Marcke. Richthofen sent one down in flames and out of control. He received credit for his 57th victory. The second RE8 was brought down in a spinning nose-dive by *Leutnant* Groos and, as had become customary, was not publicly recorded as his third victory until over a month later.

While it was too early to attribute success to Richthofen's massed *Geschwader* flights, he quickly gained a reputation across the lines for changing German air tactics. In early July, the German Air Force Commanding General's weekly report stated: 'Many prisoners believe firmly in the existence of the Richthofen Wandering Circus. It is said to fly along the (90-kilometre or 50-mile) Front from Lille to St. Quentin and to number from 18 to 30 aeroplanes and more.'

In fact, *Jagdgeschwader I* travelled farther than that – about 25 kilometres (15 miles) from its airfields to Lille and about 85 kilometres (50 miles) south to St. Quentin and back – but with fewer aeroplanes than attributed to them. Richthofen concentrated on force effectiveness in the *Geschwader*'s operational area. During his first meeting with the *Jagdstaffel* leaders, Richthofen ended individual missions carried out by pilots on their own initiative (even though that had long been his style). He stated that he would authorize *Staffel* or *Geschwader* missions based on information about enemy air activity provided by front line sources. Then, he would relay mission information by a telephone line connected to all four *Staffel* commanders simultaneously. He developed a new plan to deploy his forces in steps, as laid out in Wing Order No. 1:

> As of 6 July, the sequence of daily take-off readiness (from daybreak on) in rotation is *Jastas 11, 10, 6, 4*; the daily midday take-off sequence (from 1330 to 1500 hours) is *Jastas 10, 6, 4, 11*.

On Friday, 6 July, the day the deployment plan went into effect, Richthofen's order was countermanded. 'The green table' – the popular term for the Army Corps Headquarters staff whose members laid out their maps and aerial photographs on green felt-covered tables – directed *Jagdgeschwader I* to begin flight operations at 0800 hours. 'The *Kommandeur* hates "the green table" like the plague,' noted *Geschwader* Adjutant Bodenschatz. But, as ordered, Richthofen directed *Jasta 4* to due west toward Ypres, where British artillery-spotting aircraft were reported to be very active. Finding no intruders at the scene, the *Staffel* returned.

At about 1030 hours, Richthofen himself led a *Jasta 11* flight against ground-strafing two-seaters reported heading for Deulemont. Converging with other German fighters in the area, Richthofen and his men swung into a wide arc to get behind the enemy aircraft, which turned out to be FE2d bombers. Defiantly, the 'Fees' turned to meet the red Albatroses head-on. As the two groups approached each other in what seemed to be mutual target selection, Richthofen noticed that, in the aeroplane coming toward him, the British observer stood at the forward gun station and opened fire. At first, Richthofen was astounded by the gunner's naivety in shooting at him from such a great distance. But, then he recalled:

> ... Suddenly there was a blow to my head! I was hit! For a moment I was completely paralysed throughout my whole body. My hands dropped to the side, my legs dangled inside the fuselage. The worst part was that the blow on the head had affected my optic nerve and I was completely blinded ...

The Albatros dived down out of control and Richthofen thought he was finished. He could not believe that the FE2 gunner could have hit him from such a distance. Indeed, an examination of Richthofen's medical records from the event strongly suggest he was shot – albeit unintentionally – by a comrade flying behind him. Richthofen received a glancing blow above and behind his left ear, which could only have come from behind him. Speculatively, it could have been a less experienced pilot who, upon seeing the first FE2d open fire at his flight leader, overreacted and began firing in return, at a point behind the *Kommandeur*. There is no way of knowing who that pilot was or whether he realized what he had done.

For the moment, though, guided by basic instinct, Richthofen switched off the engine to minimize the danger of fire. Recovering from the initial shock, his vision returned in time to glimpse the altimeter registering 800 metres (2,600 feet). He restarted his engine. He knew that enemy fighters might follow him down to finish him off, but that fear vanished when he saw that two Albatroses stayed with him until he managed to land in a field of high grass outside Wervicq, Belgium, close to a German forward observation post.

There, *Leutnant der Reserve* Hans Schröder, who manned the post and watched the fight through his binoculars, ordered a Corporal to run with a field aid package to the injured pilot. Schröder, hampered by an earlier wound, got to the scene as soon as he could and tended to the flyer's wounds, while directing his subordinate to call for a field ambulance.

Richthofen opened his eyes and spoke briefly with his rescuer, identified himself and told Schröder: 'I want to go to Courtrai immediately.' After the ambulance arrived and stopped at an aid station in Menin, Richthofen demanded to be taken to Courtrai: 'Do not stay here. I want to go to Courtrai.' Schröder remained in the ambulance with Richthofen to assure that the wounded man was rushed to the field hospital *Feldlazarett 76* in Courtrai, a short distance from Marckebeke. Later, Richthofen wrote:

> I had quite a respectable hole in my head, a wound of about ten centimetres (four inches) across that could be drawn together surgically later; but in one place clear white bone as big as a *Taler* [large-size coin] remained exposed. My thick Richthofen head had once again proved itself. The skull had not been penetrated ... [but] in the X-ray photos one could notice a slight swelling. It was a skull fracture that I was not rid of for days, [and] was not very comfortable.

The next issue of the weekly aviation report for 4th Army Sector simply noted, perhaps to avoid alarming people, that Richthofen had been 'lightly wounded in aerial combat.'

That afternoon, when the *Kommandeur* was declared out of mortal danger, Adjutant Bodenschatz and the leaders of *Jastas 4, 6* and *11* were at Richthofen's bedside. He was pale and weak, but he promised them that he would be back in service soon. Most likely, *Oberleutnant* von Althaus, leader of *Jasta 10*, remained at the airfield to provide command-level leadership in the event *JG I* was called into action again.

While Richthofen convalesced, a fellow Silesian, *Oberleutnant* Kurt-Bertram von Döring, became acting *Jagdgeschwader-Kommandeur*. A graduate of the Prussian Cadet Corps, Döring had only three confirmed victories to his credit at that point, but his length of service and command experience qualified him to lead *JG I* temporarily. Now, following a normal chain of command, Döring reported directly to *Hauptmann* Otto Bufe, but apprised Richthofen of all *Geschwader* activities.

Five days later, Kurt Wolff was wounded in aerial combat and returned to Marcke with his left hand bleeding. He was sent to *Feldlazarett 76* [Field Hospital] for treatment and ended up sharing a room with his mentor, Manfred von Richthofen.

At this time, *JG I* felt the full force of increasing British air superiority. *Hauptmann* Bufe described the situation in his weekly report:

> Enemy aviation activity shows a further expansion compared with the previous week, although the opponent seems to be holding back his main force. A strong aircraft barrier has been reported along [our] Army's entire Front, reaching up to 5,500 metres (18,000 feet); according to consistent reports, [the barrier] is strongest at Boesinghe, where the objective of the opponent's reconnaissance is especially prominent ...

Manfred von Richthofen was impatient to return to the Front. He was comfortable enough in his hospital bed in Courtrai and following orders, this time from doctors. His convalescence progressed so well it was almost as if he had willed his wounds to heal. But he was bothered by daily reports he received from *Hauptmann* von Döring, the acting leader of *Jagdgeschwader I*. Even during his absence, Richthofen expected top performance from his four squadrons and recent results were not up to his standards. Then there were enemy air raids that made enough noise for him to hear as clearly as if he were at the Front. Why were his men not taking the fight to the British, to keep them away from German lines?

At first, the only information he could squeeze out of Döring was that British air activity had increased greatly since before Richthofen was shot down. Indeed records show that 12 July 1917 saw more aerial combat than since the war began. Activity was heaviest over the British Fifth Army Front, which was in *JG I*'s operational area. The report stated that the *Geschwader* was credited with eight victories that day, but lost one man in a late morning fight.

Finally, Döring admitted that Richthofen's operational orders were being countermanded by Bufe. Döring knew that Richthofen wanted *JG I*'s four *Staffeln* to operate as a unified aerial fighting force, aggressively attacking enemy aircraft on both sides of the lines. But Bufe ordered that British aircraft be hindered from crossing German lines and he directed piecemeal use of the *Geschwader*'s combined strength. In effect, Bufe reverted to the 'barrier flights' that Richthofen recalled from his time on the Verdun Front over a year earlier. They had only limited success then and did not reflect the Air Force Commanding General's current desire for new tactics – including the charge Richthofen was given to create the first of several *Jagdgeschwadern* to aggressively maintain air superiority over the battle zone.

Like Richthofen, Bufe was a product of the Royal Prussian Cadet Corps, although slightly older and with more seniority in rank. However, he had flown only as an observer, accustomed to giving orders to two-seater pilots – treating them like drivers – on reconnaissance and bombing missions. Having been both an observer and a pilot of a variety of aircraft, and then in a command position, Richthofen had a broader grasp of aerial warfare.

Richthofen came to recognize that, even in a hospital bed, he had other battles to fight, and he had to be as resourceful at bureaucratic infighting as he was at leading his men against ever increasing enemies in the air. First, he directed Döring to put his eagle's eye view of the current 'adjusted tactics' in writing, noting especially that *JG I* losses increased during the sparsely manned evening missions that Bufe had ordered. Richthofen knew that night-time combat against enemy fighter aircraft put his men at a disadvantage. British aircraft flying in the late afternoon or evening had the advantage of advancing with the sun against their backs, making them hard to see by German attackers. And sending up only one squadron at a time resulted in greater losses of German aircraft. In his report of 17 July, Döring wrote:

> After the experiences of the last few days it has been proved that single flying squadrons are in no position to do battle successfully with large British formations, which appear chiefly in the evening. For this reason, a simultaneous deployment of *Staffeln* is required ... [and they] must appear together over the Front at high altitude (4,000 to 5,000 metres (13,000 to 16,000 feet)) and, as much as possible, carry out their attacks together against the strong British formations. The *Staffeln* must make every effort to fly in such a way that they support each other ...

After receiving Döring's report, Richthofen used his access to the staff of the Commanding General of the Air Force [*Kogenluft*]. He wrote in brutally frank terms to his old friend *Oberleutnant* Fritz von Falkenhayn, who was now the *Kogenluft* staff's Technical Officer. Richthofen complained that Bufe had subverted the tactical dicta that had already been approved by *Kogenluft*. He wrote:

We have 16 *Jagdstaffeln* in the [4th] Army. These must really do the job. When [enemy aircraft were] shot down recently, it was [done] only by the *Jagdgeschwader*. What are the other 12 *Staffeln* doing?

This [situation], of course, is not due to individual pilots or *Staffel* leaders; rather, the blame lies elsewhere.

When I came to this Army, Bufe told me: "It does not matter to me that [enemy aircraft] are shot down in my Army; rather, that you with your *Jagdstaffel* [and] by your presence at the Front at a certain time will barricade the air!" This is such an insanely great mistake that one could not make a bigger one in fighter aviation ...

Bufe has arranged all the *Jagdstaffeln* on a timetable whereby each *Staffel* has a set time, a set area, [and] a prescribed altitude to barricade for an hour and a quarter. It is indeed quite clear, of course, that this will never be a fighter sortie, but rather maintains the character of a barrier flight ...

The other *Jagdstaffeln* are ... unhappy about it. The *Jagdgeschwader* is a thorn in [Bufe's] side, as from the beginning I have not got into routine barrier flights. So now he uses the opportunity of my being sick and issues the idiotic orders [regarding] how the *Geschwader* should fly, how the take-off preparations should go, etc., as if he were the *Kommandeur* of the *Geschwader*.

... This Bufe is prejudiced in such a way that it is absolutely impossible to deal with him. The [lack of] success is also strikingly clear. For [the past] three days the British have done what they want. They come over, fly wherever they want and absolutely dominate the air [and], not just over their lines, oh no, they dominate the air far over the countryside. Almost none at all are shot down, in any case [few] in proportion to the masses [of aircraft deployed] ...

Apparently independent of this criticism of Bufe, a shift of tactics was taking place at Army Corps level. The day Richthofen's letter went to Falkenhayn, the Commanding General of the 4th Army, *General der Infanterie* Friedrich Sixt von Armin, directed an increase in attacks against British tethered observation balloons and essentially 'turned loose' the fighter units: 'Likewise, *Jagdgeschwader I* is available to sweep the attack area of enemy aeroplanes.'

A week later, on Wednesday, 25 July 1917, Manfred von Richthofen was back at Marckebeke and in full command of *Jagdgeschwader I*. He must have felt a sense of personal victory and validation from the 19 July issue of the 4th Army air chief's daily report, which quoted a recently received statement from General von Hoeppner, praising the Sector's aviation matters:

> Appreciation on the part of the Commanding General [is extended] to the flyers of the 4th Army, and above all the Jagdgeschwader, in view of the superiority [gained] over enemy combat flyers in recent days.

Meanwhile, Richthofen brought good news upon his return to *JG I*. Anthony Fokker's new triplane fighters were in production and *JG I* would receive the first examples, which Richthofen had been assured would be able to out-climb and out-fight anything the British could put up.

Among the good news Richthofen received was that on the preceding evening, *Jasta 10* leader von Althaus had shot down one of the new Sopwith F.1 Camels, which was recorded as his ninth aerial victory. Richthofen demanded top pilots, led by the capable, motivational officers, who continually proved their ability, as he did. *Jasta 10* had the poorest victory record in *JG I*, and Althaus would have to improve the situation or be transferred.

On the evening of 26 July, *JG I* lost a promising pilot and Richthofen protégé, when 21-year-old *Leutnant der Reserve* Otto Brauneck was killed. As usual, the sad event, but not Althaus' latest triumph, was detailed in the last issue of the weekly aviation report for 4th Army Sector published under *Hauptmann* Otto Bufe's direction.

Despite low clouds and rain, Monday, 30 July 1917 marked the beginning of further success for *Jagdgeschwader I*. *Oberleutnant* Ernst *Freiherr* von Althaus, was transferred to the fighter pilot school in Valenciennes. The young aristocrat was a disappointment to Richthofen, who did not know that Althaus was losing his eyesight and eventually would become blind.

The new leader of *Jasta 10* was a pilot Richthofen greatly admired: *Leutnant der Reserve* Werner Voss, only 20 years old and already a 34-victory ace and a *Pour le Mérite* recipient. Voss was brave in the extreme and took incredible risks, a leadership example that would surely lead his new *Staffel* to a high level of success. Indeed, Voss was such a successful fighter pilot that, in the summer of 1917, the Inspectorate of Military Aviation recalled him from the

Front to test-fly the Fokker V 4 prototype triplane. Voss' reports about the new fighter convinced Richthofen that the Fokker Triplane would enable *JG I* to regain German aerial superiority.

But, first, the opening of the Third Battle of Ypres had to be endured. In the pre-dawn hours of Tuesday, 31 July 1917, the fighting began with a massed British-French ground attack. Despite constant rain and low clouds, waves of Royal Flying Corps and Royal Naval Air Service aircraft caused severe damage to German troops, vehicles and facilities, while Anglo-French troops advanced against German positions along the Flanders Front. The RFC and RNAS soon gained control of the skies.

JG I aircraft, which were not called out until German infantry lines were being penetrated at several points, responded with 'small flights' of fighters, rather than the full *Geschwader*. The response may have reflected Richthofen's lack of confidence in the Albatros D.V, which, in addition to the chronic, still unresolved lower wing failure problem, had lost its superior edge over the newest British fighter aircraft. Even that minimal effort became a favourable test of pilot skill, however, as *Geschwader* units scored five of the six aerial victories over the 4th Army Sector that day.

Rain storms the next three days kept German and Allied aircraft in their hangars. Meanwhile, after almost a year with the 4th Army staff, on 5 August, Bufe was reassigned as Officer in Charge of Aviation for the 8th Army, on the Eastern Front. Whether or not his departure had been hastened by Richthofen's complaints, Bufe remained a good soldier and sent a dignified farewell message:

> I leave the 4th Army with the feeling of pride and gratitude for having been commander of a flying force, which through the radiant bravery and discharge of duties by the aircrews, and through the proficiency of pilots in each and every battle made such a splendid name for themselves ... I wish for the activities of the flyers in the 4th Army to lead to new successes, to new victories and to new glory.

Just as Richthofen was quick to post non-performers out of his units, he was fiercely loyal and supportive of successful men under his command. Hence, when on 6 August, *Jasta 6* leader *Oberleutnant* Eduard Dostler was awarded the

Pour le Mérite, but the decoration itself would be some time in coming, Richthofen took off his own medal and put it on Dostler to wear for the *Geschwader's* celebration of the occasion.

Leutnant Kurt Wolff returned to Marckebeke the following day. Like Richthofen, after being discharged from the hospital in Courtrai, he was not allowed to fly for a time. There was no seeking a special favour for Wolff, as Bufe had departed only two days earlier and it would have been unseemly for the *Kommandeur* to ask for a waiver of rules from the new Officer in Charge of Aviation for the 4th Army, *Hauptmann* Helmuth Wilberg. He was a pre-war flyer and admirer of Richthofen, who wanted to preserve and cultivate the relationship.

Moreover, that morning an eight day period began for 4th Army *Jastas* to send Albatros fighters to the Army's air depot for repairs and adjustments by mechanics and riggers from the factory. Aware of Wolff's frustration, Richthofen had to be more concerned that *JG I* had adequate – if even older – aircraft on hand to provide coverage at this time.

On the morning of 10 August, for example, a British bomber crossed the lines before Richthofen could order his units into the air. He turned his explanation of JG I's lack of response into a complaint about the combined inadequacies of the front line monitoring system and his Albatros fighters being away for repairs. He urged his superiors to expedite delivery of the promised Fokker Triplanes. Richthofen wrote that:

> ... to take off against a group that has already broken through is pointless ... [as] British bombing and reconnaissance aircraft groups now fly over our lines at very high altitudes (4,500 to 5,000 metres (14,700 to 16,000 feet)). Our machines do not have sufficient climbing ability to reach the enemy in time. The possibility of approaching such a formation would occur only when the ground observers report their gathering on the other side of the Front.

Finally, after a 40-day absence, on the morning of 16 August, Manfred von Richthofen was allowed to return to the cockpit of his all-red Albatros D.V and nominally 'accompany' a patrol of four *Jasta 11* Albatroses to the Front. Irrespective of some residual weakness and constant headaches, made worse by engine noise, Richthofen yearned to be back in the aerial battlefield.

Then he spotted a flight of British Nieuport 23 Scouts strafing German trenches east of Zonnebeke. By his own account, Richthofen:

> ... attacked an opponent and . . . shot up his engine and fuel tank. The aeroplane went into a spin, [and] I followed right after it until [it was] just above the ground, [and] gave it one more shot, so that the aeroplane crashed south-west of Houthulst Forest and went right into the ground ...

The downed Nieuport was confirmed as Richthofen's 58th aerial victory. But the fight left him exhausted and, upon returning to Marckebeke, he went directly to bed.

On 17 August, four victories were recorded, including a Bristol F.2B brought down by *Leutnant* Hans-Georg von der Osten. New to *Jasta 11*, von der Osten was surprised to find himself in the limelight of a dinner party after his first air triumph. His achievement also marked *Jasta 11*'s 200th victory during its seven months of operations, which was the real reason for the party at Marckebeke Castle that evening. Richthofen sent messages that used the milestone to point out that, despite modest recent performance, his *Staffeln* were still Germany's best. The first response came from Air Force Commanding General von Hoeppner, who equated *Jasta 11*'s triumph to the amount of war booty that a highly successful ground unit might achieve: '... [*Jasta 11* has] captured 121 aeroplanes and 196 machine guns.'

Beginning to feel more like his old self, Richthofen wrote to *Hauptmann* Wilberg at 4th Army Headquarters to 'mention' a current problem:

> The *Geschwader* is being split up by deployment as individual *Staffeln*. Particularly on major combat days, the deployment of several *Staffeln* at the same time in the same place is required. The *Staffeln*, which [now] must provide escorts for attack units [*Kampfstaffeln*], are withdrawn from the *Geschwader* formations for the greatest part of the day. A pilot who has already been called upon for protective flights, long-range missions and bombing flights can no longer completely and undividedly fulfil his duty as a fighter pilot on the same day, as, for successful execution of aerial combat, he must be unfatigued and completely fresh.

Wilberg was surely aware of his predecessor's disagreements with Richthofen – and their likely outcome – and did not wish to repeat them. Consequently, he rescinded the order for *JG I* units to escort bombers or trench-strafers the following day. But there are two sides to the coin that Richthofen tossed, and he saw the other side in *General* von Hoeppner's next message. Following words of praise for *JG I* and Richthofen's 58th aerial victory, the Air Force Commanding General concluded that the *Jagdgeschwader-Kommandeur* needed to be more prudent about his own role in future aerial combats:

> ... I expect that [Richthofen] ... is conscious of the responsibility of the deployment of his person and, until the last traces of his wound are gone, he will fly only when absolute necessity justifies it.

Further disappointment came on Sunday, 19 August, a day that was to herald a new era at *Jagdgeschwader I*. *General* Ludendorff and his Staff were scheduled to visit and 'inspect the most audacious pilots in the German Army and to shake their hands ... [and to] also inspect the newly-arrived [Fokker] Triplanes, which every fighter pilot awaited longingly and which make an excellent impression.'

There was only one problem: the new fighters had not yet arrived. The first two prototype triplanes, which had made their acceptance flights at the Fokker factory only three days earlier, were sent to the 4th Army Air Park at Ghent, where Manfred von Richthofen and Werner Voss were to give the aeroplanes their first field tests. Ludendorff visited, but saw only Albatros D.V aircraft.

More bad news came on 21 August, when *Jasta 6* leader *Oberleutnant* Eduard Dostler failed to return from a morning front line flight and was later declared 'missing in action, presumed dead.' Richthofen's sadness at the loss of his friend was compounded by another message from the 4th Army air chief. Without directly mentioning the feared loss of Germany's only *Jagdgeschwader-Kommandeur*, *Hauptmann* Willberg referenced 'higher authority' to remind Richthofen that he was to take no unnecessary risks to attain personal goals: 'I refer to the Army Order of 12 August, sub-paragraph II and, if necessary, request notification in case this aspect is not being sufficiently taken into account.'

'Sub-paragraph II' virtually grounded Richthofen. He commanded the *Geschwader*, but was not to fly with it in combat unless circumstances made his presence absolutely necessary. Events of the early morning of 26 August put the restriction to a hard test. Three *JG I* airfields – Heule, Bisseghem and Marcke – were attacked by British SPAD S.7 fighters and, to Manfred von Richthofen, this bold raid on his airfields was enough for him to disregard 'sub-paragraph II' and to go after his attackers. Less than an hour after the last strafing run, Richthofen and four comrades spotted a SPAD over German advance lines north of Ypres and went after it. Richthofen attacked from out of the sun:

> [The British pilot] tried to escape by diving away, whereby I got a good shot at him and he disappeared into a thin cloud cover. Following behind, I saw him below the cloud cover, diving straight down, then at about 500 metres (1,600 feet) altitude he exploded in the air ...

Richthofen received credit for his 59th aerial victory, but his Albatros was damaged when some rounds of faulty incendiary ammunition exploded, set off by heat from his guns and engine compartment. With his pressure line, intake manifold and exhaust manifold out of commission, Richthofen had to shut off the engine and hope he could glide back to Marcke. He was successful this time, but felt lingering effects from the head wounds he had received over a month earlier. Two days later he wrote:

> I have made only two combat flights [since returning to the Front] and both were successful, but after each flight I was completely exhausted. During the first one, I almost got sick to my stomach. My wound is healing frightfully slow ...

It is worth noting that the next issue of the Notification about Activity of Flyers in the 4th Army Sector listed all of the week's aerial victories, concluding with Richthofen successfully downing the SPAD. The pre-Bufe alteration format, which had continued to be used by every other Army Corps Officer in Charge of Aviation, had been reinstated by *Hauptmann* Wilberg for his publication.

Foul weather at the end of the month had more power than 'sub-paragraph II' to keep Richthofen on the ground. On 28 August, when the first two Fokker Triplanes arrived, he was tempted to try one of the new machines during a brief period of sunshine, but gave the honour to Leutnant Werner Voss.

The bad weather did not stop British night bombers from attacking German airfields west of Courtrai on the evening of 31 August/1 September. The following morning, Richthofen cited the hours-earlier raid to justify circumventing 'sub-paragraph II' and, conveniently, make his first combat flight in a Fokker Triplane. At about 0750 hours, he and four Jasta 11 comrades attacked what he described as 'a very courageously flown [RE8] British artillery-spotting aircraft' which 'apparently...had taken me for a British triplane, as the observer stood up in his machine without making a move to attack me with his machine gun.' Richthofen sent the two-seater down out of control within German lines and the event was recorded as his 60th victory.

Combat action and aerial successes must have made Richthofen feel that the good old days had returned. He then welcomed a new *Jasta 11* pilot who turned out to be an old friend: *Leutnant* Alfred Gerstenberg. They had begun their military careers in the same regiment and later served together in *Kagohl 2*. Gerstenberg was tenacious in trying to shoot down enemy aeroplanes, but not successful. He was one of the very few non-scoring fighter pilots retained in *Jasta 11*, probably on the basis of his friendship with Richthofen.

Richthofen and the *Geschwader* were on a morning patrol on 3 September, when they attacked a flight of Sopwith Pups over Menin. *Leutnant* Eberhardt Mohnike, another *Kagohl 2* veteran, shot down one of the Pups to score the first of *JG I*'s 11 victories that day, as well as his sixth 'kill.'

Then, Richthofen ended a chase after a Pup and forced it to land. He credited his opponent with putting up a good fight, and praised his new aeroplane:

The Fokker triplane F.I 102/17 is absolutely superior to the British Sopwith.

Aircraft constructor Anthony Fokker was visiting Marcke at the time and arrived at the scene shortly after the Pup crashed and used his new cine-camera to record Richthofen and his uninjured adversary, 20-year-old Lieutenant Algernon F. Bird of No. 46 Squadron – Richthofen's 61st victory.

Richthofen's chief rival in terms of aerial victory scores, *Leutnant der Reserve* Werner Voss, flew the other Fokker Triplane on 5 September and scored his 40th and 41st aerial victories. It was not openly acknowledged, but a competition to attain the most aerial victories was under way – and Manfred von Richthofen felt up to the challenge.

11
TRIPLANE TRIUMPH

Manfred von Richthofen went on an enforced leave of absence that was cloaked in bureaucratic normality, but carefully arranged to ease him out of functional command while assuring respect for his historic role in the German Air Force. He would go on furlough and return without a single feather ruffled. The 6 September 1917 entry in *Jagdgeschwader I*'s war diary read simply:

> The *Rittmeister's* four-week convalescent leave has begun. *Oberleutnant* von Döring (Jasta 4) is for the duration of the *Rittmeister's* leave acting *Geschwader* leader. *Oberleutnant* von Boenigk (*Jasta 4*) has acting leadership of *Jasta 4*. Leutnant Groos, in the place of the wounded Oberleutnant Reinhard, has acting leadership of *Jasta 11*.

This smooth transition in the command structure assured that capable and promising men remained in charge of the *Geschwader* and its *Staffeln*. Designating *Oberleutnant* Kurt von Döring as *stellvertretender Geschwaderführer* [Acting Wing Leader], allowed Richthofen to remain the first and, up to that time, only *Jagdgeschwader-Kommandeur* [Fighter Air Wing Commander] in the German Air Force. After all, he was important to the war effort and, without being too overbearing, was aware of his importance.

Fog, mist and low clouds shrouded the airfield at Marcke, as, amid the cheers and smiles of his devoted flyers, Richthofen was driven to the nearest main railway station to begin his long ride to the city of Gotha in the Saxon Duchy of Thuringia. Carl Eduard, the Duke of Saxe-Coburg-Gotha, had invited Richthofen to relax at *Schloss* [Castle] Reinhardsbrunn, his hunting lodge south-west of Gotha. Known for its serene setting for over 800 years, the castle's pleasure garden became famous in the 19th century as the place where the young Queen Victoria of England met her future husband, Prince Albert of Saxe-Coburg-Gotha.

Even though *Freifrau* von Richthofen awaited her son in Schweidnitz, he could not decline an invitation from the first royal house to decorate him with a high award. Aside from the call of duty, hunting was a pleasure never to be missed. Furthermore, in Manfred von Richthofen's absence, *Leutnant der Reserve* Werner Voss put the new Fokker Triplane to good use. On 10 September, he shot down his 43rd, 44th and 45th enemy aircraft with it. The next day he added two more to his score, including his second Sopwith Triplane.

Also, *Leutnant* Kurt Wolff, known as '*Wölfchen*' [wolf cub] or the '*zarte Blümlein*' [gentle little flower] due to his youthful, almost frail appearance, resumed flying. On 12 September, Wolff, the victor in 33 aerial combats, received a telegram with the news that, on orders of Kaiser Wilhelm II, the fighter pilot had been promoted to *Oberleutnant* in recognition of his outstanding achievements.

On Saturday, 15 September 1917, Wolff was flying Richthofen's Fokker triplane (F.I 102/17), when he was shot down and killed by a new Sopwith F.1 Camel. His body was recovered and given a funeral befitting a Knight of the *Orden Pour le Mérite*. His remains were sent to his parents' home in what was then the German Baltic territory of Memel [today Klaipeda, Lithuania].

The Richthofen family learned of Wolff's death only in the Schweidnitz newspaper. Lothar von Richthofen was at home on convalescent leave at the time, waiting for Manfred to arrive from Thuringia.

Freifrau von Richthofen recalled Lothar's reaction:

> His features became hardened; he sat like that the whole day, glanced into a book and stared out of the window at the dark trees in the garden. None of us said anything. None of us dared, [and] each of us stayed busy, as it was absolutely necessary to begin a conversation about something else ... Lothar said nothing, but his face showed the turmoil [within him]. When twilight came, he wanted no light.
>
> When I went to the door I believe I heard some words. They were spoken very softly, definitely intended for someone far, far away.
>
> "So young ... engaged while on leave ... he should not have been allowed to do that ... a combat pilot is not allowed that."

Manfred was still in Thuringia when a telegram from *JG I* arrived at Schweidnitz on 24 September. It broke the news: '*Leutnant* Voss has not returned from a flight, [and he has] probably been killed.'

Werner Voss' body was not recovered and Manfred von Richthofen grieved in the solitude of *Schloss* Reinhardsbrunn. In fact, he was still there when, on 25 September, his brother Lothar returned to Marcke to resume command of

Jasta 11. Lothar relieved *Leutnant* Groos, who, although wounded in a fight on 14 September and needing hospital treatment, remained at his duty station. Now, Groos could depart *Jasta 11* as it gloried in the return of one of the Richthofens, who were idolized as 'models of comradeship and gallantry, models of audacity [and] fearlessness, models in every sense of the word,' to quote the *Jagdgeschwader* adjutant.

At the end of the month, Manfred von Richthofen concluded his hunting vacation with a hurried note to his mother from the Schloss Hotel in Gotha. Now refreshed and, having grieved for Wolff and Voss privately and in the solitude that was necessary for him, he wrote:

> I am mightily pleased about Lothar's rapid recovery. After being on leave, together we will be able to once again make it hot for the Englishmen, [as] I am with Lothar in the same *Staffel*. My "bag" in the last 14 days has not been bad. A strong elk stag, three very good deer and a ram. I am very proud of it, as Papa has in his whole life shot only three really big deer. Today, I travel to Berlin and, at the latest, will be with all of you in a week.

When a passenger on the train from Frankfurt to Berlin, Emil August Glogau, purchased a copy of Manfred von Richthofen's book that morning, he could not imagine that he would share a First Class compartment with the famous flyer. Glogau recorded his brief encounter with Richthofen:

> ... in Gotha a young Uhlan officer of acrobatic agility jumped on to the train as it was pulling out, dropped his hunting rifle from his shoulder into the luggage rack of my compartment, pulled the collar of his overcoat up over his chin, settled into the thick seat cushions and in the next moment was fast asleep ... Who could train himself so that in an instant he could transcend the borders of consciousness at will? The young man must possess strong resolve, I said to myself ...
>
> When he got on, did the blonde young man not have good-natured, youthful blue eyes? Was he not deliberate and determined in his movements, [and] vigorous in the way he handled his gun? The squared-off skull and the firmly set jaw belonged to an eastern

German *Junker* [country squire]. But how did worry lines get into
this motionless face from cheekbone to chin? Had the war etched
these wrinkles into this young officer? Just then I saw the two pips
on his shoulder boards ... At 20, at the most 24 years old, a
Rittmeister? That's it – he got on in Gotha, a Thuringian duchy –
[there was] a high award under the collar of his overcoat – therefore,
he must be a prince.

Suddenly the eyes popped open ... focused on my luggage rack and
sparkled with happiness ... Then he laughed like a rascal who had
just been turned loose, turned red like an author who had been
published for the first time ... and said: "Oh no, there is the book.
It amuses me very much, of course, that all of the travellers buy
such a thing ..."

I turned on the overhead light, grabbed the book, opened it to the
title page and knew then that I was sitting across from the red
combat flyer in person, Manfred *Freiherr* von Richthofen.

Richthofen entertained his cabin partner with a stream of warm and friendly
reminiscences. Glogau recorded a sombre point:

"I am after all only a combat pilot," [Richthofen] said, "but Boelcke,
he was a hero." With that he tucked the *Pour le Mérite* under his
tunic so that the people would not stare at him.

Later, when they arrived in Berlin's Anhalt Station, Richthofen was again a
proper and courteous German officer. He offered a formal handshake, bowed
slightly and clicked his heels. Then, with a boyish cheery wave, he disappeared
into the crowd.

Manfred von Richthofen had many contacts in the German capital, but he
felt most comfortable with people he knew before he became a celebrity. His
former cadet school teacher, *Hauptmann* Erich von Salzmann, hosted him often
in Berlin and recalled:

We sat together during regimental dinners complete with exquisite
music. On those occasions, of course, there were drinks. Following
the good old Silesian tradition we clinked our goblets together and

had a fine time ... Later, Richthofen was with ladies repeatedly at my home in Berlin. There, too, [he showed] the flawless manner, the naturalness that women like so much. He was not a ladies' man in the well-known sense of the word ... anything but that. He was almost the personification of modern manliness, [and] the ladies liked him, even though he did not court them in every way, as did many young cavaliers who had become famous.

Once we were together at the races in [the Berlin section] Grunewald and for a while he remained unnoticed. That morning he had been at Johannisthal, had test flown some new aircraft and his "dress" was not really very elegant racecourse attire. In general, Richthofen was little inclined toward superficial appearances, although he did not seek to neglect the way he looked. Suddenly people recognized him. Then the photographers came. I have seen other young celebrities in such moments, as they put on airs and posed. None of that for Richthofen. His complete self-confidence was obvious. The young girls rushed toward him. He was asked to sign their programmes as souvenirs.

Richthofen shrugged his shoulders and said to me: "What else should I do?" Anyone else would have gone off. Richthofen signed calmly, patiently, always with the same friendly smile ...

Richthofen also received other forms of recognition, as many German states honoured him with awards normally reserved for their own fighting men. While he was in Berlin this time, for example, he was notified that, on 22 September, the city-state of Lübeck had conferred its Hanseatic Cross on him. Two days later, Duke Ernst August of Braunschweig and Lüneburg presented Richthofen with his duchy's *Kriegsverdienstkreuz* [War Merit Cross]. Then, of course, in view of Richthofen's status as a product of the Prussian cadet system, the Kaiser sent a bronze bust of himself with the engraved inscription: 'To the praiseworthy combat flyer *Rittmeister Freiherr* von Richthofen [from] his grateful king. 10.9.17.'

Richthofen stayed in Berlin briefly this time and, on 9 October, his journey to Schweidnitz was expedited by using the two-seat reconnaissance aircraft he had flown in the past. With its bright red paint scheme, the aircraft was instantly recognizable. The pilot hero circled Schweidnitz at about 6.00 p.m., while townspeople waved to him and swarmed toward the parade ground, which had been cleared for his landing. Cheers and good wishes aside, *Freifrau* von Richthofen was concerned about his health:

> Manfred's wound is deeper than I had thought. I was distressed to notice that the hair on his head has got thinner. He looked as if he had been given tonsure. Perhaps the hair has fallen out at this spot and will grow back.
>
> To my horror I ascertained that Manfred's head injury has not yet healed. The bone is still exposed. Day after day he goes to a local medical aid station to have his bandage changed. He does not look good and is irritable. Previously, it seemed to me that he was like young Siegfried, the invulnerable.

Later, when his mother asked him to give up flying, Manfred responded: 'Who would fight the war if we all thought like that? Only the soldier in the trenches? When the professional fails at leadership, it will soon be as it is in Russia.'

'But the soldier is relieved of duty from time to time and goes to a rest area, while every day you repeatedly endure the most dangerous duels at 5,000 metres (16,000 feet) altitude,' his mother replied.

Uncharacteristically short-tempered with his mother, whom he truly adored, Manfred said gruffly: 'Would it please you if I were in some safe place and resting on my laurels?'

During this visit home, there were other manifestations of Manfred's inner turmoil and his nearly obsessive drive to return to the Front, where he felt his presence could bring some relief to the beleaguered men in the trenches.

One evening after dinner, he had such a severe headache that he went directly to bed. A short time later the members of a local club appeared on Striegauer Strasse, in front of the house, to praise the great hero, which normally elicited an embarrassed grin from him. This time however, as his mother recalled:

> ... my husband had to go upstairs and wake him. A few minutes later he appeared – with a dour expression – at the doorway. He was almost unfriendly. He didn't care to accept the ovation. He could hardly conceal his foul mood, even though all eyes were on him [as if] spellbound.

I felt sorry for the people and asked if he would be a little friendlier the next time. Manfred bolted up with an almost brusque movement, his eyes narrowed and hard [and said]: "When I fly out over the fortified trenches and the soldiers shout joyfully at me and I look into their grey faces, worn from hunger, sleeplessness and battle ... then something rejoices within me. You should see it; often they forget all danger, jump out onto the roofing, swing their rifles and wave to me. That is my reward, Mother, my nicest reward!"

Clearly, Manfred needed a change of scenery, which came in an invitation from the War College in Danzig. The long train ride north to the port city – to be among the uniformed people with whom he was most comfortable – was relaxing. After a brief visit in Danzig, he enjoyed another leisurely ride, this time along the Baltic coast, past Königsberg in East Prussia, to Labiau, where the Neu-Sternberg game preserve in the vast forest and swampland along the Deime River awaited him. After six days of sweating his way through marshes and woods – surely, a good way to release his pent-up emotions – Richthofen shot an enormous elk. Physical and emotional weariness was pushed aside. He had proved to himself that he was still a master hunter.

Refreshed by that triumph, Richthofen returned to *Schloss* Reinhardsbrunn in Thuringia, this time to attend the 18 October wedding of an old friend from *Kampfgeschwader 2* on the Verdun Front, *Hauptmann* Fritz Prestien. Richthofen believed that, at 30, Prestien was of a proper age to marry; he had joined the army at 17 and showed great promise as a career officer. Prestien was a Gotha native and his marriage to Wally von Minckwitz, daughter of the Chief Property Manager of the Court of Saxe-Coburg-Gotha, was a good match. Richthofen was acquainted with his friend's prospective father-in-law from visits to *Schloss* Reinhardsbrunn and it also accrued to Richthofen's good fortune that Fritz Prestien was then serving on the staff of the Inspectorate of Military Aviation in Berlin. A Silesian newspaper reported:

The ceremony was performed by Chief Court Pastor Scholz from Gotha. At the ceremony were about 30 persons, among others the Duke of Saxe-Coburg-Gotha together with his consort [Duchess Viktoria Adelheid], State Secretary von Bassewitz and several aviation officers.

Richthofen's role in Prestien's wedding party confused a *Gothaische Zeitung* journalist, who reported Manfred as the new husband of the former *Fräulein* von Minckwitz. The story made headlines throughout Germany. In Schweidnitz, *Freifrau* von Richthofen assured relatives and friends that Manfred had not done something rash, out of keeping with his newly-gained station in life. When Manfred returned to his room at the Hotel Continental in Berlin, he was greeted by many congratulatory telegrams and well-wishers.

The wedding gossip spread as far as the battlefield rear areas, where *Major* Albrecht *Freiherr* von Richthofen heard so much about it, he began to think the story was true. With Manfred's eager acceptance of modern ways, the Major said, he would not be surprised to learn that his son had married without consulting his father. Later, Manfred wrote:

> But, finally, he completely agreed that I was in no position to get married, for he was of the conviction that it would have been somewhat premature. I, myself, could imagine quite well enjoying my life as a carefree bachelor right up to the blessed end.

While seemingly satisfied with the single life, Manfred is thought to have had a serious romantic interest, but the rumours died when he did. His mother, to whom he confided much, including the secret in his heart, told American journalist Floyd Gibbons: 'Manfred loved this one girl. He had for her the love of an honourable man for the woman he wanted to be the mother of his children. I know that she loved him.'

Manfred was happy for his old friend Fritz Prestien, who then had a relatively safe post in Berlin, but there was always the prospect of being recalled to the Front, as, in fact, Prestien later was. In any event, Manfred's total self-control kept him devoted to his military mission. 'I cannot indulge myself in the rite of marriage as long as I am liable to die any day,' he said.

The marriage rumours and interest in his private life hastened Richthofen's return to the Front. Moreover, the first batch of new fighters was then on the way to *Jasta 11*, where Richthofen was the only leader with Fokker Triplane combat experience.

Other news only drove him harder. His old *Kagohl 2* comrade *Leutnant* Alfred Gerstenberg had taken a bullet through one lung and would be out of action for a time. Then, two days later, British bombers attacked Marcke and

Bisseghem airfields and damaged five aircraft of *Jasta 11*. When Richthofen returned the next day, the damaged areas had been cleaned and mechanics were going over a brand-new Fokker Triplane to make it ready for the *Jagdgeschwader-Kommandeur*.

The long-awaited Fokker Dr.I Triplanes did not prove to be the 'wonder weapons' that German fighter pilots anticipated. While the Triplanes could 'climb like apes and [were] as manoeuvrable as the devil,' as Richthofen promised, only skilled pilots could truly master them. Triplane controls were very sensitive and required constant attention.

As part of *JG I*'s transition to Fokker Triplanes – equipped with rotary engines, which had a different 'feel' to pilots than the in-line stationary engines in their Albatroses – Richthofen ordered orientation flights in older rotary-engine-powered Fokker D.V biplane fighters. But soon after his return to the Front, a series of incidents raised questions about the new fighters.

On Monday, 29 October, *Vizefeldwebel* Josef Lautenschlager of *Jasta 11* was on patrol in a new Fokker Triplane north of Houthulst Forest when he was shot down and killed. According to an Air Force report, the 25-year-old pilot was attacked by another German fighter pilot who took Lautenschlager's Fokker Dr.I for a Sopwith Triplane.

The following morning, Manfred and Lothar von Richthofen flew together for the first time in over five months. Both were eager to prove to their comrades and themselves that they were pilots to be reckoned with – in spite of heavy clouds and rain – in their new Fokker Triplanes. Then, without warning, the engine on Lothar's aeroplane quit and he went into a glide. Manfred circled back to ensure Lothar was safe; in fact, he made a normal landing south of Roeselare. A few minutes later, Manfred headed for a landing near the failed machine when his aeroplane cracked, burst and came apart. He was unharmed, but was shocked at the destruction caused by a seemingly minor incident.

Yet, Manfred von Richthofen had better luck than the 39-victory ace and *Pour le Mérite* recipient *Leutnant* Heinrich Gontermann, who was test-flying a Fokker Triplane over his own airfield when the top wing came off and the aircraft crashed not far from the crowd watching him below. Gontermann, age 21 and leader of *Jasta 15*, died of his injuries that evening. The next afternoon, *Leutnant* Günther Pastor, who joined *Jasta 11* five weeks earlier, was flying a Fokker Triplane north of Moorsele, when the top wing structure suddenly collapsed and his aircraft crashed fatally.

The series of accidents was too costly in manpower and equipment losses to allow continued operation of the Fokker Triplane. Consequently, on 2 November 1917, all Triplanes were grounded until the Inspectorate of Aviation determined the cause of the series of recent crashes and instituted corrective measures. During the course of the investigation by the Inspectorate's Central Acceptance Commission, *JG I*'s pilots flew only Albatros D.III and D.V and new Pfalz D.III biplanes.

Then, while Richthofen was planning *JG I*'s move to the 2nd Army Sector in anticipation of a major Allied assault there, another aircraft problem emerged. On the morning of 6 November, the day Canadian forces took Passchendaele, *Jasta 10* ace *Leutnant* Erich Loewenhardt was forced to land after a lower wing broke on his Albatros D.V. If, in addition to the removal of the Triplanes, the Albatroses had to be withdrawn or if pilots lost confidence in them, *JG I* would have only Pfalz D.III fighters, which had streamlined good looks that belied their air combat inferiority to the Albatroses.

Given the various problems facing *JG I* at the time, Manfred von Richthofen was strangely absent from the flight line for several weeks. To be sure, he did not lack in personal courage, but he had enormous propaganda value and, with the Fokker Triplanes out of action and the Albatroses again under suspicion, the 'higher-ups' could not risk having the *Jagdgeschwader-Kommandeur* flying in either aircraft. His old friend Erwin Böhme, by then leader of *Jasta Boelcke*, wrote to his fiancée of the situation. Böhme's letter of 19 November contrasted his own joy of flying with a cynical commentary by Richthofen, who had become 'public property' with the various press reports bolstered by publication of his autobiography. Böhme wrote that Richthofen's *Jagdgeschwader*:

> ... is also attached to our Army Corps and is right in the neighbourhood, but is at the disposal of the Army High Command only for special missions, while we have a prescribed sector at the Front. Of course, we do not have to stay within it meticulously; when the situation requires, very often we hunt even in the neighbouring sectors – that is what is so great indeed about fighter aviation, that one finds new tasks on every flight and then pursues them based on one's own decision.
>
> Yesterday afternoon on the flight back from the Front, I stopped for a coffee at Richthofen's airfield – they always have the best cakes

there. Richthofen is constantly spied on by artists, who want to paint his likeness. Yesterday, he said, he wanted to give up flying altogether and busy himself with self-portraiture, which is less dangerous and at least makes one famous just as quickly.

Heavy fog in Flanders on the day after Böhme's visit promised to provide *JG I* with good cover to begin moving south to the 2nd Army Sector – back to the Somme Front, where Richthofen achieved his first air combat successes as a student of Boelcke's. *Leutnant* Konstantin Krefft, the *Geschwader* Technical Officer, was ready to lead tradesmen and work crews to Avesnes le Sec, north-east of the heavily-contested Cambrai region. But the workers were not even under way when, at 0620 hours on 20 November, British forces initiated the Battle of Cambrai, aimed at cracking the stabilized German battle lines in that sector. Departing from the usual opening artillery barrage, this offensive began with a concentration of 381 British tanks, troops and aircraft attacking German lines across a four-mile stretch from Gonnelieu to Havrincourt, south-west of Cambrai. Following the tanks out of the mist and low clouds were infantry and air units of the British First and Third Armies, south and south-west of Cambrai. During two days of raging ground fighting, the men and equipment of *JG I* headed south under the cover of bad weather to their new airfields, all within three miles of each other: *Jastas 4* and *6* at *Lieu St. Amand*, *Jasta* 10 at Iwuy, and *Jasta 11* and the *Geschwader* staff at Avesnes le Sec.

Finally, on Friday, 23 November 1917, *Rittmeister* von Richthofen was back in combat, flying in the repaired Albatros fighter in which he had been shot down in July. He led combined flights from *JG I* and *Jastas 5* and 15 to clear the skies over Bourlon Wood, which had been taken by a British division, supported by its low-flying fighters. Richthofen attacked two Airco DH5 fighters over Fontaine-Notre Dame and chased them back to British lines. Later, he forced one fighter to land and closed in on the second:

> **After the first shots, the Englishman started to glide downward, but then fell into the south-east corner of Bourlon Wood ...**

Although the second DH5 was not seen to crash, it was recorded as Richthofen's 62nd victory and he later received the fabric patch bearing the serial number. *JG I* completed the move to its new airfields during the next few days of wind and rain. The heavy winds were a blessing, as they minimized the danger of personnel and equipment being strafed by enemy fighters or low-flying two-seaters looking for targets of opportunity.

On 25 November, Lothar von Richthofen wrote to his mother:

> We have moved, but at the moment I cannot tell you where – it is secret. When you read the reports: there, where the British attacks are taking place – that is where we are!
>
> On the second day of our move, Manfred and I each shot down an Englishman on the new Front.
>
> Here there is so much to do – Manfred doesn't know whether he is coming or going. (At the moment a violent storm is beginning, and my aeroplanes are standing out in the open.)

The 'secret' of the move was not well kept. British intelligence officers learned about it from prisoner interrogations, which provided valuable information about ranking German air units and their leaders. Before the move was completed, British air unit personnel already knew: 'The 2nd and 11th Pursuit Flights [*Jastas 2* and *11*] (looked upon as "Star" units) were recently withdrawn from the Flanders Front, where they had suffered many casualties, as they were unable to make much headway on such an active Front.'

Despite the Royal Flying Corps intelligence summary's comment disparaging the well-known and highly effective German fighter units, the appearance of *JG I* and its famous commander had a 'bogey-man' effect on British air operations during the last week of November. On 26 November, 12 Airco DH4 bombers of No. 49 Squadron were to be escorted by 14 new Royal Aircraft Factory SE5a fighters – twice the number usually assigned. But the RFC bomber-fighter rendezvous did not take place, due to bad weather. Hence, while *JG I* flew 37 sorties that day, no air contacts were reported between the opposing air elements.

Over the next few days, however, increased low-level German air activity – which British observers noted were marked by the appearance of 'the coloured aeroplanes of the Richthofen "Circus"' – was a strong indicator that German forces were preparing a counter-attack in the Cambrai Sector.

Improved weather on 29 November brought out large numbers of aircraft on both sides, resulting in a mixture of good and bad news for Manfred von

Richthofen. *JG I*'s morning patrol shot down five British aircraft, but, later, a report from the German 4th Army Sector revealed that Richthofen's old friend Erwin Böhme had been killed in combat. After Böhme had scored his 24th air combat success, that day, he was in turn shot down by a British two-seater crew. Had he survived, back at *Jasta 2*, Böhme would have found that his newly awarded *Orden Pour le Mérite* had arrived in the day's mail.

Just after daybreak on 30 November, heavy artillery fire heralded the German counter-offensive at Cambrai. Early that afternoon, Richthofen led *JG I* against a formation of Airco DH5s and stayed above the fray to watch one of his protégés, *Leutnant* Georg von der Osten of *Jasta 11*, shoot down one of the British fighters. It was confirmed as the new man's fourth victory.

Almost an hour later and a few kilometres away, the *JG I* flight attacked ten SE5a fighters. The Richthofen brothers and *Leutnant* Siegfried Gussmann charged into the formation and, during the ensuing fight, Manfred von Richthofen sent down an SE5a on fire into a small quarry in the woods. He was credited with his 63rd aerial victory, which would also be his last of 1917.

But the day was not without loss to *JG I*. *Leutnant der Reserve* Friedrich Demandt, a one-month veteran of *Jasta 10*, was last seen in a fight over Flesquières, pursuing a hoped-for first victory, south-east of Moeuvres. Then, as often happens in war, the 25-year-old native of Rastatt in the Grand Duchy of Baden did not return and his body was not found.

Bad news could not be allowed to linger. Successful combat pilots learned to 'steel' themselves to the sight of vacant chairs at the dining room table and to look forward to the next day's successes or a comrade's personal achievement. In addition to Richthofen's great victory that day, a telegram brought news that *Leutnant der Reserve* Hans Klein would become the seventh Richthofen protégé to receive the *Orden Pour le Mérite*.

As part of the *Jagdgeschwader-Kommandeur*'s air combat pilot development process, on 1 December, Richthofen welcomed to *Jasta 11* another ex-cavalryman with a familiar name, *Leutnant* Friedrich-Wilhelm Lübbert. Like his older brother Eduard, a *Jasta 11* member who died in aerial combat on 30 March 1917, Friedrich-Wilhelm had served in the much-admired two-seater unit *Feldflieger-Abteilung 18*. Indeed, Lübbert's observer from that *Abteilung*, *Oberleutnant* Hans-Helmut von Boddien, had been recruited to *Jasta 11* four months earlier. Both men displayed the fighting spirit Richthofen wanted.

A devoted student of the *Rittmeister*, Lübbert recalled that his mentor:

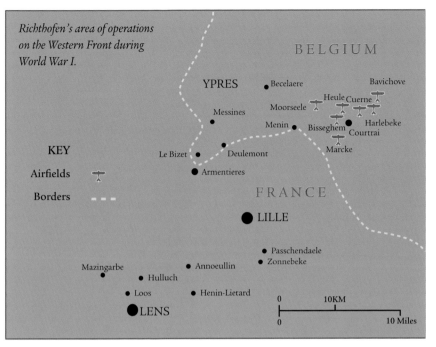

Richthofen's area of operations on the Western Front during World War I.

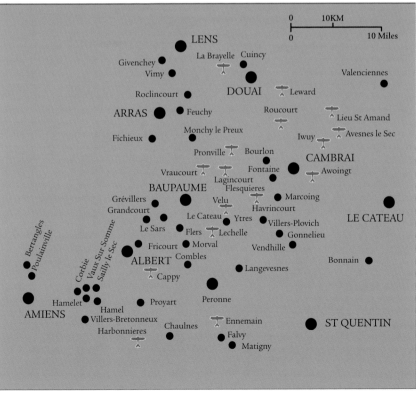

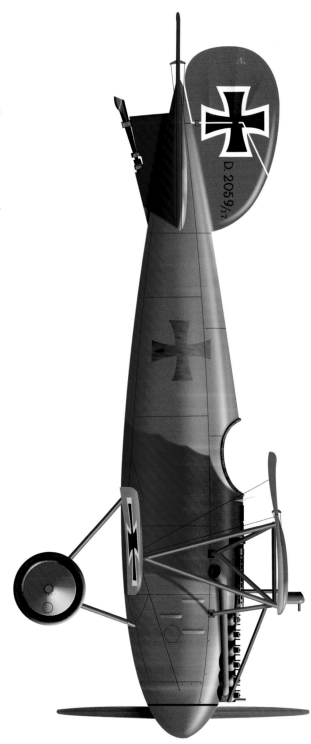

Albatros D.V 2069/17

Best known for flying all-red aeroplanes, Manfred von Richthofen had Albatros D.V 2069/17 painted red to an extreme. The aircraft serial number on the vertical stabilizer was over-painted and then re-painted and even the national insignia on the fuselage sides were given a red "wash." Richthofen scored his 58th and 59th victories while using this aeroplane.

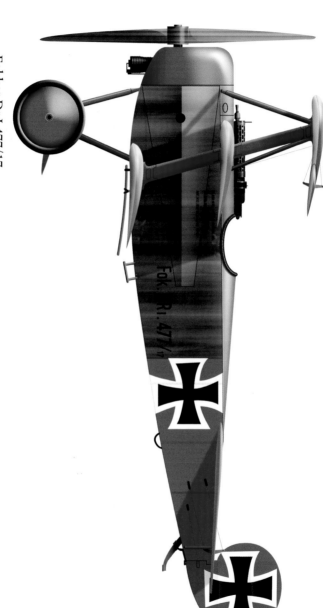

Fokker Dr.I 477/17

Not all of Manfred von Richthofen's aeroplanes were entirely coloured red. Fokker Dr.I 477/17 was delivered in the standard brown and green 'streak' camouflage pattern, and Jagdstaffel 11 ground crewmen had time only to paint the top wing, top fuselage deck, tail, cowling and wheel covers red. Richthofen scored his 67th, 68th, 69th, 70th, 72nd, 73rd, 75th 77th and 78th victories while flying this aeroplane.

While still wearing his head bandage, Manfred von Richthofen posed for this photograph with Kätie Otersdorf, his strong-willed nurse at the hospital in Courtrai. Their rigid stance and distance seems to dispel any notion of a hinted romantic link between them.

Rittmeister *Karl von Grieffenhagen, who flew with* Jasta 1 *when Richthofen began his career with* Jasta 2, *was among old comrades who visited the famous flyer at Courtrai. When he became commander of the Fighter Pilot School at Paderborn, Grieffenhagen alerted Richthofen to promising students heading for the Front.*

While JG I *aircraft provided air cover over Courtrai for* Kaiser *Wilhelm's inspection of 4th Army troops on 20 August 1917,* Richthofen *remained on the ground to salute his monarch. Standing at the right is* General der Infanterie *Friedrich Sixt von Armin, 65-year-old Commanding General of the 4th Army, whose motto* Richthofen *embraced: 'He who does not dare to take the next step has made the whole journey for nothing.'*

Manfred von Richthofen removed his full head dressing, but still wore a small bandage secured by a strap, for what would be the last family portrait at home at No. 10 Striegauer Strasse in Schweidnitz. He also wore all of his decorations on an ordinary field tunic, as did his brother Lothar. Standing with him (from left): his mother, brothers Lothar and Bolko and his sister Ilse. His father, Major *Albrecht* Freiherr *von Richthofen, was seated and out of uniform.*

Upon receiving news that Oberleutnant *Eduard Dostler, leader of* Jasta 6, *was to receive the* Pour le Mérite, *Richthofen placed his own* Pour le Mérite *around the 21-victory ace's neck, as seen in this view of the announcement festivities.*

Lieutenant Algernon F. Bird of No. 46 Squadron, RFC (right), Richthofen's 61st opponent, managed a smile when he met his victor. Bird, age 21, was one of 29 airmen to survive a fight with Richthofen; another 54 are known to have been killed.

While Richthofen was recovering from the wounds he received on 6 July, JG I operated under orders of Hauptmann *Otto Bufe (second from left), Officer in Charge of Aviation for the 4th Army Sector. Many of Bufe's tactics were counter to Richthofen's and caused friction between the two men.*

After Richthofen recruited Leutnant der Reserve *Ernst Udet and assigned him to command* Jasta 4, *Udet scored his 24th through 62nd victories and became Germany's second-highest scoring ace of the war. He had the fourth-highest victory score of all nations, following* Rittmeister *Manfred* Freiherr *von Richthofen (80),* Capitaine *René Fonck (75) and Lieutenant Colonel William A. Bishop (72). a committed acolyte of Hitler.*

When problems developed with the Fokker Dr.I Triplanes, Richthofen visited the Pfalz Aeroplane Works to test the Pfalz Dr.I as a possible replacement. His disappointment with the Pfalz Triplane is a major reason it did not go into production.

JG I flew a number of Pfalz D.IIIa biplane fighters. This Jasta 10 machine fell into British hands intact on 27 December 1917 and provided the Royal Flying Corps with an example for evaluation. In this view, German national markings have already been painted over by the British tri-colour.

Manfred von Richthofen (fifth from left) attended the wedding of his friend
Hauptmann *Fritz Prestien on 18 October 1917 at Reinhardsbrunn Castle in*
Gotha. Attendees included, from left: Wolf Freiherr *Pergler von Perglas and*
his wife, Gerda von Minckwitz and Oberjägermeister Major aD *Hans von*
Minckwitz (parents of the bride), Richthofen in full medals and wearing a
Tschapka *uhlan dress helmet, Duchess Viktoria Adelheid and Duke Carl Eduard of*
Saxe-Coburg-Gotha, three Court officials, Wally von Minckwitz and Fritz Prestien
(the bridal pair), various court, military and family members. The German press
misunderstood the story and reported that Richthofen had married Fräulein *von*
Minckwitz.

A grieving Geschwader-Kommandeur *von Richthofen pays last respects at the*
grave of Jasta 10'*s Leutnant der Reserve Franz Bohlein, who was killed at age*
21 in aerial combat on 16 March 1918 and was buried in a German-organized
cemetery at Avesnes-le-Sec, France.

To ward off chilly spring weather, Richthofen (X) wore a bulky flying suit with a Heinecke parachute harness and, on this occasion, flew a Fokker Dr.I 127/17, a mostly red Triplane. In the war's last year, aircraft parachutes were in wider use.

Manfred von Richthofen's 78th victim was a Sopwith F.1 Camel flown by Lieutenant Ronald Adams, seen here in the aircraft he flew to France on 30 March. Eight days later, flying a new Camel with No. 73 Squadron, Adams was shot down. He survived the fight and later wrote to this author: 'It was little consolation to learn that I had fought with von Richthofen or that he was killed two weeks later, to the day.'

Rittmeister *von Richthofen flew this Fokker Dr.I 425/17 in his last aerial combat, on 21 April 1918. The* original Balkenkreuz *['iron cross' type] national insignia had recently been replaced by the white-bordered Greek Cross design seen here on the all-red Triplane.*

Leutnant der Reserve *Richard Wenzl took the last photograph of Manfred von Richthofen alive, shortly before the* Rittmeister *began his last flight. Reflecting his ebullient mood after having scored his 80th victory the day before, Richthofen enjoyed playing with his Great Dane named 'Moritz.'*

Canadian-born Captain Arthur Roy Brown, age 24, had nine confirmed aerial victories to his credit when he took off on 21 April 1918, leading 'A' Flight No. 209 Squadron, RAF. In the view of some historians, Brown's tenth victory was Richthofen's Fokker Triplane. Others, this author included, believe the evidence shows that the Red Baron was shot down from the ground.

Second Lieutenant Wilfrid R. May of No. 209 Squadron was Richthofen's intended 81st victim. The 23-year-old Canadian pilot, seen here in training in 1917, was on his first combat mission when he attacked a German fighter and, when his guns jammed, turned for home. Looking around, he saw an all-red Fokker Triplane behind him, with its machine-gun firing at him. He was saved by an Australian ground gunner, who probably got a lucky hit on Richthofen.

Manfred von Richthofen was killed at about 1145 hours on 21 April 1918. He came down at Vaux-sur-Somme, France and was dead when Australian troops reached the crash site. His body was removed from the wreckage and taken to Poulainville airfield, where this photograph was taken.

Sergeant Cedric B. Popkin, assisted by Privates Weston and Marshall, of the 24th Machine-Gun Company, operated the Vickers machine-gun that very likely killed the Red Baron.

Richthofen's official obituary, as published in Germany, lauded the fallen flyer as a 'role model, advisor and friend' who would never be forgotten. It was signed by Hauptmann *Wilhelm Reinhard, who succeeded to the post of* Kommandeur *of* Jagdgeschwader I.

After Manfred von Richthofen's remains were exhumed from Fricourt, France on 14 November 1925, a government-authorized train bore them through Germany and to Berlin. There, they were placed in a zinc coffin inside a brown oak casket with Uhlan swords and Tschapkas *[Uhlan dress helmets] atop it. In front of the coffin was the original wooden cross grave marker, bearing only his name and the number 53091. An honour guard included officers from his* Jagdgeschwader *and Uhlan Regiment Nr. 1 escorted the coffin through Berlin. Seen in the foreground are two* Pour le Mérite *fighter pilots: Leutnant der Reserve Josef Veltjens, former JG II Kommandeur (left), and Leutnant der Reserve Kurt Wüsthoff, former leader of Jasta 4.*

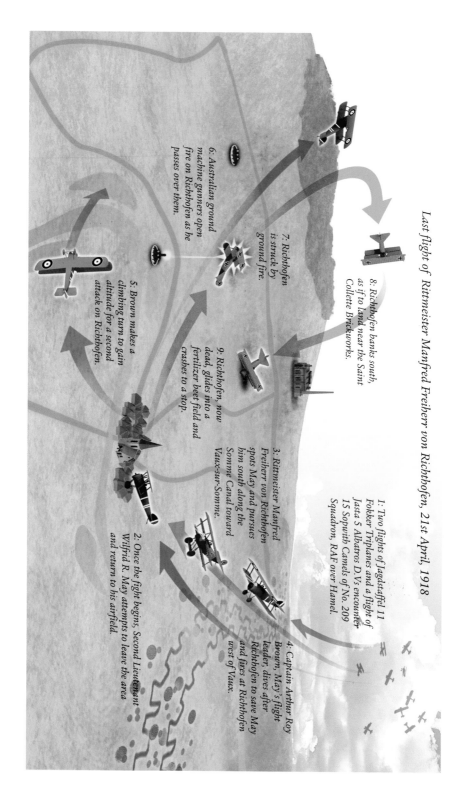

Last flight of Rittmeister Manfred Freiherr von Richthofen, 21st April, 1918

1: Two flights of Jagdstaffel 11 Fokker Triplanes and a flight of Jasta 5 Albatros D.Vs encounter 15 Sopwith Camels of No. 209 Squadron, RAF over Hamel.

2: Once the fight begins, Second Lieutenant Wilfrid R. May attempts to leave the area and return to his airfield.

3: Rittmeister Manfred Freiherr von Richthofen spots May and pursues him south along the Somme Canal toward Vaux-sur-Somme.

4: Captain Arthur Roy Brown, May's flight leader, dives after Richthofen to save May and fires at Richthofen west of Vaux.

5: Brown makes a climbing turn to gain altitude for a second attack on Richthofen.

6: Australian ground machine gunners open fire on Richthofen as he passes over them.

7: Richthofen is struck by ground fire.

8: Richthofen banks south, as if to land near the Saint Collette Brickworks.

9: Richthofen, now dead, glides into a fertilizer beet field and crashes to a stop.

EINTRITTSKARTE

zu den

Beisetzungsfeierlichkeiten für den im Weltkriege gefallenen

Rittmeister Frhr. von Richthofen

am 20. November 1925, nachmittags 1³⁰ Uhr

INHABER:

Herr

Die Kommandantur Berlin

Due to the volume of people who wanted to attend Richthofen's funeral, attendance at the church had to be restricted to invitees bearing this special card from the Berlin garrison commander.

Most of Richthofen's war trophies ended up in the family home in Lower Silesia. A British rotary engine converted into a chandelier hung from the ceiling of one room, above the small bust presented by Kaiser Wilhelm II. Serial number patches from Richthofen victims include (from top left): A.2401 from victory No. 33; N.5193 – No. 16; A.3340 – No. 36; A.5446 – No. 14; A/1108 – No. 23; A.9299 - No. 62; 6618 - No. 4; 6232 obtained by him in error, as he shot down 6231 for victory No. 20; A.6382 - No. 34; 5841 - No. 32; 2506 - No. 8; 6997 - No. 18; 6580 - No. 5; 9865 matches no known Richthofen victory; and 4997 from victory No. 43.

The Richthofen family home was at No. 10 Striegauer Strasse in Schweidnitz. Following World War I, the street was renamed Manfred-von-Richthofen-Strasse and, on the 15th anniversary of his death, the home became a private museum open to the public. Aided by family members, Kunigunde Freifrau von Richthofen showed visitors rooms filled with trophies and mementoes attesting to the success of her two eldest sons.

Former World War I fighter ace Bruno Loerzer (at the lectern) was among many German aviation dignitaries to visit the Richthofen Museum in Schweidnitz. Family members from right are the Rittmeister's sister Ilse, brother Bolko, and mother Kunigunde Freifrau von Richthofen. The woman with the fur is the widow of Major Erich Brückner, a World War I Pour le Mérite recipient from the infantry.

... possessed all of the qualities that a successful fighter pilot must have: flies well, shoots well, sees everything, [and] always stays calm and alert when approaching the enemy.

[But] he was absolutely opposed to unnecessary escapades in the air – he never in his life made a loop just for fun – and never followed the unhealthy impulse that cost many another good fighter pilot his life. "Slow but sure" seems to be his motto. "I prefer to shoot down fewer [enemies] than to be shot down myself; for then I can perform no duties for the Fatherland."

When his *Staffel* or *Geschwader* was embroiled in an aerial combat, [Richthofen] saw everything and everyone. He concerned himself not only with his own opponent, but at the same time watched over his pilots, whether to come to one's aid just in time or, during the critique afterwards, to tell him what he should not have done.

Strong winds, ground fog and snow showers made training new pilots in winter weather especially difficult. But there was hope for success on 5 December, when two new pilots attained their first victories. British withdrawal from hard-won positions in Bourlon two days later ended the Battle of Cambrai. Despite worsening weather, Richthofen continued to send out *JG I* patrols over the Front. He ordered 39 sorties on the final day of battle and 18 the next day.

Construction and design problems with the Fokker Triplanes had been identified and were being corrected, but Richthofen, leery of Albatros and Fokker failures, was still looking for a suitable replacement. His endorsement of a new aeroplane would lead to a sizeable contract for a company. Hence, management at the Pfalz Flugzeugwerke [Aeroplane Works] in Speyer am Rhein, which had also developed a triplane, invited Richthofen to consider it for use by *JG I*. The Pfalz Dr.I Triplane had a more powerful engine and was supposed to be able to climb faster than the Fokker Triplane.

During the winter lull, on 12 December, Richthofen went to the factory with high hopes. He returned ten days later to report that the Pfalz aircraft did not handle as well as the Fokker Dr.I and the Pfalz triplane's Siemens-Halske Sh III rotary engine did not meet the manufacturer's claims. Until the Fokker Dr.Is with modified wings arrived, the *Geschwader* had to face growing British superiority with its old Albatros and Pfalz D.III biplane fighters.

12
THE PRICE OF GLORY

In northern France during December 1917 it was as if nature, weary of man's destructive use of the air, intervened and made the skies inhospitable. At *Jagdgeschwader I*'s open, treeless, windswept base at Avesnes le Sec, for example, Adjutant Karl Bodenschatz wrote in *JG I*'s war diary:

> ...it grows calm. The Englishmen scarcely let themselves be heard and even less seen. Winter has set in on all Fronts and no one is opposed to it. Rain changes to fog and fog changes to snowstorms, [and] heavy ground fog lies over most of the entire landscape.

On Tuesday, 18 December, Manfred von Richthofen was the only *Jagdgeschwader* pilot who flew that day and only because he was in Germany at the Pfalz factory, testing its triplane prototype. Disappointed with the Pfalz Dr.I, Richthofen returned to Avesnes le Sec to spend Christmas with his men. The entire *Jagdgeschwader* complement rejoiced when Manfred and Lothar were joined by their father, *Major* Albrecht *Freiherr* von Richthofen. As comradeship in wartime often does, a familial quality grew in *JG I* and it became even more evident during visits by the senior Richthofen, who was affectionately known to his sons' comrades as the *Fliegervater* [Father of the Flyers].

Hauptmann Wilhelm Reinhard, who in four months would succeed Manfred von Richthofen as *Jagdgeschwader-Kommandeur*, recalled:

> It was a marvellous sight when Father Richthofen spent time with us in the company of both of his sons. Three solid soldier figures! Father Richthofen, tall and broad-shouldered, despite his age [58] still straight as a reed, [and with] a striking profile; our *Rittmeister*, somewhat compact, but a powerful figure; and Lothar, slender and sinewy, a cavalry figure. And, as their outward appearance showed them to be old-line Prussian officers, their character and conduct was soldierly through and through.
>
> ... Father Richthofen loved his sons equally in an open and sincere manner. In Silesian fashion, he was a bit stand-offish with strangers. He took an especially active interest in aviation and [flying] officers.

He never tried to stop his sons [from flying] or warned them to be cautious ...Our *Fliegervater* often sat for hours on end amidst the circle of comrades in the Officers' Mess and let them talk about their aerial combats. He enjoyed every ... tidbit about flying and, as he often was an eyewitness to many air fights from the ground, he showed great appreciation of us. He understood our flyers' talk and shared with us the joys and sorrows of fighter pilots.

No *Jagdgeschwader I* victories were recorded during the year-end lull, but 1917 did not end on a happy or hopeful note. On 27 December, a *Jasta 11* Albatros D.V was flying over its own airfield when, suddenly, the wings collapsed and the aeroplane dived into the ground, where it caught fire and the pilot was killed. The smashed aeroplane provided Technical Officer Konstantin Krefft with no clues about whether the all-too-frequent Albatros wing weakness had caused the crash. Later that day, a Pfalz D.IIIa from *Jasta 10* failed to return from its patrol. After a fight with a British two-seater, the German pilot was forced down within British lines and taken prisoner. British intelligence records make it clear that he confirmed *JG I*'s move to the Cambrai Sector.

But, by then, Manfred and Lothar von Richthofen were en route to Brest-Litovsk in Russia at the invitation of *Prinz* Leopold of Bavaria, Commander in Chief of German Forces in the East. After the abdication and murder of Czar Nikolai II, as well as the failure of the Kerenski Government's military actions, the war with Russia was over. Now, Imperial Germany and Austria-Hungary offered harsh peace terms to the revolutionary Government of V.I. Lenin. The Richthofen brothers were among German victory symbols whose presence at the peace talks was intended to impress the Bolshevik delegation.

The brothers had no known effect on the Russians, but were treated to a visit to the late Czar's palatial hunting lodge to stalk rare game. Following their return to Brest-Litovsk on 5 January 1918, it became clear that the peace conference would drag on and there was no propaganda value in keeping the Richthofens there. They returned to Germany, where Manfred made appearances when his prestige was needed, as noted in a letter to his mother:

You will surely wonder why you have been so long without news from me; but that is always a sign that I am well. In this case, to be sure, I have experienced very much. As Lothar has already written to you, we were in Brest-Litovsk ... Then for a few days we were in the Bialowicz Forest, [where] each of us shot a stag and were really splendidly refreshed in the quiet of the primeval forest. Now I am very often in Berlin. From the 20th on, I will be there for 14 days and then I hope to see you often.

In Berlin, Richthofen saw signs of the social unrest that the Bolsheviks he had met at Brest-Litovsk predicted would bring down the German Empire. Recalling the Russians' proud boasts of having 'dealt with' their former nobility and other 'enemies of the people,' Richthofen was more aware of the danger to the traditional German social order he was fighting to maintain.

He spoke with conviction to workers on strike at munitions factories in hopes of calming their protests over working conditions, food shortages and the long and costly war's other privations. Richthofen's popularity and personal manner made him a credible representative of the regime. From her conversations with Manfred, his mother recalled:

When he arrived [at the factories] they all rushed up to him and he had to speak to them. Then he made it clear to them just how important their work was and so on. For the most part, they went back to their work. But perhaps they would not do it for long. He was very gloomy on that point. The Kaiserin [Empress Auguste Victoria] often went to the striking munitions workers and spoke with the people.

I had the feeling that [Manfred] did not like to talk about such things ... he was a person of duty and discipline, whose whole life was a commitment to self-sacrifice [and] who complied with the government-sponsored tactic of "persuasion" with reluctance.

The *Jagdgeschwader-Kommandeur* much preferred his next assignment. He left *Rittmeister* Kurt von Döring temporarily in charge of the *Geschwader* so he could be at Adlershof airfield outside Berlin for the aircraft type tests on 19 January. Adlershof, German for 'eagles court,' was the site of the *Flugzeugmeisterei* [Aircraft Test Establishment], which hosted competitions between aircraft manufacturers that would result in new air weapons for Richthofen and his comrades, and lucrative production contracts for manufacturers.

The January 1918 type tests of some 28 aircraft from five different firms were critically important in determining which fighter aircraft would be produced for the coming spring offensive and beyond. Manfred von Richthofen's role at Adlershof was described by former *JG I* member Richard Wenzl:

> These *Typenprüfungen* [aircraft type tests] were an achievement of Richthofen, who was of the viewpoint that not just any old home front pilot, most of all [not] one working for one of the aircraft companies, should be the man who determines what will be flown at the Front. Thus, representatives from all of the *Jagdstaffeln* at the Front came to these tests. The individual types were test-flown, [and] then the gentlemen agreed amongst themselves on which types were best suited at the moment ...

Former *Jasta 11* member Georg von der Osten also took part in the tests at Adlershof and flew the Fokker V 11 biplane, which was later produced as the Fokker D.VII, which became an outstanding air weapon. He recalled one of the lighter moments of the time:

> On a rainy day we drove back from Adlershof to Berlin by car. Not much had been accomplished at the tests due to the rain. On the way, Richthofen said, "Well, I will get out here at Schulte's [art gallery] and have a look at the pictures that Reusing [a noted portraitist] has painted!"
> [He] wore an overcoat with a big collar, typical of the officers' coat that we had before the war. As it was raining, it acted like a disguise. He went into the gallery and came to the painting that showed him in his plane, captioned "*Rittmeister Freiherr* von Richthofen."
> An elderly gentleman came up and stood beside him. Richthofen said to him: "I beg your pardon, but I am told I have some likeness to this painting!" The gentleman put on his spectacles, took a look at the picture, took a look at Richthofen, and finally said: "I think you can forget that notion."
> Ten minutes later, Richthofen joined us at the hotel, beaming with joy, and related the incident to me.

While Richthofen and his comrades prepared to leave Berlin, another office in that city, leaving nothing to chance, made its contribution to the coming spring offensive. The Medical Section of the Air Force Commanding General's office published the second edition of its findings on flying's effects on the human body and medical advice for flyers. The report urged aviation personnel to keep themselves in the peak of health. It noted the potentially harmful effects of high-altitude flight and suggested deep breathing exercises as a way for pilots to avoid problems. The report also emphasized the need for airmen to rest and sleep between flights and to use alcohol in moderation, if at all. It particularly condemned the use of tobacco as harmful to the lungs and nervous system. In a portion titled '*Mässigkeit und Vorsicht beim Geschlechstsverkehr*' [Moderation and Caution in Sexual Intercourse], the report counselled:

> Sexual intercourse is to be taken into account as a further impairment. (The judgement from the standpoint of morality is entirely excluded here.) When ... a harmful effect through the excess [of activity] is to be feared, the great danger of infection must be remembered. Every infection makes one unfit for duty for weeks. This lack of fitness for duty is one's own fault and must in all circumstances be avoided.

With all of the command concerns on his mind, sexual pleasure seemed to be far from Richthofen's thoughts, as evident by his last visit home, at the end of January. His red two-seat aeroplane came into view against the ice-blue winter sky over Schweidnitz at about 4:00 p.m. *Freifrau* von Richthofen waited for him, joined by many townspeople to whom her son's appearances were always welcome. They waved and cheered, but made no attempt to keep the national hero from his family. Quickly, Manfred and his mother were past the crowds and into their house across the street from the landing field.

Warmed by the hearth and the affection of his mother, he told her about his two-hour flight from Berlin to Schweidnitz: flying over the Cadet Academy at Wahlstatt, where Bolko was following the family tradition. There, Manfred violated one of his own rules. With the cadets gathered on the parade ground, he swooped down and then pulled up into a great loop before continuing on. He could well imagine his brother and the other boys roaring their approval.

Freifrau von Richthofen chided Manfred and told him that Bolko was very disappointed that his famous oldest brother flew over Wahlstatt and never landed there. Manfred could only wince in mock anguish and respond that Bolko was too young to understand that even famous flyers cannot simply set down wherever they wish.

Later that evening, Manfred was visibly pained when he sorted through photographs he had brought with him from the Front. One showed him and some flying comrades in Russia. Looking over his shoulder, his mother pointed to one smiling young flyer and asked: 'What has become of him?'

'Fallen in combat.' Pointing to a second man brought Manfred's reply: 'Also dead.' Before she could inquire further, he said in a voice suddenly hoarse: 'Do not ask any more – they are all dead.'

He must have sensed what his mother was thinking and quickly reassured her: 'You don't need to worry. In the air I have nothing to fear. In the air ... we are ready for them, even when there are many of them. The worst that could happen to me would be to have to land on the other side.'

Then he became lost in thought about the perils of combat flying. His mother reassured him: 'I firmly believe that the British would treat you decently.'

He replied simply: 'I believe that also.'

Freifrau von Richthofen did not pursue the subject further, knowing that the mantle of command and the responsibilities of a public figure had changed him. But she felt that some changes – such as his moroseness and aloofness to the point of being almost unapproachable – came from one source: 'I believe he has seen death too often.'

Exercising 21st century hindsight, now it is clear that Manfred von Richthofen continued to suffer from the head wound he received the previous July. But in 1918, heroes felt obligated to bear physical and emotional injuries in dignified silence.

Some 81 years later, in an article in the prestigious British medical journal *The Lancet*, former German naval aviation physician *Dr Med* Henning Allmers wrote about the after-effects of Manfred von Richthofen's head injury:

> **The skull wound was not closed, and the bare bone was probably visible until his death. He was advised not to fly until the wound in his head had healed completely. There is a special mention of the fact that even the surgeon in charge held this opinion in the**

medical file. It was also recorded that "without a doubt there had been a severe concussion of the brain and even more probable a cerebral haemorrhage. For this reason sudden changes in air pressure during flight might lead to disturbances of his consciousness". The record ends with the statement that von Richthofen promised not to resume flying before he had been given permission by a physician.

Dr. Med Allmers also noted:

...A series of medical conferences was held in the autumn of 1916 sponsored by the Prussian Ministry of War concerning the evaluation of fitness for military and combat duty of soldiers who had received injuries or wounds ... According to those recommendations, von Richthofen should not have been allowed to return to active flight duty since he was diagnosed as having a concussion and cerebral haemorrhage. The physicians and surgeons who treated him knew this, as can be concluded from their strong recommendation to von Richthofen not to fly before his head wound had completely healed.

At the end of January 1918, *Rittmeister* Manfred von Richthofen returned to duty. His aeroplane had been removed to Breslau for maintenance and he went there by train to continue on to Berlin by air. As he and his sister Ilse drove away from their house on Striegauer Strasse, *Freifrau* von Richthofen stood by a window at the top of the stairs and called out: *'Auf Wiedersehen* – Until we meet again, my boy.'

At the railway station, Ilse reinforced the message in the candid, direct way that siblings employ: 'Please be a bit careful, [as] we do want to see you again.'

'Can you imagine, Ilse, that I could ever die in some wretched bed of straw?' he responded in a like manner.

Later that day, to keep the peace with another family member, Richthofen made a low pass over the Cadet Academy in Wahlstatt. Bolko and the other cadets ran out on to the parade ground, giving the pilot of the well-known red two-seater a good target on which to empty a box of candies. No doubt, the boys enjoyed their first aerial assault.

The *Kommandeur* spent only a short time in Berlin before returning to the Front to begin preparations for the spring offensive. Lothar had returned home with a severe inflammation of the inner ear, which made Manfred's return all the more important for morale purposes.

On 2 February, *Jagdgeschwader II* (comprising *Jastas 12, 13, 15* and *19*) was formed in the 7th Army area and *JG III* (*Jastas 2, 26, 27* and *36*) was established within the 4th Army Sector. The return of the first *Jagdgeschwader-Kommandeur*, now in the 2nd Army Sector, reflected a unity of force along the Flanders Front. Manfred wrote to his mother on 11 February:

> It is too bad that my duties in Berlin dragged on so long that I could not come back to Schweidnitz once more. It would have been so nice and I would have enjoyed it very much. Now I think I will not be able to come back to Germany for a long time.
>
> Lothar should stay at home as long as possible; he is very careless with his ears and does nothing at all to take care of them. He is missing nothing here. I want him to know that he should not come back before the 1st of March. Should things start up strongly here, I will notify him by wire.

Two days later, an old problem returned when *Jasta 11* pilot *Leutnant* Hans Joachim Wolff, flying a Fokker Triplane south of his own airfield, watched the spar and leading edge of his top wing collapse. Only an emergency landing saved him and the aeroplane, but the incident raised further doubts about the Fokker Triplane. It would be at least two months until the new Fokker D.VII biplane would be delivered to front line units; hence, Wolff's Triplane incident added to Richthofen's concerns about the coming offensive.

Another great challenge would be to have *JG I* function as an organized air fighting force. He knew that his pilots enjoyed displaying their flying skill, like knights of old, glorying more in the thrill of the fight than in the overall results. But now Richthofen needed to channel individual ambition into the group objective if the German Air Force was to defeat the combined air arms of Britain, France and the United States.

Consequently, he began to develop an air combat manual, an expanded version of Boelcke's dicta, with the added scope of Richthofen's experiences from lone pilot to *Jagdgeschwader* leadership. Highlights of the document are:

Everyone must show absolute trust in the leader in the air. If this trust is lacking, success is impossible from the outset. The *Staffel* gains trust by [the leader's] exemplary daring and the conviction that [he] sees everything and shows himself to be up to every situation ...

When a single-seater is put on the defensive, thus if his guns jam, if he is separated from the *Staffel*, or his engine is shot-up [or] is defective, if he has to come down low or something like that, [or] if far on the other side he faces a superior opponent who attacks him energetically, he is defenceless ...

I insist on target practice in flight and at high altitude in tight turns and at full throttle. If a pilot satisfies me in all of the points [just] discussed, then he will make the very image of the available types who can be trusted at the Front ...

The greatest danger for a single-seater is the surprise attack from behind. A very large number of our best and most experienced fighter pilots were surprised and shot down from behind. The opponent looks for the most favourable moment to attack the rearmost aircraft of a flight section. He dives on him from out of the sun and can cause him to go down with a few shots. Without fail, everyone must give the highest consideration [to the air space] behind him.

During this hectic time, Richthofen suffered another loss when 27-year-old *Leutnant der Reserve* Hans Klein, leader of *Jasta 10*, was wounded during a fight on 19 February. Replacing a 22-victory ace such as Klein was nearly impossible, but the *Kommandeur* had a 'system' that worked. There was an abundance of talent within *JG I*, as Richthofen – like Boelcke before him – devoted considerable time to 'driving around to the Fighter Pilot Schools and [other] *Jagdstaffeln* and had observed operations' to identify promising new pilots he could develop into skilled air fighters. Hence, he quickly replaced Klein with *Leutnant der Reserve* Hans Weiss, who at age 25 had already shot down 12 enemy aircraft.

After the United States of America entered the war on 6 April 1917, German military planners recognized America's potential to supply men and material, but knew that they still had time to achieve a decisive victory in Europe. German Air Force Commanding General von Hoeppner concluded that:

...a quite substantial increase in enemy air power must be counted on by spring 1918 at the latest.

Anticipating a race to ultimate victory, German forces on the Western Front were bolstered by the steady infusion of fresh, little-used troops from the Eastern Front, where a peace settlement had been concluded on 3 March 1918. Three attack plans were proposed: 'Michael,' on both sides of St. Quentin; 'Mars,' near Arras; and 'Georg,' near Armentières. *General* Erich Ludendorff selected 'Operation Michael' and German units prepared for it.

For his part, on 28 February, Manfred von Richthofen ordered *JG I*'s forward airfield to be established at Awoingt, about 15 kilometres (nine miles) south-west of Avesnes le Sec and closer to the front lines. Once again, Allied intelligence caught wind of this development and related moves by interrogating a German fighter pilot who had been shot down.

According to that source:

> [The] 'Pfalz [D.III] scout is not popular with pilots owing to its lack of speed and its bad manoeuvrability; an improved type is expected. Richthofen's squadron [*Geschwader*] is being equipped with Fokker Triplanes with a much improved aileron control ... [and] Fokker Triplanes have recently been received and are to take the place of the Albatros scouts; this accounts for the high number of machines at present with the flight, the normal number being 15–16 machines. The strength of pilots [in a *Jasta*] is never more than 10–12 on an average, either in his flight or in the majority of pursuit flights, but [the prisoner] believes that special steps are taken to keep the flights in von Richthofen's squadron up to higher establishment.

JG I received its complement of new Fokker Triplanes after the wing construction problem had been resolved, but now the *Jagdgeschwader* was dogged by operational problems. Richthofen felt that his units were being poorly deployed by *Hauptmann* Wilhelm Haehnelt, Officer in Charge of Aviation for the 2nd Army. As in the past, he sought intervention by Fritze von Falkenhayn, as his letter of 27 February stated:

A few days ago I sent you a report about the Rizinus-*Ersatz* [synthetic lubricant produced from coal tars] relative to rotary engines. I am of the opinion that, due to the poor [-quality] oil (Rizinus-*Ersatz*) that is available to us, rotary engines are no longer suitable for this war. Therefore, I set no high value on having rotary engines in my *Geschwader*, even when they produce 200 horsepower. As the situation is now, I would prefer to have the Fokker [D.VII] with the BMW engine or the supercharged Mercedes. Should the Fokkers be issued with unsupercharged engines, I would not refuse them.

Here there is mostly bad weather and extremely scant enemy flying activity in our Army Sector. Furthermore, I [now feel like] the leader of four [low-level ground support units] under Haehnelt and no longer as *Jagdgeschwader-Kommandeur*, which after a year-and-a-half of fighter aviation is a change. I do not want it said that the change is excessively interesting.

The British are much busier in the 17th and also the 6th Army Sectors than here on our Front. My brother will arrive here tomorrow and is again in good health, as he confirms. He has missed nothing, only some ground-support flights, which he would have put up with, but no aerial combat.

Richthofen wanted operational independence, but this time he had to accept a subordinate role and be careful about criticizing his immediate superior. *Hauptmann* Haehnelt, a pre-war military pilot with a distinguished record, also had many connections in high places. He was not to be out-manoeuvred in air operations matters as Otto Bufe had been.

In the weeks before the spring offensive, members of *JG I* used an invented word to describe their desire to meet their adversaries. They interjected into conversations the word '*kuk*,' short for '*Komme und kämpfe*' [Come over and fight].

Their wish was fulfilled late on the morning of 12 March, when ten Bristol F.2Bs were reported south-east of *JG I*'s airfields. Manfred and Lothar von Richthofen and *Leutnant* Werner Steinhäuser attacked the formation and shot down four of them. Flying a new, mostly red Fokker Triplane in combat for the first time, Manfred von Richthofen claimed his 64th victory. Lothar von Richthofen, once criticized by his brother for being more of a 'shooter' than a 'hunter,' charged into the Bristol Fighter flight and shot down two aeroplanes, credited as his 28th and 29th victories. Lothar's bold style of aerial combat – vs Manfred's more calculating manner – may have thrown the F.2B flight into disarray and driven some of its members before the guns of the other Triplanes.

For the second time, the Number 13 proved unlucky for Lothar von Richthofen, who had already been shot down on 13 May 1917. Now, on … 13 March 1918, his Triplane was one of 35 *JG I* aircraft that had massed to attack 11 Bristol Fighters, which were escorting Airco DH4 two-seaters and were joined by two flights of Sopwith F.1 Camels. Manfred shot down one of the Sopwith Camels, scoring his 65th victory, but one of the Bristol Fighter crews claimed to have shot down a Triplane that lost its top wing, thereby hastening its departure from the fight. That must have been Lothar and, just as he was approaching *Jasta 11*'s advance airfield at Awoingt, his aeroplane hit a high-tension wire and crashed.

Manfred von Richthofen's latest triumph was muted by his brother's crash. A participant in that fight, *Leutnant* Friedrich Wilhelm Lübbert, recalled:

> The *Rittmeister* was among the last to land. Only his brother Lothar was missing. When Richthofen landed, his first question was: "Is Lothar back?" The answer: "No, but it was observed that the top wing of his Triplane fell off at 5,500 metres [18,000 feet] and that he went down in a glide."
>
> Calmly, Richthofen went with the pilots to the operations hut. No news had come in yet. Suddenly there was a report by telephone: "*Leutnant* von Richthofen has crashed near Cambrai and is dead." Shortly thereafter a second report came in: "*Leutnant* von Richthofen has made an emergency landing and has badly injured an eye." No one knew which report gave the actual facts. Everyone spoke in depressed tones.
>
> The *Rittmeister*'s facial features did not change in the least. "We must wait," he said and very calmly went into a critique of the day's flight. "By the way, I have shot down two today," he said in the midst of things and rather casually.
>
> When no further news came in after a long time, he got into his crate and flew to the crash site in order to determine for himself

more about the fate of his brother, whose injuries turned out to be relatively light, fortunately, despite the hard crash.

Manfred von Richthofen reassured his mother by telegram and then, a week later, wrote:

> You have of course meanwhile received my telegram, notifying you of Lothar's crash. Thank God, he is doing very well. I visit him daily. So, please, do not worry about anything. He is really doing very well.
> His nasal bone has already healed, only the jawbone has been cracked, but all of the teeth have been saved. Over the right eye he has a big gash, but the eye itself has not been damaged. On the right knee some blood vessels have burst, [and] on the left leg from the calf down, likewise some haemorrhaging.
> The blood that he coughed up did not come from any internal injuries; rather, he swallowed it in the crash. He is in hospital in Cambrai and hopes to be up and about in fourteen days. He regrets very much only that he cannot be with us now.

Manfred von Richthofen's search for promising pilots and prospective *Staffel* leaders was voracious. Upon learning that *Jagdstaffel 37* had been transferred from the 4th Army Sector in Flanders to the 2nd Army Sector in which he now operated, he hopped into his small Opel car during the rain on Friday, 15 March, and headed to Le Cateau airfield in hopes of recruiting that *Staffel's* current commanding officer.

Bold and daring, 21-year-old *Leutnant der Reserve* Ernst Udet had shot down his first aeroplane two years earlier, went on to shoot down 19 more and had attained the criteria needed to qualify for the *Pour le Mérite*. Richthofen was certain Udet would make a fine *Staffel* leader in *JG I*. Udet recalled that Richthofen asked him about his current score of confirmed aerial victories:

> He poked his oak walking stick into the wet leaves. "Hmmm.
> So, 20 in all," he repeated. He glanced up and looked at me in a scrutinizing way. "Then you would really be ready for us. Would you like to [join us]?"

Would I like to? Of course I would like to. I would like it enormously. And if I had any say in the matter, I would have packed up immediately and gone back with him. There were many good *Jagdstaffeln* in the [2nd] Army and *Jasta 37* was not the worst. But there was only one *Jagdgeschwader Richthofen*.

"Yes, indeed, *Herr Rittmeister*," I said. We shook hands. I watched as he – small and slender – almost elegantly scrambled down the steep slope. He climbed into his car and disappeared in the next wave of the cloak of rain.

Richthofen prepared for every eventuality. That evening, he handed an envelope with the *Geschwader* wax seal on it to *Oberleutnant* Karl Bodenschatz, his adjutant. It was to be opened in the event the *Kommandeur* did not return from the Front, as the envelope contained Richthofen's official testament, designating his successor.

The following day, Richthofen made another preparation when he relieved *Leutnant* Kurt Wüsthoff of command of *Jasta 4*. Wüsthoff a 27-victory ace and *Pour le Mérite* recipient, was transferred to the *Geschwader* staff. According to his successor, *Leutnant* Georg von der Osten:

Leutnant Wüsthoff was a most dashing and successful fighter pilot. For this reason he had been assigned to command *Jasta 4* by Richthofen, at the age of 19! ... I heard that they did not like him very much there. He was ... very much younger than all of his pilots, and he had a very cheeky way. Apart from not being a very sympathetic man, he reported victories that he did not always check. So Richthofen relieved him as *Staffel* leader.

General von Hoeppner inspected *JG I* on 17 March and *Jagdgeschwader-Kommandeur* von Richthofen demonstrated its capabilities late the following morning, when a large formation of British aircraft crossed into the 2nd Army Sector, headed for Le Cateau. Richthofen led 30 aeroplanes from *Jastas 6, 10* and *11* up to 5,300 metres (17,000 feet) and targeted a formation trying to reconnoitre the German rear area. He observed as two of his pilots shot down Bristol Fighters. Then, Richthofen went after a Sopwith Camel and forced it to land within German lines, where it was recorded as his 66th victory.

A member of the German 238th Infantry Division who witnessed the fight noted that while the British fighter was landing:

> ... A German machine circled over him like a bird of prey.
> The Englishman set his aeroplane on the ground about 150 metres
> (500 feet) from us. He climbed out and we brought him into the
> village. The German flyer landed right near the enemy machine,
> climbed out and cut the serial number from the [fuselage] of the
> opponent ... [The German was in] the red machine that had
> circled over us and that everyone waved at. It was *Rittmeister* Manfred
> von Richthofen.

During the following two-day quiet time, *JG I*'s equipment was moved at night to the advance airfield at Awoingt and placed in hangar tents. *Geschwader* aircraft were flown to the new field and placed inside the hangars on the evening of 20 March.

At 0445 hours the following day, a thunderstorm of German heavy artillery fire of the 2nd, 17th and 18th Armies opened along a 70-kilometre (42-mile) battle line. The German spring offensive had begun.

German 2nd Army Air Commander Haehnelt divided the Sector into two aerial combat areas. Richthofen was in charge of Zone North, a box-shaped area bounded by Marcoing-Ytres-Longavesnes-Vendhuille. In addition to commanding *JG I*, Richthofen also had charge of the smaller fighter group *Jagdgruppe 2 (Jastas 5 and 46)* for this operation. Zone South was assigned to another Regular Army officer, *Oberleutnant* Hermann Kohze, a fighter pilot with three victories to his credit; Kohze was responsible for *Jagdgruppe 9 (Jastas 3, 37, 54 and 56)* and *Jagdgruppe 10 (Jastas 16 and 34b)*. A total of 150 German fighter aircraft were prepared to carry out a massive aerial assault against their adversaries.

Haehnelt's plan called for Richthofen and *Jasta 11* to lead the air attack, taking off at 0900 hours, 45 minutes prior to the infantry assault, to protect German reconnaissance aircraft and suppress British aircraft and tethered observation balloons. But a heavy morning mist made early flying impossible and the first *JG I* aircraft did not leave until after noon. *Jasta 10*'s 'balloon busters' destroyed two balloons, which, from among Richthofen's great air armada's 52 sorties that day, were the *Geschwader*'s only confirmed victories.

Bad weather over the next two days did not deter flying activity on both sides of the lines. On the 23rd, *JG I* flew 80 nearly full strength sorties, but had nothing to show for the effort.

On the 24th, 105 sorties were flown, including 15 aerial combats, resulting in a Fokker Triplane loss and a victory. The latter, Manfred von Richthofen's 67th air triumph, was scored while the *Kommandeur* led an overwhelming force against British fighters. He must have looked like the apparition of red death in his first combat in the red Fokker Triplane Dr.I 477/17.

The following day, he scored *JG I*'s only aerial success, which was also his 68th victory. Later that day, *Leutnant der Reserve* Ernst Udet reported for duty at Awoingt. He described Richthofen's method of greeting new pilots, even high-scoring aces:

I arrived at 10:00 [a.m.] and at 12:00 I took off on my first flight with *Jagdstaffel* 11 ... [Richthofen] attached great importance to personally testing every newcomer.

On 26 March, Udet flew again with Richthofen and watched the *Kommandeur* seal the fate of his 69th aerial victory. And then his 70th, as described in the combat report:

A quarter-hour after the first [aircraft of the day] was shot down, I encountered an RE two-seater at exactly the same location at about 700 metres (2,300 feet). I went into a dive behind it and fired about 100 rounds at close range [and] set it on fire. At first the observer defended the British [aircraft] with his machine gun. [Then] the aircraft burned until it hit the ground. A half-hour later the aeroplane was still burning on the ground.

That aeroplane from No. 15 Squadron came down less than 20 kilometres (12 miles) from its former airfield at Lechelle, which, with the rapid advance of German forces, had recently been assigned to *JG I*. That evening, the airfield was German-occupied, but could not be used until numerous shell holes in the landing area were filled. Richthofen's men expected to find better accommodation than they had at Awoingt and were disappointed to have only sturdy, unadorned Nissen huts. *Kommandeur* von Richthofen had another desire. He had hoped the British had left about 15,000 litres (4,000 U.S. gallons) of aviation fuel to bolster his meagre and lower-quality supplies, but found only 1,500 litres (400 U.S. gallons). At least the Lechelle airfield put *JG I* closer to the Front.

British air units crossed into newly gained German territory the next day and 'concentrated on low bombing and machine-gunning enemy infantry in the neighbourhood of Cambrai, Bapaume, Peronne and Chaulnes.' Richthofen anticipated the attack and was ready for it. His Adjutant commented: 'Now [Richthofen] could show the infantry that he was there when they needed him.'

27 March 1918 was one of the most successful days in *Jagdgeschwader I*'s history: 118 sorties flown, 39 inconclusive aerial combats and 13 successful air fights, including Manfred von Richthofen's 71st, 72nd and 73rd aerial victories.

The next afternoon, Richthofen shot down his 74th enemy aircraft.

Kommandeur von Richthofen attracted a variety of fighting men to *JG I*. In the case of *Oberleutnant* Walther Karjus, the man's tenacity must have moved Richthofen to recruit him to *Jasta 11*. A hard-fighting observer and recipient of the Knight's Cross of the House Order of Hohenzollern, Karjus had been so badly wounded, his right arm had to be amputated. Being fitted with a prosthetic device made aerial photography and other observer duties impossible, so he became a pilot and then a flight instructor.

When Richthofen saw Karjus flying at Army Air Park 2, he asked how a combat pilot could fly with one hand. 'Very simple,' Karjus replied, 'I have had the control column and the gun firing lever modified [to be worked with one hand].' Following his arrival on 30 March, Karjus was nicknamed 'the Götz von Berlichingen of the air,' alluding to the medieval poet and knight whose prosthetic device was an iron claw.

Richthofen was less happy to also attract political figures who wanted a link – and publicity about – their support of Germany's great heroes. The initial success of the German spring offensive led a group of *Reichstag* [Parliament] representatives to visit Lechelle.

Arriving at the airfield by limousine, the legislators paraded around as if they were at a social event. One politician even wore a cutaway coat, which, with frequent bowing and gesturing, made his coat-tails sway like the tail of a mocking bird. The pilots had to stifle their laughter.

Much less amusing, however, were long speeches at dinner in the Officers'sMess. 'When you motor on against the enemy in your flying machine, *Herr Baron* . . .' one speaker began. Manfred von Richthofen listened in stony silence.

The small Nissen huts used by *Geschwader* members were the only sleeping quarters available. No doubt, the politicians would tell their constituents that they, too, had endured front line hardships.

Among the pilots, mischief was afoot. One flyer suggested: 'They must be allowed to experience more of the war before they return home tomorrow.'

Another added: 'Air raid!'

Now being of a common mind, they and their accomplices went in different directions to put their plan into action. *Leutnant* Hans Joachim Wolff for example, 'armed' himself with a flare pistol and some colourful 'ammunition.'

Ernst Udet recalled:

> Inside the barracks there was a clattering, the crackle of gunfire and the dull thud of bombs being detonated. Right after that [there was] an outcry.
>
> It was a night with a full moon. We stood hidden in the dark shadows of the other barracks. Suddenly, across the way, the door flew open and out charged three forms in flapping white nightshirts. The Rittmeister laughed so hard that tears ran down his cheeks. "Air raid! Back into the barracks!" thundered a mighty voice across the airfield and, on a frantic run, the three white forms disappeared back behind the door.
>
> The next morning, they got under way hurriedly. They did not even have breakfast with us. We laughed for a long time afterward. The joys ... [at the Front] are very few and whenever there is a chance for some fun, one enjoys it gratefully and for a long time...

13
BLOODY APRIL 1918

At first glance, April 1918 seemed to offer Germany hope for a repeat of the history of April 1917. British air operations under clear skies on Monday, 1 April 1918 – the day the Royal Flying Corps and the Royal Naval Air Service were amalgamated to create the Royal Air Force – resulted in 'comparatively heavy' RAF casualties: 'Ten aeroplanes ... missing, 38 wrecked ... and four destroyed as a result of [a] German bombing raid ...' But the big difference in 1918 is seen in the RAF casualties: 'Of the 38 wrecked [aircraft], 12 had suffered severe damage through [German] anti-aircraft or rifle and machine gun fire. The remainder were wrecked through forced descent owing to engine failure, or through faulty landings.' Not through an onslaught of superior German aircraft, as had happened a year earlier.

Indeed, the issue of the *Nachrichtenblatt der Luftstreitkräfte*, the German Air Force Commanding General's weekly report, sent to all air units 11 days later, made no mention of flight operations on that day, although weather conditions were ideal. *Jagdgeschwader I*'s war diary entry for 1 April recorded 106 combat missions, five aerial victories and no losses. The bigger picture portrayed – or neglected – in the *Nachrichtenblatt* was further evidence that, over the previous year, Germany's technological edge was eroding and its air arm was falling further into numerical inferiority, thereby dulling its sting.

Manfred von Richthofen had no air triumphs on the first day, but he led the scoring on 2 April. During a noon patrol over the woods at Moreuil, he caught an RE8 reconnaissance aircraft unawares and sent him down in flames.

That afternoon, while a *Jasta 11* advanced airfield was being established at Harbonnières, about 34 kilometres (20 miles) south-west of Cappy, Richthofen was having a pleasant chat with *Oberleutnant* Peter Lampel, a bomber pilot passing through Lechelle who had the good fortune of being introduced to the Red Baron and then invited to stay for a late lunch. The new location provided the *Staffel* with an operating field to refuel and re-arm about eight kilometres (five miles) from the front lines, instead of having to return to Lechelle between fights.

As expected, Lampel queried his host about his current victory tally and was astounded to learn that Richthofen's 75th victim had fallen a few hours earlier.

While his guest sat in stunned silence, Richthofen took the unusual step of revealing some of his inner thinking:

> It is peculiar... but the last ten I shot down all burned. The one I got today also burned. I saw it quite well. At the beginning, it was only quite a small flame under the pilot's seat, but when the machine dived, and the tail stood up in the air, I could see that the seat had been burned through.
>
> The flames kept on showing as the machine dashed down. It crashed on the ground with a terrible explosion – worse than I have ever witnessed before. It was a two-seater, but its [crew] defended themselves well ...
>
> I had to come up quite close. I believe that observer, whoever he was, was a ... first-class fighting man. He was a devil for courage and energy. I flew within five yards of him, until he had enough, and that in spite of the fact I believe I had hit him before. Even to the very last minute, he kept shooting at me. The slightest mistake, and I should have rammed him in the air...
>
> It is a strange feeling ... when one has again shot dead a pair of human beings; they lie out there somewhere, cremated, and [I] come back here to a normal table and the food tastes as good as ever. I once said that to His Majesty, when the Kaiser invited me to dine. Yet, His Majesty said nothing more to me than: "My soldiers do not shoot people dead; my soldiers annihilate the opponent."

The conversation was interrupted when *Geschwader* Adjutant Karl Bodenschatz burst into the small dining room with an urgent telegram from Air Force Headquarters. It said that Richthofen had been awarded an unusually high decoration, the Order of the Red Eagle Third Class with Crown and Swords, in honour of his 70th victory. Bodenschatz read aloud from the Commanding General's telegram:

> It is again a great joy for me to... express to you my congratulations [upon attaining] this high and seldom-bestowed decoration. Wear it as a mark of the very highest recognition for what you have proved in three years of war, of the glittering successes that have crowned

your flying actions and of the gratitude of your King for all you have accomplished in the mighty battles of the last two weeks at the head of your *Geschwader* as the champion of German air power.

Ordinarily, that grade of the Order of the Red Eagle was presented to colonels or lieutenant-colonels at the peaks of their careers; hence, Richthofen was the lowest ranked recipient and the only airman to receive the distinction for bravery in the face of the enemy during World War I. Later that day, he confided to Peter Lampel that the award was most likely a 'consolation' arranged by high-ranking admirers whose requests for a higher honour were refused, Richthofen said:

> I know that [at the time of] my 70th victory, Ludendorff himself forwarded a nomination for me to be awarded the Oak Leaves to the *Pour le Mérite*. But the All-Highest Cabinet Council members proved quite clearly that I could not receive this award because it was [to be presented] only for winning a battle. *General* Ludendorff, of course, said: "Richthofen has won more than a battle."

Clearly, Richthofen enjoyed his fame and recognition, but he understood that his current success was short-term and he needed long-term help if his *Geschwader* were to prevail. In the sector south of Arras, for example, he knew that Germany enjoyed numerical superiority (822 vs. the RAF's 645 aircraft), but that was little compensation for the improved quality of Anglo-French aircraft.

Conditions were different on other Fronts, and the balance would change, Richthofen knew, as Anglo-French squadrons and their American allies continued to receive more new aircraft. He was certain that German superiority could be regained only by the swift arrival of new, improved fighter aircraft.

In the end on 2 April, Richthofen wrote once more to his friend and best contact at Air Force Headquarters in Berlin, *Oberleutnant* Fritze Falkenhayn, to ask when the *Jastas* would receive the badly needed new Fokker biplane fighter aircraft and improved engines he had seen demonstrated at the manufacturers' competition in January. Richthofen noted with urgency:

The superiority of British single-seat and reconnaissance aircraft makes it even more perceptibly unpleasant here. The single-seaters fight coming over [at high altitude] and stay up there. We cannot even shoot at them. The two-seaters drop their bombs without our being able to reach them. Speed is the most important point. We could shoot down five to ten times as many [enemy aircraft] if we were faster. During the offensive we liked the low cloud ceiling (100 metres (300 feet)), because at low altitude the Triplane has its advantages. We could not fly at all with the super-compressed Siemens [-Schuckert] engine, for, as we discussed, [it took] two hours to get from 50 up to 700 metres (160 to 2,300 feet). So please give me news soon about when we can count on [receiving] new machines.

The need has become very great now, as every emergency landing in the old bombarded area of the Somme wasteland leads without fail to a total wreck. After aerial combat, frequently one must land urgently; consequently, [there are] very many wrecks.

For the moment, however, Richthofen's newest aircraft were Fokker Triplanes, and he made best use of them by basing them close to the front lines so they could devote more time over the lines. Rainy weather on 5 April offered good cover to erect enough hangar tents at the Harbonnières forward airfield for two *Staffeln*.

The following day, *Jagdgeschwader I* flew 106 sorties and shot or forced down nine British aircraft. Low clouds and rain made it more difficult for the aerial combatants to find each other, but about mid-afternoon, Richthofen spotted a Sopwith Camel at the edge of Hamel Wood, and closed in for the kill. He was above and behind and at fairly low altitude when he let loose a burst of fire that hit the Sopwith's fuel tank. Richthofen reported that his 76th victim:

...began to burn after only a few shots from my guns. Then it crashed burning near the little wood north-east of Villers-Bretonneux, where it continued to burn on the ground.

During favourable weather on Sunday, 7 April, *JG I* aircraft shot down four British fighters within 35 minutes along a small corridor straddling the Roman Road east of Amiens. Two of them were Richthofen victories, one downed near Hangard, the second brought down north of Villers-Bretonneux. His 77th aerial victory was flown by Second Lieutenant Albert V. Gallie of No. 73 Squadron. The aircraft fell apart, but Gallie was uninjured.

Richthofen's next opponent was Lieutenant Ronald Adams, who went on to fame on the stage and screen under the name Ronald Adam. As related in correspondence to the author, Adams was flying a Sopwith Camel with 'B' Flight of No. 73 Squadron, RAF, that day. He and four squadronmates joined with 'A' and 'C' Flights on an offensive patrol near Amiens, looking for 'the Richthofen Circus.' As the 18 Camels headed east, Adams' mechanical fuel pump malfunctioned and he began using a hand pump to assure a steady flow of gasoline, when his squadron encountered Fokker Triplanes and Albatroses east of Villers-Brettoneux. It must have been an odd sight, he admitted, flying with one hand and pumping with the other.

Clearly, Adams fuel pump problem would not allow him to continue with his comrades and he had to withdraw from the fight. He recalled:

> No sooner had I tried to turn for our lines when, with a crash
> behind me, a bullet entered my tank and the pressure disappeared
> forever. True, I had a gravity tank, which did not need pressure.
> I had not turned it on before, as it held only a half-hour's petrol, but
> on to it I turned now.
>
> Nothing happened and 200 feet below me I saw Richthofen's
> aerodrome [at Harbonnières], with machines and mechanics out in
> front of the sheds. In a last despairing effort I pointed the nose of
> my machine at them and [as the machine guns had malfunctioned]
> pressed my useless triggers. I shouted with idiot laughter as the
> mechanics scattered and fell about in fear of me, and then madness
> seemed to take hold of me. Better dead than captured – and all the
> time the Triplane was firing into me. Better dead than captured –
> and I saw a railway line below me. I put my nose straight down and
> ... went into the rails. There was one colossal crash, a series of
> somersaults, and I came to, upside down and dangling in the
> machine by my feet, while my head and shoulders rested on the
> [railway ties]. The Triplane had at last stopped firing.

Adams was taken to a prisoner holding cell in Proyart and visited that evening by a German orderly, who informed him: '*Freiherr* von Richthofen's compliments. You are his 79th [sic] victory.' Richthofen's description of Adams aircraft as a

SPAD added confusion to the claim, but German authorities accepted it as the *Rittmeister*'s 78th air combat triumph.

As in the glory days of a year earlier, Richthofen continued to receive praise from senior commanders, including this citation from the Commanding General of the Air Force: 'In the 2nd Army Sector, despite bad weather in the time from 3 to 7 April, 943 combat flights were carried out and 29 enemy aircraft [were] shot down, 12 of which [were] by *Jasta 11* of *Jagdgeschwader I* ...'

Then, as if combat conditions were not bad enough, Richthofen received confirmation that his newest and brightest star – *Leutnant der Reserve* Ernst Udet – had a pus discharge in one ear (suppuration) and would need to be hospitalised in Germany. Always a tough character, Udet delayed treatment as long as possible, and even shot down his 23rd enemy aircraft on 6 April, despite being in excruciating pain the whole time. Udet's protests that he could continue to serve were to no avail. 'Out here at the Front one must be healthy,' Richthofen chided him.

Udet recalled Richthofen's absolute insistence on the matter:

It was very hard for me to give up my new *Staffel* now, to break off my success in the middle. [Richthofen] knew that, more or less, we all believed in the old rule of not breaking a lucky streak. Then next morning he brought me himself to the old two-seater that we flew in the rear areas. He stayed at the airfield during the take-off and waved at me with his cap. His blonde hair glistened in the sun.

Udet left for home in Bavaria on 8 April. The following day he became the 35th fighter pilot to be awarded the *Orden Pour le Mérite*. Udet was succeeded as leader of *Jasta 11* by 25-year-old *Leutnant der Reserve* Hans Weiss, a Richthofen protégé who knew the war from a ground soldier's perspective and had been an aggressive two-seater pilot. He had earned rapid promotion, a Reserve commission and was ready for the hard struggle ahead.

Richthofen would send other people away for medical treatment, but his own devotion to the *Geschwader* was such that he would not even consider changing his own status. When his father suggested days earlier that, with 75 victories to his credit, Manfred could retire honourably from combat, the son quickly cited his obligation to set an example of devotion to duty, of the driving need to succeed in aerial combat and support the men in the trenches.

Rain the following day was an ideal setting for a shift of emphasis to the Second German Drive of 1918 (also known as the Lys Offensive) along the German 4th and 6th Army Sectors. Further, that distraction brought a relatively quiet period to the 2nd Army Sector. The new offensive began on 9 April, coincidentally *General* Erich Ludendorff's 53rd birthday, and it was Germany's last opportunity to drive a wedge between the British Expeditionary Force, in the hope of impeding Allied prospects for victory on the ground.

In hopeful anticipation of German success, Richthofen took advantage of the bad weather to order a new airfield prepared south of Cappy – to bring his men some 20 kilometres (12 miles) closer to the front lines. By Friday, 12 April, the new field was operational and Richthofen ordered a midday attack, which resulted in four *JG I* aerial victories. Two casualties also occurred, with one man being wounded and another killed – losses the German Air Force could not afford. *JG I*'s four victories from 8 to 14 April were meagre results within the overall German claim of 58 confirmed victories. For that matter, the German successes compared poorly with the Royal Air Force's claim of 69 enemy aircraft shot down and another six brought down by anti-aircraft or ground machine gun fire during the same six-day period, despite the weather conditions that hampered air operations along the Front.

Indeed, the weather and lack of opportunity for victory in the air, as well as his own – albeit unadmitted – need to take leave and tromp about in a serene forest far from the Front may have contributed to a period of reflection that was not in keeping with Manfred von Richthofen's usual, if even occasionally forced, generally high spirits.

Whatever the case, at about this time Richthofen put pen to paper to record inner thoughts that were far more sombre than earlier writings. They were so out of character with other writings, in fact, that they did not appear publicly until 15 years after his death. By the time the short essay – titled 'Thoughts in a Dugout' – appeared in the 1933 edition of *Der rote Kampfflieger*, Richthofen was being portrayed as the ultimate dedicated, conscientious German hero who had given everything for his country, but had not been totally hardened by the war. It is worth noting that, even though he had not lived in a dugout since the spring of 1915, the essay's title reveals the emotional link he still felt to the ground troops:

In my dugout there hangs from the ceiling a lamp that I had made from a [rotary] aircraft engine. It came from an airplane that I had

shot down. I mounted light bulbs in the cylinders and at night, when I lie awake and let the light burn, Lord knows, this chandelier on the ceiling looks fantastic and weird enough. When I lie like that I have much to think about.

I write this down without knowing whether anyone other than my closest relatives will ever see [it]. I am thinking about doing a continuation of *Der rote Kampfflieger* and, indeed, for quite a good reason. The battle now taking place on all Fronts has become dreadfully serious; there is nothing left of the "lively, merry war," as our deeds were called in the beginning. Now we must arm ourselves against despair so that the enemy will not violate our country.

I now have the deepest impression that from [the image of] the "red battle flyer," people have been exposed to quite another Richthofen than I truly am deep inside of myself. When I read [my] book, I smile at my own insolence. No longer am I so insolent in spirit. Not because I can imagine how it would be one day when death is breathing down my neck; surely not for that reason, although I have thought about it often enough that it can happen. I have been told by [people in] high places that I should give up flying, for one day it will catch up with me. I would be miserable with myself if now, burdened with glory and decorations, I were to become a pensioner of my own dignity in order to save my precious life for the nation, while every poor fellow in the trenches endures his duty as I do mine.

I am in wretched spirits after every aerial combat. But that is surely one of the consequences of my head wound. When I put my foot on the ground again at the airfield, I go [directly] to my four walls, I do not want to see anyone or hear anything. I believe that [the war] is not as the people at home imagine it, with a hurrah and a roar; it is very serious, very grim...

But even cloudy skies early on the evening of 20 April offered some prospects for contact with the enemy. Manfred von Richthofen was in his all-red Fokker, leading a flight of Triplanes from *Jasta 11*, looking for targets along the old Roman Road near Villers-Bretonneux, when he spotted a flight of Sopwith Camels.

As he wrote in his combat report:

> With six aeroplanes of *Jasta 11*, I attacked a large enemy formation.
> During the fight, I observed that a Triplane was attacked and shot at
> from below by a Camel. I put myself behind the adversary and
> brought him down, burning, with only a few shots. The enemy
> aeroplane crashed near Hamel Forest, where it burned further on
> the ground.

The RAF flight leader, Captain Douglas J. Bell, MC, claimed to have engaged
and shot down one of the Triplanes: 'I saw one Camel in flames, and another
catch fire, but fire appeared to go out. The 'plane, when last seen, was absolutely
out of control.'

Bell may have witnessed Richthofen and Hans Weiss, each attacking a Camel
at about the same time. One Camel may have been on Weiss' tail and, in saving
his comrade, Richthofen shot down Bell's squadronmate.

After Richthofen determined that his first victim of the day was finished,
he went after another Camel from the same flight. In his next combat report,
he wrote:

> Three minutes after I brought down the first machine, I attacked a
> second Camel of the same enemy formation. The adversary dived,
> caught his machine and repeated this manoeuvre several times.
> I approached him as close as possible when fighting and fired 50
> bullets until his machine began to burn. The fuselage of the
> machine was burned in the air, the remnants dashed to the ground,
> north-east of Villers-Bretonneux.

The pilot of the second British fighter, Second Lieutenant David G. Lewis, then
age 19, came down not far from Richthofen's earlier victim, Major Richard
Raymond-Barker, commanding officer of No. 3 Squadron, RAF. Lewis, who
suffered minor burns but was largely uninjured, recalled: 'About 50 yards from
where I was, Major Barker's machine was burning fiercely, so I staggered
over to him to see if it were possible to pull him out, but was beaten back by
the flames ...'

In the sky, meanwhile, the remaining Sopwith Camels flew home and the flight of *Jasta 11* Fokker triplanes, intact and undefeated, headed back to Cappy airfield to celebrate their leader's 79th and 80th aerial victories. It was an especially joyous occasion for one member of that flight, 22-year-old Hans Joachim Wolff, who worked hard to emulate his idol. After scoring his seventh victory earlier that day, Wolff had been promised that he would accompany Richthofen on his next hunting trip to the famed Black Forest in southern Germany a few days later.

Ordinarily, *Geschwader-Kommandeur* von Richthofen forbade any form of stunt flying by his pilots, but on this noteworthy flight home, that strict rule was suspended. As Hans Joachim Wolff later wrote to Lothar von Richthofen:

> *Herr Rittmeister* must have been just awfully happy about shooting down these two. After the air fight, he flew quite low so that everyone [on the ground] could recognize his red machine and [he] waved to the troop columns and infantrymen. Everyone knew very well who was in the machine and all had seen the burning Englishmen shortly before. Excitedly, the troops waved back and tossed their caps into the air.
>
> After *Herr Rittmeister* landed, he smacked his hands together and said very happily: "Heavens above, 80 is still a decent number." And we were all happy for him and looked at him very enthusiastically.

Typical of the men Manfred von Richthofen attracted to *Jagdstaffel 11* was *Leutnant der Reserve* Richard Wenzl. At the outbreak of war in August 1914, Wenzl enlisted in Field Artillery Regiment Nr. 76 in his home town of Freiburg im Breisgau in the Grand Duchy of Baden, in south-west Germany, and then quickly transferred to the Flying Service. Two months later he gained a Reserve commission and was off for a long stint on the Eastern Front. By spring 1918, he had progressed from two-seat reconnaissance planes to single-seat fighters, gained two confirmed aerial victories and earned the Hohenzollern House Order. When he received orders to *Jasta 11* in late March, he was ready for a German combat pilot's ultimate challenge.

Wenzl was a Richthofen man through and through, as reflected in his view of the events of Sunday, 21 April 1918:

The morning ... was somewhat foggy and very misty so that there was almost no enemy air activity. After a short time, the east wind gained strength and it cleared up. We set out for the airfield. Richthofen had already been waiting a bit for "the Englishmen to get bold." He was in fine spirits. The day before he had shot down his 79th and 80th, about which he expressed his joy openly. His furlough had already been approved. He would go together with *"Wölffchen"* [wolf cub] to Freiburg im Breisgau and from there to the Black Forest for hunting. Everything was prepared, even sleeping car reservations had been obtained in case the lack of flying weather remained.

Richthofen's high spirits rubbed off on us. Everyone was in a good mood. There was all manner of mischief to be made. Richthofen started it. I was trying to take a nap when he tipped over the stretcher I was lying on and did the same to the next person who tried it. I thought it would make a good picture and fetched my camera. Meanwhile, a wise guy tied a wheel chock to the tail of Moritz, Richthofen's much-beloved dog. Richthofen cried out: "Moritz" – one jump and the poor beast succumbed to his fate and ran with the chock in circles. I photographed this moment twice. They are the last photos of the Old Master.

At this moment, some Englishmen streaked overhead toward the Front. In five minutes we were in the air. We flew ... in two flights. This time, [*Leutnant*] Weiss was lower than we [were]. Over the lines we attacked seven Sopwith Camels with red snouts [engine cowl covers] ... Now, the twisting and turning began. As the British were in superior numbers, they did not enter the fight calmly. But then Richthofen's flight came into view. At the same time that they twisted above, there were seven or eight Englishmen below. There was a massive twisting and turning, as often happened in recent days. Most [of the new men] did not come down far because everyone was ready to shoot. Only the "aces" got down into it.

The story continues in the words of *Leutnant* Hans Joachim Wolff, who – along with the *Rittmeister's* cousin *Leutnant* Wolfram *Freiherr* von Richthofen, *Oberleutnant* Walther Karjus and *Vizefeldwebel* Edgar Scholtz – flew with the *Kommandeur* that day:

Scarcely had we arrived at the Front when we saw below us, on this side of the lines in the area of Hamel, about seven Sopwith Camels. Apart from the five of us, [aircraft of] *Jasta 5* were in the area, but much farther on this side, in the vicinity of Sailly le Sec. Above us were still seven Sopwith Camels, part of which attacked *Jasta 5* and part remained above. One or two came down to us. We began to fight. In the course of the battle, I often saw *Herr Rittmeister* close by, but he had not yet shot down anything. From our flight, only *Oberleutnant* Karjus was near me. *Vizefeldwebel* Scholtz fought alongside the Albatroses in the area of Sailly le Sec. *Leutnant* [Wolfram] von Richthofen was not always quite in view, as it was probably his first aerial combat. While *Oberleutnant* Karjus and I fought against two or three Camels, suddenly I saw the red machine near me, as he fired at a Camel that began to spin and then slipped away in a deep dive in a westerly direction. This fight took place on the other side of the lines at the heights above Hamelet.

We had a somewhat strong east wind and thought no further about *Herr Rittmeister*. As I now had some space, I busied myself more with a Camel and fired at him. While the Camel dived, I looked for *Herr Rittmeister* and saw him at extremely low altitude over the Somme [Valley] near Corbie and instinctively shook my head and wondered why *Herr Rittmeister* pursued an opponent so far over the other side. While I also wanted to observe where my victim fell, suddenly I heard machine gun fire behind me. I was being attacked by yet another Camel. Incidentally, this "big gun" had already put 20 hits in my machine. When I luckily got away from him, I looked for *Herr Rittmeister*, and saw no one else there except *Oberleutnant* Karjus, but also not quite in view. It was uncanny, as I certainly had to see *Herr Rittmeister*. We circled the area for a time and were noticed by the British, for we had come down to about 900 metres (2,900 feet) over Corbie, but there was not a trace of *Herr Rittmeister*.

While Karjus and Wolff made their way back to Cappy, Wenzl had already landed and reported what he had seen to *Hauptmann* Wilhelm Reinhard, commanding officer of *Jasta 6* and next most senior officer in the *Geschwader*.

Now I made known my greatest fear. I had the nagging feeling that something had happened to Richthofen. As I flew back, on the other side of the lines, I saw a small machine that had not been there before. This machine appeared to me to be red. As I knew where the position was, *Hauptmann* Reinhard asked me to fly back and reconnoitre it with some comrades. I took off with Karjus and ... [Wolfram von] Richthofen. During the search I lost both of my partners. As it was more dangerous higher up than lower down, I went down to 200 to 300 metres (600 to 900 feet) and tried to find the machine, in the vicinity of which stood another. I could recognize nothing at this distance ...

Geschwader Adjutant Karl Bodenschatz was also busy, trying to learn what had happened to their *Kommandeur* by contacting other front line posts. As he recorded:

... Scarcely has *Leutnant* Richard Wenzl taken off than the Adjutant dragged all the Air Defence Officers to the telephones. None of them can report anything. Now all divisional headquarters in the sector are alerted. In frantic haste, over and over the same sentence: "*Staffel 11* has returned from a combat mission. The *Rittmeister* is missing. The gentlemen of the *Staffel* report that the *Rittmeister* has been brought down. Has a red triplane made an emergency landing in your sector? Has a red triplane been observed landing on this side or the other side of the lines?

... Finally, after what seems to be an eternity, the General Staff officer of the 1st Division reports the following: The artillery observation post of Field Artillery Regiment Nr. 16, *Oberleutnant* Fabian, observed the fight perfectly from Hamel-East. *Oberleutnant* Fabian saw a red triplane land smoothly on Hill 102 north of Vaux-sur-Somme. Immediately after the landing, British infantry ran up and pulled the machine behind the hill.

...*Oberleutnant* Fabian's report is immediately sent to the Commanding General of the Air Force. The *Geschwader* Adjutant requests *Hauptmann* Reinhard's permission to drive to the observation post of Field Artillery Regiment Nr. 16. Perhaps ...

with the trained eyes of a flyer ... the adjutant stares into the
telescope for a long, long time. He searches the terrain thoroughly,
practically centimetre by centimetre. He keeps the lens focused on
Hill 102 for a long, long time, and puts some short, quick questions
to *Oberleutnant* Fabian ... all in vain.

At 2 p.m. [1400 hours], the Adjutant returns ... to the airfield with
burning eyes. Some other infantry officers have passed along
reports, but they contain nothing beyond what Artillery Officer
Fabian has already reported.

More than a decade after the end of the war, several German soldiers who were
in that area also said they witnessed Manfred von Richthofen's landing within
British lines – and his summary execution by his captors. This persistent rumour
has tantalized researchers for decades, but the soldiers' account had not been laid
out in enough detail to prove or disprove the accusation of a war crime allegedly
committed against one of World War I's most celebrated figures.

Hence, it was an exciting discovery when this author happened upon a copy
of the May 1932 issue of the German veterans' magazine *Der Frontsoldat erzählt*
[The Front Line Soldier Recounts] containing the article '*Die Wahrheit über den
Tod Richthofens – Augenzeugenbericht von Hermann Bink*' [The Truth About
Richthofen's Death – Eyewitness Account by Hermann Bink].

Here is Bink's account, with slight editing of redundancies and extraneous
material, as it appeared in a national forum:

In the early days of April [1918] ... our regiment, the 3rd
Grenadiers, took up positions in the area of Hamel, which we
occupied until the beginning of May. Substantial engagements in
our assigned sector did not take place during this time, but aerial
activity on both sides increased. It was on a sunny, warm spring
morning that almost all of the trench crews were enticed out.
Then, there was a sudden whirring in the air on all sides! Everyone
in the [German] trenches cried out: "Richthofen!" Quite right!
I push my telescope to my eye and watch. An exciting event! Only a
few aeroplanes [are out]. Seasoned and determined to attack, the
"red devil," as Richthofen was known to his opponents, [they]
sought out an enemy partner and dived on him. "Bravo!" rang out

from many throats. Every further action was followed with feverish interest and almost breathless silence. The Englishman was forced to land. As customary, once again Richthofen climbed [to a position] above his opponent in order to fire down at him and put him out of action; for, his experience was in that tactic ...

In any case, we – in the 1st Company, which was next to the ominous place – also observed something similar, when we became aware of the steady tack-tack-tack-tack of the machine gun of a German aeroplane. It was about 400 metres (1,300 feet) away from us. Richthofen circled quite low, so we determined that he did not notice his position above the enemy trenches. Then, suddenly, he landed – but quite calmly in a glide – just behind the enemy trenches. Meanwhile, the enemy flyer disappeared. It is possible that the engine of Richthofen's aeroplane was hit and perhaps he was, as well. But in any event, we saw him climb out of the aeroplane alive! Several brown forms fell on him with drawn daggers – or with shiny side arms – and presumably stabbed him. They were British colonial troops, which were opposite us. The cluster of people crowded ever closer to the landing site, so that from our leading position everything had to be tried to keep the excited spectators [on both sides] from having a spontaneous battle; for it would have achieved nothing.

As a living witness of this incident, I am in contact with ... comrades of my Company who can confirm my contention ... But other troop members have also observed the incident described!

When my first account of the eyewitness reports was published in issue No. 9 of the periodical *Kyffhäuser* ... the editorial staff received a concisely worded letter dated 3 February 1930 from Richard Rex ... which said literally: "In ... your journal, comrade Hermann Bink reported about the death of Manfred von Richthofen. As the leader of a section of a signal corps of the [rifle] battalion of Grenadier-Regiment Nr. 1, at this time we were west of Hamel Forest and to the right of Hill 101. I lay on the summit and could see the terrain before me very well. I agree with everything that *Herr* Bink states. For that is the only way it happened. I have long been amazed that until now no one was disturbed by the false [British] claims. Ultimately I believed that as the only [dissenter] I had to keep silent. I am all the more pleased by the true remarks of Herr Bink."

Herr Rex also confirms that, immediately after the landing, Richthofen climbed out of the aeroplane and briskly walked towards the enemy position. At the time, *Herr* Rex gave his report to *Major* [Paul] von Homeyer, who immediately passed along the news.

Another eyewitness ... Hans Rohde of Königsberg, further confirmed my remarks in issue No. 100 of the *Königsberger Tagblatt* [Königsberg Daily News] of 10 April 1930 with the following text: "... At the time I was the leading machine-gunner of a Machine-Gun Company of Infantry Regiment Nr. 43. The position of my gun for anti-aircraft defence was on a summit near the small forest at Hamel. Before us stretched a valley in the direction of Amiens, and we had a clear view for several kilometres. In this valley the scene played out... The British fled and we noticed that von Richthofen set down in a glide with his engine off. He landed undisturbed and thoroughly in order. I followed the process with my excellent Zeiss binoculars for about 2,000 metres (6,500 feet) and saw quite clearly: von Richthofen jumped buoyantly out of the machine, during which a wound affecting his movements definitely was not noticed ... In our view, von Richthofen was healthy when he was taken prisoner. In the afternoon when news of his death became known, it appeared to us eyewitnesses as inconceivable. In addition to myself, of course, many others observed the event. Previously, I had assumed that the details would be known precisely and I am surprised that in the meantime altogether differing accounts are possible."

Due to Richthofen's landing and the spirited departure from the aeroplane, all of us eyewitnesses had the impression that in no case was he mortally wounded. A mortally wounded person no longer jumps out of an aeroplane; on the contrary, he must be hoisted out. A shot originating from the ground did not end Richthofen's career; rather, he was slain in assassination by a bestial non-European. And when a British "eyewitness" maintains he was at Richthofen's "crash" [site] that is a completely irrelevant falsehood; for there was no crash; rather, a smooth landing, which in the first place no one was able to see. When the opponents first saw the newly landed pilot leave his aeroplane, they sprang like rats from their holes to pile on to the victim. And when the feared flyer was made safe, the characters vanished in fear of the German [artillery] fire. Richthofen's aeroplane stood abandoned behind the enemy trenches until the darkness of the fatal day closed in on it, continually observed by us. By daybreak the next morning it had disappeared.

Oddly enough, none of the officially sanctioned German regimental histories of the units involved made any mention of any of their men having seen the distinctive all-red Fokker triplane that came down within their line of sight at or about noon on 21 April 1918. Given Richthofen's prominence and the legend that grew after his death, one might have expected the most miniscule connection to him to be included or highlighted in the regimental histories.

Conversely, the official Australian history of that encounter goes on at length to clarify the role of Australian (and they were not 'colonial' or non-European-ancestry) troops in such a noteworthy moment in World War I history.

This author has tried for over two years to locate survivors of members of the three German regiments mentioned in Hermann Bink's article – mostly to no avail. As the units hailed from the former German province of East Prussia, which was ceded by treaty to the Soviet Union and Poland after World War II, there is an understandable paucity of access to German civilian records from pre-World War II times. Two exceptions were a man who, in the *Frontsoldat erzählt* article, gave his residence as a Western German town that has no record of his ever having lived there, and a man from an Eastern German city, also named in the magazine article, simply 'disappeared' during the tumultuous 1930s.

The author would like to have learned more about the spectacular view of events that Hans Rohde of Infantry Regiment Nr. 43 saw through his 'excellent Zeiss binoculars' for about 2,000 metres (6,500 feet). The binoculars must have been masterpieces of optical craftsmanship to provide such detail over a mile away.

Of particular interest to the author is alleged witness Richard Rex's contention that he immediately reported what he saw of the Richthofen incident on 21 April to *Major* Paul von Homeyer of Grenadier Regiment Nr. 1 for dissemination up the chain of command. According to the regimental history, Homeyer was playing cards on the evening of 17 April, when his quarters took a direct artillery hit, killing his partner immediately and requiring Homeyer's removal to a field hospital, where he died from his wounds on 6 May 1918. By coincidence, the hospital was located in Cappy, the same town that provided airfield accommodation for Richthofen's *Jagdstaffel 11*. It is unlikely that Rex reported anything to *Major* von Homeyer, if, indeed, he had anything to report – which, based on evidence in the following chapter, this author does not believe was the case.

14
EIN DEUTSCHES REQUIEM

Initially, members of *Jagdgeschwader I* hoped that some miracle enabled Manfred von Richthofen to elude being caught between British Sopwith Camel fighters above and Australian soldiers advancing along the Somme Valley below.

But, *Geschwader* Adjutant Karl Bodenschatz wrote that, with every passing hour:

> ... the time during which the [*Geschwader*] could have helped the *Rittmeister*, somehow, some way, was just about gone. Now, they could only have hope that he had to land on the other side of the lines, wounded at worst, unwounded at best. It would not be the first time he had made an emergency landing. He even landed smoothly when he was wounded [in July 1917].
>
> At the *Geschwader*'s telephone switchboard, inquiries poured in from all sides. At Army Headquarters, it was decided to take an extraordinary step. The General allowed an inquiry to be radioed to the enemy in plain [un-coded] text: "*Rittmeister* von Richthofen landed on your side, request news about his fate."
>
> No answer followed.
>
> Silent, listening, despondent – work goes on at Cappy airfield. In the afternoon the east wind becomes stronger and cooler. This thrice cursed east wind! It drives everything that can no longer resist it to the west, toward France. And anyone whose engine failed will be driven by it. Perhaps this thrice cursed east wind drove the red triplane westward, [and] without the east wind, it would have been possible for him ... such dreams are futile.

The last German to see Manfred von Richthofen in the air, *Leutnant* Hans Joachim Wolff, was particularly distraught at his leader's failure to return. Machine gun fire from another British fighter distracted Wolff from watching the *Kommandeur* descend into the Somme Valley in pursuit of what he surely envisioned as victory No. 81. By the time Wolff slipped away from his adversary, the red triplane was out of sight.

In a letter to Lothar von Richthofen, Wolff noted that after returning to Cappy:

> Reports had already come in. A red triplane had landed smoothly north-west of Corbie. [But] that an ...Englishman could have shot him down from behind was out of the question ...
>
> That would have been the most dreadful thing for me, as I considered myself to be *Herr Rittmeister*'s personal protector. And, indeed, should *Herr Rittmeister* have shot down the Englishman, then he would have pulled up, but he suddenly went into a steep dive and landed smoothly. Now there were two possibilities. The machine was overstressed, some sort of a valve let go, and the engine quit. The other possibility [was] that shots fired from the ground hit the engine. But he had to be alive and that [thought] eased our pain somewhat. Indeed, we were happy for his parents, who would be able to see their great son again after the war.
>
> And then, the following day, *Major* Haehnelt [Officer in Charge of Aviation for the 2nd Army] came and told us that *Herr Rittmeister* had fallen ... And just then a dreadful suspicion came to me ... If the fatal shot came from the ground, then he could no longer land a triplane smoothly. But there were Australians who had seen how the British shot [him] down and how suddenly the triplane landed. No, it was not at all to be imagined ...

Following the newly-promoted *Major* Haehnelt's pronouncement, Bodenschatz fulfilled a sad duty and opened a small metal box that he knew contained instructions Richthofen wanted carried out in the event that he did not return from combat. Bodenschatz removed a grey envelope secured by the *Geschwader* seal, which he broke in Wilhelm Reinhard's presence. It contained a one-page pencilled note in Richthofen's handwriting, dated 10 March 1918, that said: 'Should I not return, then *Oberleutnant* Reinhard should succeed to command of the *Geschwader*.' Reinhard had been promoted to *Hauptmann* since Richthofen wrote his testament, and the note simply reaffirmed his qualification to be *JG I*'s new *Kommandeur*.

Reinhard's first official act was to despatch Bodenschatz to Courtrai, to personally inform *Major* Albrecht von Richthofen that his son was missing.

Later, after Bodenschatz returned to Cappy, the pilot's father sensed that harder news would follow and began to prepare the family for the worst. He sent a brief telegram to his wife: 'Manfred alive in British captivity.'

A British aeroplane subsequently dropped a message canister containing confirmation of Manfred von Richthofen's death and a photograph of the grave, as positive proof that the *Rittmeister* had not survived.

On 23 April, based on information from British and Australian sources, the Reuters News Service informed the world of Richthofen's death. The Reuters account was quoted in German news media, as well as the German Air Force's weekly *Nachrichtenblatt* publication, which stated:

> As a British war correspondent reported, *Rittmeister Freiherr* von Richthofen was shot down as he flew behind the Australian Front at the lowest altitude. To all appearances, he fell [as] the victim of fire by an Australian battery that had directed a Lewis machine gun at him. [The body of] *Rittmeister Freiherr* von Richthofen showed only one wound: a bullet had hit him in the heart.

As an avid hunter, Richthofen, under other circumstances, would have appreciated the benefit of a 'clean shot' through the heart. Death would have been almost instantaneous. In 1998, Australian physician and researcher Dr. M. Geoffrey Miller published what this author regards as the most complete medically related study of the *Rittmeister*'s demise and noted: 'Von Richthofen would have lost consciousness within 20 to 30 seconds, and certainly could not have continued to fly his aeroplane ...'

That *Nachrichtenblatt* issue also included *General* von Hoeppner's condolences to *JG I* and, specifically, to *Jagdstaffel 11*. The General concluded by invoking the spirit of Richthofen as an inspiration to all German airmen: 'Stronger than [Richthofen's] words were his deeds. It was granted to him to be confirmed and honoured to live as a leader, [and] to be cherished as a comrade. We will not direct our gaze on what he could have been; rather, from what he was we will derive [a] living force, [a] force that stays alert as a permanent memorial to his deeds.'

Only one question remained: whose bullet brought down Manfred von Richthofen?

British and German records confirm the fateful aerial encounter took place near midday, after being set in motion by a preliminary engagement, as noted in a 1933 official Australian source:

> Two [RE8 two-seat] photographing machines of No. 3 Australian Squadron ... were starting out on reconnaissance of the German lines at Hamel, when at 7,000 feet over that village, they saw a flight of enemy triplanes approaching. The weather was hazy and visibility very poor, and the Australian machines were attacked at short warning of the enemy's presence. Four triplanes dived almost at once ... [and were] met with equal resolution ... [that] beat them off with several effective bursts of fire. One triplane was plainly hit and began to go down; the other then hauled off. The Germans had sighted a formation of British scouts in the offing and abandoned the attack on the two-seaters...
>
> Meanwhile ... the red circus, having passed the lines after the first escape of the two RE8s, immediately encountered a formation of [Sopwith] Camels from a British naval air squadron operating as fighting scouts in the Amiens sector. These scouts witnessed the approach of the [Germans], and it was evidently their presence which had saved the Australian photographic machines in the first attack. The two formations flew straight at each other, and in a few seconds the infantry on the great natural grandstand of the Morlancourt Ridge were spectators of a first-class air battle ...

Two flights of *Jasta 11* Fokker triplanes and a flight of *Jasta 5* Albatros D.Vs headed toward a 15-aeroplane-strong High Offensive Patrol from No. 209 Squadron, RAF: three flights of nimble Sopwith F.1 Camel fighters, which flew from their aerodrome at Bertangles south to Hangard before turning north toward Albert. Initially distracted by the closer target of German reconnaissance aircraft, three 'B' Flight Camels initiated the day's fighting, according to American-born flight leader Captain Oliver C. LeBoutillier:

> I observed two Albatros two-seaters over Le Quesnel. Lieutenants Foster, Taylor and myself fired on one ... [which then] he burst into flames and crashed at Beaucourt [-en-Santerre].

Most of the 'B' Flight Camels attacked the German reconnaissance aircraft, while 'A' Flight leader Captain Arthur Roy Brown, 'led the remaining two Flights northwards to the Somme valley,' where the German fighters approached westward. Brown reported diving:

> ... on [a] large formation of 15-20 Albatros Scouts D-5 and Fokker triplanes, two of which got on my tail and I got out.
>
> Went back again and dived on a pure red triplane which was firing on Lieutenant May. I got a long burst into him and he went down vertical and was observed to crash by Lieutenant Mellersh and Lieutenant May. I fired on two more but did not get them.

A member of 'A' Flight, Lieutenant Francis J.W. Mellersh, confirmed:

> I followed Captain Brown down on to a large formation of Fokker triplanes and Albatros D-5s. A dogfight ensued and I managed to get on the tail of a triplane with a blue tail. I fired about 50 rounds into him when he turned and I got a long burst into him when he was turned up. The triplane then dropped his nose and went down in a vertical dive. I followed, still firing, and saw the machine crash near Cérisy.
>
> The other triplanes then dived on to me and I was forced to spin down to the ground and return to our lines at about 50 feet. Whilst so returning, a bright red triplane crashed quite close to me and in looking up I saw Captain Brown.

Brown was intent on saving Second Lieutenant Wilfrid R. May, who reported that, after firing at one German fighter:

> I then went down and was attacked by a Red triplane, which chased me over the lines low to the ground. While he was on my tail, Captain Brown attacked it and shot it down. I observed it crash into the ground.

Adding to the reports by Lieutenants Mellersh and May, Captain LeBoutillier stated:

[I] engaged Fokker triplane over Cérisy (about 15–20 machines) and fired about 100 rounds at a mottled coloured one but did not get him. Also fired on red triplane which was shot down by Captain Brown and crashed [on] our side of the lines.

Books, articles and television programmes devoted to this one aerial combat agree that *Rittmeister* Manfred *Freiherr* von Richthofen was killed while flying an all-red Fokker Dr.I triplane at about 1145 hours on 21 April 1918. He was pursuing May's Sopwith F.1 Camel along the Somme River Valley from Sailly le Sec to Vaux-sur-Somme until his aeroplane was hit and came down to earth.

The 'credit' for killing Manfred von Richthofen has been the source of long and perhaps endless debate. In addition to hasty credit accorded to Captain Brown, the 53rd Australian Field Artillery Battery, 5th Division, and the 24th Machine Gun Company also claimed to have brought down Richthofen's aeroplane. Their accounts did not mention Brown's aircraft, only the sight of a dark brown biplane being pursued by a red triplane:

Then one machine dived for the ground with the other on its tail. They darted about wildly for a few seconds. Suddenly the pursued aeroplane, evidently in desperate straits, made straight for the crest of the ridge near the [field artillery] battery. The gunners saw that it was a British machine and its pursuer a red triplane. The Lewis [machine] gun on the nearer flank of the battery made ready to fire, but at first could not, for the machines were flying so low and close that the fleeing Camel blocked the gunner's sight of the German. The German was firing rapid short bursts at the Camel just beyond his nose, and the hunted British machine was making no attempt to turn and fire ...

The machines flew on right overhead, careless of everything else except their own duel and ... at about a hundred yards' range, the artillery Lewis gunners and other machine guns from Australian camps on or behind the crest opened fire on the German. Splinters of wood were seen to fly off immediately near his engine. The triplane wobbled, side-banked up, swerved across to the left in a half-circle, obviously crippled, then dived straight into the ground about 400 yard away and was smashed to pieces ...

In fact, Richthofen's triplane made a relatively smooth descent until its wheels made contact with the ploughed soil of a mangel [fertilizer beet] field alongside the road from Corbie to Bray. Photographs of the wreckage suggest that the triplane's undercarriage collapsed, and the abrupt stop caused the pilot's face to strike the machine gun butts, thereby breaking Richthofen's top front teeth. By that time, however, he was dead.

Australian ground troops subsequently removed the pilot's body from the crumpled triplane, which, despite the shooting going on, soon drew the attention of a horde of souvenir hunters. Ultimately, the wreckage was retrieved and assigned the identification number G/5th Brigade/2, which, according to the system then in use, indicated it was the second enemy aircraft captured within the 5th Brigade area.

Richthofen's mortal remains were transported to Poulainville aerodrome, some nine miles from the crash site. Otherwise known only as the operational base for No. 3 Squadron, Australian Flying Corps, RE8 aircraft of which had tangled with *Jasta 11* earlier that day,Poulainville rapidly gained fame, as word spread that Richthofen's body was in one of the aircraft hangars there.

Richthofen's corpse was photographed fully dressed so there would be no disputing that Germany's leading fighter pilot had fallen within British territory, and that his body had been treated with respect. Then, according to Dr. Miller's research:

> [The] body was washed by an orderly and the first superficial post-mortem examination was made by a panel of doctors ... [consisting] of Colonel T. Sinclair, consulting surgeon to the Fourth Army, Captain G.C. Graham, RAMC and Lieutenant G.E. Downs, attached to the Air Force. [Australian historian Dennis] Newton, however, refers to the presence also of Colonel J.A. Dixon, consulting physician to the British Fourth Army.

According to Colonel Sinclair's report:

> We ... find that there are only the entrance and exit wounds of one rifle bullet on the trunk. The entrance wound is on the right side about the level of the ninth-rib, which is fractured, just in front of

the posterior axillary line. The bullet appears to have passed obliquely backwards through the chest striking the spinal column, from which it glanced in a forward direction and issued on the left side of the chest, at a level about two inches higher than its entrance on the right and about in the anterior axillary line. There was also a compound fracture of the lower jaw on the left side, apparently not caused by a missile – and also some minor bruises of the head and face. The body was not opened – these facts were ascertained by probing from the surface wounds.

Medical investigators of Richthofen's death have been stymied by the original examiner's lack of a proper surgical probe that would have more accurately traced the fatal bullet's trajectory. But even the manner of probing used in 1918 provided some help, as reported by Colonel George W. Barber, a member of the Medical Board that examined Richthofen's body a second time at Poulainville:

> I ... found the medical orderly washing Richthofen's body, so I made an examination. There were only two bullet wounds, one of entry, one of exit of a bullet that had evidently passed through the chest and the heart. There was no wound of the head but there was considerable bruising over the right jaw, which may have been fractured. The orderly told me that the consulting surgeon of the Army had made a post-mortem in the morning and I asked how he did it, as there was no evidence. The orderly told me that the consulting surgeon used a bit of fencing wire, which he had pushed along the track of the wound through over the heart. I used the same bit of wire for the same purpose so you see the medical examination was not a thorough one and not a post-mortem exam in the ordinary sense of the term. The bullet hole in the side of the plane coincided with the wound through the chest and I am sure he was shot from below while banking.

Dr. Miller adds:

> In my view, the "bit of fence wire" would have caught in the soft

tissues of the chest, such as the lung tissue, and could never have shown the true path of the bullet. However, used as Barber did, that is probing "over the heart", (probing into the exit wound), the probe could have confirmed that the bullet exited the heart, and caused an early demise and Barber was correct to point this out. However, a bit of fence wire, with its ragged edges, could not have shown the actual track of the bullet by probing from the entry wound.

I believe that the most likely path of the bullet was a line drawn between the entrance and exit wounds and, therefore, the bullet was more likely to have been fired from behind the body, not from in front of it.

Barber made a compelling case for the ground gunners, many of which were firing at a low angle, as opposed to Brown in his Sopwith Camel, firing from a high angle, above the German pilot.

But, in spite of strong claims that ground fire had brought down Richthofen's aeroplane – a viewpoint held even by *Generalleutnant* Ernst von Hoeppner, the Commanding General of the German Air Force – No. 209 Squadron, RAF, took credit for downing 'the red baron' and even used the device of a red hawk falling when its squadron heraldry was created, to solidify its claim of triumph.

At this late date, no one can prove conclusively who fired the fatal bullet at Manfred von Richthofen as he flew over Vaux-sur-Somme, France. The metal projectile portion of the fatal .303-calibre bullet was not recovered and, even if it had been, it would have been of a type common to bolt-action Lee-Enfield Service rifles, as well as magazine-fed Lewis and belt-fed Vickers machine guns used by British Commonwealth troops. Thus, it would have been nearly impossible to determine whose gun fired it.

Other evidence, however, offers a 'best educated guess.' This conclusion rules out RAF Captain Arthur Roy Brown's claim, as even a superficial examination of Richthofen's corpse indicated a nearly lateral bullet path with the exit wound 'at a level about two inches higher than its entrance on the right and about in the anterior axillary line.' Brown was never in position to fire such a shot.

A claim was made for Gunner Robert Buie, a member of the 53rd Australian

Field Artillery Battery, which fired Lewis machine guns at Richthofen as he pursued May. Citing Buie's statement that the triplane was approaching 'frontal and just a little to the right of me,' Dr. Miller stated that Buie 'could not have inflicted the wound that entered [Richthofen's] body from behind.'

Rather, Dr. Miller proved what other historical researchers over the years have stated: Sergeant Cedric B. Popkin of the 24th Machine Gun Company, manning a Vickers machine gun, was in the best position to shoot down Manfred von Richthofen:

> ... Popkin first fired when Richthofen was approaching him from the Somme valley, but he failed to stop Richthofen. After coming under fire from Buie and Gunner [William J.] Evans, at the Lewis gun emplacement, the German aeroplane turned away from the gunfire and it was then, when the triplane was flying away from Popkin, that he opened fire with his Vickers gun for the second time. Popkin continued firing while the triplane completed the turn and actually flew towards the Vickers gun, but there is no doubt that he could have inflicted a bullet wound that entered Richthofen from below, from the side and slightly behind, just as was found at the post-mortem examination. Neither Captain Brown nor Gunner Buie could have inflicted such a wound and it is therefore more probable than not that it was indeed Popkin who fired the fatal shot.

Given the hectic conditions that day, as Richthofen stayed on May's tail with an obsessive fury, it is also possible that a nameless Australian rifleman fired the shot that ended the life and began the legend of the Red Baron.

As Dr. Miller points out:

> All that we can be sure of is that the entry and exit wounds on von Richthofen's body means that the bullet passed through the heart, or great vessels, and that he could not have remained conscious for more than about 30 seconds after being hit. The fatal bullet had therefore to have been fired at von Richthofen at the end of the pursuit and this is likely to have been at the time when the triplane

was observed to turn away from the hill where the Lewis [machine] gun batteries were situated.

While Cedric Popkin's bullet almost surely ended Manfred von Richthofen's life, the German pilot contributed to his own demise by not following Boelcke's teachings as religiously as he urged his protégés to adhere to them. Richthofen's fate paralleled that of his fellow Boelcke student and one-time *Jasta 2* leader, *Oberleutnant* Stephan Kirmaier, who was also killed when he failed to follow Boelcke's eighth dictum: 'Over enemy territory, never forget your own escape route.'

Had Richthofen not descended so far into the cauldron of ground fire that the Somme Valley had become, and had he disengaged from his long and hazardously low-level pursuit of Wilfrid May sooner, he might have pulled up out of the ground gunners' range and had a chance to elude or shoot down Arthur Roy Brown. But Manfred von Richthofen remained intent on his target and, as a consequence, 25 years and 352 days after his birth, The Great War's highest-scoring fighter pilot was dead.

After the doctors concluded their examinations, Richthofen's body was laid out on a makeshift funeral bier in a hangar at Poulainville and members of No. 3 Squadron, AFC, paid their last respects.

At about 1600 hours the following day, 22 April, a military funeral with full honours was organized to inter Manfred von Richthofen's remains in the Christian tradition. No. 3 Squadron, AFC provided an honour guard of officers that accompanied the improvised hearse, a Crossley tender, which bore Richthofen's coffin to the cemetery in nearby Bertangles. Coincidentally, that town was also home to No. 209 Squadron. The funeral attracted other airmen in the area, including two French pilots, *Capitaine* Moreau and *Lieutenant* Olphe-Gaillard of *Escadrille Spa 93*, a fighter squadron based south-west of Amiens.

The funeral honours were documented on still and motion picture film. Shortly after the services, French residents of the area desecrated the grave in the mistaken belief that Richthofen had carried out the night-time bombing of the area.

Lacking the fallen warrior's physical remains for a proper state funeral, officials of the Imperial German Government organized a memorial service to be held in Berlin on Thursday, 2 May 1918. The day marked the first anniversary of Richthofen's first meeting with Kaiser Wilhelm II and would have been the flyer's 26th birthday. It was not feasible for a high-ranking delegation from the *Staffel* or the *Geschwader* to travel to Germany's capital for the solemn occasion, as the new *Kommandeur* of *JG I* had to remain at Cappy to work with the *Staffel* leaders and their subordinates. Consequently, *Hauptmann* Reinhard assigned *Hauptmann* Kurt Lischke, *Jasta 6*'s chief administrative officer, and *Leutnant* Hans Joachim Wolff of *Jasta 11* to travel to the Aaper Wald Clinic in Düsseldorf, where Lothar von Richthofen was convalescing, and escort him to the memorial service.

Once in Berlin, Lischke and Wolff accompanied Lothar, his parents, sister Ilse and brother Bolko to a private meeting with the Commanding General of the Air Force. General von Hoeppner tried to answer *Freifrau* von Richthofen's questions about her son's death and made a point of noting that Manfred had not fallen due to any lack of flying or fighting skill on his part. She recalled that the General believed

> that he could definitely assure me that Manfred had taken a chance hit from the ground. [Then] he said: "We have no replacement for your son in the whole Air Force."

Later that afternoon, two Mercedes limousines carried the mourners along Unter den Linden, Berlin's historic, tree-lined traditional victory route, and past the Imperial Palace. The stately vehicles proceeded a short way down Kaiser Wilhelm-Strasse and past the tall, dark, elegant buildings of Rosenstrasse out to Potsdam, to the 185-year-old *Garnisonkirche* [Garrison Church], where Frederick the Great and many Prussian generals were entombed. Berliners lined the entry road as the cortège halted at the front of the historic church. The bells tolled solemnly as mourners were greeted on the church steps by the Kaiser's representatives, *General der Kavallerie* Manfred *Freiherr* von Richthofen, for whom the fallen hero was named, and *General* von Hoeppner, who escorted them to reserved pews.

Inside the *Garnisonkirche*, the altar was draped in black, except for the image of Jesus Christ, symbolizing the Christian hope for redemption and the promise of heaven's glory. Symbols of war and the promise of Teutonic glory graced the front of the altar: four crepe-covered pedestals holding bronze founts with blazing flames licking up and four machine gun barrels protruded from beneath the catafalque bearing the black velvet *Ordenskissen* [pillow] that displayed Manfred von Richthofen's medals. He had not lived long enough to wear his final honour, the aptly named Order of the Red Eagle. Below the *Ordenskissen* stood a huge black-leaved funeral wreath through which protruded a splintered propeller.

An honour guard of eight young enlisted combat pilots in black leather jackets, each decorated with the Iron Cross and Pilot's Badge, and wearing hard leather flying helmets, flanked the altar display. Officers posted at either side of the catafalque remained at attention throughout the hour-long memorial service.

Just before the service began, the Richthofen family was accorded high tribute when members of the royal family – Kaiserin [Empress] Auguste Victoria, her nephew *Prinz* Sigismund of Prussia and his consort – were seated next to them.

Freifrau von Richthofen recalled that the pastor said that:

> **The achievements and the work of the deceased must console us. Not that he has been touched by the death of ordinary life; but, rather, [by] death in all of its heroic beauty. When the glow of the spectrum of colour was at its brightest, when the force of the action was at its most powerful, then the curtain came thundering down over this life. Only a poet could do justice to him.**

The brooding, defiant and, ultimately, celebratory music of Brahms' Mass *'Ein deutsches Requiem'* – a German requiem for a German hero – signified the triumph of life over death. After a pause, came the mournful notes of the 'Retreat,' the traditional cavalry bugle signal that has echoed across many battlefields where only fallen soldiers remained at their posts.

As the members of the royal family led the way out of the church, *Freifrau* von Richthofen's only comment to the Kaiserin was:

> **I wish that Manfred could have served his Fatherland longer.**

With the closing of the massive doors to the *Garnisonkirche*, Fate sent the mourners on to different paths. Hans Joachim Wolff, the *Rittmeister*'s devoted admirer, who was inconsolable in his grief, found relief exactly two weeks later, when he was shot down and killed not far from where Richthofen died.

Lothar von Richthofen eventually recovered from his latest wounds and returned to the Front on 19 July. He commanded *Jasta 11* until 13 August when – for the third time and once again on the 13th of the month – he was shot down and seriously injured. Returned to Germany for treatment and convalescence, Lothar was forced to retire from battle with 40 confirmed aerial victories – the same number achieved by Manfred's mentor Oswald Boelcke, but only half as many as Manfred himself. Similarly, Lothar earned nine awards, including the *Pour le Mérite* – but less than half of the 24 that had graced Manfred's full dress uniform.

Lothar's achievements were different. He survived the war, married *Gräfin* [Countess] Doris von Keyserlingk, the daughter of a former privy counsellor of Kaiser Wilhelm II, had a family and became a pilot for the new post-war civilian airline *Deutsche-Luft-Reederei*, a predecessor of today's *Deutsche Lufthansa*. He was flying a converted LVG C.VI reconnaissance aircraft on the Hamburg-Berlin run, when, on the night of 4 July 1922, the aeroplane hit a high-tension wire on its final approach to Berlin's Johannisthal Airport and crashed; the passengers survived, but Lothar von Richthofen was dead at age 27.

Lothar was also accorded a funeral at a *Garnisonkirche*, but not the official state military church in Potsdam; rather, a smaller structure in Schweidnitz commissioned by Frederick the Great. A military honour guard accompanied the coffin to the town cemetery, where his father had been laid to rest following his death at age 61 on 8 March 1920.

The post-World War I graves-registration process brought to public consciousness the need for better organization of final resting places of all of the fallen combatants. Accordingly, Manfred von Richthofen's original grave at Bertangles in France was disinterred and his remains were transferred to a large German military cemetery at Fricourt, France, east of Albert. In 1925, at the family's request, Richthofen's body was exhumed again and, this time, a special train was sent to France to bring the *Rittmeister*'s remains home to Germany for a formal state funeral in Berlin.

Freifrau von Richthofen wanted him buried in Schweidnitz, alongside his father and brother. But a defeated people in search of heroes needed to honour their peerless air warrior on a grander scale. Even in death, Manfred von Richthofen was called on to serve his country. An elaborate state funeral, presided over by Germany's most famous field marshal – now 78-year-old *Reichspräsident* Paul von Hindenburg – was carried out with military precision. The public response was so overwhelming that police barricades were set up to contain the crowds. Protected by an honour guard of famous wartime pilots, each proudly wearing the *Pour le Mérite*, Richthofen's coffin was borne into the *Garnisonkirche* in Potsdam in a manner worthy of the great Teutonic warrior he had become. Finally, his remains were interred with some of Germany's greatest heroes in the *Invalidenfriedhof* in Berlin on 20 November 1925.

Invariably, the question is raised: had he survived World War I, what would *Rittmeister* Manfred *Freiherr* von Richthofen have become? As this author has noted in the past, Richthofen 'was a daring and cool-headed leader in battle ... and a seasoned manager who knew how to use his resources to the best advantage and how to motivate his subordinates.' Surely, he could have ascended to great heights and added further honour to a name he made into a living legend.' But, as *Generalleutnant* Ernst von Hoeppner, Commanding General of the Air Force, suggested immediately after Richthofen's death, let us:

> ...not direct our gaze on what he could have been; rather, from what he was we will derive [a] living force ... that [remains] as a permanent memorial to his deeds.

Manfred von Richthofen's memory was invoked in World War II, when a fighter wing was named the *Richthofen Geschwader*. But his name was untarnished by the evil madness of the Third Reich and, consequently, remains in honoured use in the modern German *Luftwaffe*.

Politics of the so-called Cold War intruded briefly on Richthofen's eternal rest when, in 1976, officials of the former East German regime began to 'solidify' its border near the infamous Berlin Wall and the Richthofen gravesite in [then] East Berlin was found to be among those that had to be vacated. The family requested and was given the coffin for burial in a family plot in Wiesbaden in western Germany. Manfred von Richthofen's remains now rest near those of his mother, who died in 1962; his sister Ilse, who died in 1963; and his brother Bolko, who died in 1971. Sadly, the grave sites of his father and his brother Lothar were levelled and made unrecognizable after most of

Schweidnitz's German population was driven out after World War II. They were succeeded by enforced migration of Polish settlers who had suffered during the war and were encouraged by communist leaders to vent their hostility by ridding their new home territory in Lower Silesia of long-time German historical connections.

But the name and legend of Manfred von Richthofen lives on. In the pantheon of German heroes, he remains as a model of bravery, a person who inspires respect from former friends and foes alike. Mention the phrase 'the red baron' and only one man comes to mind: *Rittmeister* Manfred *Freiherr* von Richthofen, a larger-than-life figure who continues to inspire international interest to the point of fascination.

APPENDIX

MANFRED VON RICHTHOFEN AND *JAGDSTAFFEL 11* VICTORY LIST

Jasta	Date	Time	Pilot and His Victory No	Aircraft Type	Location
	1915	1.9	Lt M. Frhr von Richthofen-nc	Farman 2-seater	Flanders Sector
	26.10	1630	Lt M. Frhr von Richthofen-nc	Farman 2-seater	Somme Py
	1916	26.4	Lt M. Frhr von Richthofen-nc	Nieuport	Fleury, south of Fort Douaumont
	(1 May 1916: German time one hour ahead of Allied time)				
	17.9	1100	Lt M. Frhr von Richthofen-1	FE2b	Villers Plouich
	23.9	1100	Lt M. Frhr von Richthofen-2	Martinsyde G100	Beugny
	30.9	1150	Lt M. Frhr von Richthofen-3	FE2b	Frémicourt
	7.10	0910	Lt M. Frhr von Richthofen-4	BE12	Equanacourt
	16.10	1710	Lt M. Frhr von Richthofen-5	BE12	north of Ytres
	25.10	0935	Lt M. Frhr von Richthofen-6	BE12	north of Bapaume
	3.11	1410	Lt M. Frhr von Richthofen-7	FE2b	Loupart Wood
	9.11	1030	Lt M. Frhr von Richthofen-8	BE2c	Beugny
	20.11	0940	Lt M. Frhr von Richthofen-9	BE2c	south of Grandcourt
	20.11	1615	Lt M. Frhr von Richthofen-10	FE2b	Guedecourt
	23.11	1500	Lt M. Frhr von Richthofen-11	DH2	Bapaume
	11.12	1155	Lt M. Frhr von Richthofen-12	DH2	Mercatel
	20.12		Lt M. Frhr von Richthofen-13	DH2	Monchy au Bois
	20.12	1345	Lt M. Frhr von Richthofen-14	FE2b	Noreuil
	27.12	1625	Lt M. Frhr von Richthofen-15	FE2 / DH2	Ficheux / Arras
	1917				
	3.1	1615	Lt M. Frhr von Richthofen-16	Sopwith Pup	Metz en Couture
1	23. 1.	1605	Lt M. Frhr von Richthofen-17	FE8	south-west of Lens
2	24. 1.	1215	Lt M. Frhr von Richthofen-18	FE2b	west of Vimy
3	1. 2.	1600	Lt M. Frhr von Richthofen-19	BE2d	south-west of Thélus
4	5. 2.	1700	Vzfw Festner-1	BE2c	north-east of Arras, near Neuville
5	14. 2.	1300	Lt M. Frhr von Richthofen-20	BE2d	Lens - Hulluch road, east of Loos
6	14. 2.	1700	Lt M. Frhr von Richthofen-21	BE2c	Loos (over British lines)
7	16. 2.	1700	Vzfw Festner-2	FE8	between Liévin and Grenay
8	16. 2.	1200	Lt C. Allmenröder-1	BE2c	Roeux, east of

9	4. 3.	1200	Lt Schäfer-2	Sopwith 2-Seater	Arras south-west of Haisnes
10	4. 3.	1250	Lt M. Frhr von Richthofen-22	BE2d	north of Loos
11	4. 3.	1620	Lt M. Frhr von Richthofen-23	Sopwith 2-Seater	Acheville, south of Vimy
12	6. 3.	1145	Lt Schäfer-3	Sopwith 2-Seater	Lens
13	6. 3.	1155	Lt Schäfer-4	Sopwith 2-Seater	Lens
14	6. 3.	1230	Lt K. Wolff-1	BE2d	Givenchy
15	6. 3.	1700	Lt M. Frhr von Richthofen-24	BE2e	Souchez
16	9. 3.	1020	Lt Schäfer-5	FE8	between Meurchin and Faschoda
17	9. 3.	1020	Lt Schäfer-6	FE8	between Meurchin and Pont à Vendin
18	9. 3.	1020	Lt K. Wolff-2	FE8	between Meurchin and Annay
19	9. 3.	1020	Lt C. Allmenröder-2	FE8	Meurchin, west of Hulluch
20	9. 3.	1200	Lt M. Frhr von Richthofen-25	DH2	between Roclincourt and Bailleul
21	11. 3.	1120	Lt Schäfer-7	BE2c	Loos
22	11. 3.	1145	Lt Krefft-1	FE2b	between Givenchy and Vimy
23	11. 3.	1200	Lt M. Frhr von Richthofen-26	BE2d	Vimy
24	17. 3.	1145	Oblt M. Frhr von Richthofen-27	FE2b	between Bailleul and Oppy
25	17. 3.	1145	Lt C. Allmenröder-3	Sopwith 2-Seater	between Athies and Oppy
26	17. 3.	1145	Lt K. Wolff-3	Sopwith 2-Seater	Bailleul
27	17. 3.	1700	Oblt M. Frhr von Richthofen-28	BE2c	Souchez, west of Vimy
28	21. 3.	1530	Lt C. Allmenröder-4	Sopwith 2-Seater	south of Vermelles, near Loos
29	21. 3.	1725	Oblt M. Frhr von Richthofen-29	BE2f	north of La Neuville
30	24. 3.	1055	Lt Schäfer-8	Sopwith 2- Seater	Anzin, north of Arras
31	24. 3.	1155	Oblt M. Frhr von Richthofen-30	SPAD S7	Vimy

(25 March 1917: German time synchronized with Allied time)

32	25. 3.	1155	Oblt M. Frhr von Richthofen-31	Nieuport 17	Tilloy
33	28. 3.	1715	Lt L. Frhr von Richthofen-1	FE2b	south of Lens
34	30. 3.	1145	Lt K. Wolff-4	Nieuport 17	Gavrelle, Fresnoy, north-west of Arras
35	30. 3.	1415	Lt C. Allmenröder-5	Nieuport 17	between Fresnoy and Bailleul
36	31. 3.	0745	Lt K. Wolff-5	FE2b	Gavrelle
37	2. 4.	0835	Oblt M. Frhr von Richthofen-32	BE2d	Farbus, north-east of Arras
38	2. 4.	0930	Lt C. Allmenröder-6	BE2d	Angres, south-west of Lens
39	2. 4.	1000	Vzfw Festner-3	FE2d	Auby, north of Douai
40	2. 4.	1000	Lt Krefft-2	FE2d	Oignes, north of Douai
41	2. 4.	1120	Oblt M. Frhr von Richthofen-33	Sopwith 2-Seater	Givenchy
42	3. 4.	1615	Oblt M. Frhr von Richthofen-34	FE2d	Lens
43	3. 4.	1620	Lt Schäfer-9	FE2d	Avion, south of Lens
44	5. 4.	1100	Lt Simon-1	Bristol F2A	north of Monchecourt, near Auchy
45	5. 4.	1100	Oblt M. Frhr von Richthofen-35	Bristol F2A	Quincy
46	5. 4.	1100	Oblt M. Frhr von Richthofen-36	Bristol F2A	Lewaarde, south-east of Douai
47	5. 4.	1100	Vzfw Festner-4	Bristol F2A	Méricourt
48	5. 4.	1830	Vzfw Festner-5	Nieuport 17	south-west of Bailleul
49	6. 4.	1015	Lt K. Wolff-6	RE8	Bois Bernard
50	6. 4.	1018	Lt Schäfer-10	BE2	Givenchy
51	6. 4.	1037	Lt Schäfer-11	Sopwith	Souchez, west of Vimy
52	7. 4.	1745	Lt K. Wolff-7	Nieuport 17	Mercatel
53	7. 4.	1745	Rittm M. Frhr von Richthofen-37	Nieuport 17	Mercatel
54	7. 4.	1745	Lt Schäfer-12	Nieuport 23	Mercatel
55	7. 4.	1910	Vzfw Festner-6	Nieuport 17	between Mt. St.Eloy and Maroeuil
56	8. 4.	0930	Vzfw Festner-7	Nieuport 17	east of Vimy
57	8. 4.	1140	Rittm M. Frhr von Richthofen-38	Sopwith 2-Seater	Farbus
58	8. 4.	1445	Lt Schäfer-13	DH4	Epinoy
59	8. 4.	1445	Lt K. Wolff-8	DH4	Blecourt
60	8. 4.	1640	Rittm M. Frhr von Richthofen-39	BE2e	Vimy
61	9. 4.	1910	Lt Schäfer-14	BE2d	Aix Noulette

62	11. 4.	0905	Vzfw Festner-8	BE2d	north of Fampoux
63	11. 4.	0910	Lt Schäfer-15	Bristol F2A	forward lines, near Fampoux
64	11. 4.	0910	Lt K. Wolff-9	Bristol F2A	Mouville Ferme, south of Arras
65	11. 4.	0910	Lt L. Frhr von Richthofen-2	Bristol F2A	Mouville Ferme, north of Fresnes
66	11. 4.	0925	Rittm M. Frhr von Richthofen-40	BE2c	Willerval
67	11. 4.	1250	Lt Schäfer-16	Sopwith 2-Seater	east of Arras cemetery
68	11. 4.	1250	Lt L. Frhr von Richthofen-3	Sopwith 2-Seater	north-east of Fampoux
69	13. 4.	0851	Vzfw Festner-9	RE8	between Etaing and Dury
70	13. 4.	0855	Lt L. Frhr von Richthofen-4	RE8	north-east of Biache, near Vitry
71	13. 4.	0855	Lt L. Frhr von Richthofen-5	RE8	east of Roeux and Pelves
72	13. 4.	0856	Rittm M. Frhr von Richthofen-41	RE8	Vitry
73	13. 4.	0856	Lt K. Wolff-10	BE2	north of Vitry en Artois
74	13. 4.	1235	Lt K. Wolff-11	FE2d	south of Bailleul
75	13. 4.	1245	Rittm M. Frhr von Richthofen-42	FE2b	west of Monchy, near Feuchy
76	13. 4.	1630	Lt K. Wolff-12	Nieuport 17	South of Monchy le Preux
77	13. 4.	1640	Lt Schäfer-17	FE2b	near le Point du Jour
78	13. 4.	1852	Lt K. Wolff-13	Martinsyde G102	Rouvroy
79	13. 4.	1930	Vzfw Festner-10	FE2b	east of Harnes
80	13. 4.	1930	Rittm M. Frhr von Richthofen-43	FE2b	near Hénin-Liétard
81	14. 4.	0915	Rittm M. Frhr von Richthofen-44	Nieuport	near Fresnoy
82	14. 4.	0920	Lt K. Wolff-14	Nieuport 17	south-east of Drocourt
83	14. 4.	0920	Lt L. Frhr von Richthofen-6	Nieuport 23	east of Fourquières
84	14. 4.	0923	Vzfw Festner-11	Nieuport 17	Gavrelle
85	14. 4.	1705	Lt Schäfer-18	FE2b	between Liéven and Eleu
86	14. 4.	1720	Lt Schäfer-19	BE2	La Coulette, west of Avion
87	14. 4.	1823	Lt L. Frhr von Richthofen-7	SPAD S7	between Vimy and Farbus
88	14. 4.	1829	Lt K. Wolff-15	SPAD S7	Bailleul
89	16. 4.	1030	Lt L. Frhr von Richthofen-8	Nieuport 17	between Roeux and Pelves

90	16. 4.	1030	Lt K. Wolff-16		Nieuport 17	north-east of Roeux
91	16. 4.	1030	Vzfw Festner-12		Nieuport 17	between Fampoux and Biache
92	16. 4.	1730	Rittm M. Frhr von Richthofen-45	BE2c		Gavrelle

(17 April 1917: German time one hour ahead of Allied time)

93	21. 4.	1725	Lt Schäfer-20		Nieuport	east of Fresnes
94	21. 4.	1730	Lt L. Frhr von Richthofen-9	BE2g		north-west of Arleux, near Farbus
95	21. 4.	1730	Lt K. Wolff-17	BE2g		north-west of Arleux, near Willerval
96	21. 4.	1745	Lt K. Wolff-18		Nieuport 23	east of Fresnes
97	21. 4.	1745	Lt Schäfer-21		Sopwith 2-Seater	east of Fresnes
98	22. 4.	1710	Rittm M. Frhr von Richthofen-46	FE2b		Lagnicourt
99	22. 4.	1710	Lt K. Wolff-19	FE2b		Hendecourt
100	22. 4.	2005	Lt K. Wolff-20		Morane Parasol	Havrincourt
101	22. 4.	2020	Lt Schäfer-21	FE2b		north-west of Monchy-Tilloy
102	23. 4.	1213	Rittm M. Frhr von Richthofen-47	BE2f		east of Vimy
103	23. 4.	1215	Lt L. Frhr von Richthofen-10	BE2g		north of Vimy
104	25. 4.	1030	Lt C. Allmenröder-7	RE8		Guémappe
105	25. 4.	1045	Lt Schäfer-22	FE2b		north-west of Bailleul
106	25. 4.	2010	Lt Schäfer-23		Bristol F2A	Roeux train station
107	26. 4.	1635	Lt K. Wolff-21	BE2g		east of Gavrelle
108	26. 4.	1845	Lt L. Frhr von Richthofen-11	BE2g		between Vimy and Farbus
109	26. 4.	1848	Lt C. Allmenröder-8	BE2g		Vimy Ridge
110	27. 4.	2015	Lt L. Frhr von Richthofen-12	FE2b		Fresnes
111	27. 4.	2020	Lt K. Wolff-22	FE2b		south of Gavrelle
112	27. 4.	2025	Lt C. Allmenröder-9	BE2c		between Athies and Fampoux
113	28. 4.	0930	Rittm M. Frhr von Richthofen-48	BE2e		east of Pelves
114	28. 4.	1120	Lt K. Wolff-23	BE2f		between Oppy and Gavrelle
115	28. 4.	1745	Lt K. Wolff-24	BE2g		west of Gavrelle
116	29. 4.	1215	Rittm M. Frhr von Richthofen-49	SPAD S7		Lecluse
117	29. 4.	1215	Lt K. Wolff-25	SPAD S7		between Izel and Sailly
118	29. 4.	1215	Lt L. Frhr von Richthofen-13	SPAD S7		between Izel and Sailly
119	29. 4.	1655	Rittm M. Frhr von Richthofen-50	FE2b		Inchy
120	29. 4.	1700	Lt K. Wolff-26	FE2b		south of Pronville

121	29. 4.	1925	Rittm M. Frhr von Richthofen-51	BE2e	Roeux
122	29. 4.	1945	Rittm M. Frhr von Richthofen-52	Sopwith Triplane	between Billy-Montigny and Sallaumines
123	29. 4.	1950	Lt L. Frhr von Richthofen-14	BE2e	between Monchy and Pelves
124	30. 4.	0715	Lt L. Frhr von Richthofen-15	BE2g	betweenVimy and Willerval
125	30. 4.	0750	Lt L. Frhr von Richthofen-16	FE2d	Izel
126	30. 4.	1735	Lt Wolff-27	BE2e	west of Fresnes
127	1. 5.	1050	Lt Wolff-28	Sopwith Triplane	Phalempin, south of Seclin
128	1. 5.	1855	Lt Wolff-29	FE2b	Fresnoy, south of Bois Bernard
129	1. 5.	1900	Lt L. Frhr von Richthofen-17	FE2d	Gavrelle, West of Acheville
130	6. 5.	1050	Lt L. Frhr von Richthofen-18	AW FK 8	south-east of Givenchy
131	7. 5.	1200	Lt C. Allmenröder-10	BE2c	Fresnoy
132	7. 5.	1830	Lt L. Frhr von Richthofen-19	Nieuport 17	Gavrelle
133	7. 5.	2030	Lt L. Frhr von Richthofen-20	SE5	near Annoeullin
134	7. 5.	1830	Lt.d.R Maashoff-1	RE8	west of Fresnes
135	9. 5.	1830	Lt L. Frhr von Richthofen-21	Bristol F2B	road from Roeux to Gavrelle
136	10. 5.	0740	Lt C. Allmenröder-11	Sopwith Pup	Vitry en Artois
137	10. 5.	0750	Lt L. Frhr von Richthofen-22	Sopwith Pup	between Sailly and Vitry
138	11. 5.	1225	Lt.d.R Maashoff-2	BE2	Willerval
139	11. 5.	1710	Lt L. Frhr von Richthofen-23	Bristol F2B	Izel
140	11. 5.	1715	Lt W. Allmenröder-2	Bristol F2B	near Beaumont, north of Oppy
141	13. 5.	1135	Lt L. Frhr von Richthofen-24	BE2e	Arleux
142	13. 5.	1145	Lt C. Allmenröder-12	RE8	near Arleux
143	13. 5.	2115	Lt C. Allmenröder-13	Nieuport 23	Ostricourt
144	13. 5.	2120	Lt.d.R Hintsch-2	Nieuport 17	east of Fresnes
145	14. 5.	1130	Lt C. Allmenröder-14	BE2e	Quémappe
146	18. 5.	2005	Lt C. Allmenröder-15	BE2e	Fontaine, west of Monchy
147	19. 5.	0910	Lt C. Allmenröder-16	Sopwith	between Fosse 8 and Béthune
148	21.5	1710	Lt Mohnike-2	FE2b	Hullich
149	23. 5.	2115	Lt.d.R Hintsch-3	Sopwith Triplane	Carvin, south-west of Faschoda
150	24. 5.	0850	Lt C. Allmenröder-17	Sopwith	Boiry-Notre Dame

151	24. 5.	0902	Lt C. Allmenröder-18	Sopwith 2-Seater	Izel-Ferme, Flers, north of Douai
152	24. 5.	0915	Lt.d.R Maashoff-3	Sopwith Triplane	between Izel and Flers
153	25. 5.	1035	Lt C. Allmenröder-19	Nieuport	between Remy and Bois du Vert
154	25. 5.	2045	Lt C. Allmenröder-20	Bristol F2B	Monchy
155	28. 5.	0830	Lt C. Allmenröder-21	Sopwith Pup	between Feuchy and Tilloy
156	29. 5.	1750	Lt C. Allmenröder-22	RE8	Oppy, north of Gavrelle
157	1. 6.	1158	Lt Brauneck-7	RE8	Méricourt, near Airon
158	3. 6.	0730	Lt C. Allmenröder-23	Nieuport	Monchy
159	4. 6.	1925	Lt C. Allmenröder-24	RE8	Cagnicourt, south-east of Arras
160	4. 6.	2215	Lt C. Allmenröder-25	RE8	Monchy, south-east of Arras
161	5. 6.	1120	Lt C. Allmenröder-26	Sopwith 2-Seater	Terhand, at Wytschaete Bend
162	5. 6.	1120	Lt Brauneck-8	Sopwith 2-Seater	Terhand, at Wytschaete Bend
163	5. 6.	1120	Lt Niederhoff-3	Sopwith 2-Seater	Terhand, at Wytschaete Bend
164	18. 6.	0950	Lt C. Allmenröder-26	Nieuport	Verlorenhoek
165	18. 6.	1315	Rittm M. Frhr von Richthofen-53	RE8	north of Ypres
166	23. 6.	2115	Rittm M. Frhr von Richthofen-54	SPAD	north of Ypres
167	24. 6.	0920	Lt C. Allmenröder-28	Sopwith Triplane	Polygon Wood
168	24. 6.	0920	Lt Groos-2	Sopwith Triplane	near Zonnebeke
169	24. 6.	0930	Rittm M. Frhr von Richthofen-55	DH4	Becelaere
170	25. 6.	1735	Rittm M. Frhr von Richthofen-56	RE8	Trenches near Le Bizet
171	25. 6.	0846	Lt C. Allmenröder-29	Sopwith Triplane	west of Quesnoy
172	26. 6.	2200	Lt C. Allmenröder-30	Nieuport	near Ypres
173	2. 7.	1020	Rittm M. Frhr von Richthofen-57	RE8	Deulemont
174	2. 7.	1025	Lt Groos-3	R.E.8	near Messines
175	6. 7.	2120	Lt K. Wolff-32	RE8	Zillebeke
176	7. 7.	1100	Lt K. Wolff-33	Sopwith Triplane	Comines
177	7. 7.	1110	Lt.d.R Niederhoff-4	Sopwith Triplane	Bousbecque
178	7. 7.	1810	Vzfw. Lautenschlager-1	Sopwith 2-Seater	between Houthem and Wytschaete
179	11. 7.	2115	Lt Mohnike-3	Sopwith Triplane	Comines
180	17. 7.	1110	Lt.d.R Niederhoff-5	Nieuport 23	Nordschoote
181	20. 7.	2110	Lt.d.R Niederhoff-6	Nieuport 23	south-east of Zonnebeke
182	22. 7.	1125	Lt Brauneck-9	Sopwith Triplane	east of

183	22. 7.	1130	Lt.d.R Niederhoff-7	Sopwith 2- Seater	Kortewilde south-west of Zonnebeke
184	22. 7.	1130	Oblt Reinhard-1	Sopwith 2-Seater	Warneton
185	27. 7.	2040	Lt von Schoenebeck-1	Sopwith Triplane	Beythem
186	28. 7.	1720	Lt Bockelmann-1	Caudron	Merckem
187	28. 7.	2100	Lt Mohnike-4	BE2	between Becelaere and Moorslede
188	31. 7.	1300	Lt K. Meyer-1	RE8	Deimlingseck
189	27. 7.	1310	Lt von Schoenebeck-2	RE8	Frezenberg
190	12. 8.	0850	Lt Stapenhorst-1	Sopwith	north-west of Bixschoote
191	13. 8.	0920	Lt Bockelmann-2	Pusher Biplane	Schellebeke, east of Ghent
192	13. 8.	1045	Oblt Reinhard-2	Sopwith 2-Seater	north of Polygon Wood
193	14. 8.	1040	Oblt Reinhard-3	RE8	Boesinghe
194	14. 8.	1045	Oblt Reinhard-4	SPAD	2 km north of Boesinghe
195	14. 8.	1735	Lt.d.R F. Müller-1	Sopwith	north of Bixschoote
96	16. 8.	0755	Rittm M. Frhr von Richthofen-58	Nieuport 23	south-west of Houthulst Forest
197	16. 8.	1120	Lt Groos-4	Sopwith Triplane	Hollebeke
198	16. 8.	1220	Lt Mohnike-5	Martinsyde G100	north of Linselles
199	17. 8.	0725	Lt Groos-5	SE5a	west of Paschendaele
200	17. 8.	2055	Lt von der Osten-1	Bristol F2B	Staden
201	23. 8.	0750	Lt Groos-6	Sopwith	south of Poelcapelle
202	25. 8.	2055	Lt von der Osten-2	Sopwith Triplane	near Paschendaele
	26. 8.	0730	Rittm M. Frhr von Richthofen-59	SPAD S7	near Poelcapelle

(victory credited to *JG I*'s overall score, not *Jasta 11*)

203	26. 8.	1045	Oblt Reinhard-5	RE8	near Bixschoote
	1. 9.	0750	Rittm M. Frhr von Richthofen-60	RE8	Zonnebeke
204	1. 9.	0815	Oblt Reinhard-6	Sopwith Camel	Zonnebeke
	3. 9.	0735	Rittm M. Frhr von Richthofen-61	Sopwith Pup	south of Bousbecque
205	3. 9.	0730	Lt Mohnike-6	Sopwith Pup	south of Tenbrielen
206	3. 9.	1000	Lt von Schoenebeck-3	Sopwith Triplane	east of Hollebeke
207	3. 9.	1018	Lt Stapenhorst-2	Sopwith Triplane	near Wytschaete
208	4. 9.	0840	Lt Mohnike-7	Sopwith Camel	Becelaere
209	4. 9.	0840	Lt Stapenhorst-3	Sopwith Camel	south of Becelaere
210	9. 9.	1250	Lt Stapenhorst-4	SPAD	south-west of

					Zonnebeke
211	15. 9.	1245	Lt von der Osten-3	Sopwith	Frezenberg
212	9.10.	1430	Lt.d.R F. Müller-2	Nieuport	Gheluwe
213	9.11.	1030	Lt L. Frhr von Richthofen-25	Bristol F2B	north-west of
					Zonnebeke
	23.11.	1400	Rittm M. Frhr von Richthofen-62	DH5	south-east of
					Bourlon Wood
214	23.11.	1400	Lt L. Frhr von Richthofen-26	Bristol F2B	2 km west of
					Seranvillers
215	30.11.	1345	Lt von der Osten-4	DH5	south of Bourlon
					Wood
30.11.		1430	Rittm M. Frhr von Richthofen-63	SE5a	Moeuvres
216	30.11.	1445	Lt Gussmann-2	DH5	near Moeuvres
217	12.12.	1320	Lt.d.R Just-1	Balloon	Ruyaulcourt
218	15.12.	1025	Lt von der Osten-5	SE5a	Havrincourt
1918					
219	13. 1.	1637	Lt Steinhäuser-2	Balloon	Heudecourt
220	2. 2.	1720	Lt Steinhäuser-3	RE8	Havrincourt
					Wood

(10 March 1918: German time synchronized with Allied time)

221	11. 3.	1310	Lt L. Frhr von Richthofen-27	Bristol F2B	north-east of
					Fresnoy-le-petit
222	11. 3.	1310	Vzfw Scholtz-2	SE5a	Honon Wood
223	12. 3.	1100	Lt L. Frhr von Richthofen-28	Bristol F2B	Maretz
224	12. 3.	1100	Lt L. Frhr von Richthofen-29	Bristol F2B	Clary
225	12. 3.	1100	Lt Steinhäuser-4	Bristol F2B	Beauvais
	12. 3.	1115	Rittm M. Frhr von Richthofen-64	Bristol F2B	Nauroy
	13. 3.	1035	Rittm M. Frhr von Richthofen-65	Sopwith Camel	near Banteaux
226	13. 3.	1040	Vzfw Scholtz-3	Sopwith Camel	Vaucelles
227	18. 3.	1100	Lt.d.R Gussmann-3	Bristol F2B	south of Joncourt
18. 3.	1115		Rittm M. Frhr von Richthofen-66	Sopwith Camel	Molain-Vaux-
					Andigny road
228	18. 3.	1115	Lt H.J. Wolff-1	SE5a	Escaufort
229	18. 3.	1120	Vzfw Scholtz-4	Sopwith Camel	La Vallée Mulâtre
24. 3.	1445		Rittm M. Frhr von Richthofen-67	SE5a	Combles
25. 3.	1555		Rittm M. Frhr von Richthofen-68	Sopwith Camel	Contalmaison
26. 3.	1645		Rittm M. Frhr von Richthofen-69	SE5a	south of
					Contalmaison
26. 3.	1700		Rittm M. Frhr von Richthofen-70	RE8	north-east of
					Albert
230	26. 3.	1700	Lt.d.R Gussmann-4	Sopwith Camel	north of Albert
	27. 3.	0900	Rittm M. Frhr von Richthofen-71	Sopwith Camel	Ancre
231	27. 3.	1150	Lt.d.R Udet-21	RE8	south of Albert
232	27. 3.	1205	Vfw Scholz-5	AW FK8	south of Albert
	27. 3.	1630	Rittm M. Frhr von Richthofen-72	Sopwith Dolphin	Foucaucourt
	27. 3.	1635	Rittm M. Frhr von Richthofen-73	Bristol F2B	north-east of
					Chuignolles

233	28. 3.	1150	Lt.d.R Udet-22	Sopwith Camel	north-east of Albert
	28. 3.	1230	Rittm M. Frhr von Richthofen-74	AW FK8	east of Méricourt
234	1. 4.	0900	Lt H.J. Wolff-2	DH4	Gréviller
235	1. 4.	1700	Lt H.J. Wolff-3	SE5a	forest N.E. of Moreuil
	2. 4.	1235	Rittm M. Frhr von Richthofen-75	RE8	over Hill 104, north-east of Moreuil
236	2. 4.	1650	Lt H.J. Wolff-4	Bristol F2B	between Morcourt and Harbonnières
237	2. 4.	1700	Lt.d.R Weiss-12	Bristol F2B	between Morcourt and Harbonnières
238	6. 4.	1415	Lt.d.R Udet-23	Sopwith Camel	forest south of Hamel
239	6. 4.	1500	Lt H.J. Wolff-5	Bristol F2B	north-east of Vauvillers
	6. 4.	1545	Rittm M. Frhr von Richthofen-76 S	Sopwith Camel	north-east of Villers-Brettoneux
240	6. 4.	1555	Lt H.J. Wolff-6	Sopwith Camel	east of Lamotte
241	6. 4.	1600	Lt.d.R Weiss-13	Sopwith Camel	southern edge of Marcelcave
242	6. 4.	1605	Vzfw Scholz-6	Sopwith Camel	Cérisy
243	6. 4.	1610	Lt Just-2	Sopwith Camel	Méricourt
244	6. 4.	1750	Lt.d.R Weiss-14	Sopwith Camel	north-east of Sailley le Sec
	7. 4.	1130	Rittm M. Frhr von Richthofen-77	Sopwith Camel	Hangard
	7. 4.	1205	Rittm M. Frhr von Richthofen-78	Sopwith Camel	north of Villers-Brettoneux
	(16 April 1918: German time one hour ahead of Allied time)				
245	20. 4.	1840	Lt.d.R Weiss-15	Sopwith Camel	south of Hamel Wood
	20. 4.	1840	Rittm M. Frhr von Richthofen-79	Sopwith Camel	south of Hamel Wood
	20. 4.	1843	Rittm M. Frhr von Richthofen-80	Sopwith Camel	Villers-Brettoneux
246	21. 4.	1150	Lt H.J. Wolff-7	Sopwith Camel	south of Hamelet
247	22. 4.	1158	Lt.d.R Weiss-16	Sopwith Camel	forest north of Moreuil
248	22. 4.	1200	Lt H.J. Wolff-8	Sopwith Camel	north of Moreuil
249	9. 5.	2000	Hptm Reinhard-13	Sopwith Camel	west of Morlancourt
250	10. 5.		Oblt E. von Wedel-1	Sopwith Camel	Cérisy
251	10. 5.		Lt Steinhäuser-5	Sopwith Camel	north of Cérisy
252	10. 5.		Lt H.J. Wolff-9	Sopwith Camel	south of Sailly-Laurette

253	15. 5.	1510	Lt H.J. Wolff-10	Bristol F2B	west of Guillaucourt
254	15. 5.	1515	Oblt E. von Wedel-2	Bristol F2B	south-east of Guillaucourt
255	19. 5.	1130	Lt Steinhäuser-6	Bristol F2B	Hamel
256	19. 5.	2000	Oblt E. von Wedel-3	SPAD	east of Harbonnières
257	19. 5.	2010	Lt Steinhäuser-7	DH9	Villers-Brettoneux
258	19. 5.	2010	Vzfw Gabriel-2	DH9	north-east of Marcelcave
	31. 5.	1945	Hptm Reinhard-14	SPAD 2-Seater	Bonneserle

(victory credited to JG I's overall score, not Jasta 11)

259	31. 5.	2040	Oblt E. von Wedel-4	SPAD	Burbillon Wood
260	1. 6.	1710	Vfw Gabriel-3	French SPAD	Fleury
261	2. 6.	1745	Lt Steinhäuser-8	SPAD 2-Seater	south of Troesnes
	2. 6.	1745	Hptm Reinhard-15	SPAD 2-Seater	south of Bonnes
	2. 6.	2030	Hptm Reinhard-16	Bréguet 14	La Ferte Milon
	2. 6.	2100	Hptm Reinhard-17	SPAD 2-Seater	Buisson de Borny Wood
	4. 6.	1725	Hptm Reinhard-18	SPAD 2-Seater	Dammard
262	4. 6.	1725	Lt W. Frhr von Richthofen-1	SPAD 2-Seater	west of Dammard
263	4. 6.	2040	Oblt E. von Wedel-5	SPAD 2-Seater	Faverolles
264	9. 6.	0900	Lt Steinhäuser-9	SPAD	Cravencon
265	9. 6.	0900	Oblt E. von Wedel-6	SPAD	Longpont
	9. 6.	0900	Hptm Reinhard-19	SPAD	Dommières
266	9. 6.	1220	Lt W. Frhr von Richthofen-2	SPAD	Tartures
267	9. 6.	1220	Lt Steinhäuser-10	SPAD	St. Baudry
268	10. 6.	1635	Vzfw Gabriel-4	Balloon	
	12. 6.	0930	Hptm Reinhard-20	SPAD 2-Seater	
269	13. 6.	1605	Vzfw Gabriel-5	SPAD	
270	16. 6.	1000	Vzfw Gabriel-6	Balloon	
271	28. 6.	0900	Lt Mohnike-8	SPAD	
272	28. 6.	0905	Lt Mohnike-9	SPAD	
273	30. 6.	0930	Vzfw Gabriel-7	Sopwith 1-Seater	
	18. 7.	0815	Oblt Göring-22	SPAD	near St. Bandry

(victory credited to JG I's overall score, not Jasta 11)

274	18. 7.	0830	Oblt E. von Wedel-7	SPAD	
275	18. 7.	0950	Vzfw Gabriel-8	SPAD	
276	18. 7.	1000	Vzfw Gabriel-9	SPAD	
277	18. 7.	1022	Vzfw Gabriel-10	Bréguet	Beugneux
278	18. 7.	1530	Vzfw Gabriel-11	SPAD	
279	21. 7.	2015	Oblt E. von Wedel-8	Sopwith Camel	Fère
280	21. 7.	2015	Lt W. Frhr von Richthofen-3	Sopwith Camel	Fère
281	25. 7.	0750	Lt L. Frhr von Richthofen-30	Sopwith Camel	Fismes
282	25. 7.	2030	Lt.d.R Just-3	SPAD 2-Seater	
283	29. 7.	1215	Oblt E. von Wedel-9	Bréguet 14	
284	1. 8.	1305	Lt Groos-7	SPAD	

285	1. 8.	1310	Lt L. Frhr von Richthofen-31	SPAD	
286	1. 8.	2025	Lt L. Frhr von Richthofen-32	SPAD	
287	8. 8.	1730	Lt L. Frhr von Richthofen-33	Sopwith Camel	west of Péronne
288	8. 8.	1745	Lt L. Frhr von Richthofen-34	SE5a	
289	8. 8.	1850	Lt L. Frhr von Richthofen-35	SE5a	Estrées
290	9. 8.	0730	Lt L. Frhr von Richthofen-36	DH9	Villers-Carbonnel
291	9. 8.	0735	Lt.d.R Just-4	Sopwith Camel	Estrées
292	9. 8.	1840	Lt L. Frhr von Richthofen-37	DH9	Foucaucourt
293	10. 8.	1215	Lt.d.R Fhrh von Köckeritz-1	SE5a	
294	11. 8.	0930	Lt L. Frhr von Richthofen-38	DH9	
295	12. 8.	0930	Lt W. Frhr von Richthofen-4/5	Sopwith Camel	east of Péronne
296	12. 8.	0935	Lt.d.R Just-5	Sopwith Camel	east of Péronne
297	12. 8.	0935	Lt L. Frhr von Richthofen-39	Sopwith Camel	north-west of Péronne
298	12. 8.	0950	Lt L. Frhr von Richthofen-40	Sopwith Camel	north-west of Misery
299	31. 8.	1945	Oblt E. von Wedel-10	Sopwith Dolphin	south-west of Péronne
300	31. 8.	1945	Lt.d.R Schulte-Frohlinde-1	Sopwith Camel	near Péronne
301	31. 8.	1945	Lt.d.R Fhhr von Köckeritz-2	Sopwith Dolphin	east of Péronne
302	2. 9.	0955	Oblt E. von Wedel-11	AW FK8	Frémicourt
303	4. 9.	1715	Lt.d.R Just-6	Balloon	Barastre
304	6. 9.	0945	Lt W. Frhr von Richthofen-5	Sopwith Dolphin	east of St. Quentin
305	7. 9.	1300	Lt.d.R Schulte-Frohlinde-2	SE5a	west of Le Catelet
306	7. 9.	1940	Lt W. Frhr von Richthofen-6	SE5a	west of Le Catelet
307	7. 9.	1945	Lt W. Frhr von Richthofen-7	SE5a	west of Le Catelet
308	7. 9.	1945	Oblt E. von Wedel-12	SE5a	Le Catelet
309	19. 9.	1600	Lt.d.R Schulte- Frohlinde-3	Bristol F.2B	Bellenglise
310	16.10.	1200	Vzfw Niemz-3	SPAD	near Aure River
311	23.10.	1255	Lt.d.R Noltenius-16	Balloon	Chatel-Cheherry
312	23.10.	1605	Lt.d.R Noltenius-17	SPAD	Aure River
313	23.10.	1735	Lt.d.R Noltenius-18	Balloon	Baulny
314	28.10.	1700	Lt.d.R Noltenius-19	Balloon	Eglisfontaine
315	3.11.	1515	Lt.d.R Noltenius-20	D.H.9	Barricourt
316	3.11.	1550	Lt.d.R Frhr von Köckeritz-3	SPAD	
317	3.11.	1605	Lt.d.R Gussmann-5	Dorand AR2	
318	4.11.	1645	Vzfw Niemz-3	D.H9	
319	4.11.	1600	Lt.d.R Schulte-Frohlinde-4	D.H4	
320	5.11.	1030	Lt W. Frhr von Richthofen-8	D.H9	south of Montmedy
321	5.11.	1035	Oblt E. von Wedel-13	SPAD	

ENDNOTES

Page numbers in **bold** refer to the page the reference appears on in this edition.
Page numbers in *italic* refer to material that is originally quoted in the author's source.

Introduction

O'Connor (1990) *Aviation Awards of Imperial Germany and the*
men Who Earned Them, vol II, pp. *2, 8, 22, 24* **6**

Chapter 1

Richthofen (1933) *Der rote Kampfflieger*, pp.*91* **12**
Richthofen (1933) *Der rote Kampfflieger*, pp.*86* **12**
Richthofen (1933) *Der rote Kampfflieger*, pp.*86–7* **13**
Richthofen (1920) *Ein Heldenleben*, pp. *188* **13**
Kriegs-Echo Wochen-Chronik Nr 91, 5 May 1916, pp. *8* **13**
Bailey and Cony, (2001) *The French Air Service War Chronology 1914–1918*, pp. *46* **13**
Werner (ed) (1930) *Briefe eines deutschen Kampffliegers an ein junges Mädchen*, pp. *18* **14**
When KEK Sivry was formed, Boelcke and Ltn Werner Notzke were its first pilots; on 21 April
    1916 – two years to the day before Richthofen's death – Notzke was testing his machine guns
    in the air when he accidently struck a tethered balloon cable and crashed to his death. [Ref:
    Werner, Boelcke (1932) *der Mensch der Flieger, der Führer der deutschen Jagdfliegerei*, pp. *150*] **14**
At the time, Immelmann had 14 aerial victories to his credit and Boelcke had
    13 [Ref: Franks, Bailey and Guest (1993) *Above the Lines*, pp. *76*] **14**
Immelmann and Boelcke both received the award on 12 January 1916 [Ref: O'Connor (1990)
    Aviation Awards of Imperial Germany and the Men Who Earned Them, vol II, pp. *55, 62*] **14**
Werner, Boelcke (1932) *der Mensch der Flieger, der Führer der deutschen Jagdfliegerei*, pp. *152* **15**
Richthofen (1933) *Der rote Kampfflieger*, *88–91* **15–16**
Moncure, (1993) *Forging the King's Sword*, pp. *2* **16**
Haythornthwaite, (1994) *The World War One Source Book*, pp. *32* **16–17**
Richthofen (1933) *Der rote Kampfflieger*, pp. *91–93* **17–18**
Quoted in Supf, (1958) *Das Buch der deutschen Fluggeschichte*, vol II, pp. *437* **18**
Richthofen (1920) *Ein Heldenleben*, pp. *189* **18**

Chapter 2

Genealogisches Handbuch des Adels – Stammfolge der Freiherren v. Richthofen, (1996), pp. *215* **20**
Richthofen (1933) *Der rote Kampfflieger*, *12* **21**
The Richthofen family evolved into five Main Lines: (Hertwigswaldau, Barzdorf,
    Michelsdorf, Ruppersdorf, and Heinersdorf, respectively). Manfred von Richthofen
    and his siblings came from the Second (or Barzdorf) Line, First (or Kohlhöhe)
    Bough and the Third (or Gäbersdorf) Branch of the family lineage
Richthofen (1933) *Der rote Kampfflieger*, *13–14* **21**

'Vigilant', Richthofen – The Red Knight of the Air, (n d), pp. 1 **22**

Richthofen (1933) *Der rote Kampfflieger*, 9–17 **22**

Richthofen (1933) *Der rote Kampfflieger*, pp. 7; current English translation from
Kilduff, (1999) *The Illustrated Red Baron*, pp. 2; the original German text is:

Reicht auch der Stammbaum nicht ins graue Altertum,
Ist's dennoch ein gar altes, wackeres Geschlecht;
Christallhell, ungetrübt blieb seines Namens Ruhm,
Hoch hielt es stets die Wahrheit, Ehre und das Recht.
Treu seiner Väter Brauch, fromm, tapfer, brav und schlicht,
Hat Gottes gnäd'ge Huld vor Schaden es bewahrt.
O wank auch fürder nicht vom Pfad der Christenpflicht,
Führ deinen Namen stolz nach echter Ritterart!
Es blühe mächtig dies Geschlecht, der Ehre Bild,
Nie fall' ein Schatten auf sein Wappenschild! **22**

According to Perthes, (1921) *Ehrentafel der Kriegsopfer des reichsdeutschen Adels 1914–1919*, pp.
199, only six Richthofens in addition to Manfred died during the course of World War I:
Fahnenjunker Egbert von Richthofen, age 21, of Dragoner-Regiment Nr 8 on 29 August
1914; Ltn Gottfried von Richthofen, 19, of 1. Grenadier-Regiment zur Fuss on 18 June 1915;
Fahnenjunker Siegfried von Richthofen, 17, of Dragoner-Regiment Nr 8 on 10 November
1914; Ltn Eberhard von Richthofen, 19, of Dragoner-Regiment Nr 8 on 31 August 1918;
Ltn Wolfram von Richthofen, 24, of Dragoner-Regiment Nr 8 on 11 August 1914, and
Rittmeister der Reserve Oswald von Richthofen, 29, of 2. Garde-Ulanen-Regiment **23**

Richthofen (1920) *Ein Heldenleben*, pp. 13–14 **22–23**

Deutscher Offizier-Bund (ed) (1926) *Ehren-Rangliste des ehemaligen Deutschen Heeres*, pp. 40 **23**

Richthofen (1920) *Ein Heldenleben*, pp. 14 **23**

Quoted in Gibbons (1927) *The Red Knight of Germany*, pp. 10 **23–24**

Moncure (1993) *Forging the King's Sword*, pp. 87–88 **24**

Hindenburg (1921) *Out of My Life*, pp. 3 **24**

The statement indicates a memory lapse; as noted above, Richthofen's cousin Wolfram
was killed in action on 11 August 1914, while Ltn Helmut von Frankenburg und
Ludwigsdorf, age 20, of Grenadier-Regiment Nr 7, was killed on 22 August 1914 [Ref:
Perthes, (1921) *Ehrentafel der Kriegsopfer des reichsdeutschen Adels 1914–1919*, pp. 68] **25**

Richthofen (1920) *Ein Heldenleben*, pp. 15–16 **25**

Richthofen: Gesundheits-Nachweis, Gross Lichterfelde, 23 February 1911 **25**

Richthofen (1920) *Ein Heldenleben*, pp. 16 **25**

Prinz Friedrich Karl's father, Prinz Friedrich Leopold of Prussia (1865-1931), and Kaiser
Wilhelm II (1859-1941) were great-grandsons of König [King] Friedrich Wilhelm III
of Prussia [Ref: Louda (1981) *Heraldry of the Royal Families of Europe*, pp. 186] **25**

Rittmeister Prinz Friedrich Karl von Preussen, age 24, died of wounds suffered while
trying to escape from British captivity on 6 April; 1917 [Ref: Perthes, (1921)
Ehrentafel der Kriegsopfer des reichsdeutschen Adels 1914–1919 pp. 185] **25**

Moncure (1993) *Forging the King's Sword*, pp. 241 **26**

Richthofen (1920) *Ein Heldenleben* pp. 17 **26**

Richthofen (1920) *Ein Heldenleben* pp. 18 **26**

Richthofen (1920) *Ein Heldenleben* pp. 18–19 **27**

MacDonogh (2000) *The Last Kaiser: The Life of Wilhelm II*, pp. 353 **27**

Richthofen (1920) *Ein Heldenleben* pp. 20 **28**

Richthofen (1920) *Ein Heldenleben* pp. 20–21 **28–29**
Richthofen (1937) *Mein Kriegstagebuch*, pp. 7–9 **29**
Richhtofen (1937) *Mein Kriegstagebuch*, pp. 9–10 **29–30**
Richthofen (1920) *Ein Heldenleben* pp. 20–23 **30**
Richthofen (1920) *Ein Heldenleben* pp. 176 **30**
Richthofen (1920) *Ein Heldenleben* pp. 24–25 **31–32**
Richthofen (1937) *Mein Kriegstagebuch*, pp. 14 **32**
O'Connor, (1988) *Aviation Awards of Imperial Germany in World War I and the Men Who Earned Them*, vol I, pp. iii **32**
O'Connor, (1990) *Aviation Awards of Imperial Germany in World War I and the Men Who Earned Them*, vol II, pp. 7–9 **32**
Richthofen (1920) *Ein Heldenleben* pp. 26 **32**
Richthofen (1920) *Ein Heldenleben* pp. 27–28 **33**
Richthofen (1920) *Ein Heldenleben* pp. 177 **34**
Richthofen (1920) *Ein Heldenleben* pp. 178 **34**
Richthofen (1920) *Ein Heldenleben* pp. 178 **34**
Richthofen (1920) *Ein Heldenleben* pp. 180 **34**

Chapter 3

Richthofen (1937) *Mein Kriegstagebuch*, pp. 13–14 **36**
Richthofen (1937) *Mein Kriegstagebuch*, pp. 22 **36**
Richthofen (1920) *Ein Heldenleben*, pp. 179–180 **36–37**
Richthofen (1920) *Ein Heldenleben*, pp. 35–36 **37**
Richthofen (1937) *Mein Kriegstagebuch*, pp. 26, 27 **38**
Richthofen (1920) *Ein Heldenleben*, pp. 181-182 **38**
Kriegs-Echo Wochen-Chronik Nr 87, 7 April 1916, pp. 12-14; Haythornthwaite (1994) *The World War One Source Book*, pp. 330 **39**
Richthofen (1920) *Ein Heldenleben*, pp. 182–183 **39**
Richthofen (1920) *Ein Heldenleben*, pp. 38 **40**
Richthofen (1920) *Ein Heldenleben*, pp. 56–57 **40–41**
Cron (1966) '*Organization of the German Luftstreitkräfte,*' C&CJ, pp. 55 **41**
Richthofen (1933) *Der rote Kampfflieger*, pp. 61 **41**
Richthofen (1933) *Der rote Kampfflieger*, pp. 62 **41**
Richthofen (1933) *Der rote Kampfflieger*, pp. 63–64 **42**
Richthofen (1920) *Ein Heldenleben*, pp. 49 **42**
Kriegsministerium (organization manual), Teil 10 Abschnitt B, (1918) *Flieger-Formationen*, pp. 138 **43**
Kriegs-Echo Wochen-Chronik Nr 63, 22 October 1915, pp. 13 **43**
Richtofen (1937) *Mein Kriegstagebuch*, pp. 40–41 **43**
Grosz (2002) '*Albatros B.II,*' Windsock Datafile No 93, pp. 1 **43**
Supf, (1958) *Das Buch der deutschen Fluggeschichte*, vol II, pp. 437 **43**
Richthofen (1920) *Ein Heldenleben*, pp. 187 **44**
Richthofen (1920) *Ein Heldenleben*, pp. 42 **44**
Richthofen (1920) *Ein Heldenleben*, pp. 42–43 **45**
Richthofen (1920) *Ein Heldenleben*, pp. 44–45 **45**
Richthofen (1920) *Ein Heldenleben*, pp. 45 **46**

The unit was formally established on 6 August 1915 [Ref:
  Fliegerformationen, op.cit, pp. *158*] **46**
Werner, Boelcke (1932) *der Mensch der Flieger, der Führer der deutschen Jagdfliegerei*, pp. *136* **46**
Grosz, (1989) 'Fokker E.III,' *Windsock Datafile* No 15, pp. *1* **46**
Richthofen (1937) *Mein Kriegstagebuch*, pp.*63* **4647**
Richthofen (1920) *Ein Heldenleben* pp. *46* **47**
Not to be confused with the US-headquartered General Electric Company,
  AEG was founded in Germany in 1883 and remained in existence
  until 1985, when it was acquired by Daimler-Benz AG **47**
Richthofen (1920) *Ein Heldenleben* pp. *46-47* **48**
Richthofen (1920) *Ein Heldenleben* pp. *48–49* **49**
Richthofen (1920) *Ein Heldenleben* pp. *51* **49**
Richthofen (1920) *Ein Heldenleben* pp. *49–50* **50**
Supf, (1958) *Das Buch der deutschen Fluggeschichte*, vol I, pp. *290* **51**
Esposito (ed), (1965) *A Concise History of World War I*, pp. *85* **51**
AOK 3. Armee Bericht Nr Ia 5515, 12 September 1915 **51**
Richthofen (1920) *Ein Heldenleben* pp. *53–54* **52**
Richthofen (1920) *Ein Heldenleben* pp. *54–55* **53–54**
Richthofen (1920) *Ein Heldenleben* pp. *52-53* **54**
Bailey and Cony, (2001) *The French Air Service War Chronology 1914-1918*, pp. *28* **55**
Richthofen (1920) *Ein Heldenleben* pp. *188* **55**

Chapter 4

Haddow and Grosz (1988) *The German Giants – The German R-Planes 1914–1918*, pp. *vii* **56**
Neumann (ed) (1920) *Die deutschen Luftstreitkräfte im Weltkriege*, pp. *58–64* **56**
Richthofen (1920) *Ein Heldenleben* pp. *56* **56**
Richthofen (1920) *Ein Heldenleben* pp. *56–57* **57**
The first son, Ltn Nikolaus Christoph Freiherr von Lyncker, served with unmounted
  Grenadier Regiment Nr 1, and died of wounds at age 22 on 10 September 1914 [Ref:
  Perthes (1921) *Ehrentafel der Kriegsopfer des Reichsdeutschen Adels 1914-1919*] **58**
Richthofen (1937) *Mein Kriegstagebuch*, pp. *69* **58**
Richthofen (1937) *Mein Kriegstagebuch*, pp. *68* **59**
Richthofen (1937) *Mein Kriegstagebuch*, pp. *70–71* **59**
Richthofen (1937) *Mein Kriegstagebuch*, pp.*46* **59**
Richthofen (1920) *Ein Heldenleben* pp. *129* **60**
Kriegsministerium (organization manual), Teil 10 Abschnitt B,
  Flieger-Formationen, (1918), pp. *196–207* **60**
Ferko, *Richthofen*. (1995), pp. *8* **60**
Schweckendiek (1938) *Der Kampfflieger Lothar Freiherr von Richthofen*, pp. *18* **60**
O'Connor (1990) *Aviation Awards of Imperial Germany in World War
  I and the Men Who Earned Them*, vol II, pp. *62* **61**
Ltn Wilhelm von Schwerin, descended from Counts of Zieten-Schwerin, was shot down
  over Rethel on 28 April 1916 and died of his wounds on 2 May at age 18 [Ref: Perthes
  (1921) *Ehrentafel der Kriegsopfer des Reichsdeutschen Adels 1914-1919 pp. 225*] **61**
Richthofen (1937) *Mein Kriegstagebuch*, pp. *76* **62**
Richthofen (1920) *Ein Heldenleben* pp. *59–60* **62**
Immelmann (1934) *Der Adler von Lille*, pp. *182* **63**

Hptm Günter von Detten was shot down and killed over Génicourt, near
Verdun, on 21June 1916 at age 37 [Ref: Perthes (1921) *Ehrentafel der
Kriegsopfer des Reichsdeutschen Adels 1914-1919* pp. 50] **63**
Hptm Ernst von Gersdorff was shot down and killed near Metz on 19 June 1916 at age 38
[Ref: Perthes (1921) *Ehrentafel der Kriegsopfer des Reichsdeutschen Adels 1914-1919* pp. 75] **63**
Richthofen (1920) *Ein Heldenleben* pp. 189–190 **63**
Werner, Boelcke (1932) *der Mensch der Flieger, der Führer der deutschen Jagdfliegerei*, pp. 159 **64**
Esposito (ed) (1964) *A Concise History of World War I*, pp.154–156 **64**
Richthofen (1920) *Ein Heldenleben* pp. 195; Richthofen (1937) *Mein Kriegstagebuch*,
pp. 75–76 notes that Zeumer was shot down over Fort Vaux and subsequently
injured in an auto accident, thereby aggravating his already delicate health **64**
Richthofen (1920) *Ein Heldenleben* pp. 65–66 **65**
Richthofen (1920) *Ein Heldenleben* pp. 67–68 **65**
Esposito (ed) (1964) *A Concise History of World War I*, pp. 156 **66**
Werner, Boelcke (1932) *der Mensch der Flieger, der Führer der deutschen Jagdfliegerei*, pp. 184–185 **66**
Werner, Boelcke (1932) *der Mensch der Flieger, der Führer der deutschen Jagdfliegerei*, pp. 169 **66**
Richthofen (1920) *Ein Heldenleben* pp. 70 **66–67**
Richthofen (1920) *Ein Heldenleben* pp. 70–71 **67**
Ritter (1926) *Der Luftkrieg*, pp. 166–167 **67**
Richthofen (1937) *Mein Kriegstagebuch*, pp. 79 **67**

Chapter 5

O'Connor (1998) *Aviation Awards of Imperial Germany in World War I*, vol. V, pp. 124 **68**
Supf (1958) *Das Buch der deutschen Fluggeschichte*, vol II, pp. 342 **68**
Werner, Boelcke (1932) *der Mensch der Flieger, der Führer der deutschen Jagdfliegerei*, pp. 63 **68**
Oberleutnant Hans-Joachim Buddecke, Leutnant Kurt Wintgens, Leutnant Max
Mulzer, Leutnant Otto Parschau, Leutnant der Reserve Walter Höhndorf,
Oberleutnant Ernst Freiherr von Althaus, and Ltn Wilhelm Frankl. Of these
pilots, only Althaus outlived Richthofen and survived World War I **68**
Clark (2006) *Iron Kingdom*, pp. 610 **69**
Kriegsministerium (organization manual), Teil 10 Abschnitt
B, *Flieger-Formationen*, (1918), pp. 234 **69**
Ltn.d.Res Hansjoachim von Arnim was shot down over Le Transloy, in the Somme
Sector, on 28 August 1916 and killed at age 22 [Ref: Perthes (1921) *Ehrentafel der
Kriegsopfer des Reichsdeutschen Adels 1914-1919*, pp. 5]; at the time he was flying with
a two-seat artillery support unit and had not yet departed for Jasta 2 [Ref: Werner,
Boelcke (1932) *der Mensch der Flieger, der Führer der deutschen Jagdfliegerei*, pp. 185] **69**
Ltn.d.Res Wolfgang Günther served with Jasta 2 until 20 December
1916, when he was transferred to Flieger-Abteilung (A) 205 [Ref:
Franks, Bailey and Duiven (1996) *The Jasta Pilots*, pp. 150] **69**
The original Jagdstaffel 2 Kriegstagebuch [war diary] has not been seen since
World War II and was very likely destroyed during bombing of the Reichsarchiv
in Potsdam, outside Berlin; this excerpt appears in Werner, Boelcke (1932)
der Mensch der Flieger, der Führer der deutschen Jagdfliegerei, **69**
Werner, Boelcke (1932) *der Mensch der Flieger, der Führer der deutschen Jagdfliegerei*, pp. 185–186 **69**
Esposito (ed) (1964) *A Concise History of World War I*, pp. 89–90 **11**
Inspektion der Fliegertruppen, Erfahrungen im Luftkampf - Jagdstaffel Boelcke, (n d), pp. 8 **70**

Endnotes

Siegert in Neumann (ed) (1920) *Die deutschen Luftstreitkräfte im Weltkriege*, pp. *474–475* **70**

Werner, Boelcke (1932) *der Mensch der Flieger, der Führer der deutschen Jagdfliegerei*, pp. *186* **71**

Henshaw (1995) *The Sky Their Battlefield*, pp. *106* **71**

Werner, Boelcke (1932) *der Mensch der Flieger, der Führer der deutschen Jagdfliegerei*, pp. *188–189* **71**

Grosz, (2003) Albatros D.I/D.II,' *Windsock Datafile No 100*, pp. *4, 5* **71**

By this time, Jasta 2 had been placed under the operational authority of the German 1st
Army, which accounts for the unit's subsequent joint combined patrols with Jasta 1 [Ref:
Stabsoffizier der Flieger der 1. Armee Bericht St.O.Fl./Ib Nr 5490, 17 September 1916] **72**

Bruce (1969) *British Aeroplanes 1914-1918*, pp. *392* **72**

Bruce (1969) *British Aeroplanes 1914-1918*, **72**

Richthofen (1917) *Der rote Kampfflieger*, pp. *91–92* **72–73**

Public Record Office, file *Air 1/686/21/13/2250 XC15183*,
Richthofen Combat Reports (translations) **73**

According to the Royal Flying Corps Casualty List for that day, FE2b 7018 of No
11 Squadron: 'Left [the] aerodrome at 9.10 a.m. Two FEs [were] seen to go
down under control west of Marcoing. Information received from 2/Lt Pinkerton
that both Morris and Rees were killed. Information from a private source
[indicates] that 2/Lt Morris died at Cambrai hospital on Sept. 17th.' **73**

Hobson (1995) *Airmen Died in the Great War 1914-1918*, pp. *75, 86* **73**

Hobson (1995) *Airmen Died in the Great War 1914-1918*, **73**

Richthofen (1917) *Der rote Kampfflieger*, pp. *93*; as Richthofen mentions
only one memorial stone, it may well have been placed on the grave
of Capt Rees, who was found dead in the wreckage **73–74**

Richthofen (1917) *Der rote Kampfflieger*, **74**

Armee Oberkommando 1Tagesbefehl Nr 17, 21 September 1916 **74**

Werner (ed) (1930) *Briefe eines deutschen Kampffliegers*, pp. *54–55* **74**

Gibbons (1927) *The Red Knight of Germany*, pp. *80* **74**

Royal Flying Corps War Diary entry, 23 September 1916 **74**

Hobson (1995) *Airmen Died in the Great War 1914-1918* pp. *23* **74**

Bowyer (1972) *The Flying Elephants*, pp. *40–41* **75**

Werner, Boelcke (1932) *der Mensch der Flieger, der Führer der deutschen Jagdfliegerei*, pp. *193* **75**

Gibbons (1927) *The Red Knight of Germany*, pp. *81* **75**

Jones (1928) *The War in the Air*, vol II, pp. *296* **75**

Richthofen (1920) *Ein Heldenleben*, pp. *191–192* **75**

Stabsoffizier der Flieger der 1. Armee Wochenbericht, Teil 1, 9 October 1916, pp. *1* **75**

Stabsoffizier der Flieger der 1. Armee Wochenbericht, Teil 7, pp. *7* identified the aircraft
type as a BE12 and the serial number as 6618, which was reported as missing by
No 21 Squadron, RFC; the pilot, 2/Lt William C. Fenwick, age 19, was reported
killed [Ref: Hobson (1995) *Airmen Died in the Great War 1914-1918* pp. *45*] **76**

Siegert in Neumann (ed) (1920) *Die deutschen Luftstreitkräfte im Weltkriege*, pp. *5*; Zuerl (1938)
Pour le Mérite-Flieger, pp. *227* lists Hoeppner's command as the 75th Reserve Division **76**

Hoeppner (1921) *Deutschlands Krieg in der Luft*, pp. *82* **76**

Kriegsministerium (organization manual), Teil 10 Abschnitt B,
Flieger-Formationen, (1918), pp. *234–239* **76**

Goote (1938) *'rangehn ist Alles!*, pp. *19* **76**

Jentsch (137) *Beim Jagdflug tödlich verunglückt?*, pp. *259* **76**

Franks (2004) *Jasta Boelcke*, pp. *46* **77**

Oblt Bodo Freiherr von Lyncker was flying with Jasta 25 when he was shot down over Gjevjeli, Macedonia on 18 February 1917 and killed at age 22 [Ref: Perthes (1921) *Ehrentafel der Kriegsopfer des Reichsdeutschen Adels 1914-1919* pp. *150*] **77**

Ltn.d.Res Joachim von Arnim on 28 August 1916, Ltn.d.Res Ernst Diener on 30 September 1916, and Ltn.d.Res Herwarth Phillips on 1 October 1916; Ltn. d.Res Winand Grafe had orders to Jasta 2 when he was killed on 22 September 1916 [Ref: Jentsch (1937) *Beim Jagdflug tödlich verunglückt?*, pp. *257*] **77**

Werner, Boelcke (1932) *der Mensch der Flieger, der Führer der deutschen Jagdfliegerei*, pp. *196* **77**

Public Record Office, file *Air 1/686/21/13/2250 XC15183, Richthofen Combat Reports* (translations) **78**

Most likely this aircraft was FE2b 4292 of No 25 Squadron, RFC, the pilot of which, 2/Lt Moreton Hayne, was killed at age 18; his observer, Lt A.H.M. Copeland, was wounded and taken prisoner [Ref: Henshaw (1995) *The Sky Their Battlefield*, pp. *117*, Hobson (1995) *Airmen Died in the Great War 1914-1918* pp. *54*] **78**

Vizefeldwebel Fritz Kosmahl and Oberleutnant Josef Neubürger of Feldflieger-Abteilung 22 [Ref: O'Connor (1990) *Aviation Awards of Imperial Germany in World War I*, vol. II, pp. *147*] **78**

Bruce (1969) *British Aeroplanes 1914-1918*, pp. *380* **78**

Public Record Office, *Richthofen Combat Reports* **79**

Richthofen (1920) *Ein Heldenleben*, pp. *192* **79**

Boelcke (1916) *Hauptmann Boelckes Feldberichte*, pp. *121* **79**

Hobson (1995) *Airmen Died in the Great War 1914–1918* pp. *99* **79**

Richthofen (1920) *Ein Heldenleben*, pp. *74–75* **79**

Werner, Boelcke (1932) *der Mensch der Flieger, der Führer der deutschen Jagdfliegerei*, pp. *202* **79**

Public Record Office, *Richthofen Combat Reports* **80**

According to the RFC Combat Casualty List entry for that day: 'A BE12 was reported by 11th A.A. Battery to be seen diving down 15,000 yards N.E. of Maricourt, apparently under control pursued by a German biplane.' **80**

Werner, Böhme, pp. *67–68* **81**

Bowyer, Albert Ball (1977) *VC*, pp. *103* **81**

Werner, Boelcke (1932) *der Mensch der Flieger, der Führer der deutschen Jagdfliegerei*, pp. *205* **81**

Werner, Böhme, pp. *69–70* **82**

Richthofen (1920) *Ein Heldenleben*, pp. *75–77* **82–83**

Jones (1928) *The War in the Air*, vol II, pp. *312ff* **83**

Richthofen (1920) *Ein Heldenleben*, pp. *193* **83**

Werner, Boelcke (1932) *der Mensch der Flieger, der Führer der deutschen Jagdfliegerei*, pp. *210* **83–84**

Werner, Boelcke (1932) *der Mensch der Flieger, der Führer der deutschen Jagdfliegerei*, pp. *211–212* **84**

Richthofen (1920) *Ein Heldenleben*, pp. *192* **84**

Chapter 6

Richthofen (1920) *Ein Heldenleben*, pp. *171* **86**

Bolle, 'Jagdstaffel Boelcke' in Neumann (ed) (1923) *In der Luft unbesiegt*, pp. *41* **86**

Stabsoffizier der Flieger der 1. Armee Wochenbericht Teil 4, 14 November 1916, pp. *4* **86**

Public Record Office, file *Air 1/686/21/13/2250 XC15183, Richthofen Combat Reports* (translations); British crewmen were Sgt Cuthbert G. Baldwin, pilot, age 28; and 2/Lt G. Andrew Bentham, observer, age 21, in FE2b 7010 of No 18 Squadron [Ref: Hobson (1995) *Airmen Died in the Great War 1914-1918*, pp. *20, 23*] **86**

Stofl 1. Armee Wochenbericht, Teil 3, 6 November 1916, pp. *4* **86**

The intended target, according to Public Record Office, Royal Flying

Corps *Communiqué No 61*, 12 November 1916, pp. *2* **86**

Richthofen (1920) *Ein Heldenleben*, pp. *78*; Stofl 1. Armee Wochenbericht, Teil 4, 21 November 1916, p. *3*; the pilot was 2/Lt Ian G. Cameron, age 19, who died of his wounds in BE2c 2506; Cameron flew alone, despite Richthofen's claim of having hit a backseat crewman [Ref: Hobson (1995) *Airmen Died in the Great War 1914–1918* pp. *30*] **86–87**

The Duke of Saxe-Coburg-Gotha was then on the staff of the 38. Infanterie-Division, headquartered at Vaux-Vraulcourt [Ref: (1921) *Thüringen im Weltkrieg*, pp. *282*] **87**

Richthofen (1920) *Ein Heldenleben*, pp. *79–80*; Ltn Hans Imelmann also received the award [Ref: *Saxe-Coburg-Gotha Archiv*, fol. *107–108*] **87–88**

Louda (1981) *Heraldry of the Royal Families of Europe*, pp. *85* **88**

Winter, (ca. 1935) *Gotha als Fliegerstadt in der Vergangenheit*, pp. *37, 39, 53* **88**

Richthofen (1920) *Ein Heldenleben*, pp. *77–78* **88**

O'Connor (1990) *Aviation Awards of Imperial Germany in World War I and the Men Who Earned Them*, vol II, pp. *132, 140, 142* **89**

Stofl 1. Armee Wochenbericht, Teil 8, 14 November 1916, pp. *5* **89**

Richthofen (1937) *Mein Kriegstagebuch*, pp. *87–88* **89–90**

Richthofen (1937) *Mein Kriegstagebuch*, pp. *89* **90**

Jentsch (1937) *Beim Jagdflug tödlich verunglückt?*, pp. *260* **90**

Stofl 1. Armee Wochenbericht, Teil 2, 21 November 1916, pp. *1* **90**

Falls in Esposito (ed) (1965) *A Concise History of World War I*, pp. *90* **90**

Jones (1928) *The War in the Air*, vol II, pp. *323–324* **90**

Stofl 1. Armee Wochenbericht, Teil 4, 5 December 1916 p. *2*; BE2c 2767 of No 15 Squadron, RFC, 2/Lt James C. Lees and Lt Thomas H. Clarke, both of whom were taken prisoner [Ref: RFC Combat Casualty List for that day] **90**

Stofl 1. Armee Wochenbericht, Teil 4, 5 December 1916; FE2b 4848 of No 18 Squadron, RFC, 2/Lt Gilbert S. Hall, who died of his wounds at age 25, and 2/Lt George Doughty, who was found dead at the scene at age 21 [Ref: Hobson (1995) *Airmen Died in the Great War 1914–1918* pp. *52, 41*] **90**

Gibbons (1927) *The Red Knight of Germany*, pp. *99* **90**

Werner (ed) (1930) *Briefe eines deutschen Kampffliegers an ein junges Mädchen*, pp. *83* **90**

Kirmaier was most likely shot down by Capt John O. Andrews of No 24 Squadron; Public Record Office, *RFC War Diary and RFC Communiqué No 63*, 26 November 1916, pp. *1*, both state that Andrews 'destroyed a hostile machine, which crashed on our side of the lines near' Lesboeufs, northwest of Morval. **91**

Inspektion der Fliegertruppen, Erfahrungen im Luftkampf – Jagdstaffel Boelcke, (n d), pp. *8* **91**

Public Record Office, *RFC War Diary and RFC Communiqué No 63*, 26 November 1916, pp. *2* **91**

Public Record Office, *Richthofen Combat Reports* **91**

Bowyer (1978) *For Valour – the Air VCs*, pp. *40* **91**

Bowyer (1978) *For Valour – the Air VCs*, pp. *44* **91**

Gibbons (1927) *The Red Knight of Germany*, pp. *102–103*; None of those souvenirs – from the serial number patches to the silver victory cups – have been seen in public since 1945, as 'the contents of the museum were taken to Moscow' (or somewhere in the former Soviet Union) by a Red Army unit devoted to seizing art and other cultural treasures in former German territories, according to Manfred von Richthofen's nephew and namesake [Ref: Quoted in Kilduff (1998) *The Illustrated Red Baron*, pp. *6*] **92**

Confirmed in *Stofl 1. Armee Wochenbericht, Teil 4*, 5 December 1916 pp. *2* **92**

Born on 30 December 1890, Hawker was five weeks and two days short of his 26th birthday when he was killed; he was Commanding Officer of No 24 Squadron,

RFC [Ref: *Stofl 1. Armee Wochenbericht, Teil 4*, 5 December 1916 pp. *37, 41*] **92**

Richthofen (1920) *Ein Heldenleben*, pp. *193*; Richthofen's chronology is mystifying, as Jasta 2's only other casualty for the month was reported to have occurred on 16 November, when Ltn.d.Res König was lightly wounded in an air fight [Ref: *Stofl 1. Armee Wochenbericht, Teil 5*, 21 November 1916, pp. *4*]. That report was corrected to note that König had not been wounded [Ref: *Stofl 1. Armee Wochenbericht, Teil 5*, 19 December 1916, pp. *2*] **92**

Werner (ed) (1930) *Briefe eines deutschen Kampffliegers an ein junges Mädchen*, pp. *82* **92**

Zuerl (1938) *Pour-le-Mérite-Flieger*, pp. *467–468* **92**

O'Connor (1990) *Aviation Awards of Imperial Germany in World War I and the Men Who Earned Them*, vol II, pp. *66* **92**

Kofl 1. Armee Wochenbericht, Teil 2, 12 December 1916 pp. *1* **92**

D.H.2 5986 of No 32 Squadron piloted by 22-year-old Lt Philip B.G. Hunt; Public Record Office, RFC Combat Casualty List reported: 'A newspaper cutting from "The Times" forwarded by 5th Brigade states "Captain Philip Hunt, Yeomanry, attached RFC, who was previously reported missing is now reported to be wounded and a prisoner of war in Germany."' **92**

Public Record Office, *Richthofen Combat Reports* **92**

Werner (ed) (1930) *Briefe eines deutschen Kampffliegers an ein junges Mädchen*, pp. *83* **93**

Kofl 1. Armee Wochenbericht, Teil 4, 26 December 1916, pp. *2* **93**

Jentsch (1937) *Beim Jagdflug tödlich verunglückt?*, pp. *259–261* **93**

Werner (ed) (1930) *Briefe eines deutschen Kampffliegers an ein junges Mädchen*, pp. *83–84* **93**

Kofl 1. Armee Wochenbericht, Teil 8, 26 December 1916, pp. *3* **93**

Kofl 1. Armee Wochenbericht, Teil 2, 19 December 1916, pp. *1* **93**

Richthofen (1937) *Mein Kriegstagebuch*, pp. *93* **94**

Jones (1931) *The War in the Air*, vol III, pp. *320* **94**

Public Record Office, *Richthofen Combat Reports* **94**

Shores, Franks and Guest (1990) *Above the Trenches*, pp. *226–227* **94**

Hobson (1995) *Airmen Died in the Great War 1914–1918* pp. *63* **95**

Public Record Office, *Richthofen Combat Reports* **95**

Hobson (1995) *Airmen Died in the Great War 1914–1918* pp.*38, 107* **95**

Schweckendiek (1938) *Der Kampfflieger Lothar Freiherr von Richthofen*, pp. *19* **95**

Richthofen (1920) *Ein Heldenleben*, pp. *193–194*; Richthofen's 13th and 14th aerial victories were scored on 20 December, not 23 December, as noted in this letter **96**

Public Record Office, *Richthofen Combat Reports* **96**

Franks, Giblin and McCrery (1995) *Under the Guns of the Red Baron*, pp. *47* **96**

Jones (1931) *The War in the Air*, vol III, pp. *320* **97**

Bruce (1969) *British Aeroplanes 1914-1918*, pp. *552* **97**

Public Record Office, *Richthofen Combat Reports* **97**

Hobson (1995) *Airmen Died in the Great War 1914–1918* pp.*14* **98**

Grosz, "The Agile and Aggressive Albatros" in (1976) *Air Enthusiast*, pp. *40–41* **98**

Kofl 6. Armee Wochenbericht Nr 22400, Teil 1, 23 January 1917 **98**

Jones (1931) *The War in the Air*, vol III **98**

Richthofen (1920) *Ein Heldenleben*, pp. *82–83* **98–99**

O'Connor (1990) *Aviation Awards of Imperial Germany in World War I and the Men Who Earned Them*, vol II, pp. *219* **99**

Kofl 6. Armee Wochenbericht Nr 22400, Teil 10, 23 January 1917 **99**

Chapter 7

Jones (1934) *The War in the Air*, vol IV, pp. *395–397* **100**
Kriegsministerium (organizational manual), *Teil 10 Abschnitt
B, Flieger-Formationen*, (1918), pp. *234* **101**
According to a review of the weekly reports for that time period filed by
the Staff Officer in Charge of Aviation for the 6th Army and abbreviated
hereafter as Stofl or Kofl 6. Armee Wochenberichten **101**
Potempa (1997) *Die Königlich-Bayerische Fliegertruppe 1914-1918*, pp. *548* **101**
Stofl 6. Armee Wochenbericht, Nr. 20759, Teil 10, 28 November 1916, pp. *2* **101**
Kofl 6. Armee Wochenbericht Nr. 22180, Teil 9, 16 January 1917, pp. *2* **101**
Nowarra and Brown (1964) *von Richthofen and the 'Flying Circus,'* pp. *38* **101**
Kofl 6. Armee Wochenbericht Nr. 22400, Teil 1, 23 January 1917, pp. *1* **101**
Grosz, "The Agile and Aggressive Albatros" in (19767) *Air Enthusiast* pp. *41–42* **101**
Richthofen (1920) *Ein Heldenleben*, pp. *83* **102**
VanWyngarden (1994) *von Richthofen's Flying Circus*, pp. *2* **102**
Confirmed in Kofl 6. Armee Wochenbericht Nr. 22639, Teil 12, 30 January 1917,
p. 3; 2/Lt John Hay, age 28, killed in FE8 6388 of No 40 Squadron, RFC [Ref:
Hobson (1995) *Airmen Died in the Great War 1914-1918*, pp. *54*] **102**
Richthofen (1920) *Ein Heldenleben*, pp. *194* **102**
Richthofen (1920) *Ein Heldenleben*, pp. *84* **103**
Gibbons (1927) *The Red Knight of Germany*, pp. *116–117* **103**
Chionchio, "Defeat by Design" in (1989) *Air Enthusiast*, pp. *69* **104**
Davilla and Soltan (1997) *French Aircraft of the First World War*, pp. *355* **104**
Grosz, (2003) *Albatros D.III Windsock Datafile Special*, pp. *11* **104**
Grosz, (2003) *Albatros D.III Windsock Datafile Special*, **104**
Kofl 6. Armee Wochenbericht Nr. 22934, Teil 10, 9 February 1917, pp. *3*; Lt Percival W. Murray,
age 20, and Lt Duncan J. McRae, age 24, both died of wounds received in BE2d 6742 of No
16 Squadron [Ref: Hobson (1995) *Airmen Died in the Great War 1914–1918* pp. *76, 70*] **104**
Gibbons (1927) *The Red Knight of Germany*, pp. *119–120* **104**
Schnitzler (1927) *Carl Allmenröder - der Bergische Kampfflieger*, pp. *7* **105**
Richthofen (1937) *Mein Kriegstagebuch*, pp. *97* **105**
Richthofen (1937) *Mein Kriegstagebuch*, pp. *98–99* **106**
Richthofen (1937) *Mein Kriegstagebuch*, pp. *99* **106**
Werner (ed) (1930) *Briefe eines deutschen Kampffliegers an ein junges Mädchen*, pp. *93* **107**
Public Record Office, file *Air 1/686/21/13/2250 XC15183, Richthofen Combat Reports*
(translations); confirmed in *Kofl 6.Armee Wochenbericht Nr. 23225 Teil 10*, 15 February 1917,
pp. *3*; BE2d 6231 of No. 2 Squadron, 2/Lt Cyril D. Bennett, age 19 wounded and taken
prisoner, 2/Lt Herbert A. Croft, killed [Henshaw (1995) *The Sky Their Battlefield*, pp. *137*] **107**
Public Record Office, *Richthofen Combat Reports*; confirmed in *Kofl 6.Armee Wochenbericht
Nr. 23225 Teil 10*, 15 February 1917; BE2c 2543 of No. 2 Squadron, Capt George C.
Bailey, DSO, age 26, was wounded and 2/Lt George W.B. Hampton, age 32, survived
and returned to British lines [Henshaw (1995) *The Sky Their Battlefield*] **107**
Public Record Office, *Richthofen Combat Reports*; confirmed in *Kofl 6.Armee
Wochenbericht Nr. 23225 Teil 10*, 15 February 1917 **107**
Gibbons (1927) *The Red Knight of Germany*, pp. *125* **108**
Zuerl (1938) *Pour le Mérite-Flieger*, pp. *406* **108**

Schäfer (1917) *Vom Jäger zum Flieger*, pp. *80* **108**

Quoted in Gibbons (1927) *The Red Knight of Germany*, pp. *126* **109**

Quoted in Richthofen (1920) *Ein Heldenleben*, pp. *205–206* **109**

'Vigilant' [Claud W. Sykes], *Richthofen – The Red Knight of the Air*, (nd), pp. *131* **109–110**

Kofl 6.Armee Wochenbericht Nr. 23225 Teil 10, 15 February 1917, **110**

Kofl 6.Armee Wochenbericht Nr. 23460 Teil 8, 22 February 1917, pp. *3* **110**

Quoted in Richthofen (1920) *Ein Heldenleben*, pp. *229* **110**

Quoted in Lampel, 'Als Gast beim Rittmeister Frhr. v. Richthofen' in
  Neumann (ed) (1923) *In der Luft unbesiegt*, pp. *220, 221* **111**

Kofl 6. Armee Wochenbericht Nr 24030, Teil 1, 8 March 1917, pp. *1* **111**

Public Record Office, RFC War Diary entry weather report for this date **111**

Public Record Office, No 2 Squadron, RFC, *Combat Report* **112**

Public Record Office, *Richthofen Combat Reports; Kofl 6. Armee
  Wochenbericht Nr 24030, Teil 9a*, 8 March 1917, pp. *3* **112**

Kofl 6. Armee Wochenbericht Nr 24030, Teil 9a, 8 March 1917; 2/Lts Herbert J. Green, age
  19, and Alexander W. Reid, age 20, died in Sopwith A.1108 of No 43 Squadron, RFC
  [Ref: Hobson (1995) *Airmen Died in the Great War 1914–1918* pp. *51, 86*] **112**

Gibbons (1927) *The Red Knight of Germany*, pp. *128* **112**

Public Record Office, RFC War Diary entry weather report for this date **112**

Kofl 6. Armee Wochenbericht Nr 24030, Teil 9b, 8 March 1917 **112**

Richthofen (1937) *Mein Kriegstagebuch*, pp. *92* **112**

Ferko (1995) *Richthofen*, pp. *17–19* **112**

Public Record Office, *Richthofen Combat Reports; Kofl 6. Armee Wochenbericht Nr
  24030, Teil 9b*; 2/Lt Gerald M. Gosset-Bibbey, age 19, and Lt Geoffrey J.O.
  Brichta, age 32, perished in BE2e A.2785 of No 16 Squadron, RFC [Ref:
  Hobson (1995) *Airmen Died in the Great War 1914–1918* pp. *50, 27*] **113**

Kofl 6. Armee Wochenbericht Nr 24340, Teil 1, 16 March 1917, pp. *1* **113**

Richthofen (1920) *Ein Heldenleben*, pp. *86–87* **113**

Richthofen (1920) *Ein Heldenleben*, pp. *88-89* **113–114**

Richthofen (1920) *Ein Heldenleben*, pp. *89-90* **115**

Public Record Office, Richthofen Combat Reports; *Kofl 6. Armee Wochenbericht Nr 24340,
  Teil 7*, pp. *2*; 2/Lt Arthur J. Pearson, MC age 29, was killed in DH2 A.2571 of No. 29
  Squadron, RFC [Ref: Hobson (1995) *Airmen Died in the Great War 1914–1918* pp. *81*] **115**

Richthofen (1920) *Ein Heldenleben*, pp. *93* **115**

'Vigilant' [Claud W. Sykes], *Richthofen – The Red Knight of the Air*, (nd), pp. *164–165* **115**

His 19th to 29th aerial victories, during the period 1 February through 21 March 1917

Quoted in Richthofen (1920) *Ein Heldenleben*, pp. *221–222* **116**

Kofl 6. Armee Wochenbericht Nr 24340, Teil 7; 2/Lts James Smyth and Edward
  G. Byrne, age 35, were killed in BE2d 6232 of No. 2 Squadron, RFC [Ref:
  Hobson (1995) *Airmen Died in the Great War 1914–1918* pp. *94, 30*] **116**

Weather report in *Kofl 6. Armee Wochenbericht Nr 24620, Teil 1*, 23 March 1917, pp. *1* **116**

Falls in Esposito (ed) (1965) *A Concise History of World War I*, pp. *95* **116**

Public Record Office, Richthofen Combat Reports; *Kofl 6. Armee Wochenbericht
  Nr 24620, Teil 10*, pp. *2*; Lt Arthur E. Boultbee, age 19, and AM2 Frederick
  King, age 22, were killed in FE2b A.5439 of No. 25 Squadron, RFC [Ref:
  Hobson (1995) *Airmen Died in the Great War 1914–1918* pp. *25, 63*] **117**

Public Record Office, *Richthofen Combat Reports; Kofl 6. Armee Wochenbericht Nr
  24620, Teil 10*; 2/Lt George M. Watt, age 27, and Sgt Ernest A. Howlett,

age 26, were killed in BE2g 2814 of No. 16 Squadron, RFC [Ref: Hobson
(1995) *Airmen Died in the Great War 1914–1918* pp. *105, 58*] **117**
Public Record Office, Richthofen Combat Reports; *Kofl 6. Armee Wochenbericht Nr 24620,
Teil 10*; Fl/Sgt Sidney H. Quicke and 2/Lt William J. Lidsey, age 21, in BE2f A.3154 of
No.16 Squadron, RFC are generally considered to have been killed by Richthofen in this
fight [Ref: Hobson (1995) *Airmen Died in the Great War 1914–1918* pp. *85, 66*] **117–8**
Kofl 6. Armee, Wochenbericht Nr 25000, Teil 14, 30 March 1917, pp. *3* **118**
Richthofen (1920) *Ein Heldenleben*, pp. *195* **118**
Richthofen (1920) *Ein Heldenleben*, pp. *85–86* **118–9**
Public Record Office, *Richthofen Combat Reports*; *Kofl 6. Armee, Wochenbericht Nr 25000, Teil
10*; pp. *6*; Lt Richard B. Plunkett, age 29, was wounded in SPAD S.7 6706 of No. 19
Squadron, RFC [Ref: Henshaw (1995) *The Sky Their Battlefield*, pp. *146–147*] **119**
Kofl 6. Armee, Wochenbericht Nr 25000, Teil 10; Lt Christopher G. Gilbert,
age 24, was wounded in Nieuport 17 A.6689 of No. 29 Squadron, RFC
[Ref: Henshaw (1995) *The Sky Their Battlefield*, pp. *147*] **119**
Kriegsministerium (organization manual), *Teil 10 Abschnitt B,
Flieger-Formationen*, (1918), pp. *120* **119**
Kofl 6. Armee, Wochenbericht Nr 25000; *Teil 1*, pp. *1* **119**
Kofl 6. Armee, Verzeichnis … Fliegerverbände, pp. *2* **119**
Richthofen (1920) *Ein Heldenleben*, pp. *93* **120**
Quoted in Schmeelke,'Leutnant der Reserve Otto Brauneck' in
(1983) *Cross & Cockade Journal*, pp. *163* **120–1**

Chapter 8

Franks, Guest and Bailey (1995) *Bloody April … Black September*, pp. *110* **122**
Public Record Office, Royal Flying Corps War Diary daily weather reports, April
1917; 'Vigilant,' *Richthofen - The Red Knight of the Air*, (n d), pp. *134 ff* **122**
Jones (1931) *The War in the Air*, vol III, pp. *323* **122**
Albatros D.III 2253/17 [Ref: Franks, Giblin and McCrery (1995)
Under the Guns of the Red Baron, pp. *89*] **122**
Richthofen (1920) *Ein Heldenleben*, pp. *94–95* **122–3**
Kofl 6. Armee Wochenbericht Nr 25500, Teil 10, 7 April 1917, pp. *2*; Lt Patrick J.G. Powell,
age 20, and 1/AM Percy Bonner, age 23, perished in BE2d 5841 of No 13 Squadron
[Ref: Hobson (1995) *Airmen Died in the Great War 1914–1918*, pp.*84, 25*] **123**
Richthofen (1933) *Der rote Kampfflieger*, pp. *136* **123**
Kofl 6. Armee Wochenbericht Nr 25500, Teil 10, 7 April 1917, **123**
Richthofen (1920) *Ein Heldenleben*, pp. *96* **123**
Public Record Office, file *Air 1/686/21/13/2250 XC15183, Richthofen Combat Reports*
(translations); confirmed in *Kofl 6. Armee Wochenbericht Nr 25500, Teil 10*; 2/Lt
A. Peter Warren, age 18, was taken prisoner, and Sgt Reuel Dunn, age 24, died
after their Sopwith 1½ Strutter A.2401 of No. 43 Squadron, RFC crashed [Ref:
Hobson (1995) *Airmen Died in the Great War 1914–1918*, pp. *42*] **124**
Kofl 6. Armee Wochenbericht Nr 25500, Teil 10 pp. *3*; 2/Lt Donald P. MacDonald,
age 22, was wounded and taken prisoner, and 2/Lt John I.M. O'Bierne, age 24,
died of wounds received while flying FE2d A.6382 of No. 25 Squadron, RFC
[Ref: Hobson (1995) *Airmen Died in the Great War 1914–1918*, pp. *78*] **124**
Jones (1931) *The War in the Air*, vol III, pp. *334* **124**

Jones (1931) *The War in the Air*, vol III, pp. *334-335* **124**

Kofl 6. Armee Wochenbericht Nr 25500, Teile 10, 11, pp. *3–4* **124**

Leefe Robinson received Britain's highest award for valour for shooting down Schütte-Lanz airship SL11 on the night of 2/3 September 1916 [Ref: Bowyer (1978) *For Valour - the Air VCs*, pp. *69, 75–77*] **124**

Bowyer (1978) *For Valour - the Air VCs*, pp. *77* **124**

Public Record Office, *Richthofen Combat Reports* **125**

Kofl 6. Armee Wochenbericht Nr 25500, Teile 10, pp. *3*; Lts Alfred T. Adams was uninjured and taken prisoner, and Donald J. Stewart, age 20, was wounded and taken prisoner after landing in Bristol F.2A A.3343 of No 48 Squadron, RFC [Ref: Gibbons (1927) *The Red Knight of Germany*, pp. *181*] **125**

Leefe Robinson's death on 31 December 1918 is considered to be a result of the harsh treatment he received as a prisoner of war [Ref: Bowyer (1978) *For Valour - the Air VCs*, pp. *78–79*] **125**

Burge (ca. 1919) *The Annals of 100 Squadron*, pp. *51* **125**

Richthofen (1920) *Ein Heldenleben*, pp. *103* **125–6**

Kofl 6. Armee Wochenbericht Nr 25500, Teile 10, pp. *3* **126**

While RFC records show that No 100 Squadron and other units raided Douai on various occasions, the author has found no British or German records mentioning a raid on the evening of 6/7 April 1917; hence, Richthofen's narrative may relate to another event **126**

Richthofen (1920) *Ein Heldenleben*, pp. *104–105* **126–7**

Kofl 6. Armee Wochenbericht Nr 50151, Teil 10, 13 April 1917, pp. *3*; 2/Lt George O. Smart, age 31, perished in Nieuport 17 A.6645 of No. 60 Squadron, RFC [Ref: Hobson (1995) *Airmen Died in the Great War 1914–1918*, pp. *93*] **127**

Kofl 6. Armee Wochenbericht Nr 50151, Teil 10; 2/Lt John S. Heagerty, age 23, was wounded and taken prisoner and Lt Leonard H. Cantle, age 21, was killed in Sopwith 1½ Strutter A.2406 of No 43 Squadron, RFC [Ref: Hobson (1995) *Airmen Died in the Great War 1914–1918*, pp. *30*]; and 2/Lts Keith I. MacKenzie, age 18, and Guy Everingham, age 22, both perished in BE2g A.2815 of No 16 Squadron, RFC [Hobson (1995) *Airmen Died in the Great War 1914–1918*, pp. *69, 44*] **127**

Gibbons (1927) *The Red Knight of Germany*, pp. *206* **127**

O'Connor (1990) *Aviation Awards of Imperial Germany in World War I and the Men Who Earned Them*, vol II, pp. *62, 106, 109* **127**

O'Connor (1990) *Aviation Awards of Imperial Germany in World War I and the Men Who Earned Them*, vol II, pp. *141, 219* **128**

Kogenluft, *Nachrichtenblatt der Luftstreitkräfte*, Nr 7, 12 April 1917, pp. *3* **128**

Falls in Esposito (ed) (1965) *A Concise History of World War I*, pp. *96* **128**

Kofl 6. Armee Wochenbericht Nr 50151, Teil 10 **128**

Kofl 6. Armee Wochenbericht Nr 50151, Teil 10; very likely Lt Edward C. Derwin, age 23, and 2/AM H. Pierson, who crashed in BE2c 2501 of No 13 Squadron, RFC; both were wounded and later rescued by advancing British troops [Ref: Gibbons (1927) *The Red Knight of Germany*, pp. *208*] **128**

Quoted in Richthofen (1920) *Ein Heldenleben*, pp. *301–303* **129–130**

Wegener, 'Jagdstaffel Richthofen' in *Kriegs-Echo* Nr. 143, 4 May 1917, pp. *492* **130**

Kofl 6. Armee Wochenbericht Nr 50151, Teil 10; Capt James M. Stuart, age 20, and Lt Maurice H. Wood, age 23, died in RE8 A.3190 of No 59 Squadron, RFC [Ref: Hobson (1995) *Airmen Died in the Great War 1914–1918*, pp. *97, 109*] **131**

Wegener, 'Jagdstaffel Richthofen' in *Kriegs-Echo* Nr. 143, 4 May 1917 **131**

Richthofen (1920) *Ein Heldenleben*, pp. *306–307* **131**

Public Record Office, *Richthofen Combat Reports*; 2/Lt Allan H. Bates, age 21, and Sgt
   William A. Barnes, age 31, were killed in FE2b 4997 of No 25 Squadron, RFC [Ref:
   Hobson (1995) *Airmen Died in the Great War 1914–1918*, pp. *22, 21*] **132**

Richthofen (1920) *Ein Heldenleben*, pp. *99-100* **132**

Kofl 6. Armee Wochenbericht Nr 50369, Teil 10, 20 April 1917, pp. *3*; Lt William
   O. Russell, age 24, was flying in Nieuport 17 A..6796 of No 60 Squadron,
   RFC, when he was shot down, captured uninjured and sent to a prison
   camp [Ref: Henshaw (1995) *The Sky Their Battlefield*, pp. *159*] **132**

Quoted in Richthofen (1920) *Ein Heldenleben*, pp. *294* **132–3**

Kofl 6. Armee Wochenbericht Nr 50369, Teil 10 pp. *4*; Lt Alphonso Pascoe was wounded and sent
   home to recover and 2/Lt Frederick S. Andrews, age 28, died in the crash of BE2e 3156
   of No 13 Squadron, RFC [Ref: Henshaw (1995) *The Sky Their Battlefield*, pp. *160*] **133**

O'Connor (1993) *Aviation Awards of Imperial Germany in World War
   I and the Men Who Earned Them*, vol III, pp. *108* **133**

O'Connor (1993) *Aviation Awards of Imperial Germany in World War
   I and the Men Who Earned Them*, vol III, pp. *21* **133**

O'Connor (1998) *Aviation Awards of Imperial Germany in World War
   I and the Men Who Earned Them*, vol V, pp. *124* **133**

Esposito (ed), (1965) *A Concise History of World War I*, pp. *92–94* **133**

Kofl 6. Armee Wochenbericht Nr 50570, Teil 11, 28 April 1917, pp. *4*; Lts Waldemar
   Franklin, age 20, and William F. Fletcher, age 22, were shot down and
   wounded in FE2b 7020 of No 11 Squadron, RFC, and escaped to British
   lines [ref: Henshaw (1995) *The Sky Their Battlefield*, pp. *161*] **133**

Kofl 6. Armee Wochenbericht Nr 50570, Teil 11, 28 April 1917, pp. *3* **133**

Kogenluft, *Nachrichenblatt der Luftstreitkräfte Nr 10*, 3 May 1917, pp. *3* **133–4**

Kofl 6. Armee Wochenbericht Nr 50570, Teil 11, 28 April 1917, pp. *4*; 2/Lt Eric A. Welch, age
   23, and Sgt Amos G. Tollervey, age 21, were killed in BE2e A.3168 of No 16 Squadron,
   RFC [Ref: Hobson (1995) *Airmen Died in the Great War 1914–1918*, pp. *105, 100*] **134**

Richthofen (1920) *Ein Heldenleben*, pp. *195* **134**

Kofl 6. Armee Wochenbericht Nr 50790, Teil 14, 4 May 1917, pp. *7* **134**

Kofl 6. Armee Wochenbericht Nr 50790, Teil 14, 4 May 1917 pp. *5*; both crewmen were
   wounded and Lt Reginald W. Follitt, age 26, succumbed to his wounds, while 2/Lt
   Frederick J. Kirkham, age 23, was taken prisoner; they had been flying BE2e 7221 of
   No 13 Squadron, RFC [Ref: Henshaw (1995) *The Sky Their Battlefield*, pp. *165*] **134**

Kofl 6. Armee Wochenbericht Nr 50790, Teil 14, 4 May 1917; 2/Lt Richard Applin, age 22,
   was killed in SPAD S.7 B.1573 of No 19 Squadron, RFC [Ref: Hobson (1995) *Airmen
   Died in the Great War 1914–1918*, pp. *19*]; Sgt George Stead, age 19, and Cpl Alfred
   Beebee, age 18, were shot down in flames, fell out of their aircraft and died after flying
   FE2d 4898 of No 18 Squadron, RFC [Ref: Hobson (1995) *Airmen Died in the Great War
   1914–1918*, pp. *95, 23*]; Lts David E. Davies, age 25, and George H. Rathbone, age 21,
   died in the crash of BE2e 2738 of No 12 Squadron, RFC [Ref: Hobson (1995) *Airmen
   Died in the Great War 1914–1918*, pp. *39, 85*]; Flight Sub-Lt Albert E. Cuzner, age 26,
   was shot down in flames and died in Sopwith Triplane N.5463 of No 8 Squadron,
   RNAS [Ref: Hobson (1995) *Airmen Died in the Great War 1914–1918*, pp. *4*] **134**

Bruce (1969) *British Aeroplanes 1914–1918*, pp. *566* **134**

Public Record Office, *RFC Communiqué No 85*, 29 April 1917, pp.*3* **135**

Kofl 6. Armee Wochenbericht Nr 50790, Teil 3, pp. *1* **135**

Richthofen (1917) *Der rote Kampfflieger*, pp. *136*; for reasons never made
  clear, later editions of this book do not include the 29 April 1917 date,
  even though all evidence points to it as the occasion **135**

Jones (1931) *The War in the Air*, vol III, pp. *368–369* **135**

Public Record Office, *Combat Report, No 60 Squadron*, RFC by Capt W.A.
  Bishop, MC, in Nieuport 17 B1566, 30 April 1917 **136**

Shores, Franks and Guest (1990) *Above the Trenches*, pp. *76–78* **136**

Bishop (1918) *Winged Warfare*, pp. *149–151* **136**

Bishop (1918) *Winged Warfare*, pp. *151–152* **136–7**

Kofl 6. Armee Wochenbericht Nr 50790, Teil 11, pp. *6* **137**

Richthofen (1917) *Der rote Kampfflieger*, pp. *154–155* **137**

Quoted in von Richthofen (1937) *Mein Kriegstagebuch* pp. *107* **137**

Chapter 9

Kofl 6. Armee Wochenbericht Nr 50790, Teil 11, 4 May 1917, pp. *6* **138**

Jones (1931) *The War in the Air*, vol III, pp. *368*

Kofl 6. Armee Wochenbericht Nr 50790, Teil 11, 4 May 1917 **138**

41 confirmed victories was one more than Oswald Boelcke attained **139**

With no explanation, this date is at odds with Richthofen's other writing,
  which identified the notification date as 29 April **139**

Richthofen (1917) *Der rote Kampfflieger*, pp. *154–155* **139**

Richthofen (1920) *Ein Heldenleben*, pp. *118* **140**

Richthofen (1920) *Ein Heldenleben*, pp. *141*; surely Richthofen meant this was
  the first time he wore the Pour le Mérite in public as, prior to this furlough,
  he had been home to visit his family wearing the award **140**

Richthofen (1920) *Ein Heldenleben* **140–1**

Richthofen (1937) *Mein Kriegstagebuch*, pp. *75–76, 107–108* **141**

Schowalter (1981) *Bad Kreuznach als Sitz des Grossen Hauptquartiers im Ersten Weltkrieg*, pp. *8–9* **141**

Richthofen (1917) *Der rote Kampfflieger*, pp. *159* **141**

Gibbons, The Red Knight of Germany, (1927), pp. *259* **142**

Quoted in Lampel, 'Als Gast beim Rittmeister Frhr. v.Richthofen'
  in Neumann (1923) *In der Luft unbesiegt*, pp. *219* **142**

Richthofen (1920) *Ein Heldenleben* pp. *146* **142**

Richthofen (1920) *Ein Heldenleben* pp. *143* **142**

Richthofen (1920) *Ein Heldenleben* pp. *142* **143**

Richthofen (1920) *Ein Heldenleben* **143**

Richthofen (1920) *Ein Heldenleben* **143**

Richthofen (1920) *Ein Heldenleben* pp. *143* **144**

Quoted in Richthofen (1920) *Ein Heldenleben* pp. *223* **144**

Gibbons, The Red Knight of Germany, (1927), pp. *261* **145**

Richthofen (1920) *Ein Heldenleben* pp. *143* **145**

Richthofen (1920) *Ein Heldenleben* **145**

Falls in Esposito (ed) (1964) *A Concise History of World War I*, pp. *95* **145**

Jones (1931) *The War in the Air*, vol III, pp. *370–371* **145**

Jones (1934) *The War in the Air*, vol IV, pp. *113* **145**

Bowyer, Albert Ball (1994) *VC*, pp. *136* **146**

Kogenluft, *Nachrichteblatt der Luftstreitkräfte*, Nr 11, 10 May 1917, pp. 3 **146**

Public Record Office, *Royal Flying Corps Casualty List*, 1917 **146**

Richthofen (1920) *Ein Heldenleben* pp. *196* **146**

Richthofen (1917) *Der rote Kampfflieger*, pp. *163* **147**

Richthofen (1917) *Der rote Kampfflieger*, pp. *173* **147**

O'Connor (1998) *Aviation Awards of Imperial Germany in World War I and the Men Who Earned Them*, vol V, pp. *219, 64* **147**

Richthofen (1937) *Mein Kriegstagebuch*, pp. *108–109* **148**

Richthofen (1937) *Mein Kriegstagebuch*, **149**

Richthofen (1937) *Mein Kriegstagebuch*, pp. *113* **149–50**

Schowalter (1981) *Bad Kreuznach als Sitz des Grossen Hauptquartiers im Ersten Weltkrieg*, pp. *8* **150**

Richthofen (1917) *Der rote Kampfflieger*, pp. *176–179* **150–1**

Richthofen (1920) *Ein Heldenleben* pp. *223–224* **151**

Grosz, 'The Agile and Aggressive Albatros' in (1976) *Air Enthusiast*, pp. *46–47* **151–2**

Jones (1931) *The War in the Air*, vol III, pp. *370–371* **152**

Bruce, 'The Fokker Dr.I' in (1965) *Aircraft Profiles* pp. *3* **152**

Grosz and Ferko, 'The Fokker Dr.I A Reappraisal' in (1978) *Air Enthusiast*, pp. *10* **152**

Grosz and Ferko, 'The Fokker Dr.I A Reappraisal' in (1978) *Air Enthusiast*, pp. *14* **152**

Richthofen (1937) *Mein Kriegstagebuch*, pp. *141* **153**

Richthofen (1920) *Ein Heldenleben* pp. *333* **153**

Later confirmed in *Kofl 6. Armee Wochenbericht Nr. 469 I, Teil 13*, 8 June 1917, pp. *7* **153**

Richthofen (1937) *Mein Kriegstagebuch*, pp. *118–119* **153**

Kofl 6. Armee Wochenbericht Nr. 469 I, Teil 4, pp. *2* **153**

Kofl 6. Armee Wochenbericht Nr. 469 I, Teil 1 **153**

Richthofen (1937) *Mein Kriegstagebuch*, pp. *196–197* **153–4**

Kofl 4. Armee Meldung Nr 30652/19, Teil 2f, 9 June 1917, pp. *4*; *Kofl 6. Armee Wochenbericht Nr 469 I, Teil 12*, pp. *6* **154**

O'Connor (1990) *Aviation Awards of Imperial Germany in World War I and the Men Who Earned* Them, vol II, pp. *141* **154**

Quoted in Nowarra, 'Reminiscences of Jasta 11' in (1960) *Cross & Cockade Journal*, pp. *60–61* **154–5**

Chapter 10

Falls in Esposito (ed) (1965) *A Concise History of World War I*, pp. *97* **156**

Air Ministry (1995) *Handbook of German Military and Naval Aviation (War)*, pp. *43* **156**

Kofl 4. Armee Meldung Nr. 20652/19, Teil 3f, 9 June 1917, pp. *2* **156**

Stammliste der Offiziere des 6. Badischen Infanterie-Regiments (Kaiser Friedrich III) Nr. 114, (1904), listing 293, pp. *122* **156**

Bufe: Personal-Bogen, (1920), pp. *2–3* **156**

Kofl 4. Armee Meldung Nr. 20690, Teil 3f, 22 June 1917, pp. *6* **157**

Public Record Office, file *Air 1/686/21/13/2250 XC15183, Richthofen Combat Reports* (translations); Lts Ralph W.E. Ellis and Harold C. Barlow, age 27, were killed in RE8 A.4290 of No. 9 Squadron, RFC; Franks, et al., (1995) *Under the Guns of the Red Baron*, pp. *137* give the location as 'Stray Farm,' east of Pilckem and north of Ypres **157**

Public Record Office, *Richthofen Combat Reports* (translations); this claim, unsupported by other witness, has been questioned by aviation historians Franks, et al., (1995) *Under the Guns of the Red Baron*, pp. *139–141* contend the aircraft was SPAD B.1530 of No. 23 Squadron,

RFC, piloted 2/Lt Robert W. Farquhar, who was unwounded and whose aeroplane was not struck off squadron strength due to combat damage and was not counted as a loss **157**

Kogenluft, *Nachrichtenblatt der Luftstreitkräfte Nr 18*, 28 June 1917, pp. *2*;
Capt Norman G. McNaughton, MC, age 27, and Capt Angus H. Mearns, age 22, perished in DH4 A.7473 of No 57 Squadron, RFC [Ref: Hobson, (1995) *Airmen Died in the Great War 1914-1918*, pp. *70, 72*] **157**

Bodenschatz (1935) *Jagd in Flanderns Himmel*, pp. *147* **157**

Kriegsministerium (organization manual), *Teil 10 Abschnitt B, Flieger-Formationen*, (1918), pp. *208–209* **157**

Bodenschatz, (1935) *Jagd in Flanderns Himmel*, pp. *14* **157**

Hoeppner (1921) *Deutschlands Krieg in der Luft*, pp. *115* **158**

Oblt Hans Joachim Buddecke, Ltn Wilhelm Frankl and Obltn Ernst Frhr von Althaus [Ref: Zuerl (1938) *Pour-le-Mérite-Flieger*, pp. *124, 32*; Theilhaber (!924) *Jüdische Flieger im Weltkrieg*, pp. *87*] **158**

Ltn Albert Dossenbach and Obltn Ernst Frhr von Althaus [Ref: Zuerl (1938) *Pour-le-Mérite-Flieger*, pp. *179, 32*] **158**

Kogenluft, *Nachrichtenblatt der Luftstreitkräfte Nr 18*, 28 June 1917, pp. *45*; Lt Leslie S. Bowman, age 20, and 2/Lt James E. Power-Clutterbuck, age 23, were both killed in RE8 A.3847 of No 53 Squadron, RFC [Ref: Hobson, (1995) *Airmen Died in the Great War 1914-1918*, pp. *26, 84*] **158**

Kogenluft, *Nachrichtenblatt der Luftstreitkräfte Nr 18*, 28 June 1917 **158**

Kogenluft, *Nachrichtenblatt Nr 21*, 19 July 1917, pp. *95* **159**

O'Connor (1990) *Aviation Awards of Imperial Germany in World War I*, vol II, *Appendix XIX* **159**

Schnitzler, (1927) *Carl Allmenröder - der Bergische Kampfflieger*, pp. *7* **159**

Schmeelke, 'Leutnant der Reserve Otto Brauneck Part II' in (1986) *Over the Front* pp. *197* **159**

Richthofen (1937) *Mein Kriegstagebuch*, pp. *124* **159**

This was surely an exaggeration, as even the biggest bombers of the time were not 50 metres long **159**

Richthofen (1937) *Mein Kriegstagebuch*, pp. *124–125*; the parentheses are Richthofen's; the brackets are the author's **159**

Hildebrand (1990) *Die Generale der deutschen Luftwaffe 1935-1945*, vol I, pp. *203–204*; by the end of World War I, Kurt-Betram von Döring commanded Jagdgruppe 4 **159–60**

O'Connor (1990) *Aviation Awards of Imperial Germany in World War I*, vol II, pp. *219* **160**

Bodenschatz (1935) *Jagd in Flanderns Himmel*, pp. *147* **160**

Bodenschatz (1935) *Jagd in Flanderns Himmel*, pp. *11–13* **160**

Kogenluft, *Nachrichtenblatt Nr 19*, 5 July 1917, pp. *58*; Sergeant Hubert A. Whatley, age 19, and 2/Lt Frank G.B. Pascoe, age 20, died in RE8 A.3538 of No. 53 Squadron, RFC [Ref: Hobson, (1995) *Airmen Died in the Great War 1914-1918*, pp. *106, 80*] **160**

Kogenluft, *Nachrichtenblatt Nr. 24*, 9 August 1917, pp. *140* **160**

Bodenschatz (1935) *Jagd in Flanderns Himmel*, pp. *17* **161**

Bodenschatz (1935) *Jagd in Flanderns Himmel*, pp. *147* **161**

Bodenschatz (1935) *Jagd in Flanderns Himmel*, pp. *19* **161**

Richthofen (1920) *Ein Heldenleben*, pp. *148* **162**

Richthofen: Krankengeschichte, Krankenbuch 286, Feldlazarett 76 Kortrijk, 25 July 1917 **162**

Bodenschatz (1935) *Jagd in Flanderns Himmel*, pp. *22* **162**

Schröder (ca. 1934) *Erlebter Krieg*, pp. *255–256* **163**

Richthofen (1920) *Ein Heldenleben*, pp. *150* **163**

Kofl 4. Armee Meldung Nr. 24406/19, Teil 7b, 13 July 1917, pp. *7* **163**

Bodenschatz (1935) *Jagd in Flanderns Himmel,* pp. *23* **163**
Bodenschatz (1935) *Jagd in Flanderns Himmel,* pp. *148* **163**
Bodenschatz (1935) *Jagd in Flanderns Himmel,* pp. *25, 149* **163**
Kofl 4. Armee Meldung Nr. 24406/19, Teil 2, pp. *1* **164**
Public Record Office, *Royal Flying Corps Communiqué No 96,* 15 July 1917, pp. *4* **164**
Bodenschatz (1935) *Jagd in Flanderns Himmel,* pp. *149* **164**
Bodenschatz (1935) *Jagd in Flanderns Himmel,* pp. *28–29* **165**
Letter from the Falkenhayn family via a private source **166**
Quoted in Bodenschatz (1935) *Jagd in Flanderns Himmel,* pp. *30* **166**
Kofl 4 Tagesbericht Nr 26 quoted in Bodenschatz (1935) *Jagd in Flanderns Himmel,* pp. *150* **167**
Bodenschatz (1935) *Jagd in Flanderns Himmel,* pp. *33* **167**
Kogenluft, Nachrichtenblatt Nr 25, 16 August 1917, pp. *157* **167**
Kofl 4. Armee Meldung Nr. 26952/19, Teil 7, 2 August 1917, pp. *11* **167**
Zuerl (1938) *Pour le Mérite-Flieger,* pp. *32* **167**
Jones (1934) *The War in the Air,* vol IV, pp. *160–169* **168**
Bodenschatz (1935) *Jagd in Flanderns Himmel,* pp. *152* **168**
Kogenluft, *Nachrichtenblatt Nr 26,* 23 August 1917, pp. *174* **168**
Bufe: Auszug, (1918), pp. *3* **168**
Kommander der Flieger der 4. Armee Besonderer Tagesbefehl Nr. 29171, 4 August 1917 **168**
O'Connor (1988) *Aviation Awards of Imperial Germany in World War I,* vol. I, pp. *39* **168**
Zuerl (1938) *Pour le Mérite-Flieger,* pp. *482* **169**
Kofl 4. Armee Tagesbefehl Nr. 38, 7 August 1917 **169**
Bodenschatz (1935) *Jagd in Flanderns Himmel,* pp. *37* **169**
Quoted in Bodenschatz (1935) *Jagd in Flanderns Himmel,* pp. *38* **170**
Kogenluft, *Nachrichtenblatt Nr. 30,* 20 September 1917, pp. *247;* Bodenschatz
    (1935) *Jagd in Flanderns Himmel,* pp. *153;* 2/Lt William H.T. Williams, age 19, died
    of wounds received while flying Nieuport 23 A.6611 of No 29 Squadron, RFC
    [Ref: Hobson, (1995) *Airmen Died in the Great War 1914-1918,* pp. *108*] **170**
Kogenluft, *Nachrichtenblatt Nr. 30,* 20 September 1917 **170**
Quoted in Bodenschatz (1935) *Jagd in Flanderns Himmel,* pp. *39* **170**
Bodenschatz (1935) *Jagd in Flanderns Himmel,* pp. *39–40* **170**
Bodenschatz (1935) *Jagd in Flanderns Himmel,* pp. *40* **171**
Bodenschatz (1935) *Jagd in Flanderns Himmel,* pp. *41, 154* **171**
Grosz and Ferko, 'The Fokker Dr.I A Reappraisal' in (1978) *Air Enthusiast,* pp. *18* **171**
Bodenschatz (1935) *Jagd in Flanderns Himmel; Kofl 4. Armee Meldung
    Nr. 158 op, Teil 7,* 6 September 1917, pp. *5* **171**
Bodenschatz (1935) *Jagd in Flanderns Himmel; Kofl 4. Armee Meldung
    Nr. 158, Teil 7,* 6 September 1917, pp. *41–42* **171**
Public Record Office, Royal Flying Corps Communiqué No 103, 2 september
    1917, p. 3; aircraft were identified as SPADs from No 19 Squadron, RFC
Bodenschatz (1935) *Jagd in Flanderns Himmel,* pp. *42;* 2/Lt Collingsby P.
    Williams was killed in SPAD S.7 B.3492 of No. 19 Squadron, RFC [Ref:
    Hobson, (1995) *Airmen Died in the Great War 1914-1918,* pp. *108*] **172**
Richthofen (1920) *Ein Heldenleben,* pp. *198* **172**
Kofl 4. Armee Meldung Nr. 116 op, Anlage 1, 30 August 1917, pp. *3* **172**
Bodenschatz (1935) *Jagd in Flanderns Himmel,* pp. *155* **172**
Public Record Office, *RFC Communiqué No. 104,* 9 September 1917, pp. *1* **172**
Bodenschatz (1935) *Jagd in Flanderns Himmel,* pp. *43* **173**

Kofl 4. Armee Meldung Nr. 158, Anlage 2, pp. 3; 2/Lt John B.C. Madge, age 25, was wounded and
taken prisoner, and 2/Lt Walter Kember, age 26, was killed in RE8 B.782 of No. 6 Squadron,
RFC [Ref: Hobson, (1995) *Airmen Died in the Great War 1914-1918*, pp. 254, 62] **173**
Kofl 4. Armee Tagesbefehl Nr. 63, 4 September 1917 **173**
Ulanen-Regiment Kaiser Alexander III. von Russland (Westpreussisches) Nr. 1 [Ref: *Ehren-
Rangliste des ehemaligen Deutschen Heeres*, (1926), pp. 442–443] **173**
Bodenschatz (1935) *Jagd in Flanderns Himmel*, pp. 43 **173**
Kogenluft, Nachrichtenblatt Nr. 33, 10 October 1917, pp. 306 **173**

Chapter 11

Bodenschatz, (1935) *Jagd in Flanderns Himmel*, pp. 156 **174**
Richthofen (1937) *Mein Kriegstagebuch*, pp. 132–133 **175**
Bodenschatz, (1935) *Jagd in Flanderns Himmel*, pp. 47, 159 **175**
Bodenschatz, (1935) *Jagd in Flanderns Himmel*, pp. 54 **176**
Richthofen (1920) *Ein Heldenleben*, pp. 199 **176**
Quoted in Richthofen (1920) *Ein Heldenleben*, pp. 328–330 **176-7**
Quoted in Richthofen (1920) *Ein Heldenleben* **177**
Salzmann, 'Richthofen' in (1918) *Der Weltkrieg – Illustrierte Kriegs-
Chronik des Daheim*, pp. 179–180 **177-8**
Bodenschatz, (1935) *Jagd in Flanderns Himmel*, pp. 160 **178**
Richthofen (1937) *Mein Kriegstagebuch*, pp. 127–128 **179**
Richthofen (1937) *Mein Kriegstagebuch*, pp. 128–129 **179**
Richthofen (1937) *Mein Kriegstagebuch*, pp. 129–130 **179-80**
Richthofen (1920) *Ein Heldenleben*, pp. 155–156 **180**
Prestien: Personal-Bogen, (1920), pp. 2–3 **180**
Quoted in Richthofen (1937) *Mein Kriegstagebuch*, pp. 141
Quoted in Richthofen (1937) *Mein Kriegstagebuch*, pp. 142 **181**
Richthofen (1920) *Ein Heldenleben*, pp. 154 **181**
Quoted in Gibbons (1927) *The Red Knight of Germany*, pp. 108 **181**
Bodenschatz, (1935) *Jagd in Flanderns Himmel*, pp. 160, 161 **181**
Bodenschatz, (1935) *Jagd in Flanderns Himmel*, pp. 161 **181**
Grosz and Ferko, 'The Fokker Dr.I A Reappraisal' in (1978) *Air Enthusiast*, pp. 22 **182**
The propeller is bolted to the rotary engine, which itself spins on an axis, powering
the propeller and cooling the engine, but producing a gyroscopic effect as the
engine pulls the aeroplane in the direction the engine is rotating **182**
Kogenluft, *Nachrichtenblatt der Luftstreitkräfte Nr. 36*, 1 November 1917, pp. 351 **182**
Bodenschatz, (1935) *Jagd in Flanderns Himmel*, pp. 54–55
Kogenluft, *Nachrichtenblatt der Luftstreitkräfte Nr. 36*, 1 November 1917, pp. 355
noted Gontermann's death, but not the aircraft in which he died **182**
Vanoverbeke (1993) *Moorsele - één dorp, twee vliegvelden*, pp. 165 **182**
Bodenschatz, (1935) *Jagd in Flanderns Himmel*, pp. 162 **183**
Gray, 'The Pfalz D.III,' (1965) *Aircraft Profiles*, pp. 8 **183**
Werner (ed) (1930) *Briefe eines deutschen Kampffliegers an ein junges Mädchen*, pp. 186–187 **183-4**
Public Record Office, *Royal Flying Corps Communiqué No 115*, 29 November 1917, pp. 1 **184**
Kogenluft, *Nachrichtenblatt Nr. 43*, 20 December 1917, pp. 469; Lt James A.V. Boddy age
22, flying DH5 A.9299 of No. 64 Squadron, RFC, was wounded in action **184**
Quoted in Richthofen (1937) *Mein Kriegstagebuch*, pp. 142–143 **185**

Public Record Office, *Periodical Summary of Aeronautical Information*
No. 23, 16 November 1917, pp. 7 **185**
Jones (1934) *The War in the Air*, vol IV, pp. 248 **185**
Bodenschatz, (1935) *Jagd in Flanderns Himmel* **185**
Jones (1934) *The War in the Air*, vol IV, pp. 249 **185**
Zuerl (1938) *Pour le Mérite-Flieger*, pp. 81 **186**
Kogenluft, *Nachrichtenblatt der Luftstreitkräfte Nr 41*, 6 December 1917, pp. 431; Lt Donald
A.D.I. MacGregor, age 22, was killed in SE5a B.644 of No 41 Squadron, RFC **186**
Kilduff, 'Honor Roll of the Fallen Fliers of Baden' in (1989) *Over the Front*, pp. 367 **186**
Bodenschatz, (1935) *Jagd in Flanderns Himmel* pp. 58, 165; O'Connor (1990)
Aviation Awards of Imperial Germany in World War I and the Men Who Earned Them,
vol II, pp. 219 lists the date of award as 4 December 1917 **186**
Quoted in Richthofen (1920) *Ein Heldenleben*, pp. 311 **187**
Grosz and Ferko, 'The Fokker Dr.I A Reappraisal' in (1978) *Air Enthusiast*, pp. 19–21 **187**
Lamberton (1960) *Fighter Aircraft of the 1914-1918 War*, pp. 158 **187**

Chapter 12

Bodenschatz, (1935) *Jagd in Flanderns Himmel* pp. 58 **188**
Richthofen (1920) *Ein Heldenleben*, pp. 199 **188**
Quoted in Richthofen (1920) *Ein Heldenleben*, pp. 318–320 **188–9**
Bodenschatz, (1935) *Jagd in Flanderns Himmel* pp. 60, 166 **189**
Public Record Office, *Periodical Summary of Aeronautical Information*
No 26, 31 December 1917, pp. 1 **189**
Public Record Office, *Periodical Summary of Aeronautical Information*
No 26, 31 December 1917, pp. 199--200 **189–90**
Richthofen (1937) *Mein Kriegstagebuch*, pp. 148–149 **190**
Bodenschatz, (1935) *Jagd in Flanderns Himmel* pp. 167 **190**
Cron, 'Organization of the German Luftstreitkräfte' in
(1966) *Cross & Cockade Journal*, pp. 55 **190**
Van Ishoven (1979) *The Fall of an Eagle*, pp. 54 **191**
Wenzl (ca. 1930) *Richthofen-Flieger*, pp. 46–47 **191**
von der Osten, 'Memoirs of World War I with Jagdstaffeln 11 and 4' in (1974) *Cross & Cockade
Journal*, pp. 224; Richthofen (1920) *Ein Heldenleben*, pp. 224 contains the same anecdote **191**
Kogenluft, *Einflüsse des Fliegens auf den menschlichen Körper und ärtzliche
Ratschläge für Flieger*, January 1918, pp. 21 **192**
Richthofen (1937) *Mein Kriegstagebuch*, pp. 148 **193**
Richthofen (1937) *Mein Kriegstagebuch*, pp. 149 **193**
Richthofen (1937) *Mein Kriegstagebuch*, pp. 151 **193**
Allmers, 'Manfred von Richthofen's medical record – was the "Red
Baron" fit to fly?' in (1999) *The Lancet*, pp. 503 **193–4**
Allmers, 'Manfred von Richthofen's medical record – was the "Red
Baron" fit to fly?' in (1999) *The Lancet*, pp. 503–504 **194**
Richthofen (1937) *Mein Kriegstagebuch*, pp. 152 **194**
Kriegsministerium (organization manual), *Teil 10 Abschnitt B, Flieger-Formationen*, (1918),
p. 208; Möller (1939) *Kampf und Sieg eines Jagdgeschwaders*, pp. 15 **195**
Richthofen (1920) *Ein Heldenleben*, pp. 200 **195**
Richthofen, (1938 ed.) *Sein militärisches Vermächtnis*, pp. 9–10, 12–13, 14, 15 **196**

Bodenschatz, (1935) *Jagd in Flanderns Himmel* pp. *63* **196**

Hoeppner (1921) *Deutschlands Krieg in der Luft*, pp. *140* **197**

Esposito (1965) *A Concise History of World War I*, pp. *104* **197**

Jones, (1934) *The War in the Air*, vol IV pp. *264ff* **197**

Public Record Office, *Summary of Air Intelligence No 17*, 1 March 1918, pp. *1* **197**

Winans, 'World War I Aircraft Fuels and Lubricating Oils' in
  (1961) *Cross & Cockade Journal*, pp. *236* **197**

Letter from the Falkenhayn family via a private source *197–8*

Supf (1958) *Das Buch der deutschen Fluggeschichte*, vol 2, pp. *272* **198**

Bodenschatz, (1935) *Jagd in Flanderns Himmel* pp. *64* **198**

Public Record Office, file *Air 1/686/21/13/2250 XC15183, Richthofen Combat Reports*
  (translations); 2/Lts Leonard C.F. Clutterbuck and Henry J. Sparks, age 27, came down
  in Bristol F.2B B.1251of No 62 Squadron, RFC, and was taken prisoner **198**

Public Record Office, *Richthofen Combat Reports*; Lt Elmer E. Heath was wounded in
  Sopwith F.1 Camel B.5590 of No 73 Squadron, RFC, and taken prisoner **199**

Public Record Office, *Royal Flying Corps War Diary*, 13 March 1918 **199**

Bodenschatz, (1935) *Jagd in Flanderns Himmel* pp. *65* **199**

Richthofen (1920) *Ein Heldenleben*, pp. *313–314* **199**

Richthofen (1920) *Ein Heldenleben*, pp. *200–201* **200**

Udet, (1935) *Mein Fliegerleben*, pp. *65–66* **200–1**

Bodenschatz, (1935) *Jagd in Flanderns Himmel* pp. *70* **201**

von der Osten, 'Memoirs of World War I with Jagdstaffeln 11 and
  4' in (1974) *Cross & Cockade Journal*, pp. *224* **201**

Bodenschatz, (1935) *Jagd in Flanderns Himmel* pp. *65, 171* **201**

Bodenschatz, (1935) *Jagd in Flanderns Himmel* pp. *68* **201**

Bodenschatz, (1935) *Jagd in Flanderns Himmel* pp. *69*; 2/Lt William G. Ivamy landed in
  Sopwith F.1 Camel B.5243 of No 54 Squadron, RFC, and was taken prisoner **202**

Bodenschatz, (1935) *Jagd in Flanderns Himmel* pp. *71*; Jones,
  (1934) *The War in the Air*, vol IV pp. *292–293* **202**

Duiven, 'German Jagdstaffel and Jagdgeschwader Commanding
  Officers, 1916-1918' in (1988) *Over the Front*, pp. *145* **202**

Bodenschatz, (1935) *Jagd in Flanderns Himmel* pp. *72-73, 172* **202**

Public Record Office, *Richthofen Combat Reports*; Lt John P. McCone, age
  27, was killed in SE5a C.1054 of No 41 Squadron, RFC [Ref: Hobson
  (1995) *Airmen Died in the Great War 1914-1918*, pp. *67*] **203**

Public Record Office, *Richthofen Combat Reports*; 2/Lt Donald Cameron, age 18,
  died in Sopwith F.1 Camel C.1562 of No 3 Squadron, RFC [Ref: Hobson
  (1995) *Airmen Died in the Great War 1914-1918*, pp. *30*] **203**

Udet, (1935) *Mein Fliegerleben*, pp. *67* **203**

Public Record Office, *Richthofen Combat Reports*; 2/Lt Allan M. Denovan,
  age 23, died in SE5a B.511 of No 1 Squadron, RFC [Ref: Hobson
  (1995) *Airmen Died in the Great War 1914-1918*, pp. *40*] **203**

Public Record Office, *Richthofen Combat Reports*; 2/Lts Vernon J. Reading, age 22, and Matthew
  Leggat. Age 22, died in RE8 B.742 of No 15 Squadron, RFC
  [Ref: Hobson (1995) *Airmen Died in the Great War 1914-1918*, pp. *86, 65*] **203**

Vann and Bowyer, '15 Squadron RFC/RAF 1915-1919' in (1973)
  Cross & Cockade (Great Britain), pp. *66* **203**

Vann and Bowyer, '15 Squadron RFC/RAF 1915-1919' in (1973)

Cross & Cockade (Great Britain), pp. *75-76, 173* **203**

Public Record Office, RFC *Communiqué No 133*, 10 April 1918, pp. *2* **204**

Bodenschatz, (1935) *Jagd in Flanderns Himmel* pp. *76* **204**

Bodenschatz, (1935) *Jagd in Flanderns Himmel* pp. *76–77, 174*; Kogenluft, *Nachrichtenblatt der Luftstreitkräfte, 2. Jg, Nr 6*, 4 April 1918, pp. *76*; Capt Thomas S. Sharpe, DFC, age 29, was wounded and taken prisoner after crashing in Sopwith F.1 Camel C.6733 of No 73 Squadron, RFC; 2/Lts Edward T. Smart, age 20, and Kenneth P. Barford, age 19, were killed in Armstrong Whitworth FK 8 B.288 of No 2 Squadron, RFC; and 2/Lt George H. Harding, age 24, was killed in Sopwith 7F.1 Dolphin C.4016 of No 79 Squadron, RFC [Ref: Hobson (1995) *Airmen Died in the Great War 1914-1918*, pp. *93, 21, 53*] **204**

Kogenluft, *Nachrichtenblatt der Luftstreitkräfte, 2. Jg, Nr 6*, 4 April 1918, pp. Lts Joseph B. Taylor, age 19, and Eric Betley, age 21, were killed in Armstrong Whitworth FK8 C.8444 of No 82 Squadron, RFC [Ref: Hobson (1995) *Airmen Died in the Great War 1914-1918*, pp. *98, 24*] **204**

Quoted in Lampel, 'Als Gast beim Rittmeister Frhr. v.Richthofen' in Neumann (ed) (1923) *In der Luft unbesiegt*, pp. *215* **204**

Zuerl (1938) *Pour le Mérite-Flieger*, pp. *546*; Götz von Berlichingen is also known in German literature for his scatological contributions, which would not have been lost on Karjus's contemporaries **204**

Udet, (1935) *Mein Fliegerleben*, pp. *71–73* **205**

Chapter 13

Cole (1968) *Royal Air Force 1918*, pp. *9* **206**

Jones (1934) *The War in the Air*, vol. IV, pp. *346* **206**

Jones (1934) *The War in the Air*, vol. IV, **206**

Kogenluft, *Nachrichtenblatt der Luftstreirkräfte, 2. Jahrgang Nr. 7*, 11 April 1918, pp. *91* **206**

Bodenschatz, (1935) *Jagd in Flanderns Himmel* pp. *175* **206**

Public Record Office, file *Air 1/686/21/13/2250 XC15183, Richthofen Combat Reports* (translations); 2/Lts Ernest D. Jones, age 19, and Robert F. Newton perished in RE8 A.3868 of No 52 Squadron, RAF [Ref: Hobson (1995) *Airmen Died in the Great War 1914-1918*, pp. *156, 173*] **206**

Nowarra and Brown, (1959) *von Richthofen and the 'Flying Circus,'* pp. *101* **206**

Quoted in Richthofen (1920) *Ein Heldenleben*, pp. *326* **207**

Quoted in Lampel, 'Als Gast beim Rittmeister Frhr. v. Richthofen' in Neumann (ed) (1923), *In der Luft unbesiegt*, pp. *215* **207**

Quoted in Bodenschatz, (1935) *Jagd in Flanderns Himmel* pp. *79, 176* **207–8**

O'Connor, (1990) *Aviation Awards of Imperial Germany in World War I and the Men Who Earned Them*, vol II, pp. *18* **208**

Quoted in Lampel, 'Als Gast beim Rittmeister Frhr. v. Richthofen' in Neumann (ed) (1923), *In der Luft unbesiegt*, pp. *216* **208**

Jones (1934) *The War in the Air*, vol. IV, pp. *349-350* **208**

Letter from the Falkenhayn family via a private source **209**

Bodenschatz, (1935) *Jagd in Flanderns Himmel* pp. *176* **209**

Public Record Office, *Richthofen Combat Reports*; Capt Sydney P. Smith, age 22, was killed in Sopwith F.1 Camel D.6491 of No. 46 Squadron, RAF [Ref: Hobson (1995) *Airmen Died in the Great War 1914-1918*, pp. *190*] **209**

Bodenschatz, (1935) *Jagd in Flanderns Himmel* **209**

Sopwith F.1 Camel D.6550 [Ref: Franks, et al., (1995) *Under the Guns of the Red Baron*, pp. *196–197*] **210**

Adam, 'Episodes' in (1972) *Cross & Cockade Journal*, pp. *263–267* **210**

Quoted from Ronald Adam's PoW Diary (unpublished); 2/Lt R.G.H. Adam crash-landed in Sopwith F.1 Camel D.6554 and was take prisoner **210**

Quoted from Ronald Adam's PoW Diary (unpublished); 2/Lt R.G.H. Adam crash-landed in Sopwith F.1 Camel D.6554 and was take prisoner **210-1**

Kogenluft, *Nachrichtenblatt 2. Jg. Nr. 19*, 4 July 1918, pp. *280* **211**

Kogenluft, *Nachrichtenblatt 2. Jg. Nr. 8*, 18 April 1918, pp. *110* **211**

Van Ishoven (1979) *The Fall of an Eagle*, pp. *59* **211**

Udet (1935) *Mein Fliegerleben*, pp. *79* **211**

O'Connor, (1990) *Aviation Awards of Imperial Germany in World War I and the Men Who Earned Them*, vol II, pp. *220* **211**

Zuerl (1938) *Pour le Mérite-Flieger*, pp. *544–545* **211**

Richthofen (1920) *Ein Heldenleben*, pp. *319* **211**

Esposito (1965) *A Concise History of World War I*, pp. *111* **212**

Bodenschatz, (1935) *Jagd in Flanderns Himmel* pp. *177* **212**

Kogenluft, *Nachrichtenblatt Nr. 19*, pp. *280–281* **212**

PRO, *Royal Air Force Communiqué No. 2*, 18 April 1918, pp. *1* **212**

Richthofen (1933) *Der rote Kampfflieger*, pp. *203–204* **212-3**

Public Record Office, Richthofen Combat Reports; confirmed in Bodenschatz, op.cit, p. 178; Major Richard Raymond-Barker, MC, age 23, was killed in Sopwith F.1 Camel D.6439 of No. 3 Squadron, RAF [Ref: Hobson (1995) *Airmen Died in the Great War 1914-1918*, pp. *181*] **214**

No. 3 Squadron Combat Report No. 55 of Capt D.J. Bell, MC, in Sopwith F.1 Camel C.6730; there is no record of a corresponding German loss Public Record Office, *Richthofen Combat Reports*; confirmed in Bodenschatz, (1935) *Jagd in Flanderns Himmel* **214**

Quoted in Gibbons (1927) *The Red Knight of Germany*, pp. *345* **214**

Richthofen (1920) *Ein Heldenleben*, pp. *260* **215**

Wenzl (ca. 1930) *Richthofen-Flieger*, pp. *22–23* **215-6**

Quoted in Richthofen (1920) *Ein Heldenleben*, pp. *261–262* **216-7**

Wenzl (ca. 1930) *Richthofen-Flieger*, pp. *24* **217-8**

Bodenschatz, (1935) *Jagd in Flanderns Himmel* pp. *83–84* **218-9**

Bink in Der Frontsoldat erzält, (1932), pp. *266–268* **219-222**

Cutlack, *The Official History of Australia in the War of 1914-1918*, vol viii, The Australian Flying Corps, 1933, pp. *249–252* **222**

von Gottberg (ed) (1929) *Das Grenadier-Regiment Kronprinz (1. Ostpreussisches) Nr 1 im Weltkriege*, pp. *182* **222**

Chapter 14

Bodenschatz, (1935) *Jagd in Flanderns Himmel* pp. *84* **224**

Quoted in Richthofen (1920) *Ein Heldenleben*, pp. *262–263* **225**

Bodenschatz, (1935) *Jagd in Flanderns Himmel* pp. *85* **225**

Richthofen (1937) Mein Kriegstagebuch, pp. *162* **225**

Bodenschatz, 'Das Jagdgeschwader Frhr. v.Richthofen Nr.1 im Verbande der 2. Armee' in Neumann (ed) (1923) *In der Luft unbesiegt*, pp. *232–233* **226**

Kogenluft, *Nachrichtenblatt der deutschen Luftstreitkräfte, 2. Jahrgang, Nr 9*, 25 April 1918, pp. *128-A* **226**

Miller, 'The death of Manfred von Richthofen: Who fired the
   fatal shot?' in Sabretache, (1998), pp. *20* **226**
Kogenluft, *Nachrichtenblatt der deutschen Luftstreitkräfte, 2. Jahrgang, Nr 9*, 25 April 1918 **226**
This potential loss of a Fokker Dr.I triplane does not match
   German casualties reported that day **227**
Prior to the amalgamation of the Royal Flying Corps and the Royal Naval Air Service
   into the Royal Air Force on 1 April 1918, Jasta 11's new opponents from No 209
   Squadron, RAF, had been designated as No 9 Squadron, RNAS, and and all former
   RNAS units were referred to as 'naval' squadrons for some time thereafter **227**
Cutlack (1933) *The Official History of Australia in the War of 1914-1918*, vol VIII, pp. *250* **227**
Jones (1934) *The War in the Air*, vol IV, pp. *389* **227**
Public Record Office, *No. 209 Squadron Combat Report of Capt
   O.C. LeBoutillier in Sopwith F.1 Camel B.3338* **227**
Jones (1934) *The War in the Air*, vol IV **227**
Public Record Office, *No. 209 Squadron Combat Report of Capt
   A.R. Brown, DSC, in Sopwith F.1 Camel B.7270* **228**
Public Record Office, *No. 209 Squadron Combat Report of Lt
   F.J.W. Mellersh in Sopwith F.1 Camel B.6257* **228**
Public Record Office, *No. 209 Squadron Combat Report of 2/
   Lt W.R. May in Sopwith F.1 Camel D.3326* **228**
Public Record Office, *No. 209 Squadron Combat Report of Capt
   O.C. LeBoutillier in Sopwith F.1 Camel B.3338* **228**
Jones (1934) *The War in the Air*, vol IV pp. *251* **229**
Carisella and Ryan (1969) *Who Killed the Red Baron?* pp. *133–149* **230**
Puglisi, 'German Aircraft Down in British Lines, Part 2' in
   (1969) *Cross & Cockade Journal*, pp. *278* **230**
Cutlack (1933) *The Official History of Australia in the War of 1914-1918*, vol VIII, pp. *249–250*
Miller, 'The death of Manfred von Richthofen: Who fired the
   fatal shot?' in Sabretache, (1998), pp. *17* **230**
Quoted in Miller, 'The death of Manfred von Richthofen:
   Who fired the fatal shot?' in Sabretache, (1998) **230-1**
Quoted in Miller, 'The death of Manfred von Richthofen:
   Who fired the fatal shot?' in Sabretache, (1998) **231**
Additional information from Dr Miller to the author, 23 June 2007 **231-2**
Hoeppner (1921) *Deutschlands Krieg in der Luft*, pp. *157* **232**
Woodman (1989) *Early Aircraft Armament – The Aeroplane and the Gun up to 1918*, pp. *34, 43* **232**
As quoted in Dr. Sinclair's report in Miller, 'The death of Manfred von Richthofen:
   Who fired the fatal shot?' in Sabretache, (1998) pp. *17* **232**
Miller, 'The death of Manfred von Richthofen: Who fired the
   fatal shot?' in Sabretache, (1998) pp. *27* **232**
Miller, 'The death of Manfred von Richthofen: Who fired the
   fatal shot?' in Sabretache, (1998) pp. *28* **233**
Miller, 'The death of Manfred von Richthofen: Who fired
   the fatal shot?' in Sabretache, (1998) **233**
Inspektion der Fliegertruppen, *Erfahrungen im Luftkampf – Jagdstaffel Boelcke*, (n d), p. *8* **234**
Chamberlain and Bailey, 'History of Escadrille Spa 93' in (1978)
   Cross & Cockade (Great Britain), pp. *70* **234**
Carisella and Ryan (1969) *Who Killed the Red Baron?* pp. *179* **234**

Bodenschatz, (1935) *Jagd in Flanderns Himmel* pp. *180* **234**

Richthofen (1937) Mein Kriegstagebuch, pp. *169* **235**

Baedecker, Berlin, (1927), pp. *145*; the church was razed by
the post-World War II communist régime **235**

Richthofen (1937) Mein Kriegstagebuch, pp. *169–170* **236**

Richthofen (1937) Mein Kriegstagebuch, pp. *170* **236**

Richthofen (1937) Mein Kriegstagebuch, **236**

Bodenschatz, (1935) *Jagd in Flanderns Himmel* pp. *100, 183* **236**

Schweckendieck (1938) *Der Kampfflieger Lothar Freiherr von Richthofen*, pp. *65* **236**

O'Connor, (1990) *Aviation Awards of Imperial Germany in World War I
and the Men Who Earned Them,* vol II, pp. *238–239* **236**

Schweckendieck (1938) *Der Kampfflieger Lothar Freiherr von Richthofen*, pp. *76–79* **237**

Schweckendieck (1938) *Der Kampfflieger Lothar Freiherr von Richthofen*, pp. *81* **237**

Genealogisches Handbuch des Adels – Stammfolge der Freiherren v. Richthofen, (1996), pp. *263* **237**

Kilduff (1993) *Richthofen – Beyond the Legend of the Red Baron,* pp. *8* **238**

Kogenluft, *Nachrichtenblatt der deutschen Luftstreitkräfte, 2. Jahrgang, Nr 9,* 25 April 1918 **238**

BIBLIOGRAPHY AND SOURCES

Published Books:

Air Ministry, *Handbook of German Military and Naval Aviation (War) 1914–1918*, London, 1919 (1995 reprint ed)

Bailey. F, and Cony, C., *The French Air Service War Chronology 1914–1918*, London, 2001
Bishop, W., *Winged Warfare*, London, 1918
Bodenschatz, K., *Jagd in Flanderns Himmel – Aus den sechzehn Kampfmonaten des Jagdgeschwaders Freiherr von Richthofen*, Munich, 1935
Böhme, E. (ed J. Werner), *Briefe eines deutschen Kampffliegers an ein junges Mädchen*, Leipzig, 1930
Boelcke, O., *Hauptmann Boelckes Feldberichte*, Gotha, 1916
Bowyer, C., *The Flying Elephants*, London, 1972
– *For Valour – The Air VCs*, London, 1978
–*Albert Ball, VC*, London, 1994
Bruce, J., *British Aeroplanes 1914–1918*, London, 1969
Burge, C., *The Annals of 100 Squadron*, London, ca. 1919

Carisella, P. and Ryan, J., *Who Killed the Red Baron?* Wakefield, 1969
Clark, C., *Iron Kingdom – The Rise and Downfall of Prussia 1600-1947*, Cambridge 2006
Cole, C., *Royal Air Force 1918*, London, 1968
Cutlack, F., *The Official History of Australia in the War of 1914–1918*, Vol IV,   Sydney, 2nd ed, 1933

Davilla J, and Soltan, A, *French Aircraft of the First World War*, Stratford, 1997
Deutscher Offizer-Bund (ed), *Ehren-Rangliste des ehemaligen Deutschen Heeres*, Berlin, 1926
Dickhuth-Harrach, G. (ed), *Im Felde unbesiegt*, Vol I, Munich, 1921
Dorndorf, G (ed), *Das Infanterie-Regiment Herzog Karl von Mecklenburg-Strelitz (6. Ospreussissches) Nr 43*, Oldenburg, 1923

Eberhardt, W. von (ed), *Unsere Luftstreitkrafte 1914–1918*, Berlin, 1930
Esposito, V. (ed), *A Concise History of World War I*, New York, 1965

Ferko, A., *Richthofen*, Berkhamsted, 1995
Foerster, W. and Greiner, H. (ed), *Wir Kämpfer im Weltkrieg – Selbstzeugnisse deutscher*

Frontsoldaten, Berlin, (n d)
Franks, N., *Jasta Boelcke – The History of Jasta 2, 1916–1918*, London, 2004
– Bailey, F. and Duiven, R. *The Jasta Pilots*, London, 1996
– Bailey, F. and Duiven, R. *Casualties of the German Air Service 1914–1920*, London, 1999
– Giblin, B., and McCrery, N., *Under the Guns of the Red Baron*, London, 1995
– Guest, R., and Bailey, F., *Bloody April ... Black September*, London, 1995

Genealogisches Handbuch des Adels – Stammfolge der Freiherren v. Richthofen, Limburg an der Lahn, 1996
Gibbons, F., *The Red Knight of Germany*, New York, 1927
Goote, T. [W. Von Langsdorff], *'... rangehn ist Alles!* Berlin, 1938
Gottberg, F. von (ed), *Das Grenadier-Regiment Kronpriz (1. Ostpreussisches) Nr 1 im Weltkriege*, Berlin, 1929

Haddow, G., and Grosz, P., *The German Giants – The German R-Planes 1914–1918*, London, 3rd ed, 1988
Haythornthwaite, P., *The World War One Source Book*, London, 1994
Henshaw, T., *The Sky Their Battlefield*, London, 1995
Hildebrand, K., *Die Generale der deutschen Luftwaffe 1935-1945*, vol I, Osnabrück, 1990
Hindenburg, P. von, *Out of My Life*, London, 1921
Hobson, C., *Airmen Died in the Great War 1914–1918*, Suffolk, 1995
Hoeppner, E. von, *Deutschlands Krieg in der Luft*, Leipzig, 1921
Hoffmann, R. (ed), *Der deutsche Soldat – Briefe aus dem Weltkrieg*, Munich, 1937

Immelmann, F., *Der Adler von Lille*, Leipzig, 1934

Jentsch, K., *Beim Jagdflug tödlich verunglückt?* Magdeburg, 1937
Jones, H., *The War In the Air*, Vol II, Oxford, 1928
–*The War In the Air*, Vol III, Oxford, 1931
–*The War In the Air*, Vol IV, Oxford, 1934

Kilduff, P., *Germany's First Air Force 1914–1918*, London, 1991
– *Richthofen - Beyond the Legend of the Red Baron*, London, 1993
– *The Red Baron Combat Wing – Jagdgeschwader Richthofen in Battle*, London, 1997
– *The Illustrated Red Baron – The Life and Times of Manfred von Richthofen*, London, 1999
Kriegsarchiv der Universitätsbibliothek Jena, *Thüringen im Weltkrieg*, Vol I, Leipzig, 1921

Lamberton, W., *Fighter Aircraft of the 1914–1918 War*, Letchworth, 1960
Langsdorff, W. von, *Flieger am Feind*, Gütersloh, 1934
Louda, *Heraldry of the Royal Families o of Europe*, New York, 1981

MacDonogh, G., *The Last Kaiser: The Life of Wilhelm II*, London, 2000
Moncure, J., *Forging the King's Sword*, New York, 1993
Möller, H., *Kampf und Sieg eines Jagdgeschwaders*, Berlin, 1939

Neumann, G., (ed), *Die deutschen Luftstreitkräfte im Weltkriege*, Berlin, 1920
– *In der Luft unbesiegt*, Munich, 1923
Nowarra, H. and Brown, K., *von Richthofen and the Flying Circus*, Letchworth, 1964

O'Connor, N., *Aviation Awards of Imperial Germany in World War I*, Vol I
   The Aviation Awards of the Kingdom of Bavaria, Princeton, 1988
Aviation Awards of Imperial Germany in World War I and the Men Who Earned Them, Vol II
   The Aviation Awards of the Kingdom of Prussia, Princeton, 1990
Aviation Awards of Imperial Germany in World War I and the Men Who Earned Them, Vol III
   The Aviation Awards of the Kingdom of Saxony, Princeton, 1993
Aviation Awards of Imperial Germany in World War I and the Men Who Earned Them, Vol V
   The Aviation Awards of the Eight Thuringian States and the Duchy of Anhalt, Princeton, 1998

Perthes, J., *Ehrentafel der Kriegsopfer des reichsdeutschen Adels 1914–1918*, Gotha, 1921
Potempa, H., *Die Königlich-Bayerische Fliegertruppe 1914–1918*, Frankfurt am Main, 1997

Richthofen, K. von, *Mein Kriegstagebuch*, Berlin, 1937
Richthofen, M. von, *Ein Heldenleben*, Berlin, 1920
Der rote Kampfflieger, Berlin, 1917
Der rote Kampfflieger, Berlin, 1933
[transl. P. Kilduff], *The Red Baron*, New York, 1969
Ritter, H., *Der Luftkrieg*, Berlin, 1926

Schäfer, K., *Vom Jäger zum Flieger*, Berlin, 1918
Schillman, F (ed), *Grenadier-Regiment König Friedrich Wilhelm I. (2. Ostpreussisches) Nr 3 im Weltkriege 1914–1918*, Oldenburg, 1924
Schnitzler, E., *Carl Allmenröder der Bergische Kampfflieger*, Wald, 1927
Schröder, H., *Erlebter Krieg*, Bern, ca. 1934
Schweckendiek, O., *Der Kampfflieger Lothar von Richthofen*, Hamburg, 1938.
Shores, C., Franks, N. and Guest, R., *Above the Trenches*, London, 1990
Showalter, *Bad Kreuznach als Sitz des Grossen Hauptquartiers im Ersten Weltkrieg*, Bad Kreuznach, 1981
Supf, P., *Das Buch der deutschen Fluggeschichte*, Vol I, Stuttgart, 1958
– *Das Buch der deutschen Fluggeschichte*, Vol II, Stuttgart, 1958
Stammliste der Offiziere des 6. Badischen Infanterie-Regiments (Kaiser Friedrich III) Nr. 114, Karlsruhe, 1904

Theilhaber, F., *Jüdische Flieger im Weltkrieg*, Berlin, 1924

Udet, E., *Mein Fliegerleben*, Berlin, 1935

Van Ishoven, A. (ed C. Bowyer). *The Fall of an Eagle*, London, 1977
Vanoverbeke, L., *Moorsele – één dorp, twee vliegendene*, Kortrijk, 1993
'Vigilant' [C. Sykes], *Richthofen - The Red Knight of the Air*, London, (n d)

Wenzl, R., *Richthofen-Flieger*, Freiburg im Breisgau, ca 1930
Werner, J. (ed) *Briefe eines*

*deutschen Kampffliegers an eines
junges Mädchen*, Leipzig, 1930
*Boelcke der Mensch, der Flieger, der Führer
der deutschen Jagdfliegerei*, Leipzig, 1932
Winter, P., *Gotha als Fliegerstadt in der
Vergangenheit*, Gotha, ca. 1935
Woodman, H., *Early Aircraft
Armament – The Aeroplane and the
Gun up to 1918*, London, 1989

Zuerl, W., *Pour le Mérite-Flieger*, Munich, 1938

Documents:

Armee Oberkommando 1,
Tagesbefehle, in the field, 1917

Bufe: *Auszug*, in the field, 1918
– *Personal-Bogen*, Berlin, 1920

Inspektion der Fliegertruppen, *Erfahrungen im
Luftkampf – Jagdstaffel Boelcke*, Berlin, (n d)

Jagdstaffel 11, *Berichte*, in
the field, 1917, 1918

Kommander der Flieger der 4. Armee,
Wochenberichte, in the field, 1917
– *Tagesberichte*, in the field, 1917

Kommander der Flieger der 6. Armee,
Wochenberichte, in the field, 1917

Kommandeur der Flieger der 7. Armee,
Fliegertagesmeldungen, in the field, 1918

Kommandierende General der
Luftstreitkräfte, *Nachrichtenblatt der
Luftstreitkräfte* Vol I, Berlin, 1917
Nachrichtenblatt der Luftstreitkräfte
Vol II, Berlin, 1918

Kriegsminsterium (organizational; manual),
Teil 10 Abschnitt B, Flieger-Formationen, Berlin,
1918

Prestien: *Personal-Bogen*, Berlin, 1920

National Archives (formerly Public Record
Office, London), No 2 Squadron,
RFC, *Combat Report*, in the field, 1917
No. 3 Squadron, RAF, *Combat*

Report, in the field, 1918
No 60 Squadron, RFC, *Combat
Report*, in the field, 1917
No 209 Squadron, RAF, Combat
Reports, in the field, 1918
*Periodical Summary of Aeronautical
Information*, in the field, 1917
Royal Air Force Communiqués, in the field,
1918 (PRO File No Air
1/2097/207/14/1)
Royal Flying Corps Communiqués, in the field,
1917
Royal Flying Corps Communiqués, in the field,
1916
Richthofen Combat Reports
(Translations), London, (PRO File
No Air 1/686/21/13/2250 XC15183)
Royal Flying Corps War Diary, in
the field, 1916, 1917, 1918
Western Front Combat Casualty List, in the
field, 1916, 1917, 1918 (PRO File
Nos Air 1/967/204/5/1097–
969/204/5/1102)

Richthofen: *Gesundheits-Nachweis*,
Gross Lichterfelde, 1911

Stabsoffizier der Flieger der 1. Armee,
Wochenberichte, in the field, 1916

Stabsoffizier der Flieger der 6. Armee,
Wochenberichte, in the field, 1916

Articles, Monographs
and Periodicals:

Adam, R., 'Episodes – Wing
Commander Ronald Adam, OBE'
in *Cross & Cockade Journal*, 1972
Allmers, H., 'Manfred von Richthofen's
medical record – was the "Red
Baron" fit to fly?' in *The Lancet*, 1999

Bink, H., 'Die Wahrheit über
den Tod Richthofens' in *Der
Frontsoldat erzählt*, Kiel, 1932
Bodenschatz, K., '*Das Jagdgeschwader Frhr
v.Richthofen Nr 1 im Verbande der 2. Armee*,'
In der Luft unbesiegt, Munich, 1923
Bruce, J., 'The Fokker Dr.I,' *Aircraft Profile
No 55*, Leatherhead, Surrey, 1965

Chamberlain. P. and Bailey, F.,
'History of Escadrille Spa 93' in *Cross &*
Cockade (Great Britain), 1978
Chionchio, J., 'Defeat by Design'
in *Air Enthusiast*, 1989
Cron, H. (transl. P. Grosz), "Organization
of the German Luftstreitkräfte,"
Cross & Cockade Journal, 1966

Duiven, R., 'German Jagdstaffel and
Jagdgeschwader Commanding Officers,
1916-1918' in *Over the Front*, 1988

Ferko, A., *Fliegertruppe 1914–*
1918, Salem, Ohio, 1980
'The Origin of the First Jagdstaffeln,'
Cross & Cockade Journal, 1965
Richthofen, Berkhamsted, 1995
and Grosz, P., 'The Circus Master
Falls: Comments on a Newly Discovered
Photograph,' *Cross &*
Cockade Journal, 1968

Genealogisches Handbuch des Adels
Stammfolge der Freiherren v. Richthofen,
Limburg an der Lahn, 1996
Gray, P., 'Albatros D.V,' *Aircraft Profile*
No. 9, Leatherhead, Surrey, 1965
'Pfalz D.III,' *Aircraft Profile No.43*,
Leatherhead, Surrey, 1965
Grosz, P., 'The Agile and Aggressive
Albatros' in *Air Enthusiast*, 1976
'Fokker E.III,' *Windsock Datafile*
No 15, Berkhamsted, 1989
'Albatros B.II,' *Windsock Datafile*
No 93, Berkhamsted, 2002
'Albatros D.I/D.II,' *Windsock Datafile*
No 100, Berkhamsted, 2003
and Ferko, A., 'The Fokker Dr.I –
A Reappraisal,' *Air Enthusiast*, 1978

Kilduff, P., 'Honor Roll of the Fallen
Fliers of Baden' in *Over the Front*, 1989
Kriegs-Echo, Berlin, 1916, 1917, 1918

Lampel, P., '*Als Gast beim Rittmeister Frhr*
v.Richthofen,' In der Luft
unbesiegt, Munich, 1923

Miller,G., 'The death of Manfred
von Richthofen: Who fired the fatal
shot?' in *Sabretache*, Sydney, 1998

Puglisi, W., 'German Aircraft Down in British

Lines, Part 2' in *Cross & Cockade Journal*, 1969

Richthofen, M. von, *Rittmeister*
Manfred Freiherr von Richthofen – Sein
militärisches Vermächtnis, Berlin, 1938

Salzmann, E. von, 'Richthofen' in *Der*
Weltkrieg – Illustrierte Kriegs-Chronik des
Daheim, 9. Bd,, Bielefeld/Leipzig, 1918
Schmeelke, M., 'Leutnant der Reserve Otto
Brauneck,' *Cross & Cockade Journal*, 1983

VanWyngarden, *von Richthofen's Flying*
Circus, Berkhamsted, 1994

von der Osten, 'Memoirs of World
War I with Jagdstaffeln 11 and 4'
in *Cross & Cockade Journal*, 1974

Winans, D., 'World War I Aircraft
Fuels and Lubricating Oils' in
Cross & Cockade Journal, 1961

INDEX

Air Units:

Further Information

Readers interested in obtaining additional information about military aviation of the First World War may wish to contact the websites of research-oriented, non-profit organizations, including:

Australian Society of World War I Aero Historians
URL: http://asww1ah.0catch.com

Cross & Cockade International (UK)
URL: http://www.crossandcockade.com

League of World War I Aviation Historians (USA)
URL: http://www.overthefront.com

Das Propellerblatt (Germany)
URL: www.Propellerblatt.de

World War One Aeroplanes (USA)
URL: http://www.avation-history.com/ww1aero.htm